WORLD TRADE ORGANIZATION

Dispute Settlement Reports

1998
Volume V

Pages 1831-2197

CAMBRIDGE
UNIVERSITY PRESS

PUBLISHED BY THE PRESS SYNDICATE OF THE UNIVERSITY OF CAMBRIDGE
The Pitt Building, Trumpington Street, Cambridge, United Kingdom

CAMBRIDGE UNIVERSITY PRESS
The Edinburgh Building, Cambridge CB2 2RU, UK
40 West 20th Street, New York, NY 10011–4211, USA
10 Stamford Road, Oakleigh, VIC 3166, Australia
Ruiz de Alarcón 13, 28014 Madrid, Spain
Dock House, The Waterfront, Cape Town 8001, South Africa

http://www.cambridge.org

Printed in the United Kingdom at the University Press, Cambridge

French edition and Spanish edition paperbacks of this title are both available directly from WTO Publications, World Trade Organization, Centre William Rappard, 154 rue de Lausanne, CH-1211 Geneva 21, Switzerland http://www.wto.org

ISBN 0 521 80096 X hardback
ISBN 0 521 80501 5 paperback

THE WTO DISPUTE SETTLEMENT REPORTS

The *Dispute Settlement Reports* of the World Trade Organization (the "WTO") include panel and Appellate Body reports, as well as arbitration awards, in disputes concerning the rights and obligations of WTO Members under the provisions of the *Marrakesh Agreement Establishing the World Trade Organization*. The *Dispute Settlement Reports* are available in English, French and Spanish.

This volume may be cited as DSR 1998:V

TABLE OF CONTENTS

EUROPEAN COMMUNITIES - MEASURES CONCERNING MEAT AND MEAT PRODUCTS (HORMONES)

Arbitration under Article 21.3(c) of the Understanding on Rules and Procedures Governing the Settlement of Disputes

Award of the Arbitrator
Julio Lacarte-Muró
WT/DS26/15, WT/DS48/13

Circulated to Members on 29 May 1998

I. INTRODUCTION

1. On 13 February 1998, the Dispute Settlement Body (the "DSB") adopted the Appellate Body Report[1] and the Panel Reports[2], as modified by the Appellate Body Report, in *EC Measures Concerning Meat and Meat Products (Hormones)*.[3] On 13 March 1998, the European Communities informed the DSB, pursuant to Article 21.3 of the *Understanding on Rules and Procedures Governing the Settlement of Disputes* (the "DSU"), that it intended to fulfil its obligations under the *Marrakesh Agreement Establishing the World Trade Organization*[4] (the "*WTO Agreement*") in respect of this matter, and that it had initiated the process to examine the options for compliance with a view to implementation in as short a period of time as possible, and that it would require a reasonable period of time for this process.[5]

2. On 26 March 1998, consultations were held between the European Communities and the United States and Canada in order to reach agreement on a "reasonable period of time" for the implementation of the recommendations and rulings of the DSB adopted on 13 February 1998. These consultations, and further written communications between the parties, did not lead to an agreement. There-

[1] WT/DS26/AB/R, WT/DS48/AB/R.

[2] Complaint by the United States, WT/DS26/R ("US Panel Report"); Complaint by Canada, WT/DS48/R ("Canada Panel Report").

[3] As noted at paragraphs 2-5 of the Appellate Body Report, the "measures" at issue in this dispute were Council Directive 81/602/EEC of 31 July 1981, Council Directive 88/146/EEC of 7 March 1988 and Council Directive 88/299/EEC of 17 May 1988, which were codified and replaced by Council Directive 96/22/EC of 29 April 1996 ("Directive 96/22"), which came into effect on 1 July 1997, Official Journal, No. L 125, 23 May 1996, p. 3.

[4] Done at Marrakesh, Morocco, 15 April 1994.

[5] WT/DSB/M/43, 8 April 1998, p. 8.

fore, the European Communities requested, on 8 April 1998, that the "reasonable period of time" be determined by binding arbitration pursuant to Article 21.3(c) of the DSU.[6]

3. In the absence of an agreement between the parties on the appointment of an arbitrator within 10 days after referring the matter to arbitration, the European Communities requested, in a letter dated 18 April 1998 and received on 20 April 1998, and the United States and Canada requested, on 20 April 1998, the Director-General of the World Trade Organization ("WTO") to appoint the arbitrator, as provided for in footnote 12 to Article 21.3(c) of the DSU. After consultations with the parties, the Director-General decided, on 30 April 1998, to appoint H.E. Mr. Celso Lafer and myself as the arbitrators in this matter. Subsequently, Ambassador Lafer informed the Director-General that he was unable to accept the nomination. The Director-General informed the parties on 7 May 1998 that, given the very strict timeframe within which this arbitration must be conducted, he believed that the best course of action was to continue this arbitration with me acting as the sole arbitrator.

4. Written submissions were received from the European Communities, the United States and Canada on 6 May 1998, and an oral hearing was held on 12 May 1998.

II. ARGUMENTS OF THE PARTIES

A. *European Communities*

5. The European Communities concluded in its written submission that the "reasonable period of time" for implementation of the recommendations and rulings of the DSB in this case should be approximately four years, comprising two years for a risk assessment and approximately two years for any legislative action which may be necessary in the light of the results of the risk assessment. Later, in the oral hearing, the European Communities stated that the "reasonable period of time" could be reduced to, in total, 39 months: two years for a risk assessment and 15 months for any necessary legislative action thereafter.

6. In the view of the European Communities, the period of time that is necessary to implement the DSB recommendations and rulings in this case cannot be shorter than what is reasonably required by sound science to respond to the findings in the Appellate Body Report that the EC measures banning imports of meat and meat products derived from cattle administered with certain hormones for growth promotion purposes are inconsistent with Articles 5.1 and 3.3 of the *Agreement on the Application of Sanitary and Phytosanitary Measures* (the "*SPS Agreement*"). The intention of the European Communities is to take action composed of two elements: first, to conduct hormone-specific and residue-specific

---

6 WT/DS26/14, WT/DS48/12, G/L/235, 16 April 1998.

risk assessments for all the hormones, as clarified by the Appellate Body, including an evaluation of the risks posed to human health from failure to observe good veterinary practice; and second, to review the measure at issue in the light of the results of that risk assessment and propose to abolish, amend or maintain it, as appropriate.[7]

7. The European Communities asserts that the period of time to complete the first "preparatory" phase, consisting of the various scientific studies, cannot be shorter than two years. With respect to the second or "conclusive" phase, the European Communities argues that a sufficient period of time should be made available to it in order to allow for the necessary legislative measures to be taken. While the European Communities stated in its written submission that this second phase would require approximately two years, the European Communities stated in the oral hearing that it would need 15 months to conclude this phase.

8. The European Communities asserts that while Article 21.3 of the DSU imposes an obligation on the Member concerned to inform the DSB of its intentions regarding implementation, what is specifically required by the obligation to "implement" is not spelled out either in this provision or elsewhere in the DSU. Under the DSU, the required act of implementation is the removal of the inconsistency found by the DSB to exist between a measure and a covered agreement. An implementing Member has options concerning the precise means of implementation. In the present case, "[t]here is *no* recommendation or ruling of the Appellate Body about *how* the EC must bring its measures into conformity."[8] Therefore, the inconsistency can be eliminated "either by abolishing the measure *or* by providing the hormone-specific and residue-specific risk assessments that the Appellate Body held to be required under Article 5.1 of the SPS Agreement."[9] The European Communities asserts that:

> ... the Appellate Body did not find that the EC's import prohibition *per se* was inconsistent with the SPS Agreement, but only that the EC had violated its obligations under the SPS Agreement by not conducting a proper risk assessment within the meaning of Article 5.1 as the basis for the import prohibition. The EC is entitled, therefore, to bring its measure into conformity with the SPS Agreement by basing it on a properly specific risk assessment, as this concept has now been clarified for the first time by the Appellate Body.[10]

Referring to the finding of the Appellate Body at paragraph 129 of the Appellate Body Report that the phrase "as appropriate to the circumstances" in Article 5.1 "makes clear that the Members have a certain degree of flexibility in meeting the

---

7 Written submission of the European Communities, para. 74.

8 Written submission of the European Communities, para. 24.

9 *Ibid.*

10 Written submission of the European Communities, para. 64.

requirements of Article 5.1", the European Communities asserts that "the flexibility to which Members are entitled" under Article 5.1 "would be wrongfully abrogated if this arbitration does not allow the EC a reasonable period of time in which to perform the hormone-specific and residue-specific risk assessment which the Appellate Body for the first time in this case held is required."[11]

9. According to the European Communities, the recommendation in paragraph 255 of the Appellate Body Report must be read in the context of the reasoning in the Appellate Body Report, and "[a] careful examination of the Appellate Body's findings in paragraphs 198-201 and 206-208 leads to the conclusion that the essence of the Appellate Body's endorsement of the Panel's finding of inconsistency with Article 5.1 was the absence of a suitably specific risk assessment. In other words, the Appellate Body's findings and conclusions in respect of this matter rest on the proposition that no risk assessment sufficient for the purpose had been undertaken or presented to the Panel."[12]

10. The European Communities contends that the statement in Article 21.3 of the DSU that the reasonable period of time "may be shorter or longer [than 15 months], depending upon the particular circumstances" mandates a case-by-case approach in the determination of the reasonable period. The "type and technical complexity of the measure which the respondent Member is required to draft, adopt and implement within the minimum period of time can constitute 'particular circumstances'."[13] In the present case, "these 'particular circumstances' comprise the methods of implementation available to the EC under the SPS Agreement and the period of time required to accomplish them."[14] The European Communities maintains that "[s]ince there is a need ... to conduct a hormone-specific and residue-specific risk assessment in order to implement the DSB recommendations and rulings, the question of what constitutes a 'reasonable period' depends upon the time it normally takes scientists in the EC (and around the world) to conduct this type of risk assessment and to review the inconsistent measure in the light of the results of that risk assessment."[15]

11. With respect to the first phase of its proposed implementation of the DSB recommendations and rulings, the European Communities states that it intends to carry out a series of research projects that, it considers, constitute "the risk assessment specified by the Appellate Body report."[16] In view of the type and nature of the experiments involved, some of these projects, such as those testing the carcinogenicity and genotoxicity of residues in meat of the parent compounds and their metabolites, cannot be completed in less than two years from the time they are commenced. This time period of two years is incompressible. The Euro-

---

[11] Written submission of the European Communities, para. 52.

[12] Written submission of the European Communities, para. 56.

[13] Written submission of the European Communities, para. 71.

[14] *Ibid*.

[15] *Ibid*.

[16] Written submission of the European Communities, para. 79.

pean Communities states that in order to identify missing scientific information, avoid duplication of scientific work and reduce as far as possible the time necessary to complete the risk assessment, the EC Commission requested in writing, on 8 April 1998, relevant information from the United States, Canada, Australia and New Zealand. It also intends to send a similar request for information to the Codex Alimentarius Commission.

12. With respect to what it terms the "second" or "conclusive" phase of its proposed implementation process, the European Communities asserts that it cannot take definitive legislative measures before the results of the risk assessment become available, as it cannot prejudge the outcome of the risk assessment.[17] Nevertheless, the European Communities states that the EC Commission has already initiated the process of exploring the various legislative options that would be available and the relevant decision-making procedures, and that this process will continue as the risk assessment progresses. According to the European Communities, the aim is to prepare the ground as well as possible so that, when the definitive results of the risk assessment become available, the proposal of the EC Commission to the other EC institutions can be presented within the shortest period of time possible.

13. The European Communities maintained in its written submission that if the results of the risk assessment indicate the need to take legislative action, the legislative process for the implementation of the DSB recommendations and rulings in this case could be completed within approximately two years. In the oral hearing, the European Communities stated that it would need 15 months for the legislative process. The European Communities disagrees with the United States and Canada concerning the appropriate legislative basis - and, consequently, concerning the legislative process that must be followed within the European Communities - for any measure abolishing or amending the current measure banning imports of meat and meat products derived from cattle administered with certain hormones for growth promotion purposes. According to the European Communities, even if Directive 96/22 was based on Article 43 of the *Treaty Establishing the European Community*[18] (the "*EC Treaty*") and was adopted pursuant to the consultation procedure, this is no longer the correct legal situation in the European Communities.[19] As the principal objective of the measure in question is to protect human health, an act to abolish or amend Directive 96/22 will require a Directive of the Council and the European Parliament based on Article 100a of

---

[17] Written submission of the European Communities, para. 101.

[18] Done at Rome, 25 March 1957, as amended. Before the entry into force of the *Treaty on European Union* on 1 November 1993, this Treaty was referred to as the *Treaty Establishing the European Economic Community* (the "*EEC Treaty*").

[19] The European Communities refers for this proposition to a case pending before the European Court of Justice, Case C-269/97, *Commission v. Council*, the pleadings of which are summarized in Official Journal No. C 295, 27 September 1997, p. 17.

the *EC Treaty*. Any act based on Article 100a must be adopted in accordance with the co-decision procedure provided for in Article 189b of the *EC Treaty*.[20]

14. In any case, the European Communities claims that the debate on the appropriate legal basis for an act to abolish or amend Directive 96/22 will become irrelevant after the entry into force of the *Treaty of Amsterdam* on 1 January 1999. That treaty modifies Article 129 of the existing *EC Treaty* by explicitly requiring in Article 152(4)(b) that "measures in the veterinary and phytosanitary fields which have as their direct objective the protection of public health" must be adopted on the basis of the co-decision procedure. The European Communities stated that upon the adoption of the *Treaty of Amsterdam*, any pending legislation would have to be withdrawn and a new legislative process would have to be commenced.

B. United States

15. The United States argues that the "reasonable period of time" for implementation of the DSB recommendations and rulings in this case is 10 months, i.e., by 1 January 1999. The most relevant factors affecting the decision on the length of the reasonable period of time for implementation are: (i) the legal form of implementation necessary (e.g., legislation, regulations, decree, etc.); (ii) the nature of the legislative or regulatory changes to be made; and (iii) the period of time in which the implementing Member can achieve the proposed legal form of implementation, assuming that the Member applies itself in good faith. Based on these criteria, an implementation period of 10 months is "reasonable" in this instance in light of the action that is required of the European Communities to comply with the DSB recommendations and rulings, i.e., removal of the import ban, and the nature of the regulatory/legislative process applicable to issues involving agriculture, such as the import ban in question, under the current law of the European Communities.

16. In the view of the United States, the burden rests on the implementing Member to justify the period of time necessary for implementation of DSB recommendations and rulings. The burden of demonstrating that a certain period of time is "reasonable" becomes heavier when that period exceeds the 15-month guideline set out in Article 21.3(c) of the DSU. If the European Communities believes that immediate implementation is impracticable, it must demonstrate why this is so and must also substantiate its request for a particular period of time within which to implement.

---

20 Written submission of the European Communities, para. 106. The *Single European Act*, effective 1 July 1987, amended the *EEC Treaty* by adding Article 100a, which required the use of the cooperation procedure. The *Treaty on European Union*, which entered into force on 1 November 1993 (thereafter, the *EEC Treaty* was known as the *EC Treaty*), amended Article 100a and added Article 189b. Together, these provisions require the use of the co-decision procedure for legislation aimed at the protection of human health.

17. According to the United States, the period of time proposed by the European Communities for implementation is unreasonable and is based on two false premises. First, while the European Communities is free to conduct a risk assessment, such a risk assessment is irrelevant to implementation of the DSB's recommendations and rulings and cannot be used to delay the "reasonable period of time" for compliance. The DSB recommendations and rulings do not require another risk assessment. The DSB has ruled that the European Communities has no human health basis for its ban. As a result, the ban is not justified under the *SPS Agreement*. Withdrawal of the measures that were found to be inconsistent with the obligations of the European Communities under Articles 3.3 and 5.1 of the *SPS Agreement* is the only action consistent with the findings of the Panel and Appellate Body and the DSB recommendations and rulings in this case. The import ban in question has already been in place for nine years, and the dispute settlement proceedings in this case have already taken two years. During this time, benefits accruing to the United States under the *WTO Agreement* have been denied. The United States should not have to wait for a further period of two years before the European Communities even begins the necessary legislative process to bring its measure into conformity with the *SPS Agreement*.[21]

18. Second, the United States submits that the legislative procedures necessary to repeal the import ban in question can be accomplished within less than 10 months. The regulation of hormones used in the production of animals is an agricultural matter subject to Article 43 of the *EC Treaty*[22], which provides that legislation pertaining to the common market in agriculture shall be taken pursuant to the consultation procedure. Directive 96/22 was based on Article 43 of the *EC Treaty* and the European Communities is not now legally required to base a legislative measure on Article 100a of the *EC Treaty* and to use the co-decision procedure provided for in Article 189b of the *EC Treaty* in order to remove the import ban. The *Treaty of Amsterdam*, containing the modified Article 129 "that would allow the European Union to adopt legislation in the areas of health and consumer protection with the full participation of the Parliament, *i.e.*, pursuant to co-decision"[23], has not yet entered into effect. The consultation procedure is, therefore, applicable to any legislative measure implementing the recommendations and rulings of the DSB in this case. This procedure may be completed within five or six months. Even if the co-decision procedure were necessary in order to lift the hormone ban, it can be completed in less than 15 months.

---

21 Statements of the United States at the oral hearing.

22 The United States refers to Case 68/86, *United Kingdom v. Council*, [1988] E.C.R 855. The United States also refers to Opinion 1/94 of the European Court of Justice for the proposition that the implementation by the European Communities of the commitments in the *SPS Agreement* "will require measures to be adopted on the basis of Article 43 of the [EC] Treaty." Opinion 1/94, [1994] E.C.R. I-5271.

23 Written submission of the United States, para. 45.

C. Canada

19. Canada submits that the "reasonable period of time" for implementation of the recommendations and rulings in this case should be no more than 10 months. Given that the European Communities is under an obligation to implement the recommendations and rulings of the DSB in this case, Canada argues that the onus lies with the European Communities to demonstrate that the period it requests constitutes a "reasonable period of time". Canada submits that the proposed period is manifestly unreasonable, and that there are no "particular circumstances" that would justify such a time period under Article 21.3(c) of the DSU.

20. In Canada's view, the "reasonable period of time" does not include time for the European Communities to conduct a risk assessment. Rather, the "reasonable period of time" is provided to allow the European Communities to take the necessary legislative steps to remove its inconsistent measures. In the present case, the impugned measures of the European Communities have been found inconsistent with the obligations of the European Communities under the *SPS Agreement*. Withdrawal of the measures is the only way to bring them into conformity with the *SPS Agreement*. While the European Communities is free to undertake risk assessments for any of the hormones concerned at any time, conducting such a risk assessment does not constitute compliance with the DSB recommendations and rulings. Accordingly, the European Communities should have already started taking the necessary legislative steps to withdraw the inconsistent measures.

21. Canada submits that condoning the EC request for two years to conduct a risk assessment would "reward" the European Communities for failing to base its impugned measures on a risk assessment, as required by Article 5.1 of the *SPS Agreement*. This would permit the European Communities to continue to block imports of beef from Canada for a further two years before the European Communities even initiates the necessary legislative process to bring its measures into compliance with the *SPS Agreement*, and would invite abuse of Article 5.1 of the *SPS Agreement*. The European Communities has not argued that its measures were provisionally adopted pursuant to Article 5.7 of the *SPS Agreement* because relevant scientific information was insufficient. However, on the basis of the Appellate Body Report, the European Communities purports to require time to undertake a risk assessment. The European Communities is, in effect, claiming the benefits of Article 5.7 of the *SPS Agreement* in the guise of implementing the DSB recommendations and rulings. It has been two years since the United States and Canada requested separate consultations with the European Communities in this dispute. Thus, the European Communities has had ample reason and opportunity to conduct the risk assessment it argues that it now must conduct.

22. Finally, Canada submits that the European Communities could complete the required legislative process in significantly less than 15 months. As the measures that must be brought into conformity with the *SPS Agreement* are based on Article 43 of the *EC Treaty*, amendment or repeal of these measures could be done pursuant to the consultation procedure and, under the existing law of the

European Communities[24], would not legally require the co-decision procedure under Articles 100a and 189b of the *EC Treaty*. The consultation procedure required by Article 43 of the *EC Treaty* can be completed in a period much shorter than 15 months, i.e., in a period of approximately eight months. Canada submits that a policy choice by the European Communities in favour of the co-decision procedure under Article 189b of the *EC Treaty*, which goes beyond the strictly legal requirements of European Community law, should not be taken into account as "particular circumstances" that would impact on the determination of what constitutes a "reasonable period of time". Even if the co-decision procedure were necessary, there is evidence that this procedure would take 18 months on average, and can take less than 15 months.

III. ARTICLE 21.3 OF THE DSU

23. Article 21.3 of the DSU provides, in part, as follows:

> ... the Member concerned shall inform the DSB of its intentions in respect of implementation of the recommendations and rulings of the DSB. If it is impracticable to comply immediately with the recommendations and rulings, the Member concerned shall have a reasonable period of time in which to do so. The reasonable period of time shall be:
>
> ...
>
> (c) a period of time determined through binding arbitration within 90 days after the date of adoption of the recommendations and rulings. In such arbitration, a guideline for the arbitrator should be that the reasonable period of time to implement panel or Appellate Body recommendations should not exceed 15 months from the date of adoption of a panel or Appellate Body report. However, that time may be shorter or longer, depending upon the particular circumstances.

24. My mandate in this arbitration is to determine the reasonable period of time within which the European Communities is required to implement the recommendations and rulings of the DSB. As a "guideline", Article 21.3(c) provides that the reasonable period of time "should not exceed 15 months from the date of adoption of a panel or Appellate Body report." However, "that time may be shorter or longer, depending upon the particular circumstances."

---

24 Canada states that regardless of any case that may currently be pending before the European Court of Justice, existing case law holds that Article 43 of the *EC Treaty* is the appropriate legal basis for modifying an agricultural measure such as the one at issue in this case.

25. The ordinary meaning of the terms of Article 21.3(c) indicates that 15 months is a "guideline for the arbitrator", and not a rule. This guideline is stated expressly to be that "the reasonable period of time ... *should not exceed* 15 months from the date of adoption of a panel or Appellate Body report"(emphasis added). In other words, the 15-month guideline is an outer limit or a maximum in the usual case. For example, when implementation can be effected by administrative means, the reasonable period of time should be considerably shorter than 15 months. However, the reasonable period of time could be shorter or longer, depending upon the particular circumstances, as specified in Article 21.3(c).

26. Article 21.3(c) also should be interpreted in its context and in light of the object and purpose of the DSU. Relevant considerations in this respect include other provisions of the DSU, including, in particular, Articles 21.1 and 3.3. Article 21.1 stipulates that: "*Prompt compliance* with recommendations and rulings of the DSB is essential in order to ensure effective resolution of disputes to the benefit of all Members"(emphasis added). Article 3.3 states: "The *prompt* settlement of situations in which a Member considers that any benefits accruing to it directly or indirectly under the covered agreements are being impaired by measures taken by another Member is essential to the effective functioning of the WTO and the maintenance of a proper balance between the rights and obligations of Members"(emphasis added). *The Concise Oxford Dictionary* defines the word, "prompt", as meaning "a. acting with alacrity; ready. b. made, done, etc. readily or at once".[25] Read in context, it is clear that the reasonable period of time, as determined under Article 21.3(c), should be the shortest period possible within the legal system of the Member to implement the recommendations and rulings of the DSB. In the usual case, this should not be greater than 15 months, but could also be less.

27. In my view, the party seeking to prove that there are "particular circumstances" justifying a shorter or a longer time has the burden of proof under Article 21.3(c). In this arbitration, therefore, the onus is on the European Communities to demonstrate that there are particular circumstances which call for a reasonable period of time of 39 months, and it is likewise up to the United States and Canada to demonstrate that there are particular circumstances which lead to the conclusion that 10 months is reasonable.

IV. LONGER PERIOD THAN 15 MONTHS

28. The European Communities maintains that, in this case, there are "particular circumstances" justifying a reasonable period of time of 39 months[26] in

---

[25] D. Thomson (ed.), *The Concise Oxford Dictionary of Current English*, ninth ed. (Clarendon Press, 1995), p. 1096.

[26] In its written submission, para. 115, the European Communities stated that it would require a period of approximately four years, consisting of two years to conduct a risk assessment and approximately two years for any legislative process that may be necessary in light of the results of the

total. It argues that the reasonable period of time needed to implement the recommendations and rulings of the DSB can be separated into two distinct phases: (a) a minimum of two years to complete the hormone-specific and residue-specific risk assessments for all the hormones concerned, including an evaluation of the risks posed to human health from failure to observe good veterinary practice[27]; and (b) a period of 15 months to take any legislative action required, in light of the results of the risk assessments.[28]

29. I will first address whether "the particular circumstances" in this case allow the European Communities an initial phase of two years to conduct the risk assessments which it maintains are "mandated"[29] by the findings and conclusions of the Appellate Body Report.

30. Article 19.1 of the DSU reads as follows:

> Where a panel or the Appellate Body concludes that a measure is inconsistent with a covered agreement, it shall recommend that the Member concerned bring the measure into conformity with that agreement. In addition to its recommendations, the panel or Appellate Body may suggest ways in which the Member concerned could implement the recommendations.

31. The recommendations and rulings of the DSB in this case consist of the findings and conclusions of the Appellate Body Report and the Panel Reports, as modified by the Appellate Body Report, which were adopted by the DSB pursuant to Articles 16.4 and 17.14 of the DSU on 13 February 1998. The Appellate Body Report contained the following recommendation:

> The Appellate Body *recommends* that the Dispute Settlement Body request the European Communities to bring the SPS measures found in this Report and in the Panel Reports, as modified by this Report, to be inconsistent with the *SPS Agreement* into conformity with the obligations of the European Communities under that Agreement.[30]

The Panel Reports contained the following recommendation:

> We *recommend* that the Dispute Settlement Body requests the European Communities to bring its measures in dispute

---

risk assessment. However, in its concluding statement at the oral hearing, the European Communities reduced the time needed for any legislative process to 15 months. Therefore, the final position of the European Communities was that a reasonable period of time for implementation of the DSB recommendations and rulings would be approximately two years and 15 months, that is, 39 months.

27 Written submission of the European Communities, para. 74.

28 Statements of the European Communities at the oral hearing.

29 Written submission of the European Communities, heading 3), page 23; statements of the European Communities at the oral hearing.

30 Appellate Body Report, para. 255.

> into conformity with its obligations under the Agreement on the Application of Sanitary and Phytosanitary Measures.[31]

32. There is an issue in this arbitration as to what constitutes "implementation of the recommendations and rulings of the DSB" under Article 21.3 of the DSU. The European Communities maintains that the Appellate Body Report "mandates" hat a number of scientific studies constituting a risk assessment be conducted as "a necessary first step" to bringing the EC measures into conformity with the *SPS Agreement*.[32] The United States and Canada, on the other hand, argue that as the EC measures were found to be inconsistent with the obligations of the European Communities under the *SPS Agreement*, the *only* means of bringing them into conformity with the DSB's recommendations and rulings is by withdrawing them.

33. The Appellate Body Report and the Panel Reports, as modified by the Appellate Body Report, found the EC import prohibition to be inconsistent with the obligations of the European Communities under the *SPS Agreement*, and recommended that the European Communities bring its "measures" found to be inconsistent with the *SPS Agreement* into conformity with its obligations under that Agreement. Neither the Appellate Body nor the Panel suggested ways, under Article 19.1 of the DSU, in which the European Communities should implement the recommendations and rulings of the DSB.

34. The Appellate Body concluded that the EC import prohibition of meat and meat products derived from cattle to which certain hormones had been administered for growth promotion purposes was inconsistent with the requirements of Articles 5.1 and 3.3 of the *SPS Agreement*.[33] The Appellate Body agreed with the Panel that "Article 5.1 may be viewed as a specific application of the basic obligations contained in Article 2.2 of the *SPS Agreement*", and stressed that "Articles 2.2 and 5.1 should constantly be read together."[34] The Appellate Body stated:

> We believe that Article 5.1, when contextually read as it should be, in conjunction with and as informed by Article 2.2 of the *SPS Agreement*, requires that the results of the risk assessment must sufficiently warrant - that is to say, reasonably support - the SPS measure at stake. The requirement that an SPS measure be "based on" a risk assessment is a substantive requirement that there be a rational relationship between the measure and the risk assessment.[35]

---

31 US Panel Report, para. 9.2; Canada Panel Report, para. 9.2.

32 Written submission of the European Communities, para. 72 and p. 23.

33 Appellate Body Report, paras. 208, 209, 253(l).

34 Appellate Body Report, para. 180.

35 Appellate Body Report, para. 193.

35. The Appellate Body confirmed the legal conclusions of the Panel Reports that the EC import prohibition was inconsistent with Articles 5.1 and 3.3 of the *SPS Agreement*. As indicated above, the Appellate Body stated that Article 5.1 must be read together with Article 2.2 of the *SPS Agreement*, and requires that "the results of the risk assessment must sufficiently warrant - that is to say, reasonably support - the SPS measure at stake." For an SPS measure to be *based on* a risk assessment, as required under Article 5.1, there must "be a *rational relationship* between the measure and the risk assessment"(emphasis added). The Appellate Body examined the scientific studies presented to the Panel by the European Communities in support of its measures, and affirmed "the *ultimate conclusion* of the Panel that the EC import prohibition is not based on a risk assessment within the meaning of Articles 5.1 and 5.2 of the *SPS Agreement* and is, therefore, *inconsistent* with the requirements of Article 5.1"(emphasis added).[36] It is important to note that, despite differences in the interpretation of Articles 3.1 and 5.2 of the *SPS Agreement* by the Panel and the Appellate Body, the Appellate Body agreed with the Panel's conclusions on every major point relating to whether the EC Directives at issue were "based on an assessment, as appropriate to the circumstances, of the risks to human ... health" in accordance with Article 5.1 of the *SPS Agreement*.

36. In the Appellate Body Report, as in the Panel Reports, the "measures" found to be inconsistent with the obligations of the European Communities under the *SPS Agreement* were the Directives[37] maintaining the import prohibition of meat and meat products derived from cattle to which certain hormones had been administered for growth promotion purposes. These Directives were codified and replaced by Directive 96/22, effective 1 July 1997, and it is Directive 96/22, therefore, which must be brought into conformity with the obligations of the European Communities under the *SPS Agreement*.

37. The ultimate holding of the Appellate Body Report, affirming the Panel Reports, is that the EC import prohibition is not based on a risk assessment within the meaning of Articles 5.1 and 5.2 of the *SPS Agreement*. "The essence of the Appellate Body's endorsement of the Panel's finding of inconsistency with Article 5.1"was *not*, as maintained by the European Communities, "the absence of a suitably specific risk assessment".[38] That is not what the Appellate Body found. Rather, the Appellate Body, agreeing with the Panel, concluded that the EC import prohibition was *not based on* a risk assessment in accordance with the provisions of the *SPS Agreement*. These findings constitute the recommendations and rulings of the DSB, adopted on 13 February 1998 under Articles 16.4 and 17.14 of the DSU, which must be implemented by the European Communities within the reasonable period of time as determined by this arbitration.

---

[36] Appellate Body Report, para. 208.

[37] See footnote 3.

[38] Written submission of the European Communities, para. 56.

38. It is not within my mandate under Article 21.3(c) of the DSU, to suggest ways or means to the European Communities to implement the recommendations and rulings of the Appellate Body Report and Panel Reports. My task is to determine the reasonable period of time within which implementation must be completed. Article 3.7 of the DSU provides, in relevant part, that "the first objective of the dispute settlement mechanism is *usually to secure the withdrawal of the measures concerned* if these are found to be inconsistent with the provisions of any of the covered agreements"(emphasis added). Although withdrawal of an inconsistent measure is the *preferred* means of complying with the recommendations and rulings of the DSB in a violation case[39], it is not necessarily the *only* means of implementation consistent with the covered agreements. An implementing Member, therefore, has a measure of discretion in choosing the *means* of implementation, as long as the means chosen are consistent with the recommendations and rulings of the DSB and with the covered agreements.

39. Withdrawal is the *preferred* means of implementation under Article 3.7 of the DSU, and *prompt compliance* with the recommendations and rulings of the DSB is essential under Article 21.1. It would not be in keeping with the requirement of *prompt* compliance to include in the reasonable period of time, time to conduct studies or to consult experts to demonstrate the *consistency* of a measure already judged to be *inconsistent*. That cannot be considered as "particular circumstances" justifying a longer period than the guideline suggested in Article 21.3(c). This is not to say that the commissioning of scientific studies or consultations with experts *cannot* form part of a domestic implementation process in a particular case. However, such considerations are not pertinent to the determination of the reasonable period of time.

40. I would like to emphasize that the obligation of the European Communities to base its measures on an assessment of the risks to human health, in conformity with the provisions of the *SPS Agreement*, commenced on 1 January 1995 when the *WTO Agreement* came into force.[40] Article XVI:4 of the *WTO Agreement* specifically requires every Member to "ensure the conformity of its laws, regulations and administrative procedures with its obligations" under the covered agreements. Contrary to the European Communities' arguments that it did not know that hormone-specific and residue-specific assessments were re-

---

[39] By contrast, in a non-violation case, brought under Article XXIII:1(b) of the GATT 1994, Article 26.1(b) of the DSU states explicitly that "there is no obligation to withdraw".

[40] The Appellate Body affirmed the Panel's finding that the *SPS Agreement* does not limit the temporal application of its provisions to SPS measures adopted *after* 1 January 1995, but also applies to measures which *continued* in effect after the entry into force of the *WTO Agreement*. The Appellate Body also noted that "the measure at issue in this appeal is, since 1 July 1997, no longer embodied in the pre-1995 Directives referred to above, but rather in Directive 96/22, which was elaborated and enacted *after* the entry into force of the *WTO Agreement*. None of the parties contests that the currently applicable measure is subject to the disciplines of Articles 5.1 and 5.5 of the *SPS Agreement*." Appellate Body Report, paras. 128-130.

quired by Article 5.1 of the *SPS Agreement*[41], the European Communities did not need to wait for the Appellate Body Report before commissioning scientific studies to support its import ban. Indeed, the European Communities seemed to recognize this when it convened the *Scientific Conference on Growth Promotion in Meat Production* from 29 November to 1 December 1995 specifically to assess whether there were risks to human health from hormone-treated beef. However, the studies from that *Scientific Conference* were found by the Panel, and confirmed by the Appellate Body, to *not* rationally support the EC import prohibition.[42]

41. To grant the European Communities a further two years, from the date of adoption by the DSB of the Appellate Body Report and Panel Reports, to conduct the risk assessment that was required as of 1 January 1995 would not be consistent with the provisions of the DSU requiring prompt compliance with DSB recommendations and rulings, nor with the obligations of the European Communities under the *SPS Agreement*.

42. For the foregoing reasons, it would not be proper to include in the reasonable period of time granted to the European Communities under Article 21.3(c) of the DSU, an initial phase of two years for the conduct and completion of scientific studies to determine if there is a risk to human health from hormone-treated beef.

V. SHORTER PERIOD THAN 15 MONTHS

43. Having determined that the time required for conducting a risk assessment cannot be considered as "particular circumstances" justifying an extension of the reasonable period of time beyond 15 months, I will turn to the arguments made by the United States and Canada that there are "particular circumstances" which would justify a reasonable period of time of 10 months.

44. The United States and Canada argue that compliance with the recommendations and rulings of the DSB in this case can only be achieved by the repeal of the existing import prohibition, and that within the European legislative system, full implementation is practicable within a period of 10 months, i.e., by 1 January 1999. In their view, the repeal of Directive 96/22 can be effected by means of the consultation procedure under Article 43 of the *EC Treaty*. The European Communities contests this point and maintains that any modification of Directive 96/22 must be based on Article 100a of the *EC Treaty,* and must be adopted, therefore, under the co-decision procedure provided for in Article 189b of the *EC Treaty*. In its written submission, the European Communities asserts that:

---

41 Written submission of the European Communities, para. 52; statements of the European Communities at the oral hearing.

42 Appellate Body Report, para. 197; US Panel Report, para. 8.124; Canada Panel Report, para. 8.127.

> ... the Services of the Commission have come to the conclusion that an act to abolish or amend the Council Directive currently in force that prohibits the use of hormones (i.e. Directive 96/22/EC) will require another Directive of the Council and the European Parliament based on Article 100A of the EC Treaty. This is because the principal objective of the measure in question is to protect human health. Any act based on Article 100A must be adopted in accordance with the special co-decision procedure provided for in Article 189b of the EC Treaty. In addition, the opinion of the Economic and Social Committee is required.[43]

During the oral hearing in this arbitration, the European Communities asserted that, if determined necessary in the light of the results of the risk assessment, it would take the necessary legislative steps to amend or repeal the existing Directive 96/22 within a period of 15 months, using the co-decision procedure provided for in Article 189b of the *EC Treaty*.

45. The United States and Canada argued that the legal basis for any legislative act abolishing or amending Directive 96/22 should be Article 43, not Article 100a, of the *EC Treaty*, since this Directive was based on Article 43 in the first place. They rely on the decision of the European Court of Justice in *United Kingdom* v. *Council*[44], in which the Court found that Article 43 of the *EEC Treaty* applied where the legislation proposed was directed *both* to the objectives of agricultural policy and to other objectives which were pursued on the basis of Article 100 of the *EEC Treaty*. However, the European Communities states that this is no longer good law, and refers to an action brought on 22 July 1997 by the EC Commission challenging the legality of Council Regulation (EC) No. 820/97 of 21 April 1997, which establishes a system for the identification and registration of bovine animals and the labelling of beef and beef products. The Council adopted that Regulation under the provisions of Article 43 of the *EC Treaty* as a measure concerning the production and marketing of beef. The Commission has asked the Court to annul the Regulation for the following reasons:

> ... where such an act has at [*sic*] its principal objective the protection of human health, it must be based on Article 100a of the EC Treaty, even though the act concerns a product included in Annex II of the Treaty and might make a contribution, ancillary to the principal objective, to the attainment of one or more objectives of the common agricultural policy. The Commission considers that the development of the provisions of the EC Treaty relating to public health warrant *a reconsideration* of the interpretation given

43 Written submission of the European Communities, para. 106.

44 Case 68/86, [1988] E.C.R. 855.

> by the Court in the past of the relationship between Article 43 and Article 100 of the EC Treaty.[45] (emphasis added)

46. The European Communities maintains, furthermore, that regardless of the current state of EC law on this issue, the question will be moot when the *Treaty of Amsterdam* comes into force, which could be as early as 1 January 1999. Article 152(4)(b) of the *Treaty of Amsterdam* explicitly provides that "measures in the veterinary and phytosanitary fields which have as their direct objective the protection of public health" must be adopted following the co-decision procedure provided for in Article 189b of the *EC Treaty*.

47. Strictly as a matter of *current* EC law, it would appear that a proposal to repeal or modify Directive 96/22 could be initiated under the provisions of Article 43 of the *EC Treaty*. However, I am mindful that when the *Treaty of Amsterdam* enters into force, which could be as early as 1 January 1999, veterinary and phytosanitary measures which have as their objective the protection of public health must be adopted by means of the co-decision procedure provided for in Article 189b of the *EC Treaty*. The European Communities has also stated that upon the entry into force of the *Treaty of Amsterdam*, any legislative proposal initiated under the consultation procedure provided for in Article 43 would have to be withdrawn and reinitiated under the co-decision procedure provided for in Article 189b of the *EC Treaty*.[46]

VI. AWARD

48. In light of the above considerations, I determine that the reasonable period of time for the European Communities to implement the recommendations and rulings of the DSB in this case is *15 months* from the date of adoption of the Appellate Body and Panel Reports by the DSB, that is, 15 months from 13 February 1998.

---

[45] Case C-269/97, Official Journal No. C 295, 27 September 1997, p. 17.

[46] Statement of the European Communities at the oral hearing.

EUROPEAN COMMUNITIES - CUSTOMS CLASSIFICATION OF CERTAIN COMPUTER EQUIPMENT

Report of the Appellate Body

WT/DS62/AB/R, WT/DS67/AB/R, WT/DS68/AB/R

Adopted by the Dispute Settlement Body on 22 June 1998

European Communities, *Appellant*	Present:
United States, *Appellee*	Beeby, Presiding Member
Japan, *Third Participant*	Ehlermann, Member
	Lacarte-Muró, Member

I. INTRODUCTION

1. The European Communities appeals from certain issues of law covered in the Panel Report, *European Communities - Customs Classification of Certain Computer Equipment*[1] (the "Panel Report") and certain legal interpretations developed by the Panel in that Report. The Panel was established to consider complaints by the United States against the European Communities, Ireland and the United Kingdom concerning the tariff treatment of Local Area Network ("LAN") equipment and personal computers with multimedia capability ("PCs with multimedia capability").[2] The United States claimed that the European Communities, Ireland and the United Kingdom accorded to LAN equipment and/or PCs with multimedia capability treatment less favourable than that provided for in Schedule LXXX of the European Communities[3] ("Schedule LXXX") and, therefore, acted inconsistently with their obligations under Article II:1 of the *General Agreement on Tariffs and Trade 1994* (the "GATT 1994").

---

1 WT/DS62/R, WT/DS67/R and WT/DS68/R, 5 February 1998.

2 The United States submitted three requests for the establishment of a panel: *European Communities - Customs Classification of Certain Computer Equipment*, WT/DS62/4, 13 February 1997; *United Kingdom - Customs Classification of Certain Computer Equipment*, WT/DS67/3, 10 March 1997; and *Ireland - Customs Classification of Certain Computer Equipment*, WT/DS68/2, 10 March 1997. At its meeting of 20 March 1997, the Dispute Settlement Body (the "DSB") agreed to modify, at the request of the parties to the dispute, the terms of reference of the Panel established against the European Communities, so that the panel requests by the United States contained in documents WT/DS67/3 and WT/DS68/2 might be incorporated into the mandate of the Panel established pursuant to document WT/DS62/4. See WT/DS62/5, 25 April 1997.

3 Schedule LXXX of the European Communities, *Final Act Embodying the Results of the Uruguay Round of Multilateral Trade Negotiations*, done at Marrakesh, 15 April 1994.

2. The Panel Report was circulated to the Members of the World Trade Organization (the "WTO") on 5 February 1998. The Panel reached the conclusion that:

> ... the European Communities, by failing to accord imports of LAN equipment from the United States treatment no less favourable than that provided for under heading 84.71 or heading 84.73, as the case may be, in Part I of Schedule LXXX, acted inconsistently with the requirements of Article II:1 of GATT 1994.[4]

The Panel made the following recommendation:

> The Panel recommends that the Dispute Settlement Body request the European Communities to bring its tariff treatment of LAN equipment into conformity with its obligations under GATT 1994.[5]

3. On 24 March 1998, the European Communities notified the DSB[6] of its intention to appeal certain issues of law covered in the Panel Report and legal interpretations developed by the Panel, pursuant to paragraph 4 of Article 16 of the *Understanding on Rules and Procedures Governing the Settlement of Disputes* (the "DSU"), and filed a Notice of Appeal with the Appellate Body, pursuant to Rule 20 of the *Working Procedures for Appellate Review* (the "*Working Procedures*"). On 3 April 1998, the European Communities filed an appellant's submission.[7] On 20 April 1998, the United States filed an appellee's submission[8] and on the same day, Japan filed a third participant's submission.[9] The oral hearing, provided for in Rule 27 of the *Working Procedures*, was held on 27 April 1998. At the oral hearing, the participants and the third participant presented their arguments and answered questions from the Division of the Appellate Body hearing the appeal.

II. ARGUMENTS OF THE PARTICIPANTS

A. Appellant - European Communities

4. The European Communities requests the Appellate Body to review a number of errors of law and certain legal interpretations developed by the Panel. The European Communities submits that the Panel erred in law when it rejected the procedural objections of the European Communities concerning the lack of specificity of the request for the establishment of a panel of the United States,

---

[4] Panel Report, para. 9.1.

[5] Panel Report, para. 9.2.

[6] WT/DS62/8, WT/DS67/6 and WT/DS68/5, 24 March 1998.

[7] Pursuant to Rule 21(1) of the *Working Procedures.*

[8] Pursuant to Rule 22 of the *Working Procedures.*

[9] Pursuant to Rule 24 of the *Working Procedures.*

thus hampering the rights of defence of the responding Member and violating Article 6.2 of the DSU. The European Communities asserts that the Panel also erred in considering that the meaning of a particular heading of the Schedule of a WTO Member should be read in the light of the "legitimate expectations" of an exporting Member outside the context of a non-violation complaint under Article XXIII:1(b) of the GATT 1994. The European Communities also asserts that the Panel erred in finding that Article II:5 of the GATT 1994 confirms this view. Subordinately, the European Communities argues that even if the notion of "legitimate expectations" was relevant in the context of a violation complaint under Article XXIII:1(a) of the GATT 1994, those legitimate expectations should not be based on the classification practices for individual importers and individual consignments, or on the subjective perception of a number of exporting companies of an exporting Member. The European Communities submits that the Panel also erred in considering that, in any case, the onus of clarifying the scope of a tariff concession during a multilateral tariff negotiation under the auspices of the GATT/WTO shall necessarily be on the importing Member. The European Communities asserts that by so doing, the Panel has created new rules on the burden of proof which are inconsistent with the ones applicable to WTO dispute settlement procedures.

1. Request for the Establishment of a Panel

5. The European Communities submits that the Panel erred in finding that the measures under dispute and the products affected by such measures were sufficiently identified by the United States to include measures other than Commission Regulation (EC) No. 1165/95 as far as it concerns LAN adapter cards.[10] The European Communities asserts that the findings of the Panel are based on several legal errors. First, the Panel disregarded the requirement under Article 6.2 of the DSU providing that the request for the establishment of a panel shall "identify the specific measures at issue". Second, the Panel misapplied the established procedural requirement according to which the product coverage of a claim has to be specified prior to the commencement of the Panel's examination. Third, neglecting these procedural requirements which the European Communities invoked before the Panel results in a serious violation of the rights of defence of the European Communities and, as such, constitutes a breach of the demands of due process that are implicit in the DSU.

6. With respect to the identification of the specific measures at issue, the European Communities submits that the request of the United States for the establishment of a panel does not meet the minimum standards contained in Article 6.2 of the DSU. The European Communities asserts that in *European Communi-*

---

[10] Commission Regulation (EC) No. 1165/95 of 23 May 1995 concerning the classification of certain goods in the combined nomenclature, Official Journal No. L 117, 24 May 1995, p. 15.

ties - Regime for the Importation, Sale and Distribution of Bananas[11] ("*European Communities - Bananas*"), the Appellate Body confirmed that the measures at issue in that dispute were adequately identified under Article 6.2 of the DSU by referring to the basic EC regulation at issue, by place and date of publication, in the request for the establishment of a panel. The European Communities states that this reading of Article 6.2 of the DSU, pursuant to which the request must at least specify one basic legal measure, is fully in line with the general rules of interpretation of public international law. In the view of the European Communities, the request of the United States for the establishment of a panel only identifies one specific measure, namely Commission Regulation (EC) No. 1165/95, which is said to "reclassify" LAN adapter cards and which, unlike the regulation at issue in *European Communities - Bananas*, is not a basic measure on which all the other actions complained about are founded. In response to a question asked at the oral hearing, the European Communities expressly accepted that the application of a tariff in an individual case on a consignment is a measure within the meaning of Article 6.2 of the DSU. However, in the view of the European Communities, the measures in question are only vaguely described in the request of the United States for the establishment of a panel. The type of measure, the responsible authority, the date of issue or the reference are not clearly defined. Furthermore, the European Communities argues that it is even unclear how many of these alleged measures are under dispute.

7. The European Communities also submits that under the minimum standard laid down in Article 6.2 of the DSU, relating to the identification of specific measures, it is also necessary to clearly define the product coverage of a claim raised in the framework of a dispute settlement procedure. The European Communities asserts that the Panel erroneously distinguished the present case from *EEC - Quantitative Restrictions Against Imports of Certain Products from Hong Kong*[12] ("*EEC - Quantitative Restrictions Against Hong Kong*") when holding that no new product was added by the United States in the course of the proceedings, and that the definition of LAN equipment provided by the United States, in responding to a question by the Panel, was an elucidation of the product coverage already specified in the request of the United States for the establishment of a panel. According to the European Communities, this reasoning is based on at least two flawed assumptions: first, that LAN equipment and PCs with multimedia capability could each be considered as a single product; and, second, that the explanations of the United States before the Panel concerning product coverage were an "elucidation" rather than an unlawful "curing" of the defective product description in the request for the establishment of a panel.

8. With respect to the first assumption, the European Communities submits that LAN equipment is not a single product but a wide variety of different prod-

---

11 Adopted 25 September 1997, WT/DS27/AB/R.
12 Adopted 12 July 1983, BISD 30S/129.

ucts used in a local area network. Furthermore, the United States has not been consistent regarding the definition of LAN equipment in the course of the panel proceedings. The European Communities also asserts that, like LAN equipment, PCs with multimedia capability are not a single product category. It is further argued by the European Communities that using such broad product categories when defining the scope of a claim is equivalent to adding the convenient phrase "including but not necessarily limited to" in the request for the establishment of a panel. In the view of the European Communities, the Appellate Body in *India - Patent Protection for Pharmaceutical and Agricultural Chemical Products*[13] ("*India - Patents*") vigorously rejected the use of this kind of loose language when holding that "the convenient phrase, 'including but not necessarily limited to', is simply not adequate to 'identify the specific measures at issue and provide a brief summary of the legal basis of the complaint sufficient to present the problem clearly' as required by Article 6.2 of the DSU".[14]

9. The European Communities submits that the second assumption on which the Panel based its reasoning was that the United States elucidated the product coverage of its panel request. The European Communities argues that the Panel appeared to agree that the United States had left the precise scope of the dispute in the dark and, after the first meeting of the Panel with the parties, allowed the United States to provide a definitive list of products with respect to which it alleged there had been a violation. The European Communities asserts that the Panel accepted this list as an "elucidation" and sufficient specification of the product coverage, thus regarding the vague product definition of the United States as cured. In the view of the European Communities, this finding of the Panel amounts to an error in law.

10. The European Communities asserts that in any judicial or quasi-judicial procedure, it is an essential procedural right of the responding party to be aware of the case held against it, and that the WTO dispute settlement system can only produce acceptable solutions to conflicts between WTO Members if this fundamental rule of due process is adequately observed. The European Communities submits that the Appellate Body should, therefore, guarantee this essential procedural right by continuing to interpret Article 6.2 of the DSU strictly.

2. *"Legitimate Expectations" in the Interpretation of a Schedule*

11. According to the European Communities, the existence of a *common* intention forms the basis for the mutual consent of the signatories to be bound by an international agreement. This common intention finds its authentic expression in the text of the treaty, not in the subjective expectations of one or other of the

[13] Adopted 16 January 1998, WT/DS50/AB/R.
[14] *Ibid*., para. 90.

parties to the agreement. The European Communities states that the rules of the *Vienna Convention on the Law of Treaties*[15] (the "*Vienna Convention*") on the interpretation of international agreements are based on this fundamental consideration. Furthermore, the European Communities asserts that the report in *Panel on Newsprint*[16] is based on the correct assumption that a Schedule is an agreed commitment between the contracting parties and is not just the unilateral perception of one of the Members involved in the multilateral negotiations. The European Communities also submits that "protocols and certifications relating to tariff concessions" are an integral part of the GATT 1994[17] and, therefore, are part of an international multilateral agreement which is the result of a "meeting of the minds" and not the sum of subjective perceptions or expectations.

12. The European Communities asserts that the complaint of the United States was founded *only* on the allegation that the European Communities had violated its obligations under Article II:1 of the GATT 1994, which indicates that the claim was based *only* on Article XXIII:1(a) of the GATT 1994. The European Communities also submits that it appears that, when presenting its legal position, the United States used the notion of "reasonable expectations" and "legitimate expectations" as synonymous. The European Communities states that the Panel has not drawn any particular conclusion from the varied definitions of this notion and has apparently, albeit implicitly, decided to consider that the two definitions can be used indifferently to describe the same concept. In the view of the European Communities, the same approach was used by the Appellate Body, in paragraphs 41-42 of its Report in *India - Patents* and, therefore, the European Communities suggests that for the sake of this appeal, the Appellate Body continues to consider the notion of "legitimate expectations" used by the Panel and the parties to this dispute as equivalent to that of "reasonable expectations".

13. The European Communities submits that the Panel erred in law by *not* considering the object and purpose of the tariff concession in Schedule LXXX with respect to the products concerned but rather a supposed and erroneous object and purpose of Article II of the GATT 1994, i.e., the protection of "legitimate expectations". In the view of the European Communities, the Panel should have proceeded, pursuant to Article 31 of the *Vienna Convention*, with the interpretation of the *words* used in Schedule LXXX in the light of *their* object and purpose and within *their* context. The European Communities asserts that the context of the Schedule must include the negotiations, the legal situation in both the exporting and importing Members (including the classification practice of the United States during the entire period of the negotiations), the EC internal legislation applicable to such tariff treatment, the EC customs nomenclature existing

---

[15] Done at Vienna, 23 May 1969, 1155 U.N.T.S. 331; 8 International Legal Materials 679.

[16] Adopted 20 November 1984, BISD 31S/114.

[17] See paragraph 1(b)(i) of the language of Annex 1 A incorporating the GATT 1994 into the *Marrakesh Agreement Establishing the World Trade Organization* (the "*WTO Agreement*"), done at Marrakesh, Morocco, 15 April 1994.

at the time of the drafting of the Schedule and so on. Responding to a question asked by the Appellate Body during the oral hearing, the European Communities stated that on the basis of Article 31(3)(c) of the *Vienna Convention*, the *International Convention on the Harmonized Commodity Description and Coding System*[18] (the "*Harmonized System*") and its *Explanatory Notes*[19] would be relevant in interpreting the obligations of the European Communities under Schedule LXXX *vis-à-vis* WTO Members which are also Members of the World Customs Organization (the "WCO").

14. The European Communities argues that the Panel limited itself to an unmotivated affirmation that the context to be considered pursuant to Article 31 of the *Vienna Convention* was *only* Article II of the GATT 1994, and has proceeded to the totally separate and not directly relevant interpretation of the object and purpose of Article II and *not* of the Schedule. The European Communities asserts that "even more erroneously, [the Panel's] interpretation of Article II has been achieved through the reference to previous case law in a non-violation case, notwithstanding the fact that the present procedure is only concerned with a violation complaint".[20] Therefore, the context that the present Panel considered to be relevant for the interpretation of Schedule LXXX in a violation complaint has been deduced from the interpretation of Article II in a non-violation complaint. The European Communities further asserts that in paragraph 36 of the Appellate Body Report in *India - Patents*, the Appellate Body clearly indicates that the concept of the protection of reasonable expectations of contracting parties relating to market access was developed in the context of non-violation complaints under Article XXIII:1(b) of the GATT. Thus, according to the European Communities, the Panel's finding in paragraph 8.23 contradicts this interpretation and "melds the legally-distinct bases for 'violation' and 'non-violation' complaints under Article XXIII of the GATT 1994 into a uniform cause of action"[21] which is not consistent with Article XXIII.

15. It is further argued by the European Communities that, independently of the legal issues that were at stake in the two dispute settlement procedures, there is an extraordinary resemblance in the legal approach followed by the panel in *India - Patents* and that followed by the present Panel. The European Communities submits that as in *India - Patents*, this Panel: (i) was not about an Article XXIII:1(b) "non-violation" complaint but only about an Article XXIII:1(a) "violation" complaint; (ii) was not about a violation complaint concerning Articles III or XI of the GATT; (iii) was not concerned with the affectation of competitive relationship between imported and domestic products, but rather with the tariff treatment of certain products compared to the concessions scheduled by the

[18] Done at Brussels on 14 June 1983.

[19] *Explanatory Notes to the Harmonized Commodity Description and Coding System*, Customs Cooperation Council, Brussels, 1986.

[20] Appellant's submission of the European Communities, para. 50.

[21] Appellate Body Report, *India - Patents*, adopted 16 January 1998, WT/DS50/AB/R, para. 42.

European Communities in the WTO; and (iv) has considered the "legitimate expectations" of the parties not by examining whether they were reflected in the words of the treaty - Schedule LXXX in this case - but rather by "imputing" into the treaty considerations and subjective "understandings" which the Panel has considered to be the expectations of a Member and of private companies involved in the trade of the covered products and which were never reflected in the wording of the Schedule.

16. The European Communities also submits that the Panel's findings lead to "absurd practical consequences".[22] The European Communities questions how it is possible to determine the content of MFN tariff treatment on the basis of the "legitimate expectations" of *one* Member among all WTO Members. If the "legitimate expectations" of that Member diverges from the "legitimate expectations" of other Members, the consequence would be that a Member, in order to know exactly what is the tariff treatment to grant a given product, would have to verify the potentially divergent "legitimate expectations" of all other WTO Members. This is at odds with the aim affirmed by the Panel to protect the predictability and stability of the tariff treatment of that particular product. Moreover, in the view of the European Communities, the *balance* of mutual concessions among Members, which is the result of the successive rounds of tariff negotiations in the framework of the GATT/WTO, would be severely upset: the "legitimate expectations" of one Member would, through the MFN provision, apply to all other Members whose balance of reciprocal concessions was based on substantially different and variable "legitimate expectations". The European Communities further claims that, if the Panel's findings on this point were upheld, the whole purpose of Article II of the GATT 1994 and of the Members' Schedules would be altered. In the view of the European Communities, a tariff concession bound by a Member in its Schedule would no longer define a limit to the duty applicable upon importation of a given product, but would rather be determined by a unilateral perception of the advantages expected by the exporting Member.

17. The European Communities submits that the Panel violated the rules of interpretation of Articles 31 and 32 of the *Vienna Convention* and Articles 3.2 and 19.2 of the DSU by affirming that "[although] in nearly all instances, the ordinary meaning of the terms of the actual description in a tariff schedule accurately reflects and exhausts the content of the legitimate expectations ... [i]t must remain possible, at least in principle, that parties have legitimately formed expectations based on other particular supplementary factors".[23] According to the European Communities, what the Panel appears to pronounce here is the power to add elements which are not present in the text of the Schedules whereas, under Articles 3.2 and 19.2 of the DSU, a panel is required simply to clarify the provisions of the covered agreements. The European Communities submits that this

[22] Appellant's submission of the European Communities, para. 54.
[23] Panel Report, para. 8.26.

would inevitably alter the very nature of the panel procedure which would be seen as replacing, or attempting to replace, the signatories of the *WTO Agreement.*

18. It is further claimed by the European Communities that the Panel erred by stating that the importance of "legitimate expectations" in interpreting tariff commitments can be confirmed by the text of Article II:5 of the GATT 1994. The European Communities submits that the Panel made two contradictory statements. On the one hand, the Panel stated that Article II:5 confirms the existence of the "legitimate expectations" in Article II:1. One the other hand, however, it stated that Article II:5 is a provision for the special bilateral procedure regarding tariff classification, which is not directly at issue in this case. In the view of the European Communities, there is a clear *non-sequitur* between the affirmation of the inapplicability of Article II:5 to the present case and its use for the interpretation of a different provision which is declared applicable to this case. According to the European Communities, either Article II:5 is relevant and applicable to the present case, in particular for the interpretation of Schedule LXXX, or it is not. It cannot be both at the same time. It is further argued by the European Communities that the only relevance of Article II:5 of the GATT 1994 could have been in the context of a procedure aimed at requesting a compensatory adjustment, which was never pursued by the United States. Thus, according to the European Communities, if the Panel was of the opinion that Article II:5 was relevant, it should have come to the conclusion that it was only relevant in establishing that the United States had never correctly followed it. Alternatively, the European Communities argues that Article II:5 is simply irrelevant.

19. The European Communities also submits that Article II:5 does not prove the existence of a notion of "legitimate expectations" in Article II of the GATT 1994 or, more generally, in the tariff treatment of a given product under the Schedule of a Member. The European Communities notes that the words "believes to have been contemplated" and "contemplated" in the first and second sentence of this provision are highlighted in the Panel Report and, therefore, argues that the Panel attached a special value to them in order to support its findings. The European Communities cannot see how these words, read in their context, could in any way be assimilated to the notion of "legitimate expectations" that was developed in the context of non-violation cases. In the view of the European Communities, there is nothing in the words "believes" or "contemplated" that indicates any reference to an objective entitlement to a tariff treatment that would be different from the one that derives from the *objective* interpretation of the content of the Schedule of the importing Member.

20. In the event that the Appellate Body considers that the notion of "legitimate/reasonable expectations" is relevant in the context of a violation dispute under Article XXIII:1(a) of the GATT 1994, the European Communities submits the following arguments for its consideration. According to the European Communities, the core of the Panel's argument regarding the notion of "legitimate expectations" can be summarized as follows: during a multilateral trade negotiation, the tariff treatment of a given product subject to negotiation is considered

with respect to the "actual normal" tariff treatment at the time of the negotiation, unless there is a "manifestly anomalous" treatment that would indicate "the contrary". Therefore, the meaning of the tariff treatment which is bound in the importing Member's Schedule must correspond to the "actual normal" tariff treatment at the time of the negotiation. Otherwise, there will be a breach of the "legitimate expectations" of the exporting Member and, therefore, a violation of Article II:1 of the GATT 1994.

21. The European Communities submits that the Panel's reasoning is affected by errors in law and in logic in at least three respects. First, the European Communities argues that a duty imposed at a level which is currently lower than the duty bound in a Schedule does not constitute a right for the Members which temporarily benefit from the reduction. Second, the European Communities submits that it is not correct to assert, as the Panel does, that the current duty treatment is taken as the basis for the negotiations and, therefore, that treatment will be continued unless such treatment is manifestly anomalous or there is information readily available to the exporting Member that clearly indicates the contrary. Third, the European Communities argues that elements of subjective judgement such as "normally based", "manifestly anomalous", "information readily available" and "clearly indicates" are not legal elements that must, or even can, be taken into account when interpreting a Member's Schedule and/or Article II of the GATT 1994. These subjective appreciations are not included in Articles 31 and 32 of the *Vienna Convention*. Thus, in the view of the European Communities, irrespective of the existence of any normality or abnormality, or of information readily or not readily available, the actual or current tariff treatment of a certain product could not be considered as an obligation under Article II if it cannot be demonstrated that it is reflected in the Schedule.

22. The European Communities also submits that the Panel should not have dealt with classification issues as the WTO system does deal with these issues in the covered agreements. According to the European Communities, there is no obligation under the GATT to follow any particular system for classifying goods, and a Member has the right to introduce in its customs tariff new positions or sub-positions as appropriate. The European Communities also argues that "[w]hat the Panel has *de facto* done here is weighing the number of *individual* EC *classification* decisions presented as evidence by the US against the opposite EC *individual classification* decisions presented as evidence by the EC in order to achieve the result that the former are correct and the latter are not".[24] The European Communities asserts that this is nothing less than a classification decision by the Panel in spite of the fact that the Panel itself rightly considers classification issues to be outside its terms of reference.

[24] Appellant's submission of the European Communities, para. 82.

3. *Clarification of the Scope of Tariff Concessions*

23. The European Communities submits that the Panel erred in considering that the onus of clarifying the scope of a tariff concession during a multilateral tariff negotiation under the auspices of the GATT/WTO shall necessarily be placed on the side of the importing Member. In the view of the European Communities, the issue at stake in this dispute is not whether a requirement of clarification was on the United States or on the European Communities, but rather whether the agreement, which the United States claims it reached with the European Communities and other WTO Members, on certain tariff treatment of LAN equipment, really existed and was reflected in Schedule LXXX.

24. The European Communities asserts that the Panel dedicated three pages to the totally irrelevant issue of the burden of "clarification", which is treated separately from the issue of whether the United States has proven its assertion that Schedule LXXX contains an obligation to provide tariff treatment lower than the one applied. It is further argued by the European Communities that the Panel cannot rely on two contradictory assertions at the same time. *Either* the burden of proof and the burden of clarification are different notions, in which case the Panel should have explained to the parties and to the Members of the WTO how this is relevant in the present dispute, *or* the burden of clarification is identical with the notion of burden of proof or has, in any case, a bearing on the burden of proof in such a way as to determine a different distribution of that burden between the party which asserts and the party which responds.

25. The European Communities submits that in this second scenario, the Panel has in fact created a newly invented rule on the burden of proof. According to this burden of proof, "the exporting Member that could show the existence of *practices* on the current classification of individual shipments by some 'prevailing' customs authorities of a Member would have proved its assertion that a tariff treatment was *agreed* in the Schedule, ... irrespective of whether it has actually *proved* that the existence of the *agreement* on a certain tariff treatment was actually reflected in the text of the agreement (or of the agreed Schedule). The burden of clarifying the content of the Schedule is on the importing Member: as a result, that Member is to blame for any misunderstanding".[25]

26. The European Communities cannot agree with this newly invented rule. This rule would allow the Member who asserts that a certain agreement was passed on the tariff treatment of a given product to shift the burden of proof to the responding Member without any need to submit evidence related to the words of the agreement. In the view of the European Communities, the result of such an "easy" shift of the burden of proof on the responding Member would be that, failing any written document, it would find itself in the practical impossibility of rebutting that assumption. An assertion would amount to a proof, and an almost unrebuttable one, which is fundamentally at odds with the finding of the Appel-

[25] Appellant's submission of the European Communities, para. 88.

late Body in *United States - Measure Affecting Imports of Woven Wool Shirts and Blouses from India* [26] ("*United States - Shirts and Blouses*").

B. Appellee - United States

27. The United States endorses the findings and conclusions of the Panel. The United States submits that the Panel was correct in determining that the request of the United States for the establishment of a panel sufficiently identified the measures and products at issue. The United States also asserts that regardless of whether the Appellate Body accepts the Panel's reasoning and interpretation of "legitimate expectations", the findings of the Panel Report support its ultimate conclusion that the impairment of treatment resulting from actions of customs authorities in the European Communities is inconsistent with Article II:1 of the GATT 1994. The United States also submits that the Panel correctly followed the standard laid down by the Appellate Body in *United States - Shirts and Blouses* and that, contrary to the arguments of the European Communities, the Panel did not establish a new burden of proof rule.

1. Request for the Establishment of a Panel

28. The United States asserts that the Panel correctly followed the guidance of the Appellate Body decision in *European Communities - Bananas* in determining that the United States sufficiently identified the measures and products at issue. According to the United States, the meaning of the term "specific measures", as used in Article 6.2 of the DSU, was addressed in *European Communities - Bananas* where the panel found that the panel request complied with the requirements of Article 6.2 of the DSU because the measures contested by the complainants were "adequately identified", even though they were not listed explicitly. In the view of the United States, the panel and Appellate Body decisions in *European Communities - Bananas* "teach that the specificity requirement of Article 6.2 will be met if the responding party is provided sufficient notice and identification of the measure(s) at issue, even if those measures are not specifically identified".[27]

29. It is further argued by the United States that its panel request identified both the timing and nature of the measures at issue which, in the application since June 1995 by the customs authorities in the European Communities, consist of tariffs to LAN equipment higher than those provided for in Schedule LXXX.[28] The United States also submits that as of March 1997, both the European Communities and the United States agreed that Member State customs authorities

---

[26] Adopted 23 May 1997, WT/DS33/AB/R.

[27] Appellee's submission of the United States, para. 33.

[28] We note that the United States also argued with regard to its two additional requests for the establishment of a panel (WT/DS67/3 and WT/DS68/2) that they also identified both the timing and nature of the measures at issue (appellee's submission of the United States, paras. 34 and 35).

were applying the higher tariff rates, under heading 85.17, to imports of LAN equipment. Accordingly, in the view of the United States, the European Communities has never had any basis to claim that it lacked sufficient information about the measures the United States sought to have modified at the time of the establishment of the panel. In applying the "adequate" or "sufficient" notice test of *European Communities - Bananas*, the United States submits that the European Communities had clear notice from the explicit terms used in the panel requests of the United States that the complaint concerned the application of higher tariffs for LAN equipment by customs authorities of Member States. Since the panel request identified the same measures which the European Communities acknowledged its customs officials were applying, the European Communities suffered, in the view of the United States, no prejudice, let alone prejudice sufficient to rise to the level of a violation of due process.

30. The United States submits that there is no basis for the assertion of the European Communities that the description of the United States of "all types of LAN equipment" and the allegedly inappropriate "curing" of the request for the establishment of a panel have led to a "serious violation of the European Communities' rights of defence". According to the United States, these arguments ignore the fact that the term, LAN equipment, is a recognized term of the trade and that, beginning as early as the pre-consultation stage of this dispute through the panel proceedings, the European Communities was made sufficiently aware of which products were the subject of the dispute. According to the United States, the argument of the European Communities also ignores the many contacts between officials of the European Communities and the United States prior to the submission of the panel request, in which the term, LAN equipment, was routinely used and understood. The United States disagrees with the European Communities regarding the need for parties to exhaustively detail every conceivable sub-grouping of more broader categories of products which are detailed in a request for the establishment of a panel. In the view of the United States, the appropriate standard to be applied to product coverage should be similar to that applied by the panel in *European Communities - Bananas* to the specificity of measures: whether the products are "sufficiently identified". According to the United States, applying the logic followed in *European Communities - Bananas*, such a test would be met if the complaining party identifies the general product grouping of the products concerned in terms of the ordinary meaning in a commercial context.

31. The United States submits that the Panel was correct when it stated that the more detailed definition of LAN equipment, provided by the United States to the Panel in response to a question, was an "elucidation" of the product coverage already specified in the requests of the United States for the establishment of a panel. According to the United States, the present case is quite different from the situation in *European Communities - Bananas* and *India - Patents* with respect to

the addition of a new claim. In the request for the establishment of a panel against the European Communities[29], the United States first defined the parameters of the products at issue - all LAN products - and then provided examples of some types of LAN products. The United States submits that it need not have provided any such examples to have complied with Article 6.2 of the DSU because the term LAN products is a sufficiently precise term of the trade. Nor should the United States or any other WTO Member be required to exhaustively enumerate all product category sub-groups in its panel request. The United States also asserts that since its request for the establishment of a panel properly identified LAN equipment, the Panel was correct in distinguishing the present case from the panel decision in *EEC - Quantitative Restrictions Against Hong Kong*.

32. In the view of the United States, if the arguments of the European Communities on the specificity of product definition are accepted, there inevitably will be long, drawn-out procedural battles at the early stage of the panel process in every proceeding. The United States submits that according to the theory of the European Communities, a complaining party would be required to list each and every product in detail in its panel request.

2. *"Legitimate Expectations" in the Interpretation of a Schedule*

33. The United States submits that the attack of the European Communities on the Panel's reasoning places form over substance. In the view of the United States, the substance of the findings of the Panel is its fact-finding which supports the conclusion that the ordinary meaning of "automatic data-processing machines and units thereof" includes LAN equipment. The Panel found that the meaning of the text of the concession in heading 84.71 can include LAN equipment and that, as a matter of fact, Member State customs authorities treated LAN equipment as automatic data-processing machines ("ADP machines") during the Uruguay Round and that the European Communities had given the United States and other trading partners reason to believe that this treatment would be continued. It is further argued by the United States that during the panel proceeding, the European Communities did not produce or prove facts demonstrating that LAN equipment was intended to be included in the binding in heading 85.17 of Schedule LXXX.[30]

34. Thus, in the view of the United States, regardless of whether the Appellate Body accepts the Panel's reasoning and interpretation of "legitimate expectations", the findings of the Panel Report support its ultimate conclusion that the European Communities, by failing to accord to imports of LAN equipment treat-

---

29 See footnote 2 of this Report.

30 Heading 85.17 relates to "electrical apparatus for line telephony or line telegraphy, including such apparatus for carrier-current line systems"(hereinafter referred to as "telecommunications equipment").

ment no less favourable than that provided for in headings 84.71 or 84.73 of Schedule LXXX[31], has acted inconsistently with its obligations under Article II:1 of the GATT 1994. The United States argues that the Panel's reasoning was correct but that, even if the Appellate Body should reverse certain aspects of this reasoning, the Appellate Body should affirm the Panel's ultimate conclusion.

35. The United States submits that the Panel has properly interpreted the obligations of the European Communities under Schedule LXXX and Article II of the GATT 1994 in accordance with Articles 31 and 32 of the *Vienna Convention*. The text of the concession in heading 84.71 of Schedule LXXX provides that this concession applies to "automatic data processing machines and units thereof". According to the United States, the ordinary meaning of "automatic data processing machines and units thereof" includes computers and computer systems, as well as units of computers such as computer networking equipment, i.e., LAN equipment. The United States submits that the function of LAN equipment is not "line telephony or line telegraphy" but that of facilitation of shared processing and storage of data within a computer network or an extended computer system. The Panel found that the text of this concession *can* include LAN equipment and that to the extent the ordinary meaning of the concession is ambiguous, that ordinary meaning can be clarified by the practice of the importing Member. In the view of the United States, these findings are eminently reasonable and are consistent with prior GATT and WTO practice. They can and should be affirmed.

36. The United States asserts that an important factor in determining the "ordinary meaning" of a term used in a Schedule is how the negotiating Members treated the particular product at issue - in this case, how the European Communities, the United States and interested third parties treated LAN equipment. According to the United States, while the Panel's analysis in paragraphs 8.23-8.28 labels such treatment as an element of "legitimate expectations", this label is not essential to the Panel's conclusion. The United States submits that regardless of the label, what is important is that the factual findings of the Panel, concerning the actual treatment of LAN equipment during the Uruguay Round, amount to a determination that the parties assumed and intended that the concession under heading 84.71 in Schedule LXXX would cover LAN equipment.

37. The United States argues that "factual indicia" of "legitimate expectations" which the Panel actually considered can also be regarded as the factual context of the concessions in Schedule LXXX as facts indicating the object and purpose of the concessions in Schedule LXXX, or as a "supplementary means of interpretation" admissible under Article 32 of the *Vienna Convention*. According to the United States, whether the Panel's analysis was phrased as an interpretation of "legitimate expectations", or whether it was an interpretation of the intentions

31 Heading 84.71 relates to "automatic data-processing machines and units thereof ..."and heading 84.73 relates to "parts and accessories (other than covers, carrying cases and the like) suitable for use solely or principally with machines of heading Nos. 84.69 to 84.72"(hereinafter referred to together as "ADP machines").

and understandings of the negotiating parties, the conclusion is the same. The United States submits that the important point here is that the intentions of the United States, as well as the third parties in this dispute, were a relevant factor for the Panel to consider in interpreting the ordinary meaning of the terms used in Schedule LXXX.

38. Responding to a question asked by the Appellate Body during the oral hearing, the United States asserted that the *Harmonized System* and its *Explanatory Notes* could be deemed as part of the "circumstances of the conclusion" of the *WTO Agreement* within the meaning of Article 32 of the *Vienna Convention* and, therefore, could be used as a "supplementary means of interpretation" of Schedule LXXX. However, the United States also submitted that the *Explanatory Notes* are not generally treated as binding because they contain certain contradictions and are occasionally outdated. Thus, the United States considered that although the *Explanatory Notes* are relevant under Article 32 of the *Vienna Convention*, they should be treated with caution.

39. The United States submits that the European Communities argues that the text is the *only* permissible input for interpreting a Schedule. According to the United States, such a position leads to the conclusion that whenever a treaty interpreter cannot determine whether a given product falls within the exact product composition of a concession on the basis of the text of that concession, the importing Member can make this determination unilaterally. If this is the case, then the tariff obligations provided for under Articles II:1(a) and (b) of the GATT 1994, and the tariff concessions in the Schedules, would be reduced to inutility.

40. The United States further argues that the Panel properly considered the concept of "legitimate expectations" of WTO Members in analyzing whether LAN equipment is included within the scope of the EC's concession in heading 84.71. The United States believes that the Panel properly relied on the concept of "legitimate expectations" and that the decision in *India - Patents* does not require the rejection of the Panel's use of "legitimate expectations" as a factor in its analysis of whether the European Communities is in violation of its obligations under Article II of the GATT 1994.

41. The issue, as the United States sees it, is really whether the "legitimate expectations" of an exporting Member are a relevant factor in determining the intentions of the negotiators and thus in determining the ordinary meaning of the terms used in the concession in heading 84.71 of Schedule LXXX. The United States submits that the Panel properly used the concept of "legitimate expectations" in determining and clarifying the intentions of the parties in this case. According to the United States, such an interpretation is supported by the text and context of Article II, as well as its object and purpose. In the view of the United States, the concept of "legitimate expectations" is entirely relevant in the context of any dispute concerning the application of actual tariff concessions. Contrary to the argument of the European Communities, the United States submits that the Panel's analysis has nothing to do with a "melding" of a basis for complaint under

Articles III or XI of the GATT and a basis for a "non-violation nullification or impairment" complaint.

42. The United States argues that the argument of the European Communities confuses and distorts the Appellate Body's reasoning in *India - Patents*, and that it twists this reasoning into an instrument for undermining the enforcement of bargained-for tariff concessions. In the view of the United States, the conclusions argued by the European Communities are by no means ordained by the Appellate Body's findings and conclusions in *India - Patents*. The United States asserts that the European Communities has attempted to conflate the concept of "legitimate expectations", as used by the Panel, with the concept of "reasonable expectations" in the context of Article XXIII:1(b) of the GATT. The United States submits that these concepts are not the same thing. The phrases may exhibit accidental linguistic convergence, but are legally and historically distinct and deal with different situations. In the view of the United States, it is both possible and necessary to distinguish between the concepts employed in enforcing obligations under Articles III or XI of the GATT, the concepts involved in a "non-violation nullification or impairment complaint" and the concept of "legitimate expectations" employed by the Panel in the present dispute. According to the United States, all three concepts are intellectually and historically distinct and independent. They need not be distorted and conflated in the manner advocated by the European Communities.

43. The United States submits that as the Appellate Body pointed out in *India - Patents*, panels considering violation complaints concerning Articles III and XI of the GATT have developed the concept of protecting the expectations of contracting parties concerning the competitive relationship between their products and the products of other contracting parties. According to the United States, Article II of the GATT 1994 is different in nature from Article III. The obligations of Article II only apply to the extent that a Member has made tariff bindings in a Schedule. The United States asserts that Article II also has nothing to do with guaranteeing the equality of opportunity with regard to competitive conditions. The provisions of Article II permit and recognize the existence of tariffs and "other duties and charges" imposed at the border which imply an intentional competitive *inequality* between imports and like domestic products.

44. According to the United States, as the Appellate Body has noted in *India - Patents*, the non-violation provision of Article XXIII:1(b) was aimed at preventing contracting parties from using non-tariff barriers, or other policy measures, to negate the benefits of negotiated tariff concessions. Like Article II of the GATT 1994, the non-violation remedy under Article XXIII:1(b) recognizes the existence of tariff barriers at the border, as well as the terms, conditions or qualifications of tariff concessions, which create intentional competitive *inequality* between imports and like domestic products. Thus, the United States submits that Article II and the non-violation remedy are broadly alike in that they both protect bargained-for market access and the integrity of Schedules. However, Article II protects and enforces the tariff concession itself. According to the United States, tariff concessions safeguard the right to a particular tariff rate, and a Member's

responsibility to charge a duty no higher than the level bound in its Schedule, on products covered by the tariff binding in question.

45. The United States submits that the Panel, in the present dispute, used "legitimate expectations" as an interpretative aid to determine what the concession in heading 84.71 means, as well as whether LAN equipment was meant to be within the product composition of heading 84.71. If it is further argued by the United States that, on the other hand, the concept of "actions that could not reasonably have been anticipated" or "reasonable expectations" has been used in non-violation cases to answer the question that Article XXIII:1(b) raises, namely what GATT-legal impediments to market access an importing Member may impose without taking away the value of the concession (as opposed to violating the obligation to maintain the concession itself). Therefore, in the view of the United States, "legitimate expectations" are relevant in the interpretation of obligations under Article II of the GATT 1994, and actions which "could not reasonably have been anticipated" are relevant in the application of the non-violation remedy under Article XXIII:1(b). However, these two concepts apply under different conditions and for different purposes. The United States argues that the concept of "legitimate expectations" is entirely relevant in the context of any dispute concerning the violation of tariff concessions; the Panel's analysis has nothing to do with a "melding" of a basis for complaint under Articles III or XI of the GATT and a basis for a "non-violation nullification or impairment" complaint.

46. It is further argued by the United States that the context of the Uruguay Round Schedules, as defined by Article 31(2) of the *Vienna Convention*, clearly includes the GATT 1994 and, in particular, Article II thereof. The United States submits that the text of Article II:5 of the GATT 1994 is, therefore, a relevant part of this context and the Panel properly interpreted the meaning of tariff obligations in the light of Article II:5. According to the United States, in the text of Article II:5 the "treatment provided for" is to be understood as the "treatment contemplated by a concession". The United States asserts that the term used in Article II:5 is "contemplated" and that such a provision does not require that treatment has been "discussed" or "expressly agreed". In the view of the United States, the ordinary meaning of "contemplate" in this context is "to expect"; the "treatment" in question must be the treatment by the importing Member which was contemplated at the time. Thus, the United States concludes that the "treatment" provided by a concession is the treatment legitimately expected by the trading partners of the Member making the concession. According to the United States, in the present case, that treatment is the treatment these products were known to be receiving in the European Communities, openly and legally, at the time the binding was negotiated.

47. The United States asserts that it properly invoked Article II:5 of the GATT 1994 and complied with all its procedural requirements. However, discussions under Article II:5 stopped short when, as the European Communities itself recognizes, the European Communities refused to agree that the treatment contemplated was that claimed by the United States. According to the United States, it was this refusal that prevented any negotiations under Article II:5 with regard

to a compensatory adjustment. Therefore, in the view of the United States, having frustrated the procedures of Article II:5, the European Communities may not claim them as a defence to its own violation of Article II:1.

48. The United States disagrees with the alternative argument of the European Communities that the Panel erred in relying on particular types of evidence, namely Binding Tariff Information ("BTIs") and actual trade data, as a factual basis for its findings of fact concerning actual tariff treatment during the Uruguay Round and the "legitimate expectations" based on that treatment. According to the United States, the European Communities distorts the Panel Report by arguing that the Panel found that the tariff treatment bound in Schedules must correspond to the actual tariff treatment, or else there is a breach of the "legitimate expectations" of the exporting Member and therefore a violation of Article II:1 of the GATT 1994. The United States submits that the substance of the Panel's findings amounted to an interpretation of the ordinary meaning of the concession in heading 84.71, on the basis of its text, context, object and purpose. Thus, in the view of the United States, the Panel has, in essence, interpreted the intentions of the parties and has determined what, in fact, the actual tariff treatment of LAN equipment was as a factor in evaluating those intentions.

49. The United States asserts that the European Communities is arguing that, when interpreting a Schedule, the only evidence that may be taken into account is the text of the Schedule itself. The United States submits that this "text only" approach not only contradicts the guidance of the *Vienna Convention* and the Appellate Body, with regard to the interpretation of treaties, but also leads to establishing the right of an importing Member to arbitrarily change the duty treatment of products whenever the text of the relevant concession is ambiguous.

50. According to the United States, the Panel did not use BTIs in order to determine how LAN equipment should be classified. Rather, it used BTIs as a form of factual evidence concerning the actual tariff treatment of certain products during a particular historical period. Therefore, the United States submits that the Panel properly relied on the evidence before it, including BTIs, affidavits by exporters and actual trade data, as a basis for its findings of fact concerning the actual tariff treatment of LAN equipment during the Uruguay Round and the legitimate expectations based on that treatment. In the view of the United States, the Panel's fact-finding was within the scope of its discretion under Article 11 of the DSU and, because these findings are factual, they do not fall within the permissible scope of an appeal under Article 17.6 of the DSU.

3. Clarification of the Scope of Tariff Concessions

51. According to the United States, when the Panel rejected the assertion of the European Communities that the exporting Member bears the burden of clarifying the product composition of concessions during tariff negotiations, the Panel did not, as the European Communities suggests, create a new rule on the burden of proof in dispute settlement proceedings. Rather, the Panel correctly followed the standard laid down by the Appellate Body in *United States - Shirts and*

Blouses. The United States submits that the Panel examined first, whether the United States had presented factual information sufficient to raise the presumption that its claim concerning the actual treatment of LAN equipment during the Uruguay Round was true and, second, whether the European Communities had presented evidence sufficient to rebut that presumption once raised. In the view of the United States, the Panel correctly found that the United States had raised such a presumption as a matter of fact and that the European Communities had failed to rebut that presumption.

52. Regarding the argument of the European Communities that the Panel Report dedicates three pages to the totally irrelevant issue of the burden of clarification, the United States submits that it finds this claim curious because it is in this section of the Panel Report[32] that the Panel addressed the purported defence of the European Communities that the United States should have clarified, during the negotiations, where LAN equipment would be classified. If the Panel had accepted this defence from the European Communities, the Panel would have imposed, according to the United States, a new rule limiting the scope of proof that could be brought forward by an exporting Member, in this situation, by restricting the exporting Member to textual arguments concerning the meaning of the terms in Schedule LXXX. Thus, the United States argues that if any change in the burden of proof is suggested, that suggestion comes from the European Communities and not the Panel or the United States.

53. The United States submits that the European Communities is wrong in asserting that the Panel's findings permitting exporting Members to present evidence of tariff treatment of individual shipments, practices of current classification and other such evidence, would permit the exporting Member to shift the burden of proof to the responding Member without any need to submit evidence related to the words of the agreement. The United States asserts that it submitted to the Panel evidence concerning the meaning of the term ADP machines in Schedule LXXX and the various products falling within that definition based on treatment by the WCO, the European Communities and industry. According to the United States, it never argued to the Panel - and does not assert now - that it could sustain its burden of proof in this case without setting out the meaning of the terms of the agreement. The United States sustained its burden of demonstrating that the term ADP machines included all types of LAN equipment.

C. Third Participant - Japan

54. Japan submits that the Panel's legal reasoning regarding "legitimate expectations" and the requirement of clarification was correct and, therefore, requests that the European Communities respect the conclusion of the Panel and

[32] Panel Report, paras. 8.48-8.55.

bring its tariff treatment of LAN equipment into conformity with its obligations under the GATT 1994.

55. Japan asserts that "[g]enerally, ... the importing Member is obliged to identify products and relevant duties in its tariff schedules ... if the importing Member requests to limit or determine a scope of the tariff concession and relevant duties for the products, which are not classified under the heading of the Harmonized System Committee (HSC) of the CCC and therefore classified differently in several countries".[33] It is further argued by Japan that, "[i]n particular, the classification of the LAN equipment among the Members of the EC was not identical before the Uruguay Round. In other words, the common classification of the LAN equipment within the Members of the EC had not been established before the Uruguay Round, and the responsibility, the EC was required to discharge in this context, was inevitable".[34]

56. Japan submits that it agrees with the Panel that a tariff commitment is an instrument in the hands of an importing Member, in the light of its function to protect its own industry. Therefore, in the view of Japan, "[i]f the importing Member wishes to prove the expectations of the exporting Member, that a certain practice of its tariff classification will continue, are not legitimate, the importing Member as the effective bearer of its rights and responsibilities, will be in a position to correctly identify products and relevant duties in its tariff schedules, including such limitations or modifications as it intends to apply. Otherwise, no proof will be required to deny the legitimate expectations of the exporting Member that the tariff classification will continue and the predictability of protection through the imposition of tariffs would not be maintained".[35]

III. ISSUES RAISED IN THIS APPEAL

57. The appellant, the European Communities, raises the following issues in this appeal:

(a) Whether the measures in dispute, and the products affected by such measures, were identified with sufficient specificity by the United States in its request for the establishment of a panel under Article 6.2 of the DSU;

(b) Whether the Panel erred in interpreting Schedule LXXX, in particular, by reading Schedule LXXX in the light of the "legitimate expectations" of an exporting Member, and by considering that Article II:5 of the GATT 1994 confirms the interpretative value of "legitimate expectations"; and

---

33 Japan's third participant's submission, para. 8.

34 *Ibid.*

35 *Ibid.*, para. 9.

(c) Whether the Panel erred in putting the onus of clarifying the scope of a tariff concession during a multilateral tariff negotiation conducted under the auspices of the GATT/WTO, solely on the importing Member.

IV. REQUEST FOR THE ESTABLISHMENT OF A PANEL

58. The first issue that we have to address is whether the measures in dispute, and the products affected by such measures, were identified with sufficient specificity by the United States in its request for the establishment of a panel under Article 6.2 of the DSU.

59. Article 6.2 of the DSU provides, in part, that the request for the establishment of a panel shall:

> ... identify the specific measures at issue and provide a brief summary of the legal basis of the complaint sufficient to present the problem clearly. ...

60. The Panel considered that:

> ... the substance of the present case is the actual tariff treatment by customs authorities in the European Communities and the evaluation of that treatment in the light of the tariff commitments in Schedule LXXX.[36]

The Panel found that:

> Viewed from this perspective, ... the United States has sufficiently identified the measures subject to the dispute, which concerns tariff treatment of LAN equipment and multimedia PCs by customs authorities in the European Communities.[37]

61. The Panel found that the definitions given by the United States of the terms, LAN equipment and PCs with multimedia capability, are "sufficiently specific for the purposes of our consideration of this dispute".[38]

62. The European Communities appeals these findings and submits that:

> The Panel erred where it found that the measures under dispute and the products affected by such measures were identified sufficiently specifically by the United States to include measures other than Commission Regulation (EC)

[36] Panel Report, para. 8.12.
[37] *Ibid.*
[38] Panel Report, paras. 8.9-8.10.

> No. 1165/95 as far as it concerns Local Area Network (LAN) adapter cards.[39]

63. According to the European Communities, the request of the United States for the establishment of a panel:

> ... identifies one specific measure, namely Commission Regulation (EC) No. 1165/95 ... [relating to] LAN adapter cards. The other alleged measures are only vaguely described, without clearly identifying the type of measure, the responsible authority, the date of issue and the reference.[40]

64. We note that the request of the United States for the establishment of a panel reads in relevant part:

> Since June 1995, customs authorities in the European Communities, including but not limited to those in the United Kingdom and Ireland, have been applying tariffs to imports of all types of LAN equipment - including hubs, in-line repeaters, converters, concentrators, bridges and routers - in excess of those provided for in the EC Schedules. Those products were previously dutiable as automatic data-processing equipment under category 8471, but, as a result of the customs authorities' action, are now subject to the higher tariff rates applicable to category 8517, "telecommunications apparatus". In addition, since 1995, customs authorities in the European Communities, particularly those in the United Kingdom, have increased tariffs on imports of certain personal computers ("PCs") from 3.5 per cent to 14 per cent, which is above the rate provided for in the EC Schedules. These increases have resulted from the reclassification of PCs with multimedia capability from category 8471 to other categories with higher duty rates.[41]

65. We consider that "measures" within the meaning of Article 6.2 of the DSU are not only measures of general application, i.e., normative rules, but also can be the application of tariffs by customs authorities.[42] Since the request for the establishment of a panel explicitly refers to the application of tariffs on LAN equipment and PCs with multimedia capability by customs authorities in the European Communities, we agree with the Panel that the measures in dispute

---

39 Notice of Appeal of the European Communities, para. 1.

40 Appellant's submission of the European Communities, para. 19.

41 WT/DS62/4, 13 February 1997.

42 In an answer to a question at the oral hearing, the European Communities expressly accepted that "the application of a tariff in an individual case on a consignment is a measure" within the meaning of Article 6.2 of the DSU.

were properly identified in accordance with the requirements of Article 6.2 of the DSU.

66. With respect to the products affected by such measures, we note that the European Communities and the United States disagree on the scope of the terms, LAN equipment and PCs with multimedia capability. Regarding LAN equipment, the disagreement concerns, in particular, whether multiplexers and modems are covered by this term.

67. We note that Article 6.2 of the DSU does *not* explicitly require that the products to which the "specific measures at issue" apply be identified. However, with respect to certain WTO obligations, in order to identify "the specific measures at issue", it may also be necessary to identify the products subject to the measures in dispute.

68. LAN equipment and PCs with multimedia capacity are both generic terms. Whether these terms are sufficiently precise to "identify the specific measure at issue" under Article 6.2 of the DSU depends, in our view, upon whether they satisfy the purposes of the requirements of that provision.

69. In *European Communities - Bananas*, we stated that:

> It is important that a panel request be sufficiently precise for two reasons: first, it often forms the basis for the terms of reference of the panel pursuant to Article 7 of the DSU; and, second, it informs the defending party and the third parties of the legal basis of the complaint.[43]

70. The European Communities argues that the lack of precision of the term, LAN equipment, resulted in a violation of its right to due process which is implicit in the DSU. We note, however, that the European Communities does not contest that the term, LAN equipment, is a commercial term which is readily understandable in the trade. The disagreement between the European Communities and the United States concerns its exact definition and its precise product coverage.[44] We also note that the term, LAN equipment, was used in the consultations between the European Communities and the United States prior to the submission of the request for the establishment of a panel[45] and, in particular, in an "Information Fiche" provided by the European Communities to the United States during informal consultations in Geneva in March 1997.[46] We do not see how the

[43] Appellate Body Report, adopted 25 September 1997, WT/DS27/AB/R, para. 142.

[44] Answer of the European Communities to a question at the oral hearing.

[45] See, for example, the letter from the Vice-President of the Commission of the European Communities, Sir Leon Brittan, to the United States Trade Representative, Ambassador Michael Kantor, dated 7 December 1995 (first submission of the United States to the Panel, Attachment 26); and the letter from the United States Trade Representative, Ambassador Michael Kantor, to the Vice-President of the Commission of the European Communities, Sir Leon Brittan, dated 8 March 1996 (first submission of the United States to the Panel, Attachment 28).

[46] "Information Fiche" attached to letter from the Head of Permanent Delegation of the European Commission to the International Organizations in Geneva, Ambassador R.E. Abbott, to the Chargé

alleged lack of precision of the terms, LAN equipment and PCs with multimedia capability, in the request for the establishment of a panel affected the rights of defence of the European Communities *in the course* of the panel proceedings. As the ability of the European Communities to defend itself was not prejudiced by a lack of knowing the measures at issue, we do not believe that the fundamental rule of due process was violated by the Panel.

71. The United States has stressed that "if the EC arguments on specificity of product definition are accepted, there will inevitably be long, drawn-out procedural battles at the early stage of the panel process in every proceeding. The parties will contest every product definition, and the defending party in each case will seek to exclude all products that the complaining parties may have identified by broader grouping, but not spelled out in 'sufficient' detail".[47] We share this concern.

72. We agree with the Panel that the present case should be distinguished from *EEC - Quantitative Restrictions Against Hong Kong*. The request of the United States for the establishment of a panel refers to "all types of LAN equipment". Individual types of LAN equipment were only mentioned as examples. Therefore, unlike the panel in *EEC - Quantitative Restrictions Against Hong Kong*, we are not confronted with a situation in which an additional product item was added in the course of the panel proceedings.[48] This is not a case in which an attempt was made to "cure" a faulty panel request by a complaining party.[49]

73. In conclusion, we agree with the Panel that the request of the United States for the establishment of a panel fulfilled the requirements of Article 6.2 of the DSU.

---

d'Affaires of the United States to the WTO, Mr. A.L. Stoler, 13 March 1997 (first submission of United States to the Panel, Attachment 23).

[47] Appellee's submission of the United States, para. 50.

[48] In paragraph 30 of the panel report in *EEC - Quantitative Restrictions against Hong Kong*, the panel stated:

> The Panel considered that just as the terms of reference must be agreed between the parties prior to the commencement of the Panel's examination, similarly the product coverage must be clearly understood and agreed between the parties to the dispute.

We have already noted that Article 6.2 of the DSU does *not* require that the products at issue be specified in a request for the establishment of a panel. Also, Article 7 of the DSU provides that panels shall have standard terms of reference, unless the parties to the dispute agree otherwise within 20 days from the establishment of the panel.

[49] We recall that in our report in *European Communities - Bananas*, para. 143, we found that:

> If a *claim* is not specified in the request for the establishment of a panel, then a faulty request cannot be subsequently 'cured' by a complaining party's argumentation in its first written submission to the panel or in any other submission or statement made later in the panel proceeding.

V. "LEGITIMATE EXPECTATIONS" IN THE INTERPRETATION OF A SCHEDULE

74. The European Communities also submits that the Panel erred in interpreting Schedule LXXX, in particular, by:

(a) reading Schedule LXXX in the light of the "legitimate expectations" of an exporting Member; and

(b) considering that Article II:5 of the GATT 1994 confirms the interpretative value of "legitimate expectations".

Subordinately, the European Communities submits that the Panel erred in considering that the "legitimate expectations" of an exporting Member with regard to the interpretation of tariff concessions should be based on the classification practices for individual importers and individual consignments, or on the subjective perception of a number of exporting companies of that exporting Member.

75. Schedule LXXX provides tariff concessions for ADP machines under headings 84.71 and 84.73 and for telecommunications equipment under heading 85.17. The customs duties set forth in Schedule LXXX on telecommunications equipment are generally higher than those on ADP machines.[50] We note that Schedule LXXX does not contain any explicit reference to "LAN equipment" and that the European Communities currently treats LAN equipment as telecommunications equipment. The United States, however, considers that the EC tariff concessions on ADP machines, and not its tariff concessions on telecommunications equipment, apply to LAN equipment. The United States claimed before the Panel, therefore, that the European Communities accords to imports of LAN equipment treatment less favourable than that provided for in its Schedule, and thus has acted inconsistently with Article II:1 of the GATT 1994. The United States argued that the treatment provided for by a concession is the treatment reasonably expected by the trading partners of the Member which made the concession.[51] On the basis of the negotiating history of the Uruguay Round tariff negotiations and the actual tariff treatment accorded to LAN equipment by customs authorities in the European Communities during these negotiations, the United States argued that it reasonably expected the European Communities to treat LAN equipment as ADP machines, not as telecommunications equipment.

76. The Panel found that:

> ... for the purposes of Article II:1, it is impossible to determine whether LAN equipment should be regarded as an ADP machine purely on the basis of the ordinary meaning of the terms used in Schedule LXXX taken in isolation. However, as noted above, the meaning of the term "ADP

---

[50] See Panel Report, paras. 2.10 and 8.1.

[51] See Panel Report, para. 5.15.

> machines" in this context may be determined in light of the legitimate expectations of an exporting Member.[52]

77. In support of this finding, the Panel explained that:

> The meaning of a particular expression in a tariff schedule cannot be determined in isolation from its context. It has to be interpreted in the context of Article II of GATT 1994 ... It should be noted in this regard that the protection of legitimate expectations in respect of tariff treatment of a bound item is one of the most important functions of Article II.[53]

The Panel justified this latter statement by relying on the panel report in *European Economic Community - Payments and Subsidies Paid to Processors and Producers of Oilseeds and Related Animal-Feed Proteins*[54] ("*EEC - Oilseeds*"), and stated that:

> The fact that the *Oilseeds* panel report concerns a non-violation complaint does not affect the validity of this reasoning in cases where an actual violation of tariff commitments is alleged. If anything, such a direct violation would involve a situation where expectations concerning tariff concessions were even more firmly grounded.[55]

78. The Panel also relied on Article II:5 of the GATT 1994, and stated that:

> Although Article II:5 is a provision for the special bilateral procedure regarding tariff classification, not directly at issue in this case, the existence of this provision confirms that legitimate expectations are a vital element in the interpretation of Article II and tariff schedules.[56]

79. Finally, the Panel observed that its proposition that the terms of a Member's Schedule may be determined in the light of the "legitimate expectations" of an exporting Member:

> ... is also supported by the object and purpose of the WTO Agreement and those of GATT 1994. The security and predictability of "the reciprocal and mutually advantageous arrangements directed to the substantial reduction of tariffs and other barriers to trade"(expression common in the preambles to the two agreements) cannot be maintained without protection of such legitimate expectations. This is con-

---

52 Panel Report, para. 8.31.

53 Panel Report, para. 8.23.

54 Adopted 25 January 1990, BISD 37S/86, para. 148.

55 Panel Report, para. 8.23.

56 Panel Report, para. 8.24.

> sistent with the principle of good faith interpretation under Article 31 of the Vienna Convention.[57]

80. We disagree with the Panel's conclusion that the meaning of a tariff concession in a Member's Schedule may be determined in the light of the "legitimate expectations" of an exporting Member. First, we fail to see the relevance of the *EEC - Oilseeds* panel report with respect to the interpretation of a Member's Schedule in the context of a violation complaint made under Article XXIII:1(a) of the GATT 1994. The *EEC - Oilseeds* panel report dealt with a non-violation complaint under Article XXIII:1(b) of the GATT 1994, and is not legally relevant to the case before us. Article XXIII:1 of the GATT 1994 provides for three legally-distinct causes of action on which a Member may base a complaint; it distinguishes between so-called *violation* complaints, *non-violation* complaints and *situation* complaints under paragraphs (a), (b) and (c). The concept of "reasonable expectations", which the Panel refers to as "legitimate expectations", is a concept that was developed in the context of *non-violation* complaints.[58] As we stated in *India - Patents*, for the Panel to use this concept in the context of a violation complaint "melds the legally-distinct bases for 'violation' and 'non-violation' complaints under Article XXIII of the GATT 1994 into one uniform cause of action"[59], and is not in accordance with established GATT practice.

81. Second, we reject the Panel's view that Article II:5 of the GATT 1994 confirms that "legitimate expectations are a vital element in the interpretation" of Article II:1 of the GATT 1994 and of Members' Schedules.[60] It is clear from the wording of Article II:5 that it does not support the Panel's view. This paragraph recognizes the possibility that the treatment *contemplated* in a concession, provided for in a Member's Schedule, on a particular product, may differ from the treatment *accorded* to that product and provides for a compensatory mechanism to rebalance the concessions between the two Members concerned in such a situation. However, nothing in Article II:5 suggests that the expectations of *only* the exporting Member can be the basis for interpreting a concession in a Member's Schedule for the purposes of determining whether that Member has acted consistently with its obligations under Article II:1. In discussing Article II:5, the Panel overlooked the second sentence of that provision, which clarifies that the "contemplated treatment" referred to in that provision is the treatment contemplated by *both* Members.

82. Third, we agree with the Panel that the security and predictability of "the reciprocal and mutually advantageous arrangements directed to the substantial reduction of tariffs and other barriers to trade" is an object and purpose of the

---

57 Panel Report, para. 8.25.

58 See Appellate Body Report, *India - Patents*, adopted 16 January 1998, WT/DS50/AB/R, paras. 36 and 41.

59 Adopted 16 January 1998, WT/DS50/AB/R, para. 42.

60 See Panel Report, para. 8.24.

WTO Agreement, generally, as well as of the GATT 1994.[61] However, we disagree with the Panel that the maintenance of the security and predictability of tariff concessions allows the interpretation of a concession in the light of the "legitimate expectations" of exporting Members, i.e., their *subjective* views as to what the agreement reached during tariff negotiations was. The security and predictability of tariff concessions would be seriously undermined if the concessions in Members' Schedules were to be interpreted on the basis of the subjective views of certain exporting Members alone. Article II:1 of the GATT 1994 ensures the maintenance of the security and predictability of tariff concessions by requiring that Members not accord treatment less favourable to the commerce of *other* Members than that provided for in their Schedules.

83. Furthermore, we do not agree with the Panel that interpreting the meaning of a concession in a Member's Schedule in the light of the "legitimate expectations" of exporting Members is consistent with the principle of good faith interpretation under Article 31 of the *Vienna Convention*. Recently, in *India - Patents*, the panel stated that good faith interpretation under Article 31 required "the protection of legitimate expectations".[62] We found that the panel had misapplied Article 31 of the *Vienna Convention* and stated that:

> The duty of a treaty interpreter is to examine the words of the treaty to determine the intentions of the parties. This should be done in accordance with the principles of treaty interpretation set out in Article 31 of the *Vienna Convention*. But these principles of interpretation neither require nor condone the imputation into a treaty of words that are not there or the importation into a treaty of concepts that were not intended.[63]

84. The purpose of treaty interpretation under Article 31 of the *Vienna Convention* is to ascertain the *common* intentions of the parties. These *common* intentions cannot be ascertained on the basis of the subjective and unilaterally determined "expectations" of *one* of the parties to a treaty. Tariff concessions provided for in a Member's Schedule - the interpretation of which is at issue here - are reciprocal and result from a mutually-advantageous negotiation between importing and exporting Members. A Schedule is made an integral part of the GATT 1994 by Article II:7 of the GATT 1994. Therefore, the concessions provided for in that Schedule are part of the terms of the treaty. As such, the only rules which may be applied in interpreting the meaning of a concession are the general rules of treaty interpretation set out in the *Vienna Convention*.

85. Pursuant to Article 31(1) of the *Vienna Convention*, the meaning of a term of a treaty is to be determined in accordance with the ordinary meaning to be

61 See Panel Report, para. 8.25.
62 Panel Report, *India - Patents*, adopted 16 January 1998, WT/DS50/R, para. 7.18.
63 Appellate Body Report, *India - Patents*, adopted 16 January 1998, WT/DS50/AB/R, para. 45.

given to this term in its context and in the light of the object and purpose of the treaty. Article 31(2) of the *Vienna Convention* stipulates that:

> The context, for the purpose of the interpretation of a treaty shall comprise, in addition to the text, including its preamble and annexes:
>
> (a) any agreement relating to the treaty which was made between all the parties in connexion with the conclusion of the treaty;
>
> (b) any instrument which was made by one or more parties in connexion with the conclusion of the treaty and accepted by the other parties as an instrument related to the treaty.

Furthermore, Article 31(3) provides that:

> There shall be taken into account together with the context:
>
> (a) any subsequent agreement between the parties regarding the interpretation of the treaty or the application of its provisions;
>
> (b) any subsequent practice in the application of the treaty which establishes the agreement of the parties regarding its interpretation;
>
> (c) any relevant rules of international law applicable in the relations between the parties.

Finally, Article 31(4) of the *Vienna Convention* stipulates that:

> A special meaning shall be given to a term if it is established that the parties so intended.

86. The application of these rules in Article 31 of the *Vienna Convention* will usually allow a treaty interpreter to establish the meaning of a term.[64] However, if after applying Article 31 the meaning of the term remains ambiguous or obscure, or leads to a result which is manifestly absurd or unreasonable, Article 32 allows a treaty interpreter to have recourse to:

> ... supplementary means of interpretation, including the preparatory work of the treaty and the circumstances of its conclusion.

[64] R. Jennings and A. Watts (eds.), *Oppenheim's International Law*, 9th ed., Vol. I (Longman, 1992), p. 1275.

With regard to "the circumstances of [the] conclusion" of a treaty, this permits, in appropriate cases, the examination of the historical background against which the treaty was negotiated.[65]

87. In paragraphs 8.20 and 8.21 of the Panel Report, the Panel quoted Articles 31 and 32 of the *Vienna Convention* and explicitly recognized that these fundamental rules of treaty interpretation applied "in determining whether the tariff treatment of LAN equipment ... is in conformity with the tariff commitments contained in Schedule LXXX".[66] As we have already noted above, the Panel, after a textual analysis [67], came to the conclusion that:

> ... for the purposes of Article II:1, it is impossible to determine whether LAN equipment should be regarded as an ADP machine purely on the basis of the ordinary meaning of the terms used in Schedule LXXX taken in isolation.[68]

Subsequently, the Panel abandoned its effort to interpret the terms of Schedule LXXX in accordance with Articles 31 and 32 of the *Vienna Convention* .[69] In doing this, the Panel erred.

88. As already discussed above, the Panel referred to the *context* of Schedule LXXX[70] as well as to the *object and purpose* of the *WTO Agreement* and the GATT 1994, of which Schedule LXXX is an integral part.[71] However, it did so to support its proposition that the terms of a Schedule may be interpreted in the light of the "legitimate expectations" of an exporting Member. The Panel failed to examine the context of Schedule LXXX and the object and purpose of the *WTO Agreement* and the GATT 1994 in accordance with the rules of treaty interpretation set out in the *Vienna Convention.*

89. We are puzzled by the fact that the Panel, in its effort to interpret the terms of Schedule LXXX, did not consider the *Harmonized System* and its *Explanatory Notes*. We note that during the Uruguay Round negotiations, both the European Communities and the United States were parties to the *Harmonized System*. Furthermore, it appears to be undisputed that the Uruguay Round tariff negotiations were held on the basis of the *Harmonized System's* nomenclature and that requests for, and offers of, concessions were normally made in terms of

---

65 I. Sinclair, *The Vienna Convention on the Law of Treaties*, 2nd ed., (Manchester University Press, 1984), p. 141:

> ... the reference in Article 32 of the Convention to the circumstances of the conclusion of a treaty may have some value in emphasising the need for the interpreter to bear constantly in mind the historical background against which the treaty has been negotiated.

66 Panel Report, para. 8.22.

67 See Panel Report, para. 8.30.

68 Panel Report, para. 8.31.

69 As discussed above in paragraphs 76-84, the Panel relied instead on the concept of "legitimate expectations"as a means of treaty interpretation.

70 See Panel Report, paras. 8.23-8.24.

71 See Panel Report, para. 8.25.

this nomenclature. Neither the European Communities nor the United States argued before the Panel[72] that the *Harmonized System* and its *Explanatory Notes* were relevant in the interpretation of the terms of Schedule LXXX. We believe, however, that a proper interpretation of Schedule LXXX should have included an examination of the *Harmonized System* and its *Explanatory Notes*.

90. A proper interpretation also would have included an examination of the existence and relevance of subsequent practice. We note that the United States referred, before the Panel, to the decisions taken by the Harmonized System Committee of the WCO in April 1997 on the classification of certain LAN equipment as ADP machines.[73] Singapore, a third party in the panel proceedings, also referred to these decisions.[74] The European Communities observed that it had introduced reservations with regard to these decisions and that, even if they were to become final as they stood, they would not affect the outcome of the present dispute for two reasons: first, because these decisions could not confirm that LAN equipment was classified as ADP machines in 1993 and 1994; and, second, because this dispute "was about duty treatment and not about product classification".[75] We note that the United States agrees with the European Communities that this dispute is not a dispute on the *correct* classification of LAN equipment, but a dispute on whether the tariff treatment accorded to LAN equipment was less favourable than that provided for in Schedule LXXX.[76] However, we consider that in interpreting the tariff concessions in Schedule LXXX, decisions of the WCO may be relevant; and, therefore, they should have been examined by the Panel.

91. We note that the European Communities stated that the question whether LAN equipment was bound as ADP machines, under headings 84.71 and 84.73, or as telecommunications equipment, under heading 85.17, was *not* addressed

---

72 We recall, however, that in reply to our questions at the oral hearing, both the European Communities and the United States accepted the relevance of the *Harmonized System* and its *Explanatory Notes* in interpreting the tariff concessions of Schedule LXXX. See paras. 13 and 38 of this Report.

73 See Panel Report, para. 5.12.

74 As noted in para. 6.34 of the Panel Report, Singapore pointed out, before the Panel, that:

> ... the WCO's HS Committee had recently decided that LAN equipment was properly classifiable in heading 84.71 of the HS. The HS Committee had specifically declined to adopt the position advanced that heading 85.17 was the appropriate category ... The EC had suggested that the HS Committee decision was intended solely to establish the appropriate HS classification for future imports. It ignored that the language interpreted by the HS Committee was the same language appearing in the EC's HS nomenclature and in the EC's concession schedule at the time of the negotiations and afterwards.

75 Panel Report, para. 5.13.

76 See Panel Report, para. 5.3.

during the Uruguay Round tariff negotiations with the United States.[77] We also note that the United States asserted that:

> In many, perhaps most, cases, the detailed product composition of tariff commitments was *never* discussed in detail during the tariff negotiations of the Uruguay Round ...[78] (emphasis added)

and that:

> The US-EC negotiation on Chapter 84 provided an example of how two groups of busy negotiators dealing with billions of dollars of trade and hundreds of tariff lines relied on *a continuation of the status quo*.[79] (emphasis added)

This may well be correct and, in any case, seems central to the position of the United States. Therefore, we are surprised that the Panel did not examine whether, during the Tokyo Round tariff negotiations, the European Communities bound LAN equipment as ADP machines or as telecommunications equipment.[80]

92. Albeit, with the mistaken aim of establishing whether the United States "was entitled to legitimate expectations"[81] regarding the tariff treatment of LAN equipment by the European Communities, the Panel examined, in paragraphs 8.35 to 8.44 of the Panel Report, the classification practice regarding LAN equipment in the European Communities during the Uruguay Round tariff negotiations. The Panel did this on the basis of certain BTIs and other decisions relating to the customs classification of LAN equipment, issued by customs authorities in the European Communities during the Uruguay Round.[82] In the light of our observations on "the circumstances of [the] conclusion" of a treaty as a supplementary means of interpretation under Article 32 of the *Vienna Convention*[83], we consider that the classification practice in the European Communities during the Uruguay Round is part of "the circumstances of [the] conclusion" of the *WTO Agreement* and may be used as a supplementary means of interpretation within the meaning of Article 32 of the *Vienna Convention*. However, two important observations must be made: first, the Panel did *not* examine the classification practice in the European Communities during the Uruguay Round negotiations *as a supplementary means of interpretation* within the meaning of Article

---

77 See Panel Report, para. 5.28.

78 Appellee's submission of the United States, para. 26.

79 Panel Report, para. 5.31.

80 We note that in paragraph 8 of its third participant's submission, Japan stated that: "[i]n particular, the classification of the LAN equipment among the Members of the EC was not identical before the Uruguay Round".

81 Panel Report, para. 8.60.

82 The lists of the BTIs and classification decisions in the form of a letter, submitted by the parties and considered by the Panel, were attached to the Panel Report as Annex 4 and Annex 6 thereof.

83 See para. 86 of this Report.

32 of the *Vienna Convention*[84]; and, second, the value of the classification practice as a supplementary means of interpretation is subject to certain qualifications discussed below.

93. We note that the Panel examined the classification practice of only the European Communities[85], and found that the classification of LAN equipment by the United States during the Uruguay Round tariff negotiations was not relevant.[86] The purpose of treaty interpretation is to establish the *common* intention of the parties to the treaty. To establish this intention, the prior practice of only *one* of the parties may be relevant, but it is clearly of more limited value than the practice of all parties. In the specific case of the interpretation of a tariff concession in a Schedule, the classification practice of the importing Member, in fact, may be of great importance. However, the Panel was mistaken in finding that the classification practice of the United States was *not* relevant.

94. In this context, we also note that while the Panel examined the classification practice during the Uruguay Round negotiations, it did not consider the EC legislation on customs classification of goods that was applicable at that time. In particular, it did not consider the "General Rules for the Interpretation of the Combined Nomenclature" as set out in Council Regulation 2658/87 on the Common Customs Tariff.[87] If the classification practice of the importing Member at the time of the tariff negotiations is relevant in interpreting tariff concessions in a Member's Schedule, surely that Member's legislation on customs classification at that time is also relevant.

95. Then there is the question of the *consistency* of prior practice. Consistent prior classification practice may often be significant. Inconsistent classification practice, however, *cannot* be relevant in interpreting the meaning of a tariff concession. We note that the Panel, on the basis of evidence relating to *only* five out of the then 12 Member States[88], made the following factual findings with regard to the classification practice in the European Communities:

> To rebut the presumption raised by the United States, the European Communities has produced documents which *indicate* that LAN equipment had been treated as telecommu-

---

[84] It examined the actual classification practice to determine whether the United States could have "legitimate expectations" with regard to the tariff treatment of LAN equipment.

[85] See Panel Report, paras. 8.36-8.44.

[86] See Panel Report, para. 8.60. We note that in paragraph 8.58 of the Panel Report, the Panel stated that the classification of LAN equipment by other WTO Members was not relevant either.

[87] Title I, Part I of Annex I of Council Regulation (EEC) No. 2658/87 of 23 July 1987, Official Journal No. L 256, 7 September 1987, p. 1.

[88] With regard to the manner in which the Panel evaluated the evidence regarding classification practice during the Uruguay Round tariff negotiations, we note that in paragraph 8.37 of the Panel Report, the Panel accepted certain BTIs submitted by the United States as relevant evidence, while in footnote 152 of the Panel Report, it considered similar BTIs submitted by the European Communities to be irrelevant.

> nication apparatus by other customs authorities in the European Communities.[89] (emphasis added)
>
> ... it would be reasonable to conclude at least that the practice [regarding classification of LAN equipment] was not uniform in France during the Uruguay Round.[90]
>
> Germany appears to have consistently treated LAN equipment as telecommunication apparatus.[91]
>
> ... LAN equipment was *generally* treated as ADP machines in Ireland and the United Kingdom during the Uruguay Round.[92] (emphasis added)

As a matter of logic, these factual findings of the Panel lead to the conclusion that, during the Uruguay Round tariff negotiations, the practice regarding the classification of LAN equipment by customs authorities throughout the European Communities was *not* consistent.

96. We also note that in paragraphs 8.44 and 8.60 of the Panel Report, the Panel identified Ireland and the United Kingdom as the "largest" and "major" market for LAN equipment exported from the United States. On the basis of this assumption, the Panel gave special importance to the classification practice by customs authorities in these two Member States. However, the European Communities constitutes a customs union, and as such, once goods are imported into any Member State, they circulate freely within the territory of the entire customs union. The export market, therefore, is the European Communities, not an individual Member State.

97. For the reasons set out above, we conclude that the Panel erred in finding that the "legitimate expectations" of an exporting Member are relevant for the purposes of interpreting the terms of Schedule LXXX and of determining whether the European Communities violated Article II:1 of the GATT 1994. We also conclude that the Panel misinterpreted Article II:5 of the GATT 1994.

---

89 Panel Report, para. 8.40.

90 Panel Report, para. 8.42.

91 Panel Report, para. 8.43.

92 Panel Report, para. 8.41. In this paragraph, the Panel stated that the only direct counter-evidence against the claim of the United States that customs authorities in Ireland and the United Kingdom consistently classified LAN equipment as ADP machines during the Uruguay Round negotiations is a BTI issued by the UK customs authority to CISCO, classifying one type of LAN equipment (routers) as telecommunications apparatus. The Panel dismisses the value of this BTI as evidence on the basis that it "became effective only a week or so before the conclusion of the Uruguay Round negotiations [15 December 1993]". Similarly, in footnote 152 of the Panel Report, the Panel did not consider other BTIs issued by the UK customs authorities to be relevant because they became valid after the conclusion of the Uruguay Round negotiations. We note, however, that all of these BTIs became valid in December 1993 or February 1994, i.e., before the end of the verification process, to which all Schedules were submitted and which took place between 15 February 1994 and 25 March 1994 (MTN.TNC/W/131, 21 January 1994). Therefore, in our view, the Panel should have considered these BTIs.

98. On the basis of the erroneous legal reasoning developed and the selective evidence considered, the Panel was not justified in coming to the conclusion that the United States was entitled to "legitimate expectations" that LAN equipment would be accorded tariff treatment as ADP machines in the European Communities[93] and, therefore, that the European Communities acted inconsistently with the requirements of Article II:1 of the GATT 1994 by failing to accord imports of LAN equipment from the United States treatment no less favourable than that provided for in Schedule LXXX.[94]

99. In the light of our conclusion that the "legitimate expectations" of an exporting Member are not relevant in determining whether the European Communities violated Article II:1 of the GATT 1994, we see no reason to examine the subordinate claim of error of the European Communities relating to the evidence on which the "legitimate expectations" of exporting Members were based.

VI. CLARIFICATION OF THE SCOPE OF TARIFF CONCESSIONS

100. The last issue raised by the European Communities in this appeal is whether the Panel erred in placing the onus of clarifying the scope of a tariff concession during a multilateral tariff negotiation, held under the auspices of the GATT/WTO, solely on the importing Member.

101. In paragraph 8.60 of the Panel Report, the Panel concluded that:

> We find that the United States was entitled to legitimate expectations that LAN equipment would continue to be accorded tariff treatment as ADP machines in the European Communities, based on the actual tariff treatment during the Uruguay Round, particularly in Ireland and the United Kingdom ... We further find that the United States was not required to *clarify the scope* of the European Communities' *tariff concessions* on LAN equipment ... (emphasis added)

Prior to this conclusion, the Panel stated the following:

> ... we find that the European Communities cannot place the burden of clarification on the United States in cases where it has created, through its own practice, the expectations regarding the continuation of the actual tariff treatment prevailing at the time of the tariff negotiations. It would not be reasonable to expect the US Government to seek clarification when it had not heard any complaints from its exporters, who were apparently satisfied with the current tariff

[93] See Panel Report, para. 8.60.
[94] See Panel Report, para. 9.1.

> treatment of LAN equipment in their major export market - Ireland and the United Kingdom.[95]

102. The European Communities appeals these findings, and argues that:

> ... the Panel erred where it considered that, in any case, the onus of clarifying the scope of a tariff concession during a multilateral tariff negotiation ... shall necessarily be put on the side of the importing Member. By doing so, the Panel has created and applied a new rule on the burden of proof in the dispute settlement procedure which is outside its terms of reference and is beyond the powers of a panel.[96]

103. We do not agree that the Panel has created and applied a new rule on the burden of proof. The rules on the burden of proof are those which we clarified in *United States - Shirts and Blouses*.[97]

104. The Panel's findings in paragraphs 8.55 and 8.60 on the "requirement of clarification" are linked to the Panel's reliance on "legitimate expectations" as a means of interpretation of the tariff concessions in Schedule LXXX. They serve to complete and buttress the Panel's conclusion that "the United States was entitled to legitimate expectations that LAN equipment would continue to be accorded tariff treatment as ADP machines in the European Communities".[98]

105. We note that the Panel's findings in paragraphs 8.55 and 8.60 on the "requirement of clarification" were, in fact, the Panel's response to the question whether:

> ... the exporting Member has any inherent obligation to seek clarification when it has been otherwise given a basis to expect that actual tariff treatment by the importing Member will be maintained.[99]

106. We also note the Panel's references[100] to the panel report in *Panel on Newsprint* and the report by the Group of Experts in *Greek Increase in Bound Duty*.[101] In both of these reports, the conclusions on the obligations of the importing contracting party under Article II:1 of the GATT 1994 were reached on the basis of the ordinary meaning of the wording of the respective Schedules. These reports also assume that the tariff concessions made by the importing con-

---

[95] Panel Report, para. 8.55.

[96] Notice of Appeal of the European Communities, para. 4.

[97] Adopted 23 May 1997, WT/DS33/AB/R, DSR 1997:I, 323 at 337. See also, Appellate Body Report, *EC Measures Concerning Meat and Meat Products (Hormones)*, adopted 13 February 1998, WT/DS26/AB/R, WT/DS48/AB/R, paras. 97-109.

[98] Panel Report, para. 8.60.

[99] Panel Report, para. 8.48.

[100] See Panel Report, paras. 8.51-8.54.

[101] L/580, 9 November 1956. We note that while the panel report in *Panel on Newsprint* was adopted by the CONTRACTING PARTIES, the report by the Group of Experts in *Greek Increase in Bound Duty* was not.

tracting party would have had to be limited by "conditions or qualifications" if they were to be interpreted restrictively. That the Panel reads these two reports in this way is evident from the Panel's concluding remark that "these cases ... confirm that the onus of clarifying tariff *commitment* is generally placed on the importing Member"(emphasis added).[102]

107. However, the case before us raises a different problem. The question here is whether the European Communities has committed itself to treat LAN equipment as ADP machines under headings 84.71 or 84.73, rather than as telecommunications equipment under heading 85.17 of Schedule LXXX. We do not believe that the "requirement of clarification", as discussed by the Panel, is relevant to this question.

108. The Panel also based its conclusions on the "requirement of clarification" on a certain perception of the nature of tariff commitments. The Panel stated:

> ... that a tariff commitment is an instrument in the hands of an importing Member which inherently serves the importing Member's "protection needs and its requirements for the purposes of tariff and trade negotiations". ... It is for this reason that it behooves the importing party, as the effective bearer of its rights and responsibilities, to correctly identify products and relevant duties in its tariff schedules, including such limitations or modifications as it intends to apply.[103]

109. We do not share this perception of the nature of tariff commitments. Tariff negotiations are a process of reciprocal demands and concessions, of "give and take". It is only normal that importing Members define their offers (and their ensuing obligations) in terms which suit their needs. On the other hand, exporting Members have to ensure that their corresponding rights are described in such a manner in the Schedules of importing Members that their export interests, as agreed in the negotiations, are guaranteed. There was a special arrangement made for this in the Uruguay Round. For this purpose, a process of verification of tariff schedules took place from 15 February through 25 March 1994, which allowed Uruguay Round participants to check and control, through consultations with their negotiating partners, the scope and definition of tariff concessions.[104] Indeed, the fact that Members' Schedules are an integral part of the GATT 1994 indicates that, while each Schedule represents the tariff commitments made by *one* Member, they represent a common agreement among *all* Members.

110. For the reasons stated above, we conclude that the Panel erred in finding that "the United States was not required to clarify the scope of the European

[102] Panel Report, para. 8.54.
[103] Panel Report, para. 8.50.
[104] MTN.TNC/W/131, 21 January 1994. See also *Marrakesh Protocol to the General Agreement on Tariffs and Trade 1994*, para. 3.

Communities' tariff concessions on LAN equipment".[105] We consider that any clarification of the scope of tariff concessions that may be required during the negotiations is a task for *all* interested parties.

VII. CONCLUSIONS

111. For the reasons set out in this Report, the Appellate Body:

(a) upholds the finding of the Panel that the request of the United States for the establishment of a panel met the requirements of Article 6.2 of the DSU;

(b) reverses the findings of the Panel that the United States was entitled to "legitimate expectations" that LAN equipment would be accorded tariff treatment as ADP machines in the European Communities and, therefore, that the European Communities acted inconsistently with the requirements of Article II:1 of the GATT 1994 by failing to accord imports of LAN equipment from the United States treatment no less favourable than that provided for in Schedule LXXX; and

(c) reverses the ancillary finding of the Panel that the United States was not required to clarify the scope of the European Communities' tariff concessions on LAN equipment.

105 Panel Report, para. 8.60.

EUROPEAN COMMUNITIES - CUSTOMS CLASSIFICATION OF CERTAIN COMPUTER EQUIPMENT

Report of the Panel

WT/DS62/R, WT/DS67/R, WT/DS68/R

Adopted by the Dispute Settlement Body on 22 June 1998 as modified by the Appellate Body Report

TABLE OF CONTENTS

I. INTRODUCTION

1.1 On 8 November 1996, the United States requested consultations with the European Communities (EC) pursuant to Article 4 of the Understanding on Rules and Procedures Governing the Settlement of Disputes (DSU) and Article XXII:1

of the General Agreement on Tariffs and Trade 1994 (GATT 1994) regarding tariff reclassification by the customs authorities of the EC and their member States of Local Area Network (LAN) equipment and personal computers (PCs) with multimedia capability (WT/DS62/1).

1.2 Korea and Canada requested, in communications dated 22 and 25 November 1996, respectively (WT/DS62/2 and WT/DS62/3), to be joined in the consultations, pursuant to paragraph 11 of Article 4 of the DSU.

1.3 Consultations were held between the United States and the EC on 23 January 1997, with Korea and Canada participating. The consultations did not result in a resolution of the dispute. As a result, in a communication dated 11 February 1997 (WT/DS62/4), the United States requested the establishment of a Panel. Accordingly, the Dispute Settlement Body (DSB) at its meeting of 25 February 1997 established a panel with the following terms of reference:

> "To examine, in the light of the relevant provisions of the covered agreements cited by the United States in document WT/DS62/4, the matter referred to the DSB by the United States in that document and to make such findings as will assist the DSB in making the recommendations or in giving the rulings provided for in those agreements".

1.4 The United States, in communications dated 14 February 1997 (WT/DS67/1 and WT/DS68/1), requested consultations with the United Kingdom and Ireland. These requests were made pursuant to Article 4 of the DSU and Article XXII:1 of the GATT 1994 and concerned the tariff reclassification by the customs authorities of the United Kingdom of LAN equipment and PCs with multimedia capability, and the tariff reclassification by the customs authorities of Ireland of LAN equipment.

1.5 Korea requested in a communication dated 28 February 1997 (WT/DS67/2) to join in the consultations requested by the United States with the United Kingdom.

1.6 On 24 February 1997, the United Kingdom and Ireland responded by referring the United States to a letter of the same date, in which the European Communities officially informed the United States that the requested consultations would not be entered into. As the United Kingdom as well as Ireland had declined to enter into consultations, the United States, in communications dated 7 March 1997, proceeded directly to request the establishment of two Panels; one to examine the measures taken by the United Kingdom (WT/DS67/3), and the other to examine the measures taken by Ireland (WT/DS68/2).

1.7 At its meeting of 20 March 1997, the DSB agreed to modify, at the request of the parties to the dispute, the terms of reference of the Panel established at its meeting on 25 February 1997 so that the panel requests by the United States contained in documents WT/DS67/3 and WT/DS68/2 would be incorporated into the mandate of the already existing Panel.

1.8 The modified terms of reference of the Panel are as follows:

> "To examine, in light of the relevant provisions in the GATT 1994, the matters referred to the DSB by the United States in documents WT/DS62/4, WT/DS67/3 and WT/DS68/2, and to make such findings as will assist the DSB in making the recommendations or in giving the rulings provided for in that agreement".

1.9 In light of this decision, the DSB agreed not to establish separate panels pursuant to the requests submitted by the United States and circulated as documents WT/DS67/3 and WT/DS68/2.

1.10 The DSB also took note that the parties had agreed that the "panel established on 25 February 1997, with the terms of reference as modified at the present meeting, will be able to consider, and rule upon, any matter that might have been considered if separate panels had been established in response to those panel requests".

1.11 Furthermore, the DSB took note "that the modification of the terms of reference of the panel established on 25 February 1997 is without prejudice to the interpretation of the European Communities and its member States of the provisions of Article 4, paragraph 3 of the DSU, with regard to the 30-day period referred to in the second sentence of that paragraph".

1.12 The parties to the dispute agreed on 18 April 1997 to the following composition of the Panel:

Chairman: Mr. Crawford Falconer

Members: Mr. Ernesto de La Guardia

Mr. Carlos Antonio da Rocha Paranhos

India, Japan, Korea and Singapore reserved their rights as third parties to the dispute.

II. FACTUAL ASPECTS

A. *Product Description*

1. *Local Area Network Equipment*[1]

2.1 A LAN is an interconnection of a number of computers and computer peripherals (for example, printers, input units, memory units, etc.) using a cabling system. These cables physically interconnect all the individual devices to enable them to communicate through the transmission of data. The principal types of LANs are *Ethernet, Token Ring* and *Fibre Distributed Data Interface* (FDDI). A

---

[1] This description of certain LAN equipment has been given using information provided by the EC and the United States. It is understood that the products described do not present an exhaustive list of all LAN components.

LAN is distinguished from other types of data networks in that the communication is usually limited to a discrete area such as a single office building, a warehouse or a campus.

2.2 In order for PCs to participate in a LAN, they must be connected to each other. This connection has traditionally been made via an adapter, which is inserted in the PC. An *adapter card* or *network card* is a small electronic card generally incorporated into the PC within a network. It converts, processes and formats data for transmission within the computing environment or outside of the network thereby acting as the interface between multiple systems that may employ different technologies.

2.3 If the LAN becomes bigger (for example, larger number of PCs are concerned or larger distances to be covered), more components are needed to connect the different elements of the LAN. Examples of such components are a *hub* (or concentrator). With a hub all the PCs in the LAN have a wire or cable leading from the LAN adapter card to a shared hub. The computers connected to the hub "see" all the packets[2] sent over the network. However, only the intended recipient PC "recognizes" the destination address, which triggers it to process the incoming packet. In this arrangement, only one computer in the LAN can transmit data at a time. Hubs may also act as network managers, by collecting information about the status of each network port and activating or shutting down a port where necessary.

2.4 Computers sharing a single hub are referred to as a *LAN segment*. Segments can be connected to other segments by means of a device called a *bridge*. A *bridge* hands data from one segment to the next, and affords security within a network as segments are partitioned from one another, thereby permitting restricted access to individual segments where necessary. In a typical LAN bridge architecture, a number of networks or segments will be bridged to each other creating a circle of bridges, one of which acts as an inactive back-up which will activate or "boot" on failure of an existing active bridge.

2.5 A *router* is another device used to link segments within a local area network or to link more than one local area network. Unlike the bridge, it is aware of exact destination addresses within a network and can optimize the route by which the data is to be delivered within the network. It segments a network in the same manner as a bridge, filters data, offers security, and protects data from "traffic jams".

2.6 Another way to organize a LAN is to use *LAN switches*. As noted above, the limitation of using a hub is that only one computer can transmit data at a time. With a switch, packets are directed only to their intended destination and there-

---

[2] Specialized software formats data into "packets", which can then be sent from one PC to another. The formatted data will include a source address, a destination address and control information which is used by the network to direct packet through the network.

fore the system can direct packets from several sources to several destinations at one time.

2.7 A *repeater* is a device that regenerates data which is being routed from one part of the computer network to another. The repeater receives, builds and passes on the signal within a LAN, so that it can still be "heard" by the time it reaches its destination.

2.8 A network may use a variety of media to link up the various units operating on the LAN, for example *optical fibre converter, thick or thin coaxial cable, shielded or unshielded twisted pair cable. Media interface modules (MIMs)* are used to allow these different media to be connected into one network. A *multi-station access unit* or *multi media access center* is a unit combining a repeater module and a number of media interface modules.

2. *Personal Computers with Multimedia Capabilities*[3]

2.9 From their inception, computers have had the ability to process data in the form of digital, video and audio media. However, factors such as cost, memory capacity and speed rendered it impractical to incorporate these types of functions into most early PC models. In the late 1980s and early 1990s, continuing technological developments enabled PCs to process digital data streams more effectively and efficiently, resulting in the appearance of personal computers with multimedia capabilities. Such equipment, which may include a large capacity data storage unit such as a CD-ROM drive, is able to use computing technology to produce sounds, images or video, and may have specialized circuitry (i.e. a TV tuner card) which allows the computer to convert a television reception signal into a digital data stream for display on the computer's monitor.

B. *Tariff Concessions Contained in EC Schedule - LXXX Relating to Items under Tariff Headings 84.71, 84.73, 85.17, 85.21 and 85.28*

2.10 Schedule LXXX provides that the base rate on "automatic data processing machines and units" under HS heading 84.71 will be reduced from 4.9 per cent to a final bound rate of either 2.5 per cent or duty free depending on the product. For "parts and accessories of machines under 84.71"covered by HS heading 84.73, and more particularly electronic assemblies, the base rate of 4 per cent is to be reduced to 2 per cent. In the case of parts and accessories of such machines other than electronic assemblies, the base rate of 4 per cent will be reduced to duty free. In the case of "electrical apparatus for line telephony or telegraphy" under HS heading 85.17, the base rate of 7.5 per cent is to be reduced to 3.6 per cent or duty free, and the base rate of 4.6 per cent to 3.6 per cent or

[3] The description has been given using information provided by the EC and the United States.

3 per cent. For products under HS heading 85.21 concerning video recording or reproducing apparatus, no reduction is envisaged and the bound rates are either duty free, 8 per cent or 14 per cent. Heading 85.28 pertaining to television receivers have bound rates of 8 per cent and 14 per cent with no reduction envisaged on any item with the exception of black and white or other monochrome television receivers which will have their base rate of 14 per cent reduced to 2 per cent. Regarding the staging of these tariff reductions, according to the Marrakesh Protocol to the GATT 1994, "... The tariff reductions agreed upon by each Member shall be implemented in five equal rate reductions, except as may be otherwise specified in a Member's Schedule." The first such reduction was to be made effective upon the entry into force of the WTO Agreement and each successive reduction is to be made effective on 1 January of each following year.[4]

C. *Classification Determinations in the EC, Ireland and the United Kingdom*

1. *Commission Regulations*

(a) Classification Procedure in the EC

2.11 The European Communities form a customs union.[5] Accordingly, on imports from third countries, a Common Customs Tariff (CCT) is applied.[6] While the CCT is adopted centrally by the EC, the member States' customs authorities are involved for the purpose of administration. When goods arrive at the Community frontier for customs clearance, the customs authorities of the member State through which the goods are imported in the EC territory apply the CCT determined for that year.[7] The customs authorities check which heading of the CN the importer has mentioned on the declaration forms and apply the corresponding duty of the CCT. It is possible that, as may occur in any customs administration, customs authorities in different member States classify a product

---

4 See Annex 1. Additionally, a note on "Implementation of Concessions" in Section II (Other Products) of Part I (Most-Favoured-Nation Tariff) of Schedule LXXX reads as follows: "Should the US not implement its concessions under the conditions set out in Note 2 to Chapter 84 and Note 12 to Chapter 85 in its schedule, the EC reserves the right to do the same with respect to the concessions indicated in this schedule for the following headings: ... Chapter 85; 85.17.10.00; 85.17.20.00; 85.17.30.00; 85.17.40.00: 85.17.81.10; 85.17.81.90; 85.17.82.00; 85.17.90.90; Ex1 New, Ex2 New; 85.17.90.91; Ex1 New, Ex2 New; 85.17.90.90, Ex1 New, Ex2 New; ...". Consequently, the applied duty rate in the European Communities for these products under heading 85,17 has been 7.5 per cent since 1995.

5 Articles 12 to 17 of the Treaty Establishing the European Communities.

6 Articles 18 to 29 of the Treaty Establishing the European Communities.

7 "The Commission shall adopt each year by means of a Regulation a complete version of the combined nomenclature together with the corresponding autonomous and conventional rates of duty of the Common Customs Tariff, as it results from measures adopted by the Council or by the Commission. The said Regulation shall be published not later than 31 October in the *Official Journal of the European Communities* and it shall apply from 1 January of the following year."(Article 12 of Council Regulation (EEC) No. 2658/87, OJ 1987 L 256/1).

differently, which could lead to different duties being applied. It was indicated that, for this reason, the EC has put into place mechanisms in order to detect and remedy any such divergent practices.[8]

2.12 When divergences on a classification matter have been detected, the Tariff and Statistical Nomenclature Section (TSNS) of the Customs Code Committee which is composed of representatives of the member States and chaired by representatives of the Commission[9], examines the issue and advises on what it views the correct classification to be. The Committee may examine a matter referred to it by its Chairman either on the Chairman's initiative or at the request of a representative of a member State. Following the opinion of the Committee, the Commission may adopt a Regulation concerning the classification of goods. Where the Commission does not agree with the Committee's opinion, or where no opinion is delivered within the time-limit set out by its Chairman, the Commission presents its proposal to the Council, which takes a decision through a qualified majority. A classification Regulation, adopted either by the Commission or the Council is binding in its entirety and directly applicable in all member States of the European Communities.

2.13 It is also possible that where an individual believes that a customs decision is based on an incorrect classification of goods, the customs decision may be attacked before the national tribunals and courts of the member State in question. If the national tribunal or court considers it unclear how the product should be classified, it may refer the case to the European Court of Justice (ECJ).[10] As such the ECJ can clarify classification issues in its case law.

(b) Commission Regulation (EC) No 1165/95[11] on LAN Adapter Cards

2.14 On 23 May 1995, the Commission of the EC adopted Regulation (EC) No. 1165/95 which classified LAN adapter cards under the Combined Nomenclature (CN) Code[12] 8517.8290 which covers:

8 In particular, the EC has created a data base containing all Binding Tariff Information (BTI - see section 2(a) for "Definition and Evolution of BTIs within the EC") issued within the EC. Customs authorities must consult this data base before issuing a new BTI in order to make sure that they are aware of the classification practices as contained in the BTIs of all other customs authorities in the EC. If they discover in the data base that their own classification practice differs from that of any other customs authority in the EC for a similar product, they must consult with such other customs authority. If the customs authorities directly concerned cannot agree on a common approach, the internal co-ordination process of the EC is set in motion.

9 Article 7 of Council Regulation 2658/87, OJ 1987 L 256/1.

10 Article 177 of the Treaty Establishing the European Communities.

11 See Annex 2.

12 The EC's Combined Nomenclature (CN) Code provided for in Council Regulation (EEC) 2658/87 of 23 July 1987, is based on the Harmonized Commodity Description and Coding System. The Harmonized System (HS) was established by the International Convention on the Harmonized Commodity Description and Coding System on 14 June 1983, and the EC adhered to this Conven-

"Electrical apparatus for line telephony or line telegraphy, including such apparatus for carrier-current line systems:

- Other apparatus

-- Telegraphic

--- Other"

2.15 The stated intention of this Regulation was to ensure that henceforth LAN adapter cards were classified in HS heading 8517.8290 in face of the fact that certain member States had issued Binding Tariff Information[13] under a heading other than the one considered appropriate for this product. The Regulation states that an adapter card is for "incorporation in cable linked digital automatic data-processing (ADP) machines enabling the exchange of data over a local area network (LAN) without using a modem. With such a card, an ADP-machine can be used as an input-output device for another machine or a central processing unit. The card constitutes a printed circuit of a size of about 10x21 cm incorporating integrated circuits and active and passive components. It is fitted with a row of pin contacts corresponding to an expansion slot in the ADP-machine with an attachment to the connection cable of the LAN and light emitting diodes (LEDs)".

2. *Binding Tariff Information (BTI)*

(a) Definition and Evolution within the EC

2.16 A natural or legal person wishing to know how goods planned for export or import are classified by the national customs authorities of the member State through which the goods will enter the EC market, may request a BTI. A BTI constitutes a commitment of the relevant customs authorities vis-à-vis the individual applicant on how they will read the nomenclature and classify the goods described in the request for customs purposes.

2.17 Prior to 1991, BTIs only existed, on the basis of national law, in Germany and could only be obtained and used for customs clearance there. This practice was extended Community-wide with the stated rationale of encouraging import and export trade by facilitating the conclusion of medium-and long-term contracts for identical goods on the basis of reliable customs information. This was introduced in the EC by Council Regulation No. 1715/90 with rules for implementation contained in Commission Regulations Nos. 3796/90 and 2674/92. The first two of these Regulations entered into force on 1 January 1991, and on the basis of these provisions, BTIs could be obtained from a customs office in a particular member State, but could not be used for customs clearance in the customs offices of a member State other than the one whose customs authorities had is-

---

tion on 7 April 1987, by means of a Council Decision 87/369. It entered into force in the EC on 1 January 1988.

[13] See section 2(a) of this text for "Definition and Evolution of BTIs within the EC".

sued the BTI. On 1 January 1993, Commission Regulation No. 2674/92 which stipulated for the first time that BTIs issued by the customs authorities of one EC member State were binding on customs authorities of all other EC member States, came into force. These rules have now been consolidated in Council Regulation No. 2913/92 containing the Community Customs Code and by Commission Regulation No. 2454/93 containing implementing provisions for the Community Customs Code. These implementing provisions entered into force on 1 January 1994 as provided in Article 915 of Commission Regulation 2454/93.

(b) Withdrawal and Re-Issuance of BTIs by the Ireland Revenue Commission Concerning LAN equipment

2.18 By letter of 28 April 1995, the Ireland Revenue Commission withdrew BTIs it had issued on 11 August 1993 to a company Cabletron Systems LTD, in which it had classified units of bridges, routers, hubs, repeaters, media interface module and multi media access centre in CN heading 8471.99.10000, dutiable at 4.9 per cent. Simultaneously, it issued new BTIs classifying these products under 8517.8290, dutiable at 7.5 per cent. In their letter to Cabletron, the Irish authorities had stated that this action had been taken following discussions by the Tariff and Statistical Nomenclature Section (mechanical sector) of the Customs Code Committee (Nomenclature Committee) of the European Union on the classification of networking equipment and the issuance of Commission Regulation (EC) 1638/94 which classified adapters and transceivers in CN heading 85.17. The letter also indicated that discussion had been taking place at the Nomenclature Committee on the classification of network cards, that agreement had been reached that these products should be classified at CN heading 85.17, that a classification regulation was being drafted and that the Irish authorities would be amending Cabletron's BTIs for network cards as soon as the classification regulation was published. After the publication of Regulation 1165/95, the Irish authorities withdrew Cabletron's BTIs for LAN adapter cards that had been classified at CN heading 84.71. The Irish authorities simultaneously issued BTIs for these products in CN heading 85.17.

3. Customs Determination by the UK HM Customs and Excise Concerning LAN Equipment

2.19 On 23 March 1992, the UK HM Customs and Excise issued a letter stating that LAN adapter cards would be classified under heading 8471.9910.900.[14] It further specified that "This decision does not constitute Binding Tariff Information (BTI) within the meaning of Regulation (EEC) 1715/90. On 28 July 1993, UK HM Customs and Excise issued another letter specifying that LAN boards and repeaters imported in board form were dutiable at 4 per cent under

---

[14] Although not indicated in the letter, the product was dutiable at 4.9 per cent.

CN code 84.73 ("Parts and accessories of the machines of heading 84.71"); repeaters imported in complete units were to be dutiable at 4.9 per cent, under classification 8471.9910.900.

2.20 On 5 April 1994, the UK HM Customs and Excise issued a letter which reversed the decision contained in its letter of March 1992. It indicated that a review had been undertaken of the classification of networking equipment and on the basis of this review, it had concluded that all networking equipment including Local Area, Wide Area, Token Ring, Ethernet networks were "appropriately classified as data transmission apparatus in heading 8517". The reason provided was that apparatus which accepted data and transmitted it to a local or remote site was performing a data transmission function, which met the terms of heading 85.17, covering electrical apparatus for line telephony or line telegraphy which included apparatus for carrier current line systems. It considered heading 85.17 to be more specific than heading 84.71, which covered units of an automatic data processing machine. Additionally, the final paragraph of Chapter 84, note 5[15] of the Harmonized System[16] directed that heading 84.71 did not cover machines incorporating or working in conjunction with an automatic data processing machine and performing a specific function. The UK HM Customs and Excise further stated that in its letter dated 23 March 1992, it had classified LAN adapter cards under heading 8471.9910.900, but to "... note that all future importations/exportations of these products will be under heading 8517.82900, duty rate 7.5 per cent".

2.21 In another letter also dated 5 April 1994, the UK HM Customs and Excise provided the same aforementioned explanations before referring to its letter dated 28 July 1993, in which it had classified LAN Boards, Repeaters, Token Ring and Ethernet Products under headings 84.71/84.73 and noting "...that all future im-

[15] Note 5 of Chapter 84 of the HS: "(A) For the purposes of heading No. 84.71, the expression "automatic data processing machines" means: (a) Digital machines, capable of (1) storing the processing program or programs and at least the data immediately necessary for the execution of the program; (2) being freely programmed in accordance with the requirements of the user; (3) performing arithmetical computations specified by the user; and (4) executing, without human intervention, a processing program which requires them to modify their execution, by logical decision during the processing run; (b) Analogue machines capable of simulating mathematical models and comprising at least; analogue elements, control elements and programming elements; (c) Hybrid machines consisting of either a digital machine with analogue elements or an analogue machine with digital elements. (B) Automatic data processing machines may be in the form of systems consisting of a variable number of separately-housed units. A unit is to be regarded as being a part of the complete system if it meets all the following conditions: (a) it is connectable to the central processing unit either directly or through one or more units; (b) it is specifically designed as part of such a system (it must, in particular, unless it is a power supply unit, be able to accept or deliver data in a form (code or signals) which can be used by the system). Such units presented separately are also to be classified in heading No. 84.71. Heading No. 84.71 does not cover machines incorporating or working in conjunction with an automatic data processing machine and performing a specific function. Such machines are classified in the headings appropriate to their respective functions or, failing that, in residual headings".

[16] See footnote 12.

portations/exportations of these products will be under heading 8517.8290, duty rate 7.5 per cent...".

4. UK VAT and Duties Tribunal Ruling on PCTVs[17]

2.22 On 17 April 1996, the UK VAT and Duties Tribunal upheld a customs administration determination classifying as a "television receiver" under heading 85.28 a multimedia PC.

2.23 The appeal was taken by International Computer LTD (ICL) against a decision of the UK Customs and Excise Commissioners as to the tariff classification for import customs duty of a Fujitsu ICL "PCTV". The tribunal stated that this PCTV "is both a multimedia personal computer and a full function colour television set, integrated within the same unit and using the same screen". ICL contended that the machine should be classified under heading 84.71 entitled "Automatic data processing machines", which carried a duty rate on importation of 4.4 per cent. The Commissioners had decided that it fell under heading 85.28 - "Television receivers", which carried a rate of duty on importation of 14 per cent. ICL contended that the PCTV's principal function and/or its essential character was that of a personal computer. The Commissioners maintained that it was not possible to determine a principal function; so, when presented with two tariff headings which equally deserved consideration, they would classify the PCTV under that heading which occurred last in numerical order, namely 85.28 "Television receivers".

2.24 The tribunal dismissed the appeal. It did not find it possible to determine the principal function of the PCTV. The tribunal also found it doubtful that the "essential character" criterion was applicable in classifying a machine such as the PCTV. Even if that criterion was applicable, the tribunal was not persuaded that the automatic data processing machine was the component which gave the PCTV its essential character. According to the tribunal, the PCTV was "a new kind of hybrid machine which was both a PC and a TV," and neither of which gave it its essential character.

III. CLAIMS OF THE PARTIES

3.1 The **United States** requested the Panel to find that:

- the EC's reclassification of LAN adapter cards under Regulation (EC) 1165/95 resulted in treatment of those products less favourable than that provided for in Part I of Schedule LXXX and therefore was inconsistent with obligations under GATT Article II;

[17] See Annex 3.

- the EC's reclassification of other types of LAN equipment resulted in treatment of those products less favourable than that provided for in Part I of Schedule LXXX and therefore was inconsistent with obligations under GATT Article II;
- the EC's reclassification of multimedia personal computers resulted in treatment of those products less favourable than that provided for in Part I of Schedule LXXX and therefore was inconsistent with obligations under GATT Article II;
- the United Kingdom's reclassification of LAN equipment resulted in treatment of those products less favourable than that provided for in Part I of EC's Schedule of concessions and therefore was inconsistent with obligations under GATT Article II;
- the United Kingdom's reclassification of multimedia personal computers resulted in treatment of those products less favourable than that provided for in Part I of EC's Schedule of concessions and therefore was inconsistent with obligations under GATT Article II;
- Ireland's reclassification of LAN equipment resulted in treatment of those products less favourable than that provided for in Part I of EC's Schedule of concessions and therefore was inconsistent with obligations under GATT Article II;
- the above measures nullified or impaired the value of concessions accruing to the United States under the GATT 1994.

3.2 The United States also requested that the Panel specify which of these parties was responsible to the United States for this nullification or impairment and that the Panel recommend that the EC, Ireland and the United Kingdom bring the treatment of these products into conformity with obligations under GATT 1994.

3.3 The **European Communities** requested the Panel to reject the US claims in their entirety.

More specifically:

- the EC requested the Panel to reject the US claims against Ireland and the United Kingdom. As these member States had not engaged in any tariff bindings vis-à-vis the United States or any other country, they could not be considered to have violated any obligations under GATT Article II, nor had they nullified or impaired the value of concessions accruing to the United States under the GATT 1994;
- moreover, the EC requested the Panel to reject the US claims against the EC, as the EC had for none of the products concerned committed itself to apply the duty rate bound for computers during the Uruguay Round. The EC had not reclassified the products concerned, resulting in treatment of those products less favourable than that provided for in its Schedule. The EC had consequently

not violated any obligations under GATT Article II, nor had it nullified or impaired the value of concessions accruing to the United States under the GATT 1994.

IV. ISSUES REGARDING THE SCOPE OF THE CLAIM

A. *Product Coverage*

1. *LAN Equipment*

4.1 The **European Communities** noted that as established by an earlier panel "Prior to the commencement of the Panel's examination, ... the product coverage must be clearly understood and agreed between the parties to the dispute".[18] However, this was not the situation in the present case. The United States, as complainant had failed to define clearly LAN products subject to the dispute, with the exception of LAN adapter cards. In its first submission, the United States had indicated that products specifically involved in these tariff disputes were: repeaters, bridges, routers, hubs, adapters or network cards, optical fibre converters, media interface modules and multistation access units or multi media access centers. In its pleadings during the first substantive meeting of the Panel, the United States had stated in very general terms that one of the measures attacked was "the change in treatment and resulting increases in tariffs applied to other LAN equipment, including repeaters, bridges, routers, hubs, optical fibre converters, media interface modules, and multi station access units". In its responses to the questions by the Panel on this matter, the United States had presented an enumeration of LAN components, including this time LAN adapter cards, LAN controllers, LAN repeaters, LAN interface units and bridges, LAN concentrators, LAN switches, LAN hubs and LAN routers. With regard to controllers and switches the EC noted that these items were not included in the original US claim. Moreover, the United States appeared to have dropped equipment which it had originally designated as LAN equipment, notably optical fibre converters and multi media access centres. Therefore, in the EC's view, the only products relating to LAN equipment that were subject to dispute were LAN adapter cards. With regard to all other LAN equipment, the United States had failed to identify with sufficient precision and consistency which items were concerned by its original complaint.

4.2 The **United States** asserted that it had specified that the products at issue were LAN equipment, both LAN adapter cards and other LAN equipment. There was nothing vague about the consultation or panel requests by the United States in this respect: the term used in the trade was LAN equipment. Those products were classifiable as "automatic data processing equipment" in the Schedule

---

[18] Panel Report on *EEC - Quantitative Restrictions against Imports of Certain Products from Hong Kong*, adopted on 12 July 1983, BISD 30S/129, para. 30.

maintained by the EC, Ireland and the United Kingdom. The United States had provided further detail when requested by the Panel[19], but the answer could have been ten pages long or hundred pages long, depending on the level of detail desired. But the answer would not have been more complete, because the terms "LAN equipment", "LAN adapter cards" and "other LAN equipment" were meaningful phrases in the trade.

2. *Personal Computers with Multimedia Capability*

4.3 The **European Communities** stated that with regard to PCTVs, the scope of the US claim was even more confusing. The United States had stated on different occasions that the claim concerned "personal computers", "personal computers with multimedia capability" and "all personal computers the tariff treatment of which had been impaired relative to the treatment such products received during the relevant period". At the same time the United States had stated that its complaint was "provoked" by the UK tribunal decision of 1996 in the ICL case and had continued to suggest that its claim was limited to the specific type of PCTV dealt with in that case. As a result, the EC submitted that the only item subject to the dispute was the PCTV implicated in the 1996 judgement.

4.4 The **United States** argued that it sought restoration of the concession negotiated during the Uruguay Round for those personal computers for which tariff treatment had been impaired. This included multimedia PCs with television capability. It also included a broader range of personal computers, such as those which utilized storage devices based on laser-reading technology (i.e., CD-ROMs) and those which also had attendant audio or video capabilities. These were the products which had been subjected to duties in excess of the tariff commitments made by the EC and its member States under heading 84.71. The personal computers involved in this dispute were dealt with in EC Regulation No. 1153/97, issued on 24 June 1997 and which had entered into force on 1 July 1997. That regulation amended the EC tariff schedule to reflect a tariff rate of 3.8 per cent applicable to computers "capable of receiving and processing television, telecommunication, audio and video signals," and of 10.5 per cent applica-

---

[19] US response to the Panel's question: "... violation of tariff commitments under Schedule LXXX ... has taken place with respect to all LAN equipment. Sometimes referred to as "modules," "LAN boards," or "LAN cards," this product area includes the following general categories: - LAN adapter cards, including but not limited to LAN adapter cards and LAN network cards of all types, including those for Token Ring, Ethernet and FDDI systems; - LAN controllers, including but not limited to disk controllers, memory controllers, cluster controllers (including remote control units), storage system controllers, device drivers, and similar controller units; - LAN repeaters, including but not limited to frame relay devices, multi station access units and media interface modules; - LAN interface units and bridges, including but not limited to access servers (analogous to computer network servers), LAN extenders (low end LAN access devices), media interface modules, multi station access units and network computers; LAN concentrators; LAN switches; LAN hubs, including hublets; and LAN routers, including terminal servers not otherwise described as routers".

ble to computers "capable of receiving and processing television signals but having no other specific subsidiary functions".[20]

4.5 The **European Communities** asserted that the United States was trying to expand the scope of the dispute, by mentioning for the first time in its second written submission, EC Regulation No. 1153/97 issued on 24 June 1997, which was unacceptable.

B. Measures at Issue

4.6 The **European Communities** stated that the United States had neglected to indicate for each of the items mentioned in its list, how the EC was supposed to have violated its tariff commitments. The only products for which the United States had identified violating measure were with respect to LAN adapter cards and the PCTV implicated in the 1996 UK judgement; so in its view, those were the only products subject to this dispute.

4.7 The **United States** asserted that (i) on 23 May 1995, EC Commission Regulation (EC) No. 1165/95 mandated reclassification of LAN adapter cards to heading 85.17. It became binding on all member States; (ii) In 1995 and 1996, following adoption of Regulation No. 1165/95, the Irish Revenue Commission withdrew earlier BTIs on various types of LAN equipment and issued a series of new rulings reclassifying them as telecommunications apparatus under heading 85.17. The UK likewise reversed previously issued written determinations confirming treatment of LAN equipment under headings 84.71 and 84.73. In the wake of Regulation No. 1165/95, customs authorities in several other member States, including France, Belgium and Luxembourg also reclassified other types of LAN equipment under heading 85.17[21]; (iii) since 1996 UK customs authori-

[20] In its response to the questions posed by the Panel at the first substantive meeting, the United States had stated that, in March 1997, the EC had submitted to the WTO a document specifying how the appropriate duty treatment to carry out the information Technology Agreement ("ITA") would be provided in its WTO schedule of concessions, pursuant to paragraph 2 of the Ministerial Declaration on Trade in Information Technology Products. This notification concerning the EC's ITA implementation indicated that, as of the 1 July 1997 implementation date for the ITA, the EC and its member States would apply tariffs to these products in excess of the 1997 bound rate for computers provided in Schedule LXXX. However, as the details of ITA implementation by the EC and its member States were not known to the United States at the time of its response, it was not clear whether this implementation would eliminate the violation of tariff commitments by the EC, and its member States. In its second submission, the United States had indicated that the EC had on 24 June 1997 issued its regulation implementing its ITA commitments - Regulation No. 1153/97. As a result, the EC's Common Customs Tariff now explicitly reflected that tariffs were being applied to computers with multimedia capability provided for in heading 84.71 at rates higher than the concession rates agreed to by the EC and its member States during the Uruguay Round.

[21] The US also wished to point out that after the EC published the LAN adapter card regulation in May 1995, the United States had expressed its concerns to the EC. In a 7 December 1995 letter, the EC Commissioner Sir Leon Brittan had responded to Ambassador Kantor that "... The product in question is variously called a network or LAN card. These are the adapter cards permitting exchange of data over a local area network without using a modem. Some Member States in 1994 were classi-

ties had reclassified certain personal computers to heading 85.28. Specifically, the United Kingdom had reclassified and continued to classify, certain personal computers as "television receivers" under CN heading 85.28 as they were capable of receiving and processing television signals. The United States also argued that the amendment of Annex 1 to Council Regulation (EEC) 2658/87 on the tariff and statistical nomenclature and on the Common Customs Tariff through the issuance of Regulation No. 1153/97, confirmed that the EC and its member States had increased the tariff rates applicable to computers with multimedia capability, and confirmed that these products were specifically provided for in heading 84.71.

4.8 In summary, the reclassification of LAN adapter cards and other LAN equipment as "telecommunications apparatus" had resulted in an increase in the applicable tariff to 7.5 per cent from the current applicable bound rate of 2 per cent under heading 84.71. Reclassification of personal computers as "television receivers" had resulted in an increase in the applicable tariff to 14 per cent, from the current bound rate of 3.5 per cent for personal computers under heading 84.71.

C. *Status of Defending Parties*

4.9 The **European Communities** argued that the United States had not always been clear about who the parties to the present dispute were. While the Panel was established on the understanding that the EC replies would address all the claims made by the United States against Ireland and the United Kingdom, there were indications that the United States considered these two member States to be somehow parties to the dispute, which was not the case, in the view of the EC.

4.10 Since the late 1950s and the early 1960s, with the inception of the EC there had been a transfer of sovereignty from the EC member States to the EC, in particular in the area of customs tariffs and associated measures. For this reason, EC member States' individual schedules of tariff concessions had been withdrawn in the GATT and replaced by a (single) EC Schedule of tariff concessions. This happened most recently at the occasion of the accession of Austria, Finland and Sweden at the beginning of 1995 under the aegis of the WTO. When compared to the Schedule of commitments in the area of services, which had as a heading "European Communities and their member States", it became clear that in the

---

fying these items under heading 8473, as parts of automatic data-processing machines, while others (and indeed the majority) were classifying them under heading 8517, as electrical apparatus for line telephony or line telegraphy performing a specific function ... ". Responding to a letter from Ambassador Kantor as to the classification of "additional LAN equipment including bridges, routers and other products", Sir Leon Brittan wrote in a letter dated 28 March 1996 that "there is no current decision or planned action to classify the products you mention as telecoms apparatus." He also noted that he intended "to follow classification proposals closely since they are not just a technical matter".

present EC Schedule of tariff concessions, which had as a heading "European Communities", such tariff concessions were bound in the GATT 1994 (like in the GATT 1947) exclusively at the level of the EC and not at the level of individual member States. This was entirely compatible with Article XI:1 of the WTO Agreement which was negotiated in full knowledge of the above and which did not require EC member States to submit individual schedules of tariff concessions. The EC was an original WTO Member, in its own right.

4.11 In addition, the EC recalled the understanding reached in the present dispute by the joint letter of 20 March 1997 addressed to the Chairman of the DSB, Ambassador Wade Armstrong, which stated that ".. any argument that the United States may wish to put forward relating to the tariff treatment actually applied by the UK or Irish authorities, or related to classification decisions that lie behind such tariff treatment, can be put forward to the Panel established on 25 February 1997 (with terms of reference modified), and ... the European Communities will address any such point in their replies to the US submissions". Moreover, it was agreed in that letter that the Panel already established against the EC would also deal with the claims raised by the United States in documents WT/DS67/3 and WT/DS68/2 with regard to Ireland and the United Kingdom, respectively.

4.12 The **United States** claimed that the present dispute was directed against WTO Members in addition to the EC, as Ireland and the United Kingdom were defending parties in this dispute. Consultation requests had first been addressed to each Member pursuant to Article 4 of the DSU, and subsequently, requests for the establishment of a panel. Indeed, the United States was forced to ask for consultations and establishment of a panel with respect to Ireland and the United Kingdom because it was told during consultations with the EC that there was no centralized EC customs authority and that the Community could not control the classification practices of member State customs authorities.

4.13 The Panel's terms of reference were clear in that they incorporated three dispute settlement matters - one with respect to the measures of the EC, another with respect to the measures of the United Kingdom, and the third with respect to the measures of Ireland. If there had been only one matter before the Panel (i.e., that with respect to the Communities), then the DSB would have adopted terms of reference concerning a single matter. The understanding enshrined in the joint letter of 20 March 1997 dealt with form rather than substance. The European Commission had wished to avoid the establishment of three separate panels. The United States had wished to pursue its rights pursuant to each of the three panel requests and wished to avoid certain procedural delays. The United States had, in fact, traded its right to request three separate panels for the certainty that the existing panel would address its claims in all three of the matters raised, based on the assurances of the Commission that the United States would not be prejudiced in a single panel in its choice of arguments. The EC, Ireland and the United Kingdom were Members of the WTO. As independent Members, Ireland and the United Kingdom hid behind no other Member. Nothing in the text of the GATT 1994 or the DSU limited the scope of application of the provisions of these two agreements with respect to either Member as to its status in a dispute brought under these agreements.

4.14 Moreover, the Commission appeared to suggest that a transfer of sovereignty within the internal legal framework of the EC had resulted in fewer rights and obligations being allotted to the member States. That might be the case in the internal legal framework of the Communities, but that framework was not at issue in this dispute. What was at issue were the WTO rights of the United States and the WTO obligations of the EC, Ireland and the United Kingdom. As such, the obligations of Ireland and the United Kingdom under Article II:1 of GATT 1994 and the concessions reflected in the tariff schedule for the customs union of which Ireland and the United Kingdom were constituents, were in dispute. The United States sought nothing more or less than the benefit of the bargain it had struck in the Uruguay Round. That bargain was reflected in, *inter alia*, those tariff concessions. Whether the European Commission negotiated the tariff concessions on behalf of the member States was beside the point. The legally relevant fact was that a Schedule of Tariff Concessions had been annexed with respect to Ireland and the United Kingdom.

4.15 The **European Communities** disagreed with the US allegation that the transfer of sovereignty between EC member States and the EC was irrelevant on the external plane. The EC had bound a tariff schedule of its own in GATT 1994 and was an original Member of the WTO. This indicated that the transfer of sovereignty had been recognized by Members, and that the EC was more than a simple customs union. The EC was ready to assume its international obligations, but was not ready to allow an attack on its constitution in the WTO.

V. MAIN ARGUMENTS

5.1 The **United States** claimed that the tariff concession granted on heading 84.71 in the EC-Schedule LXXX legally benefited and applied with respect to LAN equipment and multimedia PCs. The imposition of higher duties by the EC, Ireland and the United Kingdom on these products benefiting from this concession through reclassification actions was therefore inconsistent with their obligations under Article II:1 of GATT 1994.

5.2 The **European Communities** disagreed with the US assertion that these products had been reclassified. This was because the EC had never committed itself nor could it be construed to have given the impression that it would classify LAN equipment and PCs with multimedia capabilities under heading 84.71 and apply the corresponding duty.[22] Accordingly, the US complaint could not be in-

[22] The EC argued that it had always considered LAN equipment to be classified under heading 85.17, due to its data transmission function. When considering PCs with "multimedia capabilities", one had to look at the overall situation. When applying the classification rules to individual cases, the EC had determined that these products essentially fell into four categories. One type would be the

terpreted in any other way than as an attempt to revise the negotiating record of the Uruguay Round. However, the result of the Uruguay Round could not be put into question now before the Panel. Indeed, Article 3.2 of the Understanding on Rules and Procedures Governing the Settlement of Disputes (DSU) provided that: ".....Recommendations and rulings by the DSB cannot add to or diminish the rights and obligations provided in the covered agreement". India, Japan, Korea and Singapore, who intervened as third parties, seemed to have blindly adopted the allegations of the US, in particular the statement that the EC during the Uruguay Round, uniformly classified the products concerned as computers. However, they did not bring any proof to this claim either.[23]

5.3 The **United States** wished to note that this dispute did not concern reclassification as such, and that the WTO Agreement included no legal provisions concerning where products should be classified for customs purposes. Rather, this dispute concerned tariff treatment, and in particular the duty increases on LAN equipment and certain personal computers in the EC, Ireland and the United Kingdom. For this reason, the United States was of the view that the original title assigned to this dispute was incorrect.

---

product classified in heading 85.21 due to its capability of reproducing video images (this product was no longer produced). Another type would be classifiable under heading 85.28 because of its television capabilities. Yet another category would be for products with a full range of multimedia functions (i.e. TV, telecommunications, audio and video) which fell within heading 85.43. All other PCs either without or with more limited multimedia functions fell under heading 84.71. Additionally, the particular equipment implicated in the 1996 ICL case was never classified as a computer; therefore it could not have been "reclassified" by the UK customs authorities. In this case the importer had visibly given up any hope for a more favourable judgement upon appeal, because the importer had allowed the judgement of the UK court to become final by not appealing it domestically within the relevant time limit. It appeared instead, that the Panel was now being requested to act as a sort of an appellate body on a domestic court ruling handed down in an individual case. To the knowledge of the EC, challenging a domestic court ruling as a "measure" under the WTO was a novel way of attempting to obtain a more favourable ruling in an individual case. Even if it were true that the domestic court had failed to classify the imported product in a manner allowing proper tariff treatment, which the EC submitted it had not, the EC considered that Article II:5 which would be applicable in such circumstances would pre-empt the Panel from simply overturning the domestic court ruling by a *de novo* examination of the case. Rather, Article II:5 provided for the need to compensate for the loss in tariff concessions that might ensue. Additionally, as the United States itself had recognized, the equipment implicated in this case was a Taiwanese manufacture involving a Japanese company. The classification of this particular product by definition did not concern the United States, and did not prejudge the classification of other US products which might have different characteristics.

The United States noted that the EC was admitting that it was treating some multimedia computers as dutiable under headings other than 84.71 (and at higher duty rates). As for Article II:5, the United States had duly brought the reclassification-related impairment of tariff concessions on the products at issue directly to the attention of the EC, and had requested informal consultations by letter on 2 May 1996. On 4 June and 23 July 1996, the United States and the EC had held bilateral consultations, which did not resolve the matter. The United States had subsequently brought its concerns directly to the attention of the United Kingdom and Ireland, both of which had declined to discuss the matter with the United States.

[23] See also Section VI on "Third Parties Submissions."

The United States had requested that the title of the Panel's report on these disputes be corrected to read "European Communities, Ireland and the United Kingdom - Increases in Tariffs on Certain Computer Equipment".

5.4 The **European Communities** stated that the US wish to change the title of the dispute, as reflected in its second submission, indicated that it had changed its mind on what the dispute was all about. The EC disagreed with this attempt to redirect the dispute against new parties at the present stage of the procedure as the United States now seemed to insinuate that the EC, Ireland and the United Kingdom were somehow collectively responsible for the situation complained about, as was apparent from the use of the word "and" in the suggested redrafting of the title of the dispute. It would, anyhow, be extraordinary if the title of the dispute was amended in the course of the procedure, and there was not justification whatsoever for that in the present case.

A. Scope of the Concession

1. Duty Treatment of New Products or Products Affected by Harmonized System (HS)[24] Changes

5.5 The **United States** claimed that the practice of the GATT with regard to the treatment of new products or products affected by HS changes was instructive in interpreting the scope of a concession that was described generally, but for which there was no record of any discussion or agreement describing the product scope in exhaustive detail. In both instances, there would not necessarily have been any discussion of whether a particular product or variation of a product should be included in the scope of a concession. As established by the *Gramophone Records* case, the practice in such instances was to resolve silence in favour of deeming the new or undiscussed product to be covered by the existing concession. This case concerned Germany's complaint[25] that Greece had raised the tariff on long-playing gramophone records to levels above its bound rates for gramophone records. Greece considered that "long playing" records were a new item and therefore not covered by the "records" binding because they contained a higher volume of recordings, were lighter than conventional records, and were made of a different material. The Group of Experts which examined Germany's complaint reported that the "Group agreed that the practice generally followed in classifying new products was to apply the tariff item, if one existed, that specified the products by name, or, if no such item existed, to assimilate the new products to existing items in accordance with the principles established by the national tariff legislation." The Group also observed that when Greece granted the concession on records, it had not attached any qualification to the description of the product. The Group was of the opinion that "long-playing" records were covered

---

[24] See footnote 12.

[25] *Greek Increase in Bound Duties*, complaint L/575, S.R. 11/12, pages 115 and 116.

by the description of "gramophone records" in the concession and therefore the rate of duty to be applied to those records was that bound under that item in the Greek schedule.[26]

5.6 Another case worth noting in this context was when the EC proposed to modify its binding on item 9211.A.II, "sound reproducers," in order to raise the duty on digital audio disc players (DADS) in 1983.[27] The withdrawal was to be made on a preemptive basis when trade in this product was still at low levels. The EC proposal was controversial and triggered a series of discussions in the GATT Council and the Committee on Tariff Concessions. During these discussions, even the EC did not argue that the lack of any reference to DADS in the EC tariff schedule, since they were new products, meant that DADs were unbound. Eventually, this issue was taken up in the Negotiating Group on GATT Articles and resulted in the provisions of paragraph 4 of the Understanding on the Interpretation of Article XXVIII of the GATT 1994.

5.7 The United States pointed out that while there was no obligation under the GATT to follow any particular system for classifying goods, a reclassification subsequent to the making of a concession under GATT must not violate the basic commitment regarding that concession.[28] Tariff changes resulting from reclassification and their GATT legal implications were also thoroughly discussed in the early 1980s, during preparations for the introduction of the HS nomenclature. It was clear then, as it is now, that changes in nomenclature or classification which altered the bound treatment of a product were inconsistent with a Member's obligations under Article II:1 of GATT 1994. Implementation of the HS became a massive Article XXVIII exercise in negotiating compensation for the impairment of tariffs consequential to changes in nomenclature. These considerations have applied on a continual basis with respect to the implementation of HS revisions adopted by the WCO. The GATT 1947 CONTRACTING PARTIES decided that implementation of such changes "shall not involve any alteration in the scope of concessions nor any increase in bound rates of duty unless their maintenance results in undue complexity in the national tariffs. In such cases the contracting parties concerned shall inform the other contracting parties of the technical difficulties in question, e.g. why it has not been possible to create a new subheading to maintain the existing concession on a product or products transferred from within one HS 6-digit subheading to another".[29]

---

[26] Report by the Group of Experts on *Greek Increase in Bound Duty*, 9 November 1956, L/580.

[27] Notification in SECRET/296 and Add.1 with respect to "sound reproducers with laser optical reading system", dated 24 February 1983.

[28] Panel Report on *Spain - Tariff Treatment of Unroasted Coffee*, adopted on 11 June 1981, BISD 28S/102, para. 4.4 and n.1. See TAR/M/4, Committee on Tariff Concessions, Minutes of Meeting, 31 July 1981, at para. 7.14.

[29] Decision on *GATT Concessions under the Harmonized Commodity Description and Coding System, Procedures to Implement Changes in the Harmonized System*, 8 October 1991, BISD 39S/300, para.1.

5.8 If a Member could raise duties at will on new or undiscussed product variations through reclassification, it would not need to invoke Article XXVIII. Nor would it need to provide any compensation if it wished to make a preemptive withdrawal of the sort proposed by the EC in 1983 for DADS. Paragraph 4 of the Understanding on the Interpretation of Article XXVIII would be reduced to inutility. The link between Article II and Article XXVIII was recognized by ten countries that made the compromise proposal for the Understanding, when they remarked that Article II:1(a) "is designed to provide security for the future and creates a presumption that the conditions governing access at the time of negotiations will be maintained".[30]

5.9 The **European Communities** responded that the above cited case of the *Gramophone Records* did not support the US complaint at all. This case was different from the present case in that it dealt with new products. The current US complaint was limited to products which already existed during the Uruguay Round. Thus, the question which needed to be addressed was which duty rate had been bound for the products concerned and not under which heading this equipment should be classified.

5.10 Nor was the EC alleging in any way that WTO Members could somehow undo tariff bindings by reclassifying products at will, without following the procedures of Article XXVIII of GATT 1994, and thereby unravelling the results of 50 years of tariff liberalization. On the contrary, even in cases of a reclassification as a consequence of an agreement in the WCO, the EC maintained the tariff treatment originally agreed upon in the tariff negotiations. For example, the EC used to classify power supply units for computers under the tariff classification heading for computers (8471.99). As such the bound duty rate for this product was 3.9 per cent in 1995[31] and would have been 2 per cent in 1996.[32] However, following a decision of the HS Committee, power supply units were reclassified under heading 8504.40. The tariff rate normally applying to this heading was 4.8 per cent in 1996. Yet the EC created a separate subheading, 8504.4030 with the rate of 2 per cent in order to maintain the concession it had negotiated in the WTO.

2. *"Products Described"*

5.11 The **United States** claimed that the products at issue were within the scope of the EC concession on item 84.71. Article II:1(b) required that the "products described" in a Member's Schedule which were the products of territories of other Members "shall...be exempt from ordinary customs duties in excess of those set forth and provided therein.". The ordinary meaning of "describe" was

---

[30] MTN.GNG/NG7/W/59, proposal by Argentina, Canada, Colombia, Czechoslovakia Hong Kong, Hungary, Korea, Mexico, New Zealand and Singapore circulated on 3 November 1989, page 3.
[31] See the annex to EC Regulation 1395/95.
[32] See the annex to EC Regulation 3009/95.

"to state the characteristics of...". The negotiating history of Article II confirmed that the drafters deliberately chose the general term "described" in preference to the narrower term "enumerated".[33] The EC-Schedule LXXX provided a concession on item 84.71 comprising automatic data processing machines and units thereof. The characteristics of LAN equipment and of personal computers with multimedia capability corresponded, in the United States' view, to those stated in this tariff concession on 84.71, and their parts within the scope of the concession on 84.73.

5.12 Moreover, this fact had been confirmed by the World Customs Organization (WCO). The WCO HS Committee at its eighteenth session in November 1996, had decided that a PC with television and audio capabilities was properly classified as an automatic data processing machine in HS Chapter 84 at subheading 8471.49. In accordance with Article 8 of the International Convention on the Harmonized Commodity Description and Coding System the classification decision was deemed accepted by the Council on 1 February 1997, as no reservation was entered on this decision during the two-month period allowed under the Convention. The Committee also decided at its eighteenth Session to draft an opinion which embodied this decision for inclusion in the Compendium of Classification Opinions. This text[34] was adopted by the Committee at its nineteenth Session in April 1997. Unless a WCO member made a reservation and sought to have the text of the opinion reconsidered by the Committee, this text would be deemed to be accepted by the Council as of 1 July 1997, and would be included in the next set of amendments to the Compendium of Classification Opinions. The WCO HS Committee also at its nineteenth Session in April 1997, voted on the proper classification of certain LAN equipment including routers, cluster controllers, hubs, multistation access units and optical fibre converters. The overwhelming majority of HS Committee members agreed that these products were properly classified under heading 84.71. While the United States was of the view that this case was not about classification, the WCO decisions confirmed that the United States was justified in expecting the products at issue to be classifiable under heading 84.71 and subject to the bound duty rate pertaining to that heading.

5.13 The **European Communities** failed to see how these draft opinions dated 1996/97 could confirm that the products subject to the dispute were classified

---

33 EPCT/TAC/PV/23, pages 18 and 19.

34 "8471.49 Multimedia personal computer consisting of three separately housed units: a 14 inch (35 cm) colour television receiver (display) with a digital processing unit, a keyboard (input unit), and an infra-red remote control device. The unit comprises a processor (60486DX2), a memory (4 MB RAM), a diskette drive (1.44 MB), a hard disk (350 MB), a CD-ROM drive, a colour monitor television receiver, non-interlaced in PC mode and interlaced in TV mode, and stereophonic loudspeakers. The system plays audio and software CDs and records digital audio files. The different functions (PC, television or soundstack) are selected by using either a trackball incorporated in a keyboard, the keyboard itself or the infra-red remote control device. The system also plays audio and software CDs and records digital audio files."(Annex K/14 to Doc.41.100E (HSC/19/Apr.97).

under 8471 in 1993/94. If anything, the recent draft amendment merely showed that until recently it had been disputed how the products concerned should be classified. Otherwise the HS would not need to be amended. In any case the EC, had introduced reservations in respect of both classification opinions (i.e. the PCTVs and certain LAN equipment) on 26 June 1997. But, even if the draft opinions as they stood now were to become final, the EC considered that it would not affect the present case, because the case was about duty treatment and not about product classification. A decision of the WCO could not affect the balance of concessions of the respective parties agreed upon during the Uruguay Round. Tariff negotiations were about tariffs, not about customs classification. Customs classification, thus, was only the background for such tariff negotiations, but not its subject matter. If it were different, tariff negotiations would be carried out in the framework of the WCO and not in the WTO. It was possible to have divergent views between participants in tariff negotiations concerning the classification of certain products, but that question should be addressed in the WCO. Furthermore, the EC noted that in the WTO Agreement on Rules of Origin reference was made to the future elaboration of arrangements concerning the "settlement of disputes relating to customs classification".[35] Such an arrangement had not yet been considered, which was another reason why this Panel should abstain from pronouncing itself on customs classification issues.

3. *Treatment Accorded at the Time the Concession Was Negotiated*

(a) "Treatment ... Provided For" and "Treatment ... Contemplated"

5.14 The **United States** argued that interpreting Article II:1 in its context, including Article II:5, the "treatment...provided for" in a tariff concession included the "treatment...contemplated" when the concession was made. Under GATT Article II:1(a), each WTO Member had to accord to the commerce of the other Members "treatment no less favourable than that provided for in the appropriate Part of the appropriate Schedule annexed to this Agreement." The reference to "treatment....provided for" in Article II:1(a) did not mean "classification specifically provided for." Such an interpretation would mean that in all cases where a WTO Member had not specifically provided in a concession that a particular product would be given a specific tariff classification, that Member could reclassify the product at will to a higher-duty tariff position and apply higher tariffs. The reference to "treatment...provided for" had to be interpreted in the light of its context and the object and purpose of Article II. The context of Article II:1 included Article II:5.

[35] Article 9.4 of the Agreement on Rules of Origin.

5.15 Article II:5 provided that "If any contracting party considers that a product is not receiving from another contracting party the treatment which the first contracting party believes to have been contemplated by a concession provided for in the appropriate Schedule annexed to this Agreement, it shall bring the matter directly to the attention of the other contracting party. . . ." Thus, the "treatment...provided for" was to be understood as the "treatment...contemplated" by a concession. Article II:5 did not require the treatment to have been discussed or expressly agreed. The ordinary meaning of "contemplate" in this context was "to expect". The treatment in question had to be the treatment by the importing Member which was contemplated at the time. Thus, the treatment provided by a concession was the treatment reasonably expected by the trading partners of the Member making the concession.

5.16 The **European Communities** noted that in referring to "reasonable expectations" with regard to the tariff treatment of certain computer equipment, the United States had used language that was borrowed from panel reports dealing with Article XXIII:1(b) of GATT 1994, the so-called non-violation cases. But the United States had never raised formally the matter of Article XXIII:1(b) in the procedure, nor during consultations. At the same time the United States appeared to allege that the EC had violated its obligations under Article II:1 of GATT 1994, which indicated by contrast that the claim appeared to be based on Article XXIII:1(a) of GATT 1994.

5.17 The United States had justified use of this language by referring to Article II:5 of GATT 1994, in particular by quoting the words "...the first contracting party believes to have been contemplated by a concession provided for in the appropriate schedule....". From the EC's point of view, this explanation was inconsistent with the claim that the EC had allegedly violated Article II:1 of GATT 1994. The consequence of the invocation of Article II:5 could only be that there should be negotiations on how to resolve the divergence of views depending on the subjective beliefs of the interested Members, rather than the relevant exporting industry. Nowhere in Article II:5 was there an indication that the belief, which the United States translated by "reasonable expectations", could replace the objective determination of an existing agreement on a tariff binding of a particular product.

5.18 The **United States** claimed that this dispute was about the violation of the obligations of the EC, Ireland and the United Kingdom under Article II:1 of the GATT 1994 and the nullification or impairment of benefits arising from those violations. However, it was worth recalling that one of the precepts developed under GATT 1947 was that rules and disciplines governing the multilateral trading system served to protect legitimate expectations of Members as to the competitive relationship between their products and those of the other Members. As the *Superfund* panel had pointed out, such rules and disciplines "... are not only to protect current trade but also to create the predictability needed to plan future trade".[36] The protection of legitimate expectations was central to creating security and predictability in the multilateral trading system, for governments and for trade itself. Furthermore, the *Newsprint* case had made clear that "reasonable expectation" was enforceable under Article II:1. Reasonable was not based on certainty or absolute clarity. It was the treatment that a Member "believes to have been contemplated by a concession", as that phrase appeared in Article II:5. This 1984 *Newsprint* panel case concerned an EC regulation on the duty-free tariff rate quota for newsprint. The EC had agreed to give fully duty-free access to the EFTA countries for newsprint and had reduced the MFN tariff rate quota for newsprint (bound at 1.5 million tonnes) by subtracting an amount corresponding to EFTA access (1 million tonnes) The EC claimed that it was not impairing the binding on newsprint, but the Panel found that the EC was, for the following reasons: "...under long-standing GATT practice, even purely formal changes in the tariff schedule of a contracting party.... have been considered to require renegotiations. ... In granting the concession in 1973, the EC had not made it subject to any qualification or reservation in the sense of Article II:1(b) although at the time the concession was made, it was known that agreement had already been reached that the EFTA countries would obtain full duty-free access to the Community market for newsprint from 1 January 1984 onward. The Panel therefore found that although in the formal sense the EC had not modified its GATT concession, it had *in fact* changed its GATT commitment unilaterally, by limiting its duty-free tariff quota for m.f.n. suppliers for 1984 to 500,000 tonnes".[37] The Panel had concluded that "....the EC, in unilaterally establishing for 1984 a duty-free quota of 500,000 tonnes, had not acted in conformity with their obligations under Article II of the GATT. The Panel shared the view expressed before it relating to the fundamental importance of the security and predictability of GATT tariff bindings, a principle which constitutes a central obligation in the system of the General Agreement".[38]

(b) "Treatment ... Contemplated" and "Treatment Accorded"

5.19 The **United States** claimed that in the absence of explicit provision in a Schedule or specific discussions during negotiations, the "treatment ... contemplated" could be inferred from the "treatment accorded" at the time the concession was negotiated. In other words, the latter provided a basis for interpreting the product scope and the nature of the "treatment... provided for". Under Article II, Members were free to specify the terms of, and any conditions or qualifications on, the concessions they make. The Member making the concession might specify explicitly the treatment it intended or the exact product composition of

[36] Panel Report on *United States - Taxes on Petroleum and Certain Imported Substances*, adopted on 17 June 1987, BISD 34S/136, para. 5.2.2.

[37] Panel Report on *Newsprint*, adopted on 20 November 1984, BISD 31S/114, para. 50.

[38] *Ibid.*, para. 52.

the concession. Those who had made the concessions in Schedule LXXX did not do so. In fact, Schedule LXXX could have provided that the concessions therein would be subject to reclassification at will or could have provided explicitly that the trading partners of the EC, Ireland and the United Kingdom were not guaranteed a continuation of the treatment known to be provided during the negotiations. No such qualification or reservation appeared in Schedule LXXX. Nor were there any reservations for particular types of computer or computer equipment. Hence, the parties which were bound by Schedule LXXX had agreed to continue to provide the treatment contemplated by their trading partners at the time the bargain was struck.

5.20 The **European Communities** stated that the United States had created confusion by its statement that "the product scope of a concession", and thus the "treatment ... contemplated" could be determined from the treatment actually accorded at the time that the concession was negotiated. Such an approach, if followed, would mean that a decision by a local customs authority for a particular consignment would amount to a new tariff binding under Article II of the GATT which was absurd. Information by local customs offices or even by national customs authorities to individual importers on the classification of individual consignments or goods identified by name (brand and model) could not become the equivalent of a tariff binding since a tariff binding referred to a category of products identified in a generic way by the product description in the relevant tariff line of the customs tariff. Such tariff bindings needed to be agreed during tariff negotiations, as provided for under the relevant provisions of the GATT 1994 (particularly Article XXVIII bis). It might be possible to infer a tariff binding for a category of products corresponding to the product description in a given tariff line from circumstances that were not laid down in written records of the negotiations, but the party invoking such special circumstances would have to bear the burden of proof for the existence of such circumstances. It would certainly be necessary, in order to meet this burden of proof, to show that negotiators had knowledge of the circumstances and that they were relevant to a category of products coming under a particular tariff line and not for individual imports alone.

5.21 The **United States** said that the EC had conceded that a tariff binding could be inferred for a group of products corresponding to the product description in a given tariff line, on the basis of circumstances outside the written negotiating record. However, the EC argument that negotiators must have had knowledge of these circumstances and the circumstances must have been relevant to a group of products under a particular tariff line, and not for individuals alone, was calculated to deprive BTIs and other member State classification actions of any significance. It was important to note, however, that an importer who had obtained a BTI for goods of a particular type could use the BTI to import the same goods throughout the EC. In addition, the importer would know that, no matter what the ultimate EC market for the product, it could be entered through the country that issued the BTI at the rate specified in the BTI. Other importers of identical or similar products might also expect those products to receive the same tariff treatment.[39]

(c) At the Time the Concession Was Negotiated

5.22 The **United States** said that the "time" or time period relevant to defining the rights and obligations with respect to the EC's tariff commitments on the products at issue began in March 1990 when the United States tabled the offer/request for the electronics sectoral proposal. The relevant time period closed in two stages, first and primarily with the Uruguay Round on 15 December 1993 (MTN.TNC/40). The more limited second stage closed at the end of verification of tariff schedules, which took place from February 1994 through 31 March 1994. As substantive tariff negotiations closed on 15 December 1993, changes in treatment during the verification of tariff schedules were only relevant to defining rights and obligations with respect to tariff concessions to the extent that the party making such changes brought them to the attention of its negotiating partners.

5.23 The **European Communities** were of the view that the starting base for the Uruguay Round was established in the "Procedures for the Negotiations".[40] The Uruguay Round tariff negotiations were held on the basis of the HS nomenclature and had lasted until the completion of the verification process that enabled participants to raise any problems they had with regard to the reflection of concessions negotiated in proposed schedules. This process ended in March 1994 with the finalization of the verification process.

5.24 The **United States** agreed with the EC that the starting point for the relevant period was established in the text agreed to on 30 January 1990 on "Procedures for the Negotiations". The Uruguay Round tariff negotiations were held on this basis, and ended in March 1994 with the finalization of the verification process. The US trading conditions were reflected not only in the tabling of the first "zero-for-zero" request/offer but in its preparation.

5.25 The United States recalled that, at the close of substantive tariff negotiations, the delegations had agreed that "no adjustments entailing a withdrawal of an offer or elements of offers would be permitted" from then forward (MTN.TNC/W/131). As also agreed, they had submitted their draft final schedules to the Secretariat by 14 February 1994. Between 14 February and 31 March 1994, the participants had engaged in the verification process, to ensure that the final schedules accurately reflected the negotiated concessions agreed upon by the participants. In adherence to the deadlines agreed upon, the United States, the EC and the other participants had completed verification by the end of March 1994. On 15 April 1994, the contracting parties had signed the Final Act

---

39 Additional discussion on this matter is to be found in paragraphs 5.43 to 5.62.

40 *Procedures for the Negotiations*, MTN.GNG/NG1/17 of 1 February 1990.

of the Uruguay Round, at which time their schedules of concessions were annexed to the Marrakesh Protocol.

B. *Tariff Treatment of Products*

1. *LAN Equipment*

(a) Negotiating History

5.26 The **United States** claimed that inclusion of LAN equipment within heading 84.71 was supported by negotiating history. If a party had made and maintained an offer of coverage for a specific item identified as within a particular tariff heading, then that party could be assumed to have induced reasonable reliance by its trading partners on that offer; the trading partners concerned could reasonably expect that the concession would include those items; and unless the final concession explicitly provided otherwise, it could be inferred that the final concession was intended to include that item at the rate applicable to the tariff heading in question. The same was true if a party had received a request for a specific item identified as within a particular tariff heading and had not objected that the request was wrongly targeted. In the present case, the US "zero-for-zero" request/offer of 15 March 1990 had proposed elimination of duties by the United States and its trading partners, including the EC, with respect to a long list of products, including electronic articles in HS chapters 84, 85 and 90. Singapore's June 1990 request made to the EC requested duty reductions on "microcomputers desk top type" and "microcomputers other" (both 8471.20), as well as "control units", "adaptor units", "gateways" and "concentrators or multiplexers"(all 8471.99), and "printed circuit boards assembled"(8473.30). In other words, Singapore had submitted a request to the EC for tariff reduction on LAN equipment within heading 84.71 and the EC had not objected to that classification of LAN equipment at that time. Thus, the EC's own conduct showed that it intended to include LAN equipment under the concession rate for heading 84.71.

5.27 Furthermore, representatives of the US computer industry had closely monitored the Uruguay Round negotiations, and had regularly raised their concerns with the United States Trade Representative (USTR) and members of the US Congress. During this time, they did not raise any concerns with respect to EC's classification and duty treatment of LAN equipment and personal computers with multimedia capability. They assumed, in light of the fact that this issue was not raised by the EC, that headings 84.71 and 84.73 would continue to cover LAN equipment products. The industry's only concern was that the EC's reduction in tariffs on those headings would be insufficient, as reflected in a letter on 10 November 1993 to Ambassador Kantor from the US Computer and Business Equipment Manufacturers Association (CBEMA). Reviewing the tariff headings of interest to CBEMA members, the letter noted that "there is ... enormous trade in the next level of value-added, the "stuffed circuit board"(small boards are sometimes called cards), or "electronic assembly" or sometimes called in Europe the "PCB"(for "printed circuit board"). There is a wide variety of PCB's or electronic assemblies, most of which are classified in [heading 8473] as computer parts: memory boards, graphics accelerator boards, LAN cards." In the letter, CBEMA went on to criticize a proposal floated by the EC to divide HS heading 8473 into two items, "electronic assemblies," with no duty reduction, and "other," subject to zero duties. The proposal would be inadequate, CBEMA said, because "other" computer parts consisted of plastic cases and metal chassis, which had low or nonexistent trade, and "electronic assemblies" consisted of "PCBs or stuffed circuit boards" with substantial trade. Essentially, the significance of this letter was that in the face of dramatic differences in tariff rates depending upon the classification of the products - a difference of 3.5 per cent and 14 per cent in some cases - the industry advisors were noticeably silent on the treatment of LAN equipment in reacting to the EC offer. Yet they commented specifically on the offers of other products. So the industry's understanding of tariff treatment was based, in turn on the treatment their exports had actually received, as evidenced in part by the BTIs and by their attestations that the United States submitted to support its claims.[41] The US government, in turn, during the Uruguay Round negotiations had reasonably relied on the experience of its exporters and traders in actually exporting these products to the EC under Chapter 84 and reasonably expected that these products would continue to receive treatment by the EC as computers, computer units or computer parts under Chapter 84.

5.28 The **European Communities** stated that during the Uruguay Round, both the EC and the United States had made numerous tariff concessions in various areas. However, none of the products at issue were discussed by name. No specific binding was made for any of the individual products at issue. Only the tariff headings in question were bound. Singapore's request on heading 84.71 in which it identified by name "gateways, "concentrators" and "multiplexer", did not constitute any evidence that the EC had accepted that its concessions on computers would cover these components. First Singapore's product listing under heading 84.71 was derived from Singapore's own tariff classification, and secondly subsequently to this preliminary tariff request, Singapore sent a revised tariff request to the EC on 10 October 1990.[42] Significantly in the revised list, "gateways", "concentrators" and "multiplexers" were not mentioned anymore under the tariff heading 84.71. Singapore had not submitted any evidence that the EC in

---

41 See Annex 4.

42 This letter contained the following:

"Dear Paul,

I am writing with reference to my letter of 22 June wherein I forwarded to you Singapore's preliminary request list for the tariff negotiations.

Following bilateral discussions with your market access negotiators, Singapore has revised its request list. I am enclosing the revised Singapore tariff request list to EEC. It would be appreciated if you could transmit it to the appropriate authorities. I hope that these requests would be considered favourably.

Yours sincerely, [signature]"

the meantime, or afterwards, had accepted to grant the tariff treatment accorded to computers to these products. On the contrary, the EC had clearly classified multiplexers, for instance, as telecom equipment in a 1992 Regulation[43], well before the end of the Uruguay Round. If Singapore had any expectations left, this Regulation certainly must have put an end to them. For these reasons, Singapore could not legitimately claim to have established that the EC indicated or raised expectations during the Uruguay Round, that LAN equipment would be covered by the tariff concession on computers. In any event, any expectations raised by this bilateral correspondence in the mind of Singapore could not be conferred on the United States.

5.29 The EC, additionally alleged, contrary to the United States, that American industry was aware of this problem. The American Electronics Association (AEA), which represented the computer industry, had scheduled a meeting with Commission officials on 25 February 1994 in order to discuss a number of issues including classification differences in member States with respect to a number of products including LAN interface. Tariff headings to be discussed in this context included 85.17, 84.71 and 84.73. So when asking for the meeting, the AEA (and certainly some of their members manufacturing LAN) were aware that LAN equipment was not classified in a uniform manner within the EC.

5.30 The **United States** responded that during negotiations it had not inquired specifically into the treatment of these products, as there was no reason to doubt that these products would continue to be treated as dutiable under heading 84.71. The EC on its part did not provide any notice to US negotiators during the negotiations of any doubts that the EC or member State authorities might have had concerning the proper classification or duty rate applicable to these products. And, of course, given the tariff treatment applied at the time, there would have been no logical reason for the EC to do so. Moreover, tariff negotiators dealing with thousands of tariff lines could not have discussed the precise product composition of each line without taking an additional ten years to complete the Uruguay Round. Thus, the EC's position would throw into uncertainty practically every tariff concession the EC or any of its trading partners made in the Uruguay Round. As for the AEA meeting, the United States had made inquiries, and was unable to confirm whether a meeting had, in fact, taken place in February 1994 or before the end of the Uruguay Round.

5.31 The United States questioned whether the argument that no specific binding was made for any of the products at issue because they were not discussed by name during the Uruguay Round and only the tariff headings in question were bound meant that if there was no "specific binding" for these products under Chapter 84, then they were bound under Chapter 85, and if so, why there, given the evidence suggesting otherwise? And if not, were they then to be considered unbound? The implications of such an argument were disturbing when consid-

[43] EC Regulation 396/92 of 18 February 1992, OJ 1992 L44/9.

ered in relation to the Uruguay Round tariff concessions, and even more so for Tokyo Round and Kennedy Round concessions. Although the United States had negotiated in the Uruguay Round on a request/offer basis, some participants in the Round had negotiated by using a tariff reduction formula. The US-EC negotiation on Chapter 84 provided an example of how two groups of busy negotiators dealing with billions of dollars of trade and hundreds of tariff lines relied on a continuation of the status quo. Discussion of specific product coverage was even less likely when all negotiators used a formula approach to tariff reduction, as was the case in the Tokyo Round and the Kennedy Round. Was the EC arguing that whenever the formula approach was utilized, the headings were bound but the products within the headings were not, and if so an importing country could reclassify such products at will into higher-duty headings with no duty to provide compensation? If so, not only was the balance established by all previous negotiating rounds upset, but all future negotiations would require a fundamentally different, and more time-consuming and complicated, approach.

5.32 The **European Communities** stated that the allegation raised by the United States, that the EC's position was that the products subject to the dispute were unbound under the EC-Schedule LXXX, was absurd. Its real position was that these products were not bound with computers under tariff heading 84.71, but were bound with electric machinery under the relevant tariff headings of chapter 85 of the EC schedule.

5.33 It was possible that the EC and the US negotiators did not have the same understanding on what precisely were the products to which their tariff negotiations related. In fact, no party to the negotiations raised the issue that customs duty treatment of LAN equipment differed from one country to another. This meant that different concessions were negotiated by various parties for the same products. The US negotiators might find it difficult to admit now that their understanding of the tariff classification in the EC of the products they talk about now was erroneous; however, they only had themselves to blame. They should have come forward and requested clarification from the EC negotiators if they were not sure where these products should be classified in the EC especially since they themselves had reclassified these products only shortly beforehand; a fact which was conveniently omitted by the United States. During the Uruguay Round, the United States had considered LAN equipment to be covered by category 85.17, but in 1992 on its own initiative the United States had reclassified LAN equipment under heading 84.71; so, in fact, the reclassifying party was the United States and not the EC. Moreover, the United States, after having reclassified LAN equipment itself, in 1992 from telecom equipment to computers, did not acknowledge or inform trading partners of this fact, nor did it amend its offer/request to the EC during the Uruguay Round. Canada was another example of a reclassifying Member. During the NAFTA negotiations, the parties to this agreement had admitted that it was difficult to classify LAN equipment, and they had agreed to consult on this issue and to endeavour to agree, no later than 1 January 1994, on the classification of such goods in each Party's tariff schedule.[44] Following this agreement and not earlier than May 1995, Canada modified its classification practice and began to classify LAN equipment from then on under heading 84.71. In a Customs Notice of 24 May 1995, the Canadian Department of Revenue observed that: "Although valid statements can be made for classification under heading No. 85.17, the Department has decided to adopt a harmonized NAFTA classification position for LAN apparatus under heading No. 84.71"[45]

5.34 The **United States** argued that the first important point to note was that the classification by the United States of imported goods under the Tariff Schedules of the United States Annotated or the Harmonized Tariff Schedule of the United States did not affect the reasonable expectation of the United States that the EC, the United Kingdom and Ireland would provide the tariff treatment to LAN equipment according to the concessions in the EC Schedule for automatic data processing equipment or parts thereof. It was unaware of any assumptions about the classification decisions taken by EC, UK or Irish customs authorities based upon the decisions of the United States under its tariff schedule. Such assumptions would have been wholly speculative, at best. Furthermore, the impact of US classification of such goods on its GATT tariff bindings was not apparent, as the United States had negotiated during the relevant period in the context of the North American Free Trade Agreement an understanding to move to MFN duty-free treatment of imported automatic data processing equipment.

5.35 The **European Communities** stated that the change in classification or reclassification by the United States in 1992 and Canada in 1995 was important enough to be mentioned because it showed that classification of LAN equipment was unsettled during the Uruguay round. These examples illustrated that the United States had no particular reason to expect that the EC would classify LAN equipment as computers. They also helped to put the initially inconsistent classifications of some national customs authorities in the EC into better perspective. Classification of this equipment was indeed a difficult exercise for everybody. This should have forewarned EC trading partners not to draw hasty conclusions from tariff treatment in individual cases which they found favourable. Furthermore, the recent negotiations on the Information Technology Agreement showed again the many diversities between WTO trading partners in classifying LAN equipment. For instance, two of the third parties to this dispute, Japan and Korea, were still classifying some LAN equipment as telecom equipment.[46]

---

[44] Annex 308.3 to NAFTA.

[45] Canadian Customs Notice No. 963 of 24 May 1995, page 4.

[46] See Annex 5.

(b) Imports of Products

5.36 The **United States** claimed that imports of the products at issue into the EC were treated under Chapter 84 during the Uruguay Round. This treatment could be determined through examining trade figures and other data such as invoices. In conjunction with actual treatment, classification rulings by the importing country provided particularly compelling evidence of the actual product scope of a particular tariff heading.

5.37 The **European Communities** noted that as indicated before, tariff treatment was different from custom classification. The fact of classifying a product under a certain tariff heading was separate from the agreement Members might have reached on the tariff treatment for particular items during multilateral tariff negotiations. A tariff binding could not be inferred from individual classification decisions by local customs authorities on individual consignments. If as a result of such individual classification decisions, an importer obtained more favourable tariff treatment than that foreseen in the tariff schedule, this represented a windfall benefit for that company and did not have an effect on the rights and obligations held by WTO Members.

5.38 The **United States** argued that the classification actions by the importing member States of the EC were clearly relevant in determining such treatment. Such actions demonstrated where trade was expected to and did, flow. They provided particularly compelling evidence that specific products fell within the product scope of a particular tariff heading, and that the authorities in the EC were aware of that product scope. In particular, the treatment accorded to LAN equipment under BTIs and other member State classification actions prior to 1993 was especially compelling given the absence of any EC-wide classification regulations on these products or even a mechanism to obtain BTIs with EC-wide applicability. No legitimate objection could be raised that the classification of goods imported consistent with such a ruling was fraudulent or mistaken.

5.39 The **European Communities** responded that it was clear that the EC was not bound vis-à-vis its trading partners by any actions of national authorities which were inconsistent with the EC's position, but which might have benefited certain individuals. Likewise the EC would not claim to derive any rights against the US government, for instance, if a local US customs office mistakenly levied duties on EC imports that were lower than those negotiated and bound by the United States in the WTO.

5.40 The **United States** argued that the analogy was misplaced on the ground that EC member States were themselves WTO Members, as already mentioned. Moreover, the situation in the present dispute had special features because the actual treatment of any product in the EC depended on actions by the customs authorities of each EC member State.

5.41 At the same time, the United States wished to note that sufficiency of evidence such as BTIs should not be the issue in this case. It just so happened that US exporters of the products subject to this dispute sought BTIs before exporting their products and those BTIs demonstrated treatment during the Uruguay Round as automatic data processing equipment. But what if they had not? What if there had been no document from UK and Irish customs officials articulating tariff treatment? In the normal course of trade US exporters sent products to Europe, claimed tariff treatment under headings 84.71 and 84.73 (for parts) and, in the absence of review by customs authorities, paid the duties owed. The paper trail there would not have involved a piece of paper from the customs authorities themselves. What then? Legally, it would have no effect on the strength of the US claim. Trade in the product, and the mere fact of customs treatment should be enough. That was not just the US view, but also the view of the European Commission, as set out in an "Aide-Mémoire" as far back as in 1981 when the EC had wished to draw the attention of the US authorities to the tariff reclassification by US customs service of tire protection chains. These products had been classified under TSUS no. 652.24 through 652.33, but in October 1979, the US Customs Service considered this classification as erroneous and proposed to classify these chains under TSU no. 652.35, resulting in an increase of the applied duty. The Commission had indicated that it was "...of the opinion that the reclassification under TSUS no. 652.35, bearing a much higher duty rate than the concessional rates (for TSUS nos. 652.24 through 652.33) is inconsistent with the obligations of the US under the GATT. Furthermore, the Commission considers that, even if it could be maintained that the articles in question had been erroneously classified under TSUS no. 652.24 through 652.33, the fact that over a period of many years (including the period during which the relevant tariff concession was negotiated) these articles were treated as belonging to these headings would be sufficient in itself to establish the concessional rights of the EC to a continuation of the tariff treatment promised in respect of the classification for these articles".[47]

5.42 The **European Communities** noted that the "Aide Mémoire" referred to by the United States was dated 22 May 1981, which was almost sixteen years ago. It was written in a completely different context and related to different products, and therefore could not be relevant to the present case. Moreover, the background to the situation was unknown. Additionally, in that "Aide-Mémoire" the EC had referred to an acknowledgement by the US State Department that "for some cases brought up, the Community might have some GATT rights". In the present dispute, this was not the case; the EC was not acknowledging that the United States had any WTO rights.

(i) BTIs and National Classification

5.43 The **United States** claimed that classification actions by member States provided evidence that these products were treated uniformly under Chapter 84 during the Uruguay Round. In fact, prior to the conclusion of the Uruguay Round, and going back as far as 1988, many EC member States, including at least Ireland, the United Kingdom, France, Belgium and Luxembourg, treated

---

47 European Commission Aide-Mémoire, 22 May 1981.

imports from the United States of LAN adapter cards and other LAN equipment as computer equipment, dutiable at the rates applicable to products falling under heading 8471. Additionally, prior to the implementation of the European Commission's LAN adapter card Regulation, other member States, including the Netherlands and Denmark, also issued BTIs treating LAN equipment under Chapter 84. The existing treatment in these member States prior to 1994 formed the basis for the United States' expectations during the Uruguay Round negotiations.

5.44 To support this claim, in addition to the BTIs issued by Ireland[48], and classification decisions by the UK[49] Customs and Excise, in which certain LAN equipment products subject to dispute were classified under 84.71, the United States had also produced letters from four of the leading US exporters of LAN equipment to Europe[50] attesting to the fact that all of their LAN equipment exported to Ireland and the United Kingdom between 1991 and 1994 was classified by customs authorities under 84.71 or 84.73. One of them distributed its products through its primary warehousing facility in Ireland. Another distributed through a subsidiary in the United Kingdom. The four companies which submitted the letters represented over 75 per cent of LAN equipment export from the United States to the EC. The United States had also submitted four BTIs issued by the Dutch[51] customs authorities, eight BTIs issued by the French[52] customs authorities and four BTIs by the Danish[53] authorities during the period from October 1993 to January 1995 in which LAN equipment was determined to be dutiable under heading 84.71 or 84.73. Furthermore, as late as June 1995, France had asserted at a meeting of the European Commission Customs Code Committee[54] that only "real telecommunication equipment" could be classified under 85.17. US exporters of LAN equipment had also verified that routers imported into Belgium[55] in 1995 were classified under 8471.9910, and at least one manufacturer of computer products had imported routers into Luxembourg under the heading 84.71 in 1993 and 1994.

5.45 In addition to the EC-12, at least two of the three countries that acceded to the EC in 1995 provided tariff treatment for LAN equipment under heading 84.71 prior to accession. Both Finland and Sweden[56], at the time had bound their tariffs under the Uruguay Round and prior to accession to the EC had treated LAN equipment as ADP equipment under heading 84.71. Under Finland's Uruguay Round Schedule of tariff concessions, LAN equipment under heading 84.71

48 See Annex 4, Table 1, Nos. 13-44.
49 See Annex 4, Table 2, Nos. 1-3.
50 See Annex 4, Table 3, Nos. 6-9.
51 See Annex 4, Table 1, Nos. 45-48.
52 See Annex 4, Table 1, Nos. 5-12.
53 See Annex 4, Table 1, Nos. 1-4.
54 See Annex 4, Table 3, No. 5.
55 See Annex 4, Table 3, No. 1.
56 See Annex 4, Table 3, Nos. 3 and 4.

was bound at a flat rate of 0.9 per cent. Under Sweden's Uruguay Round schedule of tariff concessions, LAN equipment, under heading 8471.9910, was staged from a base rate of 3.8 per cent in 1995 to a duty free bound rate in 1999 (other products under heading 84.71 were staged from 3.8 per cent to 1.9 per cent).

5.46 The **European Communities** noted that, contrary to what the United States alleged, the EC member States did not treat these products uniformly under Chapter 84 during the Uruguay Round. Significantly, in the EC there had been a tendency since the early 1990s to classify more and more components, which could be used in LAN and other kind of networks (e.g. telephone networks), as telecom equipment. The question of proper classification of LAN equipment was litigated early on, in Germany. There, the customs authorities issued, already in 1989, BTIs classifying LAN under heading 85.17. These rulings were upheld by the German Federal Tax Court in 1991.[57] Subsequently the German customs authorities duly continued to issue BTIs for LAN equipment under heading 85.17. For example, in 1992, the German customs authorities had issued a BTI for LAN adapter cards under 85.17[58]; the Dutch customs authorities had also issued BTIs classifying LAN equipment under heading 85.17[59], as did the UK[60] and French[61] customs authorities.

5.47 It was also true that customs authorities in some member States had initially considered LAN equipment to fall under heading 84.71, for example Ireland had issued BTIs classifying some LAN equipment under heading 84.71. However, the EC wished to recall that the impact of a BTI was limited. It could only be invoked by the individual to whom it was addressed and was temporary and restricted to the specific type of product it covered; its validity was limited in time and a BTI did not guarantee that the classification of the goods was correct and could be relied upon by the individual in the future. BTIs did not represent classification decisions of the EC. As such, BTIs created no rights or legitimate expectations for governments in the context of WTO. Thus, the Community Customs Code provided explicitly that a BTI ceased to be valid where an EC regulation was adopted and the information no longer conformed to the law laid down thereby or where the BTI was incompatible with a judgement of the ECJ.

5.48 For these reasons, the BTIs issued by the Irish Customs authorities could not have created rights and expectations for the United States about future classifications or duty treatment by the EC. Especially, in that particular case, as these BTIs were all issued on the same day by one customs office to one single company. It was not as if these BTIs reflected a consistent practice of the Irish customs authorities. With respect to the United Kingdom, reference was made to a few letters from customs authorities and it was even unclear to whom they were

57 See Annex 6, Table 2, No. 1.
58 See Annex 6, Table 1, No.4.
59 See Annex 6, Table 1, Nos. 5-34.
60 See Annex 6, Table 1, Nos. 35-44.
61 See Annex 6, Table 1, Nos. 1-3.

addressed. As far as France and Belgium were concerned the United States had produced initially importers invoices to support its allegation. However, these documents were dated 1995 and 1996 and were therefore beyond the relevant period. Also, there was no indication that these documents concerned LAN equipment; they only referred to "computer parts". Finally, as far as the EC could determine, these invoices reflected only self-certification by importers, and no decision by customs authorities. Regarding France, in particular, the unofficial report of the EC's Nomenclature Committee meeting produced by the United States, reflected an opinion which the French representative was supposed to have expressed during the meeting; it did not establish that the French customs authorities actually classified LAN equipment under heading 84.71. The French BTIs which had been submitted were also issued after 1993 which indicated that they could not have formed the basis of reasonable expectations by the United States that tariff treatment was going to be that covered by 84.71. With respect to the Netherlands, the United States had submitted merely one "original" BTI issued by the competent Dutch authorities. Moreover this original contained no stamp or other means of certification In any event according to the English translation, the rulings date from 1995, which was after the conclusion of the Uruguay Round and could certainly not have created reasonable expectations for the United States during those negotiations. With regard to Denmark, the United States had produced five "original" BTIs which were unidentifiable. No date was mentioned in the English translations or identifiable in the "original rulings". With respect to Luxembourg, no document had even been submitted regarding the classification practice of its customs authorities. The United States had also claimed that Finland and Sweden at the time they had bound their tariffs under the Uruguay Round, which was prior to their accession to the EC, had treated LAN equipment under heading 84.71. This might well be true but was irrelevant. As already explained, when countries acceded to the EC, they withdrew their individual schedules. A new schedule of the enlarged Community was then negotiated with the EC trading partners. The EC and the United States had already agreed on the EC concessions under this new schedule, and therefore no reasonable expectations could be based on the withdrawn individual schedules of Finland and Sweden.

5.49 With reference to the letters which the United States had submitted from the four leading US companies exporting LAN equipment to the EC, the EC pointed out that in the evidence submitted to the Panel by the EC, the EC had included a BTI issued to one of those companies in 1993 by the UK HM Customs and Excise, which classified a router under tariff heading 85.17.[62] This seemed to contradict the claim by that company that all its export of LAN equipment to the United Kingdom was classified under 84.71 during the relevant period. This situation created serious doubt as to the reliability of the statement

[62] See Annex 4, Table 3, No. 8 and Annex 6, Table 1, No. 41.

made by that company that all its export of LAN equipment to Ireland and the United Kingdom was classified under Chapter 84.

5.50 What had been demonstrated by the above information was the fact that there was no uniform classification[63] in the EC member States with respect to LAN equipment during the Uruguay Round period. Although, the process of unifying the views on classification of LAN equipment had taken time, the EC applying the HS interpretation rules had consistently taken the view that components of data transmitting networks in general and LAN in particular should be classified under 85.17 on the basis that its principal function is the communication/transmission of data. This was reflected in a number of Regulations issued on this matter starting from 1992. In 1992, the EC had issued a Regulation which classified a multiplexer under heading 85.17, describing a multiplexer as "an electronic multiplexing appliance in its own housing which enables multiple link-ups to be made between the different connection points of a computer network.[64] In March 1994, the EC had issued another Classification Regulation in which it classified modems as telecom equipment under 85.17.[65] A few weeks later, it decided that heading 85.17 should equally apply to adapters and transceivers.[66] Finally, the Commission had adopted on 23 May 1995 a Regulation noting *inter alia* that the proper classification of LAN adapter cards was 85.17.[67]

5.51 In view of all of the above, the United States should not have formed any "reasonable expectations" as to the treatment accorded to the products subject to the dispute.

---

[63] The aim and purpose of the relevant EC law in the context of the present case was to ensure that no conflicting BTIs be issued for the same product, nor even for similar products. That did not mean that such situations would never arise in practice. The EC had put in place a data base in order to avoid such situations as much as humanly possible. However, such undesirable things did happen occasionally in practice. In this context it was important to remember that the EC customs authorities were dealing daily with hundreds of applications in eleven different official languages. Misunderstandings or even fraudulent behaviour were a reality under such circumstances (Importers were required to indicate whether they have knowledge of the existence of a BTI for the product for which they are submitting a BTI application (cf. Article 6 para. 4 lit. j. of Commission Regulation No. 2454/93). There was a delicate balance to be drawn between a thorough and efficient implementation of EC customs law in individual cases and a smooth handling of ongoing trade operations by customs authorities. Customs formalities in the EC had to allow for the thorough implementation of all customs rules, but was not to become an obstacle for trade. The only alternative to the present decentralized organization of customs services would be to have a fully centralized customs service with specialized offices for particular products. The EC did not believe that such a change would be in the interest of the trading community. Also to be recalled was the fact that something which was not provided for in law or which was prohibited by law did not mean that it did not exist. Theft was presumably prohibited by law everywhere in the world. The promulgation and implementation of the relevant legal provisions did unfortunately not mean that theft had been eradicated and no longer existed, however, thoroughly the law was applied in individual countries.

[64] Regulation 396/92, op cit.

[65] Regulation 754/94 of 30 March 1994, OJ 1994 L 89/2.

[66] Regulation 1638/94 of 5 July 1994, OJ 1994 L 172/5.

[67] Commission Regulation 1165/95, OJ 1995 L 117/15.

5.52 The **United States** disagreed with the EC argument that the BTIs issued by customs authorities from Netherlands, Denmark and France after 1993 were irrelevant. These BTIs were relevant because they reflected previous practice (i.e. during the Uruguay Round) by these countries. According to the experience of US exporters, these member States had continued to treat imports of the relevant LAN equipment as computer parts and units under headings 84.71 and 84.73 until 1995-1996. Following the EC's publication of the adapter card regulation, these and other member States began reclassifying LAN adapter cards and other LAN equipment. In some instances, customs authorities also began in 1995 to make the unwarranted demand that importers pay additional duties for past LAN equipment imports based on the difference between the 84.71 or 84.73 rate and the 85.17 rate. For example, in August 1995, the Luxembourg customs authorities sent invoices to importers seeking to reopen their duty liability and collect for shipments since January 1993 the difference between the 3.6 per cent actually charged under heading 84.71 and the 7.5 per cent applicable under 85.17. As another example, a company whose LAN equipment had entered the United Kingdom on 11 May 1995 as ADP machines under heading 84.71, received a demand note for the difference in duties on 7 June 1996, when the United Kingdom reclassified these products. In this note, the UK customs authority asked the higher tariff rate on the imports of the products for the past year.

5.53 The EC had suggested that US expectations should instead have been formed based upon a 1991 decision by the German Bundesfinanzhof affirming BTIs issued by German customs authorities to a non-US firm (Transtec) in 1989. The reference to the Transtec ruling was irrelevant as this ruling had no authority outside of Germany and did not justify tariff treatment less favourable than or inconsistent with the EC Uruguay Round bindings negotiated for heading 8471. Under EC law, national court rulings concerning the classification of products were not binding on the customs authorities of other member States. In addition, the legal basis of the Transtec decision was reversed in a later decision by the ECJ. In the case of Siemens Nixdorf, ECJ Case C-11/93, the ECJ had ruled in favour of broad product coverage under heading 84.71.[68] In so doing, the ECJ had rejected the rationale relied on by the Transtec court. In the Transtec case, the Bundesfinanzhof had ruled that certain computer network equipment were classifiable as telecommunications equipment based upon the court's interpretation of the term "specific function" in Note 5 to Chapter 84 of the HS.[69] In the German court's view, classification under heading 84.71 was precluded where the equipment in question was viewed by customs authorities as having a "specific function"(data transmission) which was distinct from "data processing." In Siemens-Nixdorf, the ECJ had rejected this reasoning, and instead interpreted Note 5 to mean that "any unit which is connected to the central processing unit of

68 See Annex 4, Table 3, No. 10.
69 See footnote 15.

a data-processing system and which is able to accept or deliver data in a form - code or signals - which can be used by the system is to be regarded as being a part of the complete system of an automatic data processing machine and classified under heading 8471".[70]

5.54 The EC had also claimed that products classified by the Regulations referred to by the EC signalled a tendency in the EC to classify LAN components under 85.17 which should have warned the United States; however, these products were outside the scope of this dispute. The EC had included multiplexers and modems in its description of LAN equipment, suggesting that these, too, were LAN products, which was not the case. Modems were combined modulators-demodulators, which operated to convert a signal in order to achieve compatibility in a telecommunications environment. Modems had been historically classified and accorded tariff treatment as telecommunications apparatus by the EC and other US trading partners. Likewise multiplexers were not LAN products. "Multiplexing" was a technique for interleaving point-to-point telecommunications calls coming from different sources and going to different destinations but passing through common telecommunications trunk lines. The most simple way to describe this was the method by which one "dials" a call on the telephone or facsimile machine. Without multiplexers, each destination (eg. a telephone) would have to be individually connected to each other's end point, rather than through common trunk lines. Such multiplexing did not operate in a LAN environment. In a LAN, all data and processing information was automatically passed to all active interfaces or stations that were connected. Only those interfaces or stations which recognized themselves as being intended destinations would copy the transmitted data from their physical interface to their processing engines.

5.55 Additionally, these Regulations were issued after the relevant negotiating period. Specifically the EC had cited its classification Regulation on LAN adapters issued in June 1994. The United States noted that given that the EC had issued the relevant Regulation several months after it had bound its tariff in the Uruguay Round, the EC had no legitimate basis to rely on the adapter regulation as evidence of the United States' expectations during the Uruguay Round regarding tariff treatment of those or other LAN products.

5.56 The BTIs submitted by the EC from 3 (France, Netherlands and the United Kingdom) of 15 member States over a four year time-period concerning a

[70] The reasoning of the ECJ in Siemens-Nixdorf was consistent with the Opinion of the Advocate General and the position of the European Commission. The ECJ issued its decision on May 19, 1994. However, the Advocate General and the European Commission provided their views, with which the ECJ concurred, well before that date. The Advocate General delivered his opinion on January 27, 1994, after receiving and reviewing the views of the parties. The Advocate General wrote that he was adopting the views expressed by the European Commission, that Note 5 to Chapter 84 of the Combined Nomenclature should be interpreted as meaning that "separately housed units which are integral parts of a data-processing system come under heading 8471, if by virtue of their design, they are not suitable for using except as part of a data-processing system."

number of narrowly-defined products from specific producers did not, as claimed by the EC, constitute evidence that the EC had changed its collective opinion of the classification of all networking equipment. The UK BTI[71] effective December 1993 related to a "statistical time division multiplexer," which was a product outside the scope of this dispute. Six UK BTIs[72] were effective as from February 1994, i.e. only after the close of substantive tariff negotiations and their existence was not drawn to the attention of US tariff negotiators during the verification process. A Dutch BTI[73] appeared also to relate to a multiplexer. One French BTI[74] referring to a "multiprotocol terminal server for server/mainframe exchanges" which was related to a front-end controller for mainframe computers, was not relevant to the products at issue.

5.57 The question raised by the EC about the apparent contradiction between the BTI issued by the UK customs classifying a router under 85.17, and the exporting US company's claim in a letter that all its exports of LAN equipment had always been classified by UK customs under 84.71 did not cast any doubts about the reliability of the company's claim. The explanation was as follows: the company's UK office had used the 84.71 classification for its import entries until the UK customs had issued the BTI of 11 October 1993 for certain router products. The company had instructed its customs broker to initiate protest procedures, and had corresponded with the UK Customs on this matter until the company's protest about the classification of this product under 85.17 had been finally rejected on 5 May 1994. Moreover, because this company used the method of distribution[75], whereby it was not the importer, it had relied on information from its customers who were the importers that the common treatment of this equipment in the EC was under 84.71 during this same period.

5.58 The point worth noting was that the United States had produced as many BTIs from as many member States where networking equipment was classified under heading 84.71 or 84.73. It would appear that this consideration begged the

71 UK 55700: See Annex 6, Table 1, No. 42.

72 UK57112, UK57127, UK57128, UK57141, UK57142, UK 57110: See Annex 6, Table 1, Nos: 35, 36, 37, 38, 39 and 40.

73 NL199109209450089-0: See Annex 6, Table 1, No. 10.

74 FR 06190199102248: See Annex 6, Table 1, No. 3.

75 Product distribution in the EC may take place in many ways, but two scenarios are the most frequent. First, if products are distributed on a Free-on-Board (FOB) Plant basis, the EC customer takes possession of the goods at the foreign manufacturer's plant and is responsible for all subsequent distribution activities, including transportation, customs clearance, and subsequent delivery to an end user in the EC; in this scenario there may be many entry points. In the second likely scenario, a foreign multinational retains title to the goods and undertakes these activities itself. To provide the customer with the lowest landed cost and maximum flexibility, distribution is often done through a centralized location. Redistribution to end customers may be done post customs clearance where the goods are in free circulation, or in bond using a T1 transit document which enables the goods to be transported to the final destination country where customs clearance will be made. A growing number of companies, including a number of the exporters of LAN equipment, are transitioning to the latter distribution strategy (Information provided by the United States).

question of what effect actions by one member State's customs authorities might have on expectations with regard to treatment under concessions for another member State. While actions at the Community level might affect expectations regarding market access with respect to trade into all member States, the treatment of a product by Greece, for instance, could not be deemed to affect the expectations of an exporter with respect to the treatment contemplated for its exports to the United Kingdom or for its exports to the entire Community. If so, then the concessions of the Community and of the member States were all fundamentally unreliable, and the Community, alone among WTO Members, was placed in the unique position in which the treatment accorded by the Community, and each of its member States, could be reduced to the least common denominator of the treatment by any of its member States. Such an interpretation should not be accorded to Article II or to these concessions. Moreover, since the EC's trading partners knew that exporters could enter goods in one member State and then ship them free of duty to any other member State, they should be able to rely on the most favourable treatment provided in any member State. The United States noted the parallel to the interpretation that had been given to GATT Article III in disputes concerning measures of provinces or states in the United States and Canada; past GATT panels had held that Article III required treatment of imported products no less favourable than the treatment accorded to the most-favoured domestic product.[76]

5.59 The **European Communities** stated that the EC considered the principal function of LAN equipment to be the transmission of data between computers. Thus the communication function was paramount. The purpose of processing data by the LAN equipment was to enable that data to be communicated. Some modems were peripheral devices that permitted a personal computer, minicomputer, or mainframe, to receive and transmit data in digital format across voice telecommunication lines. Thus, their function was not unlike that of a router. Some multiplexers also fell within the definition of LAN equipment. In a US ruling of 21 March 1989 (NY 837606), sixteen line intelligent multiplexers described as networking boards, which were to be installed in a mainframe computer chassis and which appeared to be dedicated to the transmission of signals representing symbols and data, were classified under HS heading 8517.82. Later, following the reclassification decision of LAN equipment by the United States in 1992, a product known as statistical multiplexers was classified in HS heading 8471.80 in a ruling of 13 February 1996 (NY A80132). The multiplexers in question were designed to provide interconnection between dumb terminals and/or desk-top processors with centrally located minicomputers in both LAN

[76] Panel Report on *United States - Measures Affecting Alcoholic and Malt Beverages*, adopted on 19 June 1992, BISD 39S/206, para. 5.17; Panel Report on *Canada - Import, Distribution and Sale of Certain Alcoholic Drinks by Provincial Marketing Agencies*, adopted on 18 February 1992, BISD 39S/27, note to para. 5.4; see *Analytical Index/Guide to GATT Law and Practice* (1995 ed.), page. 130.

and WAN applications. Moreover, Singapore, in its submission, had identified a multiplexer as LAN equipment.[77] In conclusion, if this dispute was about LAN equipment other than LAN adapter cards, which the EC contested, it necessarily also included certain modems and multiplexers.

5.60 In this connection, it was also important to note that the BTIs issued by France, the Netherlands and the United Kingdom submitted by the EC were relevant. They were not as asserted by the United States dealing with products outside the scope of this issue. They, in fact, dealt with those types of LAN equipment which were complete in that they were imported in their own housing and included routers, bridges, hubs, servers and multiplexers used in computer networks for data transmission. They were not limited to connecting computers within a local area network but were also used for communication between networks. For example, routers controlled the flow of information between the different LANs that made up the larger wide-area networks (WAN).

5.61 Furthermore, the ECJ ruling in the Siemens Nixdorf case had not undermined the ruling of the German Bundesfinanzhof of 1991. In the German case, the product at issue related to LAN components, including a LAN adapter device. In the Siemens-Nixdorf case, the product at issue was a video monitor that could only receive signals from a data processing machine. The two products were therefore completely different and their functions did not correspond in any way. The German court case still stood and was not only relevant for Germany, as the United States wrongly alleged, since products imported into Germany participated in the free circulation of goods in the entire EC.

5.62 Finally, the EC wished to emphasize that how many individual classifications had been made in one direction rather than in the other could certainly not be considered decisive since at best the classification practice could only be characterized as inconsistent. How under these circumstances the US negotiators could have derived certainty about an agreed tariff treatment or even simple expectations from individual classification decisions while they were negotiating tariff concessions with the EC as a whole was extremely unclear; the EC could not be held bound by such unjustified expectations.

(ii) Trade Flows

5.63 The **United States** claimed that trade data demonstrated that the EC and its member States treated imports of these products under Chapter 84. The data and documents containing trade statistics relied on during the negotiations demonstrated that there were large and increasing trade flows of the products at issue within tariff heading 84.71. The EC's trading partners had a right to rely on this

[77] It stated the following: "Significantly, Singapore's request on 8471.99 identified by name examples of LAN equipment covered by the request namely: 'gateways', 'concentrators' and 'multiplexers'".

well-known treatment in bargaining for tariff concessions and to assume that such treatment would continue in the absence of any statement to the contrary by the EC. The calculations submitted by the EC in the 1993 negotiations to justify the value of its Uruguay Round tariff offer confirmed the reasonableness of the US expectation in this regard. These data indicated that US-originating imports into the EC of products treated as automatic data processing products under Chapter 84 closely tracked US exports of computers, computer peripherals and computer parts. Trade flow trends confirmed the US claim that, in the aftermath of the Uruguay Round, the EC changed the tariff treatment of the products at issue from that which was negotiated. Thus, while US exports of LAN equipment, as reported on the Shipper's Export Declarations under expected heading 8471.99 continued to rise in 1994 and 1995, the EC's trade data indicated that the products as classified as dutiable under that heading sharply declined in 1995. At the same time, the EC's reported imports of products dutiable as telecommunications equipment under 8517.82 increased in an amount disproportionate to the US exporters reported exports of products they expected to be treated under that heading.[78]

5.64 Furthermore, interpretation of trade flows in relation to the headings in a particular schedule had to take into account the agreed context of the tariff negotiations in the Uruguay Round. The Mid-term Review decision of Ministers on Tariffs adopted at the Montreal Ministerial Meeting of December 1988 provided explicitly: "Participants have agreed that in the negotiation of tariff concessions, current nomenclatures should be employed... ."[79] Thus, the participants had agreed that the tariff negotiations would take place on the basis of the tariff treatment that was operative during the negotiations.

5.65 The **European Communities** stated that with regard to the arguments put forward by the United States on trade figures, EC import figures from the United States for 8471.99 did not show that they had "sharply declined in 1995". Indeed the volume of imports from the US trade under heading 8471.99 had remained fairly constant since 1990; this constancy was also reflected in EC imports from the United States for the products under 84.71. However, for all products falling under 85.17 there had been since 1990 growth in imports from the United States. This was due to the ever increasing use of telephone and telecommunications equipment. LAN equipment was involved in that growth but did not account for all of it. While exporters might have said that the products they had shipped to the EC under 84.71 were LAN equipment, the EC did not know whether, in all such cases, the products were declared as LAN equipment or just declared as computers or computer products. Apart from this, the following elements also had to be considered:

---

78 See Annex 7.

79 MTN.TNC/7(MIN); also referenced in the agreed text on *Procedures for the Negotiations*, op cit., para. 5: "Participants have agreed that in the negotiation on tariff concessions, current nomenclatures should be employed . . .".

- It was possible that certain companies in certain cases had received windfall benefits through BTIs which enabled them to obtain a lower duty treatment for specific LAN products in another heading, e.g. 84.71/84.73.
- In other cases, as was already mentioned, importers might not have specifically mentioned LAN equipment when declaring products under 84.71/84.73. Indeed the evidence supplied to the Panel's questions by the United States showed that the products in question were declared as computer parts under HS heading 84.73 ("accessoires d'ordinateurs" and "onderdelen voor computers")[80] and not as LAN equipment.
- It was quite possible, not to say likely, that certain exporters were regarding all products they had shipped under 84.71 to be LAN equipment. Indeed, the statements submitted by the United States were ambiguous, if not incorrect. When products were shipped they were declared according to the exporting country's classification of a particular product, and in the period referred to, the United States had classified these products under tariff heading 84.71. However, when products were imported into a third country, they should be declared in accordance with the classification as determined by the importing country. When the United States and the EC disagreed on a particular classification of an EC product, the United States did not grant tariff treatment under the heading supported by the EC but under the heading they themselves found appropriate. One example of this, which had already been mentioned, was the US company which had claimed that all its LAN equipment exported during a certain time period to the United Kingdom had been classified by UK customs authorities under 84.71. But, in fact a BTI issued by the UK customs during that time-period to the same company had classified the product under tariff heading 85.17. Moreover, it should be remembered that in order to facilitate trade, EC customs officials only verified a small proportion of imports and the accompanying declarations.

2. *Personal Computers with Multimedia Capability*

5.66 The **United States** claimed that PCs with multimedia capability were treated as products under Chapter 84 during the Uruguay Round. The EC had admitted that personal computers at issue in this dispute, including those capable of receiving and processing television signals, existed and were marketed prior to 1994. When the EC had bound its tariffs in early 1994, it had treated all PCs,

80 See Annex 4, Table 3, Nos. 1 and 2.

including those with multimedia capability, as automatic data processing machines as provided for under heading 84.71. In negotiating its Uruguay Round concessions, the EC had not made any reservations under heading 84.71 for any particular type of personal computer.

5.67 The **European Communities** responded that as more and more functionalities had been added to PCs, it had become more common to refer to such PCs as PCs with multimedia capabilities. At the same time classification of such products had become much more difficult because it was necessary to determine whether the product was a PC with multimedia capabilities or a multimedia machine with computing facilities.

5.68 However, neither during nor at the end of the Uruguay Round, could the United States have had reasonable expectations that the EC would classify PCTVs or other multimedia equipment under tariff heading 84.71 and apply the corresponding duty rate. In fact, the United States had not produced any documentation showing that the EC had indeed classified all computers with multimedia capabilities under heading 84.71 during the Uruguay Round. Moreover, on 30 March 1994, EC Regulation 754/94[81] was issued which classified "Compact Disc Interactive System"(CDI System) made by the Dutch company Philips under tariff heading 85.21, "video apparatus." This Regulation put the trading community on notice concerning treatment of "multimedia equipment". As far as PCTVs were concerned, the United States should have had even fewer reasonable expectations that the EC would apply the tariff concession regarding heading 84.71. The mere fact that importers were able to clear certain shipments of these products under heading 84.71 was, by itself, irrelevant. As already mentioned, customs clearance in the EC depended on self-certification for over 90 per cent of imports in order to keep trade flowing, and importers derived no rights from their own misstatements. Neither should the US government.

5.69 The **United States** stated that the absence of rulings on treatment suggested (1) a consensus among importers that classification was obviously under tariff heading 84.71 and (2) a general acceptance of that view by customs officials who had ample opportunity to engage importers in discussion at local ports and through other means. Long-standing trading practices confirmed this conclusion. The process of customs entry and importation was in fact designed to work without written rulings: to be self-executing based on the plain text of the Harmonized System, the guidance of the Notes to Chapters in the Harmonized System, and the advice provided by the text of the Explanatory Notes. An importer with a new product normally began by undertaking a classification analysis based on these sources, as well as any pertinent available written rulings. Knowledgeable importers did this all the time, relying on their own expertise. If the analysis resulted in an obvious classification, the importer did not seek advance advice from customs authorities in the form of written rulings. Contrary to the EC's sug-

[81] Commission Regulation 754/94, OJ 1994 L 89/2, product 5.

gestions, such advance written advice was not required. Indeed, if it were, the normal course of international trade would be seriously disrupted by a requirement which no competent customs authority was staffed to implement within commercially acceptable time limits. Instead, the importer started importing the merchandise, using the classification that its analysis indicated was correct. This was particularly the case where the change in a product was evolutionary.

5.70 The United States argued that one should not be misled by the EC's claim that only 10 per cent of shipments were physically inspected, which suggested that only 10 per cent of shipments were classified correctly. The EC and member States had their own classification experts in major product areas, such as ADP equipment. They read the trade press, kept up with technological change, and applied their knowledge of customs classification principles and the HS sources to new products. They were not hesitant to ask questions or even demand written presentations if they had questions. If customs authorities in the EC had indeed inspected 10 per cent of shipments, it was very unlikely that they would not have inspected multimedia-capable computers; if they had not accepted that the appropriate tariff treatment was that under heading 84.71, they would have treated them as subject to a different heading.

5.71 The system had to work this way, and was described in the Kyoto Convention to which the EC and the member States were parties. Importers had an affirmative obligation to classify products correctly, whether or not the products were physically inspected. The fact that there were no EC reclassification of multimedia-capable computers during the Uruguay Round in the face of substantial trade indicated that importers were doing their jobs, customs authorities were satisfied with their classifications, and customs authorities agreed that these products were properly dutiable under heading 84.71.

5.72 Furthermore, the CDI System to which the EC had referred was outside the product scope of the present dispute, as it was not a computer. The EC asserted that this product had "computing capabilities", however, this assertion was misleading. Although the user had an array of available choices, at its most basic level the CDI System could only be “programmed" to perform in a finite number of ways, like a microwave oven or a VCR. Those, too, had various computing functions, but were not computers. The EC’s tariff treatment of microwave ovens and VCRs could not reasonably be relied upon as the measure of the EC’s tariff treatment of personal computers. Nor could the EC’s treatment of the CDI unit be reasonably relied upon by the United States and its exporters of computers as an indicator of the EC’s future treatment of computers, including computers with multimedia capacity.

5.73 During consultations in this case, the EC had indicated that personal computers capable of receiving and processing television signals were treated by the United Kingdom alone among the EC member States as dutiable under heading

85.28, and that this was inconsistent with EC practice.[82] The EC had since stated that such statements were "erroneous." Subsequently, the EC stated that "PCTV's have always been classified in the EC in 85.28." This inconsistency in the EC position illustrated why the United States had found it necessary to seek clarification concerning the treatment by the United Kingdom and the EC of all types of multimedia computers.

5.74 With the issuance of EC Regulation 1153/97, the EC Commission had now admitted that such computers - as well as all computers "capable of receiving and processing television, telecommunication, audio and video signals"- were properly treated as "automatic data processing machines and units thereof" in heading 84.71. This Regulation which became effective on 1 July 1997 amended the EC Common Tariff Nomenclature and the Common Customs Tariff. It was a Regulation which was adopted to implement EC commitments under the Information Technology Agreement (ITA) reached at the Singapore Ministerial Conference. The ITA was intended "to achieve maximum freedom of world trade in information technology products" through the reduction and ultimate elimination of customs duties on information technology products. However, the Regulation blatantly imposed tariffs at higher-than-concession rates on computers provided for in the concession on heading 84.71[83].

5.75 The **European Communities** wished to point out that Regulation 754/94 which classified the CDI System under 85.21 had also classified the Commodore Dynamic Total Vision System[84], which was a product referred to by the United States as a computer with multimedia capacity, under 85.21. Therefore, this Regulation should have put the trading community on notice concerning treatment of "multimedia equipment" in the EC.

[82] Information Fiche which in the US submission was attached to a 13 March 1997 letter from R.E. Abbott, Head of the Permanent Delegation of the European Commission to the International Organizations in Geneva, to A.L. Stoler, Chargé d'Affaires of the Permanent Mission of the United States to the WTO.

[83] Other information submitted by the United States concerning multimedia computers included: a chart and catalogues describing models of multimedia personal computers on the market in 1992 and 1993; report of the 57th meeting of the Tariff and Statistical Nomenclature Section of the EC Customs Code Committee, held on 29-30 June 1995; flash sheet dated February 1996 regarding multimedia PCs, and a letter regarding the same from the UK Department of Trade and Industry dated 27 March 1996; a European Commission document entitled "Information Note with regard to Classification of Multimedia and Related Products"; minutes of the 14 March 1996 meeting of the WTO Committee on Market Access (G/MA/M/5); and trade data on multimedia PCs submitted in response to the Panel's questions.

[84] The EC claimed that the Regulation classifying the Commodore Dynamic Total Vision (CDTV) product (item 4 in Regulation 754/94) established the principle that even though a piece of equipment was capable of computing, other functionalities might be added, thus bringing the equipment into another product category in the HS nomenclature. Also, at the time when Commission Regulation (EC) No. 754/94 was adopted, the CDTV was an exceptional product compared with the standard type of PCs imported under HS heading 8471 and presumably declared under that heading as computers.

5.76 With respect to the "erroneous statement", referred to by the United States, it was contained in an "information fiche", for a meeting. This was an informal document, which had no legal value and could not be considered a formal EC position statement. It was prepared within a short deadline and it had not been possible to consult with all the Commission services involved in the matter. In fact, the statement should have read "As regards the classification of PCTVs, the general practice in the EU is that these fall under heading 85.28"instead of "84.71". It was a mistake and did not represent inconsistencies on the part of the EC.

5.77 On the last point, Regulation 1153/97 which was adopted in order to implement the results of the ITA was, in the view of the EC and as already noted, at odds with the scope of what this dispute was about; it was a new Agreement negotiated after the Uruguay Round. Following the decision in the WCO on the classification of a multimedia personal computer, the EC had had to adapt its nomenclature in accordance with the substance of that ruling which effectively moved the PCTV from HS heading 85.28 to 84.71.[85] On the US assertion that the Regulation "blatantly imposed tariffs at higher-than-concession rates on computers provided for in the concession on heading 84.71", the EC had always held that PCTVs should receive tariff treatment which was originally provided for under 85.28. The idea being that even if there was a reclassification, for instance because of discussions at the WCO, it should not affect the tariff treatment. This approach had also been taken by the GATT with regard to the introduction of the HS, and was reflected in a decision taken by the GATT Council which stated that: "The main principle to be observed in connexion with the introduction of the Harmonized System in national tariffs is that existing bindings should be maintained unchanged. The alteration of existing bindings should only be envisaged where their maintenance would result in undue complexity in the national tariffs and should not involve a significant or arbitrary increase in customs duties collected on a particular product".[86] In fact, Article II obliged Members to give tariff treatment not less favourable than that which derived from tariff negotiations.

C. *Nullification and Impairment*

5.78 The **United States** claimed that the EC-Schedule LXXX provided tariff concessions for HS heading 84.71, "automatic data-processing machines and units thereof". These concessions were negotiated and agreed to during the Uruguay Round, after intensive negotiations between the United States and the EC on behalf of the EC member States initially within the context of the US zero-for-

[85] The EC, under the WCO process, made a reservation for the reason to seek clarity with regard to the term "multimedia", which was, as already noted, broad and imprecise.

[86] *GATT Concessions under the Harmonized Commodity Description and Coding System*, adopted on 12 July 1983, BISD 30S/17, para. 2.1.

zero initiative within the electronics sector. There was no discussion, during this time-period, between the EC and the United States of treating LAN equipment and PCs with multimedia capability as anything other than computers, computer units or computer parts subject to the tariffs applicable under tariff heading 8471 and 84.73. These products were, also during this period of time, already marketed, traded and legally imported into member States of the EC under headings 84.71 and 84.73, as demonstrated by BTIs and/or written classification determinations of member State customs authorities and by other evidence. As a result, the United States was justified in reasonably expecting the products at issue being provided the treatment foreseen under the relevant tariff headings of chapter 84 of the EC Schedule LXXX. By classifying these products to tariff headings carrying higher duty rates which were in excess of the rates provided for in Schedule LXXX under the relevant tariff headings of chapter 84, the EC, Ireland and the UK had violated their obligations under Article II:1, and as a result these measures had nullified or impaired the value of concessions accruing to the United States under the GATT 1994.

5.79 The **European Communities** argued that the United States did not have a legitimate basis to claim "reasonable expectations". On the contrary, all that had been revealed with the BTIs and classification actions of EC member states' customs authorities submitted to the Panel was that during the Uruguay Round there was no uniform treatment, within the EC member states for these products, and that if anyone re-classified LAN equipment during this period of time it was the United States and not the EC. This situation demonstrated the uncertainty that existed with respect to the classification of these products within the EC member states and EC's trading partners and therefore the claim of "reasonable expectations" could not be justified. Moreover, the United States had not been able to establish the existence of a meeting of the minds of the negotiators constituting an agreement at any moment in the course of the Uruguay Round tariff negotiations concerning the tariff treatment of these products. In view of the above, the classification actions of the EC, Ireland and the United Kingdom should be viewed as having been intended to rectify a situation of divergences within the EC member states regarding the treatment of these products, and not one of re-classification. Furthermore, it should be noted that while the customs authorities of EC member States might have classified these products differently, thereby according different duty treatment to the same products, the EC itself had always held the view that these products should be classified under the relevant tariff headings of chapter 85 as the primary function of these products was data transmission and not data processing. In view of all of the above, the actions by the EC, Ireland and the United Kingdom could not have nullified or impaired the value of concessions accruing to the United States under the GATT 1994.

VI. THIRD PARTIES SUBMISSIONS

A. *India*

6.1 India requested the Panel to find that the EC's classification of LAN equipment under Regulation (EC) 1165/95, had resulted in the treatment of those products becoming less favourable than that provided for in Part I of Schedule LXXX and therefore was inconsistent with obligations under Article II of GATT 1994.

6.2 India exported approximately Rs.1 billion worth of LAN equipment to the EC in 1995-1996.[87] In addition to this substantial trade interest, India was interested in the systemic issues raised by this dispute. In particular, India was concerned with the possibility that a Member might avoid its specific obligations related to tariff rate concessions under Article II through the reclassification of bound items. In examining this matter, emphasis had to be placed on the "fundamental importance of the security and predictability of GATT tariff bindings", a principle which constituted a central obligation in the system of the General Agreement, as mentioned in 1984 Panel Report on *Newsprint*.[88]

6.3 On 27 April 1997, an overwhelming majority of the members of the WCO HS Committee voted to classify LAN equipment, under heading 84.71. Notwithstanding this decision, the EC had not adopted any measures bringing its member States into conformity with this decision. As was clear from this decision, it was India's understanding that the products subject to this dispute should be classified under heading 84.71.

6.4 One could conclude from these facts that in the Uruguay Round tariff negotiations, other Members including developing country Members like India, who were beginning to export such products to the EC, had reason to believe that the EC had agreed to bind LAN equipment as a product under the heading 84.71. Thus the EC and its member States were under obligation to provide the tariff treatment granted at the time of the Uruguay Round to LAN equipment based on the provisions under Article II of GATT 1994.

B. *Japan*

6.5 Japan argued that on the technical side, as was clear from the decision of the WCO HS Committee and as had always been Japan's understanding, that the products subject to this dispute should be classified under tariff heading 84.71. At its eighteenth Session of the Harmonized System (HS) Committee of the WCO held in November 1996, the Committee had decided to classify "PCTV" multimedia PCs under tariff heading 84.71 as a result of a vote. At its nineteenth Session held in April 1997, the HS Committee had voted to classify LAN equip-

---

87 Statistics of Foreign Trade of India (1995-96).

88 Panel Report on *Newsprint*, op cit., para. 52.

ment, especially (1) communications controllers or router, (2) cluster controllers, (3) multistation access unit and (4) optical fibre converter under heading 84.71. Notwithstanding these decisions, the EC had not adopted any measure to bring its member States into conformity with these decisions. While, the WTO Agreement imposed no obligation on Members to follow any specific nomenclature including the HS, the scope of the concession for a tariff line in the EC's Schedule which was based on the HS nomenclature, had to be considered or interpreted, unless otherwise specified in the Schedule, in light of the related HS documents, including the text of the HS nomenclature and Notes to Chapters. However, there was no such specification or qualification concerning the product coverage for the heading 84.71 or 85.28 in the EC's schedule. Moreover, in actual practice the EC had applied the same tariff rate as the bound rate on LAN equipment and PCTVs under the heading 84.71, before reclassification actions by the EC, Ireland and the United Kingdom.

6.6 From this factual background, it could be concluded that during the Uruguay Round tariff negotiations, other Members had reason to believe that the EC had agreed to bind LAN equipment and PCTVs as "automatic data processing machines" under the heading 84.71. Thus, the EC and its member States were under the obligation to provide the tariff treatment granted at the time of the Uruguay Round to LAN equipment and multimedia PCs based on the provisions of Article II of GATT 1994. Instead, the EC, Ireland and the United Kingdom had unilaterally, through reclassification, imposed higher tariff rates than those bound during Uruguay Round without initiating the procedures set forth in Article XXVIII of GATT 1994. Wherever these products were classified, the three defending parties should have maintained the value of tariff concessions at 3.9 per cent on LAN equipment and multimedia PCs, which the EC had committed to in the Uruguay Round. The three defending parties had therefore violated their obligations under Article II of GATT 1994.

6.7 The EC had argued that the EC had exclusive prerogative to decide on the classification of products under particular tariff headings, and that the application of particular tariff rates to certain products by the customs authorities of its member States should not be the basis for expectations regarding tariff concessions; therefore the Commission Regulation (EC) 1165/95 had not reclassified LAN adapter cards nor resulted in an increase in tariff rate. In fact, in Japan's view, in the absence of clear announcements or rules to show that the EC would classify those products under the heading 85.17 or 85.28, it would be natural for countries outside the EC when engaging in tariff negotiations to base themselves on the reality at that time. If the EC wished to argue otherwise, it should have been for the EC to bear the burden of proof. Japan had not found convincing evidence to that effect in the submission by the EC. In other words, the EC had not been able to produce sufficient evidence to show that the countries outside the EC should have anticipated such increases in tariff rates after the Uruguay Round.

6.8 This particular issue was systemic in that it could be a problem with regard to not only the products in dispute now but also to other products. As technology progressed, a number of new products would be coming into the market.

Whenever new negotiations took place with regard to those products, the same issue would inevitably come out. It would then be difficult to negotiate tariff concessions on those items on which the EC did not have uniform classification on tariff headings. Moreover, if the EC was allowed to change the tariff rates after the tariff negotiations in the name of proper and uniform classification, it would disturb the delicate balance of interests formulated by the tariff negotiations.

6.9 It was in this context that Japan requested the Panel to find that the unilateral increase of tariff rates as a result of the EC reclassification, or classification, of LAN adapter cards and its member States' reclassification of other types of LAN equipment and PCTVs were inconsistent with their obligations under Article II of GATT 1994.

C. Korea[89]

6.10 Korea argued that as a WTO Member, Korea had reasonable expectation during the Uruguay Round that LAN adapter cards and other LAN equipment would continue to be treated as ADP machines and units thereof under tariff heading 84.71, and that they would not be reclassified under a customs heading with a higher import duty. In addition, Korea had reasonably expected that multimedia PCs would remain under tariff heading 84.71 and not be changed to tariff heading 85.28. Systemic problems which stemmed from the propensity to classify technologically innovative multi-purpose or hybrid products under tariff headings carrying higher duty rates should be resolved pursuant to the decisions rendered by international standard setting bodies such as the WCO.

6.11 During the Uruguay Round, Korea had every reason to expect that the EC would classify LAN adapter cards and other LAN equipment as ADP machines and units thereof, as per tariff heading 84.71, not as telecommunications apparatus under category 85.17. Moreover, Korea had reasonably expected that multimedia PCs would be classified under tariff heading 84.71, not under heading 85.28.

6.12 Korea noted that the EC had claimed in its first written submission that the fundamental point of the current dispute was the "scope of the bindings negotiated in the Uruguay Round". The EC had contended that because it did not negotiate specific concessions on the customs duties applicable to LAN or multimedia equipment, Korea and other WTO Members could not have derived reasonable expectation that these products would be classified under tariff heading 84.71. However, certain salient aspects of the EC's classification practices, notably the issuance of BTIs by the customs authorities of member States, had led to the conclusion that Korea and other WTO Members could have reasonably expected that

[89] On the procedural background, Korea in its submission had also indicated that on 2 December 1996, the EC had requested the consulting parties to delay the proceedings until after the completion of the Information Technology Agreement, and it was so agreed.

the EC would treat LAN equipment and multimedia PCs as ADP machines and units thereof. These practices included the fact that:

- "The EC has no centralized administration of the Common Customs Tariff, but involved the member States' customs authorities for the purpose of administration";
- "It may occur, in particular when it is not obvious in which heading a given product should be classified, that customs authorities in different member States classify that product differently and consequently apply different duties."
- "Prior to December 1993, when substantive Uruguay Round negotiations were concluded, there was no classification regulation on LAN equipment with an EC-wide applicability that had been adopted and implemented by the EC Commission or by the Council. Nor had there been a ruling by the European Court of Justice on the classification decision of LAN equipment".

6.13 In short, the classification of LAN equipment was left to the customs authorities of the EC member States prior to the conclusion of the Uruguay Round negotiations. Based on the factual information provided in the first written submission of the EC, it could be inferred that the practices of the member States' customs authorities constituted the only source for identifying "classification rules and practices at the time of the Uruguay Round".

6.14 To show that the reasonable expectation derived by the United States and other WTO Members from BTIs was misplaced, the EC had alluded by way of examples to various contradictory BTIs issued by member States during the Uruguay Round negotiations. The customs authorities of Germany and the Netherlands had rendered BTIs which classified LAN equipment under tariff heading 85.17, whereas the BTIs issued by the customs authorities of the United Kingdom and Ireland had classified LAN equipment under 84.71. At the same time, the EC had attempted to mitigate the significance of BTIs as a source of reasonable expectation regarding the classification of a product by citing Article 12.5 of the Community Customs Code which provided that "a BTI ceases to be valid where an EC regulation is adopted and the information no longer conforms to the law laid down thereby, or where the BTI is incompatible with a judgement of the European Court of Justice." Contrary to the EC's assertion, that provision appeared to endorse the role of BTIs to supplement the absence of Community-wide rules governing the practical classification of a variety of products. The EC's first written submission failed to point out any alternative source of concrete reference, other than the BTIs, regarding the practices of some of its member States, such as the United Kingdom and Ireland, governing the classification of LAN equipment during the Uruguay Round negotiations. Because there were no EC regulations or judgments of the ECJ which specified the classification of LAN equipment, Korea was of the opinion that the BTIs provided the best available source for exporters to identify the practices of the relevant countries. No explicit reference appeared to have been made during the Uruguay Round tariff negotiations. The EC stated that "none of the products at issue were discussed by name." In the absence of any specific exceptions or explicit reservations on the part of the EC, participating countries to the Uruguay Round tariff negotiations had no choice but to expect that the then existing classification would continue to be applied.

6.15 More significantly, as was stated by the United States, the EC's Uruguay Round concessions were set forth in Schedule LXXX. Article II of the GATT 1994 obliged contracting parties to apply the established rates of duties which appeared in their respective schedules. The imposition of a duty higher than the rates appearing in the schedule would nullify or impair the value of the concessions accruing to other WTO Members. At the time of the Uruguay Round negotiations, and prior to its conclusion, the EC had treated LAN equipment as ADP machines and units thereof under tariff heading 84.71 and such products were indeed imported under that category. After the finalization of the Uruguay Round tariff concessions, the EC began to apply the higher rate of duty under tariff heading 85.17 as mandated by Regulation (EC) No. 1165/95.

6.16 A noteworthy point made by the United States was that between 14 February and 31 March 1994, participants had engaged in a verification process to confirm that negotiated concessions were accurately reflected in the final schedules. Despite the fact that the EC was aware that its trading partners relied on BTI rulings and communications in the negotiations which indicated that LAN equipment would be treated as ADP machines under heading 8471, the EC had not taken any steps to define ADP machines to exclude LAN equipment. It was only after the Uruguay Round negotiations that the EC and several of its member States had started to categorize LAN equipment under tariff heading 85.17.

6.17 In view of the treatment of LAN equipment under tariff heading 84.71 at the time of the Uruguay Round negotiations and the EC's commitment in Schedule LXXX, the EC could not refute the claim that it had committed itself to apply the duty rate bound for computer equipment to LAN equipment. Participating countries could reasonably expect that the EC would continue to classify LAN equipment under tariff heading 84.71 and apply the corresponding tariff set forth in Schedule LXXX. However, such reasonable expectation was nullified and impaired by the application of Regulation (EC) No. 1165/95 to LAN adapter cards and by the subsequent reclassification of other LAN equipment from tariff heading 84.71 to 85.17.

6.18 With respect to PCTVs, it was common in today's international marketplace for a number of technological new products to be developed by incorporating certain functions of other products into an already existing product. Unless new headings were created and new tariff rates negotiated, there was no other way to classify the new, multi-functional products but to rely on the headings of existing products, whose functions were reflected closely or remotely in the new, multi-functional product. Given the different duty rates for the existing products to which a new product might be related, there was a possibility that the WTO Members might attempt to "shop around" to apply the highest possible duty rates to the new, multi-functional products.

6.19 Allowing WTO Members to classify new, multi-functional products under the heading of the related existing product with the highest possible duty rates without appropriate justification, would undermine the value of the concessions negotiated and committed to by WTO Members. If personal computers with television capabilities replaced conventional PCs and the new breed of PCs were dutiable under the high-duty heading of television receivers, the concessions made for personal computers would become substantially affected and reduced in value. When tariff negotiations were conducted, it was reasonable to assume that the existing product containing simple functions could be replaced by a new generation of multi-functional products. As science and technology progressed, such results were inevitable, especially in the field of goods involving high technology.

6.20 By definition, multi-functional products carried out multiple functions. Therefore, it was difficult, if not impossible, to determine the appropriate classification of multi-functional devices solely on the basis of functions, as was argued by the EC. It, therefore, became essential to scrutinize the end-use and determine which existing products were replaced by the new multi-functional goods in the largest quantity. It was unlikely that consumers purchased PCTVs for the exclusive purpose of using them as ordinary television receivers, without regard to their other applications. Furthermore, it was observed that this device worked solely in conjunction with a computer (automatic data processing machine).

6.21 One way of identifying an appropriate classification for new multi-functional products was through examination and decision by the WCO. As the EC had admitted, the HS Committee of the WCO had adopted a draft amendment to the Compendium of Classification Opinions with regard to PCTVs in favour of tariff heading 84.71. This meant that the EC had not come up with a justification, even in the form of an interim decision under the WCO, for its reclassification of PCTVs under a higher tariff heading. Apart from this, the EC had failed to suggest in its first submission any justification for the reclassification.

6.22 Based on the above stated observations, Korea challenged the EC's classification of automatic data processing machines with television capabilities under tariff heading 85.28 as an act which undermined and devalued the concession on products under tariff heading 84.71 as contained in the EC Schedule. The EC had failed to justify its classification of these new multi-functional products under the heading of the related existing products with a higher tariff rate. Unless the EC was able to justify such classification, Korea was of the opinion that the EC's classification of computers with television capabilities resulted in treatment of those products less favourable than that provided for in Part I of Schedule LXXX.

6.23 For the reasons described above, the Republic of Korea requested the Panel to find that the EC's reclassification of LAN adapter cards under the Regulation (EC) No. 1165/95 and that of other LAN equipment and computers with television capabilities through measures taken by several of its member States were inconsistent with its obligations under Article II of GATT 1994.

D. Singapore

6.24 Singapore argued that during the Uruguay Round negotiations, and prior to finalization of these tariff concessions, certain EC member States classified LAN equipment under tariff heading 84.71, as evidenced by numerous BTIs and other written rulings. In addition, the EC had clear notice from the inception of the negotiations that its trading partners, including Singapore, had negotiated with the understanding that the EC offers on ADP units included LAN equipment. Through various procedures, the defending parties subsequently classified LAN equipment, including LAN adapter cards, into tariff heading 85.17 as telecommunication apparatus. This classification resulted in the imposition of customs duties on LAN equipment imports in excess of the bound rate commitments for ADP units under Schedule LXXX.

6.25 In terms of trade interest Singapore exported approximately S$2 billion worth of LAN equipment, including LAN adapter cards, to the EC between May 1996, the effective date of the reclassification, and December 1996. In addition to this substantial trade interest, Singapore was interested in the systemic issues raised by this dispute. In particular, Singapore was concerned with the possibility that Members might avoid specific obligations related to tariff rate concessions under Article II through the reclassification of bound items. In examining this matter, emphasis had to be placed on the "fundamental importance of the security and predictability of GATT tariff bindings, a principle which constitutes a central obligation in the system of the General Agreement".[90]

6.26 The EC's reclassification of LAN computer equipment violated EC's tariff concessions under Article II of GATT 1994. GATT Article II:1(b) provided that "The products described in Part I of the Schedule relating to any contracting party, which are the products of territories of other contracting parties, shall, on their importation into the territory to which the Schedule relates, and subject to the terms, conditions or qualifications set forth in that Schedule, be exempt from ordinary customs duties in excess of those set forth and provided therein." Under Article II:7 of GATT 1994, the annexed concession schedules were an integral part of the Agreement. The EC concessions on ADP units that were at issue in this matter appeared in Schedule LXXX of GATT 1994. Article II.1(b) was violated by tariff classifications, including reclassification, that resulted in increased duties on bound items. This was reflected in the Agreement itself under Article

[90] Panel Report on *Newsprint*, op cit., para. 52.

II.5, which contemplated compensatory adjustment in cases where internal classification decisions effectively prevented contracting parties from according agreed-to tariff concessions.[91] In short, it was settled that "[i]f ... there is a divergence between a national customs tariff of a contracting party to GATT and its schedule, the international obligations of that country are those described in its schedule of concessions".[92]

6.27 The dispute on *Greek Increase in Bound Duty* confirmed that contracting parties should not avoid their Article II obligations by reclassifying bound items. In that dispute, a GATT Group of Experts examined Germany's complaint that Greece had raised its tariff on long-playing gramophone records, despite the fact that "gramophone records" were bound in the Greek schedule.[93] Greece contended that the introduction of later-developed, long-playing records made of different material constituted a new item not subject to the earlier binding. The reviewing Group agreed with Germany that the disputed records were covered by the description of "gramophone records" in the bound item and found that Greece had violated its Article II obligations.[94]

6.28 As demonstrated below, the defending parties in this dispute had similarly used tariff classification authority in violation of their Article II.1(b) commitments. In reclassifying LAN equipment from the controlling categories covering ADP units, the defending parties applied customs duties in excess of the bound rates specified for such products in the EC's concession schedule. In the present matter, at the time the EC tariff bindings were negotiated, substantial volumes of LAN equipment were being imported into and classified by EC member States in the categories covering automatic data processors and units. As documented in the US submission dated 14 May 1997, such practice was widespread and highlighted by written BTIs and letter rulings by certain EC member States.[95] Accordingly, the EC had clear knowledge of the practice. The EC, however, contended that it "never committed itself nor could it be construed to have given the impression that it would classify LAN ... equipment with computer equipment under heading 84.71 and apply the corresponding duty to the products concerned".[96] Such an assertion was plainly incorrect. As pointed out in the US submission, the documents exchanged in the concession negotiations clearly indi-

---

[91] As one GATT scholar has noted: "A reclassification subsequent to the making of a GATT concession could ... be a violation of the basic commitment regarding that concession. ... Paragraph 5 of Article II recognizes the possibility that reclassification of goods can violate a GATT concession and provides for consultation and renegotiation in such cases.", Jackson, John H., *World Trade and the Law of GATT*, 1969, p. 212.

[92] See Note by the Secretariat on *Tariff Reclassification* dated 27 April 1981, Committee on Tariff Concessions, TAR/W/19, para. 1.

[93] *Greek Increase in Bound Duties*, complaint op cit., pages 115 and 116.

[94] Report by the Group of Experts on *Greek Increase in Bound Duty*, op cit., pages 168 to 170.

[95] Pursuant to such rulings, certain EC member States applied the rates for ADP units and parts to imports of LAN equipment from numerous sources.

[96] EC's first submission, 4 June 1997, para.9.

cated that the parties viewed the EC's ADP units/tariff heading 84.71 concession as encompassing LAN equipment.

6.29 The US assertion was confirmed by negotiating documents exchanged by Singapore and the EC. In particular, in its original concession request directed to the EC in June 1990, Singapore had requested the EC to reduce tariffs on sub-heading 8471.99 from 4.9 per cent to zero. Significantly, Singapore's request on 8471.99 identified by name examples of LAN equipment covered by the request, namely "gateways," "concentrators" and "multiplexers." Through such an exchange, the EC had received express notice of Singapore's expectation that any eventual EC tariff concessions on ADP units in tariff heading 84.71 would specifically include LAN equipment. The negotiations proceeded on this basis and the EC never expressed any reservations with including LAN equipment among the products subject to its concessions on ADP units/tariff heading 84.71. Consequently, Singapore had reasonably expected such treatment. Thus, contrary to the EC's assertions, its trading partners had relied not only on EC rulings classifying LAN equipment in ADP categories, but on communications in the negotiations indicating the understanding that LAN equipment would be covered by the EC's ADP concessions. With full knowledge of such an understanding, the EC had not made any reservations on LAN equipment or otherwise attempted to define its ADP concession in a manner that would not include LAN equipment. As demonstrated in the US submission, the EC had not given any indication of any contrary perception until after the agreement was finalized.

6.30 The scope of a tariff concession had to be interpreted based on the circumstances known at the time the binding was negotiated. For example, in the Panel on *Newsprint*[97] the EC had made an Article II binding that provided duty-free access to 1.5 million tonnes of newsprint per year, and then afterwards had unilaterally reduced the quantity by 1 million tonnes, which corresponded to the amount of duty-free access granted to EFTA partners under a separate agreement. Finding that the EC had not acted in conformity with Article II commitments, the Panel had emphasized that the EC had made no reservation on its 1.5 million tonnes MFN commitment even though "it was known that agreement had already been reached that the EFTA countries would obtain full duty-free access to the Community market ... ".[98] Similarly, in the present matter, the EC was aware of the understanding by its trading partners that LAN equipment was encompassed within the tariff negotiations on ADP equipment. In view of these circumstances, the EC's failure to apply to LAN equipment the bound rates for ADP units constituted a plain violation of its Article II.1(b) commitment.

6.31 The EC's violation of its Article II.1(b) commitment constituted a *prima facie* case of nullification and impairment under Article XXIII.1(a). In addition, even if the EC had not directly abrogated its Article II commitment, its failure to

97 Panel Report on *Newsprint*, op cit.
98 *Ibid.*, para. 50.

accord LAN equipment the bound rates for ADP units nullified or impaired the value of its commitment under Article XXIII.1(b). The EC had not rebutted the US contention that the EC's trade partners had good reason to believe, based on information exchanged in the negotiations, that the EC's concession on ADP units/tariff heading 84.71 would apply to LAN equipment. Any such rebuttal would not be tenable given the explicit references to LAN equipment in Singapore's concession request submitted to the EC. Such documentation demonstrated that the EC's trading partners had reasonably expected that the EC's heading 84.71 bindings covered LAN equipment.

6.32 The concept of nullification and impairment was inextricably linked to the expectations formed by parties during the negotiation process. It was well-established that Article XXIII.1(b) violations occurred where actions subsequent to undertaking a GATT commitment resulted in the frustration of reasonable expectations. For instance, in *Treatment by Germany of Imports of Sardines*[99], the Panel had considered Norway's complaint that Germany had nullified benefits accruing to Norway when Germany had reduced tariffs on certain sardines imported from other countries to levels that were lower than tariff bindings that Germany had previously committed to on competitive sardines of a type principally imported from Norway. Although Germany had technically adhered to its bound rate on imports from Norway, the Panel had determined that Germany had impaired the intended benefits of the commitment by subsequently according more favourable duty treatment to imports of competitive sardines shipped by other countries. As stated by the Panel, Germany's actions "could not reasonably have been anticipated" at the time of the negotiations and Norway "had reason to assume during these negotiations" that its exports would not be less favourably treated than other countries' exports.[100]

6.33 Similarly, Singapore had valid reasons for expecting that the ADP binding under negotiation would apply to LAN equipment. Having explicitly referred to various types of LAN equipment in its ADP concession request, which prompted no objection from the EC, Singapore had no reason to assume that the EC would resist applying its ADP binding to LAN equipment. The EC's subsequent unilateral action nullified the benefits Singapore had reasonably expected that it would derive from the concession.

---

[99] Panel Report on *Treatment by Germany of Imports of Sardines*, adopted on 31 October 1952, BISD 1S/53.

[100] *Ibid.*, para.16. See, also *Report on The Australian Subsidy on Ammonium Sulphate*, Report adopted on 3 April 1950, page 188, BISD Volume II, May 1952, (finding that although no violation occurred, contracting party "had reason to assume, during these negotiations that ... ."); and *Reports Relating to the Review of the Agreement, Quantitative Restrictions*, adopted on 2,4 and 5 March 1955, BISD 3S/170, para. 63 (contracting parties could not resort to withdrawal of concessions or suspension of obligations, "unless the effects of the measure concurred in proved to be substantially different from what could have been foreseen at the time the measure was considered ...").

6.34 Furthermore, the WCO's HS Committee had recently decided that LAN equipment was properly classifiable in heading 84.71 of the HS.[101] The HS Committee had specifically declined to adopt the position advanced that heading 85.17 was the appropriate category.[102] Given that the language interpreted by the HS Committee was identical to the EC's description in its concession schedule for heading 84.71, the decision confirmed that the EC had no valid basis for increasing the bound rates on ADP units on imports of LAN equipment.[103] The decision also provided additional corroboration of the reasonableness of EC trading partners' expectations that their LAN equipment exports would be covered by such bound rates. The EC had suggested that the HS Committee decision was intended solely to establish the appropriate HS classification for future imports. It ignored that the language interpreted by the HS Committee was the same language appearing in the EC's HS nomenclature and in the EC's concession schedule at the time of the negotiations and afterwards. The HS Committee decision did not purport to modify the language or alter prior HS Committee's interpretation. Instead, it interpreted longstanding HS provisions that were incorporated within the parties' nomenclature throughout the course of the GATT concession negotiations. As such, the decision demonstrated that the EC's trading partners had reasonably expected the ADP bindings to cover LAN equipment.

6.35 The EC submission emphasized that the HS Committee's decision was "not yet final" and noted that reservations could be made to the WCO by 1 July 1997. Significantly, the EC had not suggested that there was any chance that the HS Committee's decision would not be adopted on substantive grounds, nor could they have, given the overwhelming majority of members who were in favour of the decision. The EC instead appeared to be referring to the rules of HS Convention that permitted any member from lodging reservations to prevent the Council's adoption of the HS Committee's decisions as Classification Opinions. However, the current legal status of the decision did not negate the fact that the HS Committee had fully considered the matter and formally determined that LAN equipment was classifiable in tariff heading 84.71. Again, such determina-

---

[101] Decisions of the Harmonized System Committee, Annex H/1 to Doc.41.100E (HSC/19/Apr.97).

[102] The HS Committee's decision will be embodied in a Classification Opinion, which will be deemed to be approved by the WCO unless a party specifically requests that the matter be referred to the Council. See International Convention on the Harmonized Commodity and Coding System, Article 8.2.

[103] In interpreting the scope of a tariff concession, "the product description ... is the essential element for delimitating the coverage of the concession." The EC Schedule LXXX identified all products subject to bound rates by (1) tariff item numbers correlating with the Harmonized System; and (2) a narrative description based on the language of the corresponding HS headings. Due to the EC's election, the scope of its tariff concessions should be determined with reference to the scope of the matching descriptions contained in the HS nomenclature.

tion had confirmed the sound foundation of expectations that LAN equipment would be treated by the EC as ADP units under its concession schedule.[104]

6.36 It should also be noted that one principal function of the HS Committee and predecessor bodies was to ensure uniform classification under common nomenclatures to protect tariff bindings under Article II. Many countries had adopted the HS specifically as a means to enhance protection of Article II tariff concessions through greater tariff classification uniformity.[105] This enthusiasm was shared by GATT: "[F]rom a GATT point of view adoption of the Harmonized System would ensure greater uniformity among countries in customs classification and thus a greater ability for countries to monitor and protect the value of tariff concessions ... ".[106] These GATT expectations were seriously undermined by the EC's insistence on autonomously interpreting the scope of common product descriptions in concession schedules and harmonized tariff nomenclature. The prevailing views of the international organization that developed the uniform product descriptions, and in whom interpretative authority was entrusted, should not be so easily dismissed.

6.37 The reclassification by the defending parties could not be justified under the general rationale that GATT contracting parties were not obligated to follow any particular system for classifying goods. Member countries' authority over their own national customs tariffs had been noted by certain panels examining the Article I consistency of tariff differentiation through the addition of subcategories

---

[104] Under WCO's internal rules, any single member could have made a reservation that would have prevented the HSC from issuing its decision. The EC did not lodge any reservation and fully participated in the HS Committee proceedings, making a thorough presentation of its views. Further, the EC acknowledged (par. 97 of EC's first submission) that the intended effect of the HS Committee proceedings in which they participated was to ensure uniform classification of LAN equipment in Heading 84.71. Based on this acknowledgement and the EC's extensive participation, the EC's trading partners had been led to reasonably expect EC's compliance with the HS Committee's decision. Otherwise, individual members could abuse the HS Committee's procedures by having their positions fully considered, and then escape the consequences of the Committee's fully deliberated decisions by withholding reservations until the last minute after their positions had been rejected. To prevent such type of abuse, CCC members had agreed that compliance with HS Committee decisions was a "moral" obligation. See Report to the Customs Cooperation Council of the Fifth Session of the Harmonized System Committee, CCC Doc. No. 35.960, 12 April 1990.

[105] This was in fact one of the primary benefits envisioned by the complainant in this matter. "Adoption by the United States of the Harmonized System would, therefore, serve to protect the value of tariff concessions granted the United States." See Interim Report on the Harmonized Commodity Description and Coding System, USITC Pub. 1106 at 31-32, November 1980.

[106] Decision on *GATT Concessions under the Harmonized Commodity Description and Coding System*, op cit., para. 1.2. Consistent with this, the Article 7.1 (e) of the HS Convention indicates that one of the functions of the HS Committee is to furnish guidance on classification of specific goods under the HS system to "intergovernmental or other international organizations," including GATT. Thus, while GATT envisioned that nomenclature harmonization would protect tariff concessions, the WCO's role is to furnish advice on the HS classification of specific goods for use in GATT proceedings.

in tariff nomenclatures.[107] Each panel had plainly cautioned that classification authority must be exercised in conformity with GATT obligations. The Panel in the *Unroasted Coffee* dispute noted, in particular, that reclassification was appropriate "provided that a reclassification subsequent to the making of a tariff concession under the GATT would not be a violation of the basic commitment regarding that concession (Article II:V)".[108] Consequently, a party could not validly rely on the authority over national tariffs to reclassify goods to circumvent bound tariffs.[109]

6.38 In conclusion, the defending parties had circumvented the prescribed requirements and procedures for ensuring that tariff reclassification conformed to Article II concessions. The transition to the HS nomenclature was closely controlled and monitored by GATT to ensure that nomenclature conversions conformed with contracting parties' existing tariff concessions under GATT Article II and the requirements of Article XXVIII. In the conversion, the "main principle to be observed in connection with the introduction of the Harmonized System in national tariffs is that existing bindings should be maintained unchanged".[110] The contracting parties had agreed to detailed requirements and procedures designed to ensure orderly notification, challenge opportunities, determinations of whether any Article II concessions had been violated or impaired, and any necessary negotiations on compensation.[111] Additional procedures were adopted in 1991 to ensure adherence to Article II tariff concessions when countries implemented HS nomenclature amendments adopted by the CCC.[112] Such activity largely reaf-

---

[107] Panel Report on *Spain - Tariff Treatment of Unroasted Coffee*, op cit., para 4.4; and Panel Report on *Canada/Japan: Tariff on Imports of Spruce, Pine, Fir (SPF) Dimension Lumber*, adopted on 19 July 1989, BISD 36S/167, para. 5.9. The goods in such disputes were not subject to bound tariffs under Article II.

[108] *Spain - Tariff Treatment of Unroasted Coffee*, op cit., para. 4.4, n.1. The SPF Panel stated that it must be "borne in mind that [tariff] differentiations may lend themselves to abuse, insofar as they may serve to circumscribe tariff advantages ... ." op cit., para. 5.9.

[109] This was particularly true of parties, such as the EC, that have adopted the Harmonized System. While HS contracting parties have discretion to establish subdivisions beyond the six-digit HS Code, they were obligated to "use all the headings and subheadings of the Harmonized System without addition or modification, together with their related numerical codes". Articles 3.1(a)(i) and 3(3) of the HS Convention. Thus, the HS was purposely structured to leave no room for classifying goods outside the controlling 6-digit HS subheadings.

[110] Decision on *GATT Concessions Under the Harmonized Commodity Description and Coding System*, op cit., para. 2.1; see also the GATT Ministerial Decision on Tariffs, adopted 29 November 1982, referring to contracting parties' agreement that, if HS nomenclature is adopted, "... the general level of benefits provided by GATT concessions must be maintained ... ." BISD 29S/18, para. 2.

[111] To this end, the parties agreed to requirements specifying (1) information to be provided to the GATT Secretariat by each country adopting the HS; (2) rules to be used for conversion of duty rates when combining headings or parts of headings; and (3) procedures governing renegotiations under Article XXVIII. "GATT Concessions under the Harmonized Commodity Description and Coding System", BISD 30S/17, *supra*.

[112] See Decision on *Procedures to Implement Changes in the Harmonized System*, adopted on 8 October 1991, BISD 39S/300-301. Members who change their nomenclatures based on CCC HS amendments are required to formally submit proposed changes to their tariff concession schedules

firmed (and streamlined procedures for implementing) pre-existing obligations to formally revise concession schedules when adopting any nomenclature changes in national customs tariffs.[113]

6.39 During this process, the GATT Committee on Tariff Concessions had confirmed that the described protections and safeguards applied to reclassification decisions, as well as nomenclature amendments.[114] The contracting parties had agreed, in particular, that these requirements applied where the reclassification was occasioned by efforts to correct a perceived erroneous classification practice[115], the exact situation here. Notably, the EC itself was at the forefront of the successful initiative to extend Article II compliance procedures to reclassification decisions.[116] Such extension was a direct response to the EC and other parties' concerns that certain countries were avoiding Article II compliance requirements by reinterpreting existing tariff provisions in lieu of amending the tariff nomenclature.

6.40 In the present matter, the defending parties effected reclassification unilaterally without giving the requisite notice and without seeking the necessary GATT approval. The defending parties had also failed to comply with the mandatory requirement to submit for approval proposed amendments to concession schedules that reflected the altered tariff treatment accorded to the goods. Such non-compliance appeared contrary to the EC's historical positions which aggressively advocated that contracting parties effected product reclassification in full conformity with Article II and Article XXVIII requirements. For instance, the EC had defended its own tariff reclassification practices under these Articles, and had openly questioned adherence by other contracting parties.[117]

---

for all nomenclature revisions, whether or not such changes alter the scope of Article II concessions. *Ibid.*, paras. 2(a) and 2(b). Such proposals are subject to objections and challenges by other members, as well as negotiation or consultation requirements under Article XXVIII. *Ibid.*, paras. 4 to 6.

[113] See, e.g., Decision on *Procedures for Rectification and Modification of Schedules*, adopted 26 March 1980, BISD 27S/25, para. 2: Changes in the authentic texts of Schedules shall be made when amendments or rearrangements which do not alter the scope of a concession are introduced in national customs tariffs in respect of bound items. Such changes and other rectifications of a purely formal character shall be made by means of Certifications. If no objection is made to the Secretariat within three months, the proposed change to the tariff schedule is deemed to be approved. See 1985 Secretariat Note on "Loose-leaf Schedules Based on Harmonized System Nomenclature,"TAR/W/55/Add. 1, p. 2-3, paras. 5-7. "[U]nder longstanding GATT practice, even purely formal changes in the tariff schedule of a contracting party, which may not affect the GATT rights of other countries, such as the conversion of a specific to an ad valorem duty without an increase in the protective effect of the tariff rate in question, have been considered to require renegotiations." Panel Report on *Newsprint*, op cit., para. 50.

[114] See Note by the Secretariat on *Tariff Reclassification*, op cit, paras. 6(iii), 8 and 14.

[115] *Ibid.*, para. 6(iii).

[116] See TAR/M/3 dated 10 March 1981, Minutes of Meeting, Committee on Tariff Concessions, pages 11 and 12, para. 5.2.

[117] *Ibid.*, para. 5.2 (the EC representative "was wondering whether, through the secretariat, it would not be possible to know what were the legal possibilities available in various countries in order to be able to maintain obligations under GATT in reclassification cases.")

6.41 In its submission of 4 June 1997, the EC had not contended that it had complied with the procedural requirements or, for that matter, even acknowledged the existence of such requirements. Instead, the EC had argued that the United States should have raised the matter on its own initiative during the concession negotiations.[118] As demonstrated above, however, the party making Article II concessions had the affirmative obligation to give the requisite notice through formal GATT procedures when it altered effective duty rates through reclassification.[119] In any event, as discussed above, Singapore in fact had taken the initiative when the negotiations had commenced by specifically referring to various types of LAN equipment in its concession request for ADP units under tariff heading 84.71. Consequently, the EC was aware that trading partners such as Singapore had negotiated with the understanding that the EC offers on ADP units included LAN equipment. Accordingly, the Panel should reject the EC's attempt to shift its burden to other Members, and its attempt to alter its binding obligation that it had committed to during the course of the negotiations.

6.42 As a conclusion, during the tariff concession negotiations, Singapore and the EC's other trading partners had every reason to believe that the EC's concessions on ADP units included LAN equipment. Singapore's original request to the EC for heading 8471 concessions explicitly referred to various types of LAN equipment, and the EC had never indicated any reservations or opposition. The reasonableness of EC trading partners' expectations was subsequently corroborated by the HS Committee's determination that tariff heading 84.71 was the controlling HS category for LAN equipment. The language interpreted by the HS Committee was identical to the language appearing in tariff heading 84.71 of the EC's HS nomenclature and the language in the EC's ADP tariff concession. Consequently, the EC's reclassification of LAN equipment and resulting imposition of duties at rates that exceeded the bound rates for ADP units had violated Article II obligations, and nullified or impaired the value of the benefits EC trading partners had reasonably expected to receive.

VII. INTERIM REVIEW

7.1 On 21 October 1997, the European Communities and the United States requested the Panel to review, in accordance with Article 15.2 of the DSU, the interim report that had been issued to the parties on 7 October 1997. The European Communities also requested the Panel to hold a further meeting with the parties to discuss the points raised in its written comments. The Panel met with

118 See, e.g., para. 92. Even if EC's partners anticipated future events and raised the issue during the negotiations, such consultations would not have relieved the EC from its obligation to follow the requisite GATT requirements when it later mandated that EC member states increase the effective duty rates on the disputed items.

119 Any obligations of fellow contracting parties are triggered only upon the receipt of such formal notice.

the parties on 12 November 1997, reviewed the entire range of arguments presented by the European Communities and the United States, and finalized its report, taking into account the specific aspects of these arguments it considered to be relevant.

7.2 Regarding paragraph 7.8 of the interim report (now paragraph 8.8 of the final report), the European Communities recalled that it had argued that a wide definition of LAN equipment necessarily included certain modems and multiplexers (see paragraph 5.59) and that Singapore had also argued before the Panel that multiplexers were LAN equipment (see paragraphs 5.26 and 6.30). The European Communities questioned how the Panel could justify the exclusion of multiplexers, since the Panel had made findings that applied to "all LAN equipment". The European Communities submitted that multiplexers should be considered LAN equipment. For the same reason, the European Communities requested that the Panel reconsider the relevance of the BTIs issued by the Netherlands (see paragraph 8.40). Given the large number of BTIs issued by the Netherlands (Annex 6, Table 1, Nos 5 to 34), the European Communities argued, this reconsideration of the Dutch BTIs should lead the Panel to the conclusion that there was enough evidence on the EC side to rebut the evidence submitted by the United States in this dispute.

7.3 The Panel noted that footnote 124 made it clear that multiplexers were outside the scope of the Panel's examination. The Panel recalled that the United States - the complainant in this dispute - stated that tariff treatment of multiplexers was not part of its claims. The Panel had found the United States' technical explanation in paragraph 5.54 to provide reasonable grounds to conclude that multiplexers should not be considered to be LAN equipment. The European Communities asserted otherwise (see paragraph 5.59), but provided no rationale for its position except the United States' own classification practice, which was not relevant in this case in the Panel's view (see paragraph 7.5 below). Accordingly, the Panel did not accept the European Communities' request on this point, and decided to retain paragraph 8.8 as it originally appeared as paragraph 7.8 of the interim report. Correspondingly, there was no reason, in the Panel's view, to reconsider the relevance of the Dutch BTIs.

7.4 The European Communities noted that in paragraph 7.23 of the interim report (now paragraph 8.23 of the final report) the Panel found that "the meaning of a particular expression in a tariff schedule cannot be determined in isolation from its context". It further noted that in paragraph 7.26 of the interim report (now paragraph 8.26 of the final report) the Panel stated that "it is clearly the case that most descriptions are to be treated with the utmost care to maintain their integrity precisely because, on its face, they normally constitute the most concrete, tangible and reliable evidence of commitments made". The European Communities argued that the Panel failed to explain how it could interpret the importing country's tariff schedule in context while omitting any reference to the relevant customs legislation of the importing country with regard to the interpretation of the tariff nomenclature, which is derived from the Harmonized System. The European Communities further pointed out that it had submitted to the Panel all the relevant interpretative notes (see footnote 15) as well as the EC legislation referring to the issuance and the legal value of the BTIs. The Panel, according to the European Communities, should have taken into account these legal elements in interpreting Schedule LXXX and in doing so should have come to the conclusion that Schedule LXXX does not require the European Communities to grant LAN equipment a tariff treatment that is below the bound duty rate for telecommunication apparatus.

7.5 After carefully examining this argument by the European Communities, the Panel remained of the view that the European Communities failed to accord imports of LAN equipment treatment no less favourable than that provided for under Schedule LXXX. First, the Panel noted that the both parties considered this dispute as a case about duty treatment, not about product classification. Indeed, the European Communities itself (see paragraph 5.13) stated that "this Panel should abstain from pronouncing itself on customs classification issues". In this respect, the European Communities was in agreement with the United States, which stated "this case was not about classification"(see paragraph 5.12, see also paragraph 5.3). The Panel adopted its interpretative approach accordingly. Furthermore, in making its finding, the Panel considered that BTIs were relevant to the formation of legitimate expectations to the extent that they indicate *actual tariff treatment* of the products concerned. In dealing with the matter, the legal status of BTIs within the European Communities was fully taken into account by the Panel, but whether or not BTIs were legally binding under the EC law, in the Panel's view, did not materially affect the conclusion that they constituted evidence of actual tariff treatment. Consequently, the Panel decided to reject the European Communities' request on this point.

7.6 The European Communities argued that the Panel's findings in paragraphs 7.36, 7.41 and 7.55 of the interim report (now paragraphs 8.36, 8.41 and 8.55, respectively) regarding the tariff treatment of LAN equipment in the European Communities were not reconcilable with the fact that "The American Electronics Association (AEA), which represented the computer industry, had scheduled a meeting with Commission officials on 25 February 1994 in order to discuss a number of issues including classification difference in member States with respect to a number of products including LAN interface"(paragraph 5.29). According to the European Communities, the existence of the scheduled meeting clearly indicated that the US industry was fully aware of the difficulties in classification of LAN equipment and that some imports of LAN products were classified as telecommunication apparatus by some EC customs authorities, including those located in the United Kingdom. The European Communities further argued that tariff commitments were negotiated by government officials, not by the industry. It therefore failed to understand how it could be held responsible for the alleged failure by the US industry to properly brief the US Government during the Uruguay Round about the differences in classification within the European Communities.

7.7 The Panel was not persuaded by this argument. The AEA meeting with EC officials might have been scheduled, but it was not clear whether or when it actually took place (see paragraph 5.30). The European Communities did not put forward more detailed explanation regarding that meeting than is contained in paragraph 5.29. In the Panel's view, it was impossible to infer from this information alone that the US industry which exported LAN equipment to Ireland and the United Kingdom was fully aware of the difficulties in classification of LAN equipment and that some imports of LAN products were classified as telecommunication apparatus in Ireland or the United Kingdom during the Uruguay Round. Moreover, in the Panel's view, the Panel had not attributed to the European Communities any failure by the US industry to brief the US Government. Rather, it was the matter of whether the European Communities bore the responsibility for creating the expectations that LAN equipment would be treated as ADP machines, or whether there was sufficient evidence to indicate "a manifest anomaly"(see paragraph 8.44) which the United States should have been aware of. Consequently, the Panel did not find it necessary to change its findings in paragraphs 8.41 and 8.55. However, in order to clarify its position further, the Panel decided to expand footnote 152.

7.8 The European Communities further argued that, in view of the agreement between the parties that the relevant period for this dispute was from January 1990 to March 1994 (see paragraph 5.24), it failed to understand how the finding in paragraph 7.41 of the interim report (now paragraph 8.41 of the final report) could be based on an objective appreciation of facts as they appeared from the file. According to the European Communities, apart from the classification carried out by other EC customs authorities (e.g. Germany) the BTI issued by the UK customs authorities to CISCO showed that it had not been possible for the US industry to have a genuine understanding during the relevant period that all LAN equipment would be classified as ADP machines. Moreover, the European Communities argued, this evidence showed that CISCO, when submitting its letter referred to in Annex 4, Table 3, No. 8 was not telling the truth (see paragraph 5.49).

7.9 The Panel noted that when it made the finding in paragraph 8.41, it was fully aware that the BTI issued to CISCO had become effective within the relevant period, but in its view, the fact that the event occurred at the very end of the period as a single incidence also had to be given due weight (see also footnote 152). It also took into account the apparent contradiction between the BTI and the CISCO letter to the US Government. However, bearing in mind the plausibility of the explanation given by the United States (see paragraph 5.57), this did not itself constitute a sufficient basis to cast doubt on the veracity of other aspects of the CISCO letter. Nor had the European Communities provided any other evidence to do so. These elements did not affect the Panel's conclusion that the counter-evidence was not sufficient to rebut the presumption that US claim was true.

7.10 Regarding paragraph 7.44 of the interim report (now paragraph 8.44 of the final report), the European Communities returned to its argument in paragraph 5.48 regarding the relevance of Danish and Dutch BTIs due to the dates of their issuance and stated that these BTIs could not serve as sufficient evidence to support that the customs authorities of Denmark and the Netherlands were classifying LAN equipment as ADP machines during the relevant period.

7.11 The Panel noted that paragraph 7.37 of the interim report (now paragraph 8.37 of the final report) had been drafted with this issue directly in mind, and did not find it necessary to change its findings on this point: i.e. regarding its view that those BTIs provided supplementary support to the US claim. However, in order to clarify its position further, the Panel modified the language as used in paragraph 8.44 of the final report.

7.12 Regarding paragraph 7.56 of the interim report (now paragraph 8.56 of the final report), the European Communities pointed out that the United States itself had reclassified during the course of the Uruguay Round, namely in 1992, LAN equipment from telecommunication apparatus to ADP machines and that this reclassification had happened after the United States had made its "zero-for-zero" request/offer of 15 March 1990, which included electronic articles in HS chapters 84, 85 and 90 (see paragraph 5.26). The European Communities also noted that during the negotiations of the North American Free Trade Agreement, the parties to that agreement had admitted that it was difficult to classify LAN equipment and they had agreed to consult on this issue and to endeavour to agree no later than 1 January 1994 on the classification of such goods in each party's tariff schedule (see paragraph 5.33). The European Communities further recalled that after the conclusion of the Uruguay Round, the HS Committee of the World Customs Organization had to examine the proper classification of certain LAN equipment (see paragraph 5.12). Finally, the European Communities stated that even some third parties to this dispute, namely Japan and Korea, were currently classifying some or all LAN equipment as telecommunication apparatus (see paragraph 5.35).

7.13 Referring to paragraph 7.49 of the interim report (now paragraph 8.49 of the final report), the European Communities maintained that the facts mentioned in the previous paragraph clearly showed that there had been, and to a certain extent still was "a manifest anomaly" because of the extraordinary difficulty concerning the correct classification of LAN equipment. It also showed, according to the European Communities, the question of precise classification of LAN equipment in the EC schedule could not possibly have influenced the way in which the United States conducted the Uruguay Round tariff negotiations since the United States' "zero-for-zero" request/offer was submitted before its own reclassification of LAN equipment, i.e. without prejudice to classification details. The European Communities asked the Panel to take these elements into account and therefore come to a different conclusion.

7.14 The Panel agreed with the European Communities that these elements had indeed been presented before the Panel, and accordingly modified and expanded the relevant paragraphs in its findings. However, for reasons explained in paragraphs 8.58 and 8.59 of the final report, it did not agree with the European Communities that it should come to a different conclusion.

7.15 The United States requested that the first sentence of footnote 167 be deleted as unnecessary and potentially misleading. That sentence, according to the United States, could be misinterpreted to suggest that production of BTIs, customs rulings or actual invoices was essential to showing a violation of Article II:1 of GATT 1994. The United States argued that it could not predict what types of evidence of actual tariff treatment might exist in a future dispute between different parties, with different domestic legal systems, concerning different concessions. According to the United States, it would be unwise for this Panel to imply that these three types of evidence were inherently superior to all other types of evidence or were the only types of evidence relevant in any case. The European Communities objected to the deletion of the sentence.

7.16 In the Panel's view, there would be no danger of misinterpretation as suggested by the United States. However, in order to clarify its views on evidence in this regard, the Panel introduced certain modifications to the sentence.

7.17 The United States also made other drafting suggestions concerning the description of its arguments, some of which the Panel accepted and introduced in its final report. These changes are reflected in paragraphs 2.9, 5.52, 8.2, 8.13, 8.14 and 8.65, and footnotes 4 and 83 of the final report.

VIII. FINDINGS

A. *Claims of the Parties*

8.1 The facts leading to this dispute can be summarized as follows. At the conclusion of the Uruguay Round, the European Communities bound its tariff rate on products described as "automatic data processing machines and units thereof; magnetic or optical readers, machines for transcribing data onto data media in coded form and machines for processing such data, not elsewhere specified or included"(hereinafter referred to as "ADP machines") under heading 84.71 at 2.5 per cent - or zero per cent on some products - (to be reduced from the base rate of 4.9 per cent) in its Schedule of Concessions and Commitments annexed to the Marrakesh Protocol to the General Agreement on Tariffs and Trade 1994 (Schedule LXXX). The bound rates of duty on "parts and accessories of the machines of heading No 8471"under heading 84.73 was 2.0 per cent. The bound rates of duty on "electrical apparatus for line telephony or line telegraphy, including such apparatus for carrier current line systems"(hereinafter referred to as "telecommunication apparatus") under heading 85.17 were varied, but generally higher than those on ADP machines (3.0 to 3.6 per cent, to be reduced from the base rate of 4.6 to 7.5 per cent). The bound rate of duty on "television receivers (including video monitors and video projectors)"under heading 85.28 was 14.0 per cent.[119]

8.2 According to the United States, the customs authorities in the European Communities, particularly those of Ireland and the United Kingdom, generally treated LAN equipment as ADP machines during the Uruguay Round and for some time after its conclusion. In May 1995, the Commission adopted Regulation (EC) 1165/95 classifying LAN adapter cards as telecommunication apparatus under heading 85.17.[120] Following the adoption of this regulation, according to the United States, the customs authorities in the European Communities including those of Ireland and the United Kingdom started treating LAN adapter cards as telecommunication apparatus as mandated by the regulation, and also started classifying other LAN equipment as telecommunication apparatus.

8.3 In April 1996, a tribunal in the United Kingdom upheld a customs administration determination classifying a product known as PCTV (a combination of personal computer and colour television set, integrated in the same unit) as a television receiver under heading 85.28.[121]

8.4 In June 1997, the Commission adopted Regulation (EC) 1153/97, classifying all personal computers (hereinafter "PCs") as ADP machines, but applying higher rates of duty (as much as 14 per cent) on those with multimedia capability.

8.5 The United States claims as follows:

(a) The European Communities' reclassification of LAN adapter cards under Regulation (EC) 1165/95 has resulted in treatment of those products less favourable than that provided for in Part I of Schedule LXXX and therefore is inconsistent with the European Communities' obligations under Article II:1 of the General Agreement on Tariffs and Trade 1994 (hereinafter "GATT 1994");

(b) The European Communities' reclassification of other types of LAN equipment has resulted in treatment of those products less favourable than that provided for in Part I of Schedule LXXX and therefore is inconsistent with the European Communities' obligations under Article II:1 of GATT 1994;

(c) The European Communities' reclassification of multimedia PCs has resulted in treatment of those products less favourable than that provided for in Part I of Schedule LXXX and therefore is inconsistent with the European Communities' obligations under Article II:1 of GATT 1994;

[119] For a more detailed description of these products and their bound rates, see Annex 1. Regarding products under heading 85.17, see also footnote 4.

[120] Annex 2.

[121] Annex 3.

(d) The United Kingdom's reclassification of LAN equipment has resulted in treatment of those products less favourable than that provided for in Part I of Schedule LXXX and therefore is inconsistent with the United Kingdom's obligations under Article II:1 of GATT 1994;

(e) The United Kingdom's reclassification of multimedia PCs has resulted in treatment of those products less favourable than that provided for in Part I of Schedule LXXX and therefore is inconsistent with the United Kingdom's obligations under Article II:1 of GATT 1994;

(f) Ireland's reclassification of LAN equipment has resulted in treatment of those products less favourable than that provided for in Part I of Schedule LXXX and therefore is inconsistent with Ireland's obligations under Article II:1 of GATT 1994; and

(g) The above measures have nullified or impaired the value of concessions accruing to the United States under GATT 1994.

8.6 The European Communities rejects these claims for the following reasons:

(h) The United States' claims against Ireland and the United Kingdom (i.e., (d), (e) and (f) above) should be rejected because these member States did not engage in any tariff bindings vis-à-vis the United States or any other country and could not be considered to have violated any obligations under Article II of GATT 1994; and

(i) The United States' claims against the European Communities (i.e., (a), (b) and (c) above) should be rejected because the European Communities did not reclassify the products concerned, resulting in treatment of those products less favourable than that provided for in its tariff schedule. The European Communities has not violated any of its obligations under Article II of GATT 1994, nor has it nullified or impaired the value of concessions accruing to the United States under GATT 1994.

B. Issues Regarding the Scope of the Claim

8.7 Before examining the substantive aspects of the case, we need to rule on three preliminary issues raised by the European Communities regarding the scope of the United States' claim. These are the issues relating to product coverage, scope of the measures and the status of Ireland and the United Kingdom in this dispute.

1. Product Coverage

8.8 The European Communities argues that the United States has failed to define clearly "LAN equipment" subject to the dispute with the exception of LAN adapter cards, and suggests that all the claims on LAN equipment other than LAN adapter cards should be dismissed.[122] The United States argues that its definition of LAN equipment is clear.[123] In response to a question from the Panel, the United States has submitted that the term "LAN equipment" means all LAN equipment including LAN adapter cards, LAN controllers, LAN repeaters, LAN interface units and bridges, LAN extenders, LAN concentrators, LAN switches, LAN hubs and LAN routers.[124]

8.9 We note that the European Communities cites, in support of its position, the panel report on "EEC - Quantitative Restrictions against Imports of Certain Products from Hong Kong", which made the following observation:

> "The Panel considered that just as the terms of reference must be agreed between the parties prior to the commencement of the Panel's examination, similarly the product coverage must be clearly understood and agreed between the parties to the dispute. The Panel considered that to allow the inclusion of an additional product item about which one party had not been formally advised prior to the commencement of proceedings would be to introduce an element of inequity."[125]

In our view, however, the present case should be distinguished from the *Quantitative Restrictions* case cited by the European Communities in that no new product was added by the United States in the course of the proceedings. The definition by the United States in the previous paragraph is an elucidation of the product coverage already specified in the United States' requests for the establishment of a panel on this matter (WT/DS62/4, WT/DS67/3 and WT/DS68/2). Consequently, we find that the definition is sufficiently specific for the purposes of our consideration of this dispute and reject the European Communities' suggestion.

8.10 The European Communities also argues that the scope of the United States' claim on multimedia PCs is unclear. According to the European Communities, the only item which can be considered to be the subject of this dispute settlement proceeding is the PCTV implicated in the 1996 judgement of a United Kingdom tribunal, and the European Communities suggests that the rest of the United States' claim on multimedia PCs should be dismissed.[126] In response to a question by the Panel, the United States has submitted that its claim includes a broad range of personal computers with multimedia capability such as those which utilize storage devices based on laser-reading technology (i.e., CD-ROMs)

---

[122] See paragraph 4.1.

[123] See paragraph 4.2.

[124] See footnote 19 or a more precise description of these products. According to the United States, modems and multiplexers are not included in this definition. See paragraph 5.54. Evidence on these products is not accepted by the Panel as proof regarding the tariff treatment of LAN equipment.

[125] Panel Report on *EEC- Quantitative Restrictions against Imports of Certain Products from Hong Kong*, op cit., para. 30.

[126] See paragraph 4.3.

and those which have attendant audio and video capabilities.[127] Again, noting that the United States' reference to "PCs with multimedia capability" in its panel requests (WT/DS62/4, WT/DS67/3 and WT/DS68/2) covers all these products, we find that this definition is sufficiently specific for the purposes of our consideration of this dispute and reject the European Communities' suggestion.

8.11 For the reasons stated above, we reject the European Communities' argument and find that all LAN equipment and personal computers with multimedia capability, as specified by the United States, are the subject of this dispute.

2. *Scope of the Measures*

8.12 The European Communities argues that the United States has failed to identify measures where tariff commitments have allegedly been violated, except Regulation (EC) 1165/95 regarding LAN adapter cards and the above-mentioned UK tribunal judgement regarding PCTVs. The United States argues that in addition to these two measures, practices of the customs authorities in Ireland, the United Kingdom and other member States regarding LAN equipment, as well as the UK customs authorities' practice regarding multimedia PCs, are included within the scope of this dispute.[128] Although the United States' formulation of its claims appears to emphasize the "reclassification" aspect of the dispute, the substance of the present case is the actual tariff treatment by customs authorities in the European Communities and the evaluation of that treatment in light of the tariff commitments in Schedule LXXX. Both parties have presented their arguments on this basis.[129] Viewed from this perspective, we find that the United States has sufficiently identified the measures subject to the dispute, which concerns tariff treatment of LAN equipment and multimedia PCs by customs authorities in the European Communities.

8.13 Separately, the United States refers to Regulation (EC) 1153/97, which entered into force on 1 July 1997, as itself imposing tariffs at higher-than-concession rates under heading 84.71.[130] The European Communities objects to its inclusion for consideration by the Panel.[131]

8.14 Regarding Regulation (EC) 1153/97, we note that the regulation was issued on 24 June 1997, almost four months after the establishment of this Panel on 25 February 1997. It has been the consistent practice of previous panels not to examine measures introduced after the establishment of the panels.[132] We see no

---

[127] See paragraph 4.4.

[128] See paragraph 4.8. See also paragraph 8.5.

[129] See paragraphs 5.3 (arguments by the United States) and 5.13 (arguments by the European Communities).

[130] See paragraph 5.74.

[131] See paragraph 4.6.

[132] Panel Report on *Uruguayan Recourse to Article XXIII*, adopted on 16 November 1962, BISD 11S/95, para. 18; Panel Report on *United States - Section 337 of the Tariff Act of 1930*, adopted on 7 November 1989, BISD 36S/345, para. 5.2.

reasons to depart from this practice in the present case. The United States argues that Regulation (EC) 1153/97 "confirms" the existing measures. It does not however explain how and why this amounts to "confirmation".[133] Accordingly, we do not examine the conformity of Regulation (EC) 1153/97 with GATT 1994 in this report.

3. *Status of Ireland and the United Kingdom*

8.15 The United States has requested that the Panel specify which of the defending parties (the European Communities, Ireland and the United Kingdom) are responsible for the alleged nullification or impairment of its benefits under GATT 1994.[134] The European Communities claims that Ireland and the United Kingdom are not parties to this dispute.

8.16 The terms of reference of this Panel clearly mandates us to examine "the matters referred to the DSB by the United States in documents WT/DS62/4, WT/DS67/3 and WT/DS68/2". The respondents in these documents are the European Communities, the United Kingdom and Ireland, respectively. However, as we stated earlier, what is at issue in this dispute is tariff treatment of LAN equipment and multimedia PCs by customs authorities in the European Communities.[135] Since the European Communities, Ireland and the United Kingdom are all bound by their tariff commitments under Schedule LXXX, our examination will focus, in the first instance, on whether customs authorities in the European Communities, including those located in Ireland and the United Kingdom, have or have not deviated from the obligations assumed under that Schedule. Accordingly, we will revert to this issue in light of the conclusions of that examination.

8.17 As a related matter, the United States has requested that the title of the report of this Panel be changed to read "European Communities, Ireland and the United Kingdom - Increases in Tariffs on Certain Computer Equipment".[136] The European Communities does not agree to this change.[137] Given that the report is a consolidated response to the United States' requests contained in documents WT/DS62/4, WT/DS67/3 and WT/DS68/2, the change in the title might have been acceptable if it had been agreed upon by the parties to the dispute when they reached an agreement on the terms of reference of this Panel. However, the United States requested this change at the very end of the second substantive meeting, which in our view was rather late in the process. Considering that the current title of this report, read together with the three document symbols (WT/DS62/R, WT/DS67/R and WT/DS68/R) it carries, does not lead to any confusion or misunderstanding regarding the substance of this dispute and that, more

---

[133] See paragraph 4.8.
[134] See paragraph 3.2.
[135] See paragraph 8.12.
[136] See paragraph 5.3.
[137] See paragraph 5.4.

generally, it is desirable for the title of a dispute to remain unchanged throughout the process (from consultations to implementation), we reject the request by the United States. In so doing, we also note that the title of a particular dispute is given for the sake of convenience in reference and in no way affects the substantive rights and obligations of the parties to the dispute.

C. *General Interpretative Issue*

8.18 As indicated earlier, the substance of this dispute is whether the tariff treatment of LAN equipment and multimedia PCs by the customs authorities in the European Communities has been in compliance with the tariff concessions contained in Schedule LXXX. The pertinent provision in GATT 1994 is Article II:1, which reads in relevant parts as follows:

> "(a) Each Member shall accord to the commerce of the other Members treatment no less favourable than that provided for in the appropriate Part of the appropriate Schedule annexed to this Agreement.
>
> "(b) The products described in Part I of the Schedule relating to any Member, which are the products of territories of other Members, shall, on their importation into the territory to which the Schedule relates, and subject to the terms, conditions or qualifications set forth in that Schedule, be exempt from ordinary customs duties in excess of those set forth and provided therein. Such products shall also be exempt from all other duties or charges of any kind imposed on or in connection with the importation in excess of those imposed on the date of this Agreement or those directly and mandatorily required to be imposed thereafter by legislation in force in the importing territory on that date."

The specific question facing this Panel is whether customs authorities in the European Communities accorded tariff treatment to certain products less favourable than what is described in Part I of its tariff schedule - Schedule LXXX. Whether LAN equipment or multimedia PCs are properly classified under a certain tariff heading is not an issue before this Panel because the question of their classification *per se* has not been raised by the United States. It should also be emphasized that the object of our examination is limited to Schedule LXXX. We have no intention of passing a judgement regarding in which tariff category a certain product must be classified. Such a question is outside the terms of reference of this Panel.

8.19 Thus, it is necessary to interpret Schedule LXXX in its relation to Article II:1 of GATT 1994. As noted earlier, Schedule LXXX is annexed to the Marrakesh Protocol, which in turn forms part of GATT 1994. As such, it is an integral part of the WTO Agreement, subject to "customary rules of interpretation of public international law"(Article 3.2 of the DSU).

8.20 Article 31 of the 1969 Vienna Convention on the Law of Treaties (hereinafter referred to as "Vienna Convention") sets out the general rules of treaty interpretation as follows:

> "1. A treaty shall be interpreted in good faith in accordance with the ordinary meaning to be given to the terms of the treaty in their context and in the light of its object and purpose.
>
> "2. The context for the purpose of the interpretation of a treaty shall comprise, in addition to the text, including its preamble and annexes:
>
> (a) any agreement relating to the treaty which was made between all the parties in connexion with the conclusion of the treaty;
>
> (b) any instrument which was made by one or more parties in connexion with the conclusion of the treaty and accepted by the other parties as an instrument related to the treaty.
>
> "3. There shall be taken into account, together with the context:
>
> (a) any subsequent agreement between the parties regarding the interpretation of the treaty or the application of its provisions;
>
> (b) any subsequent practice in the application of the treaty which establishes the agreement of the parties regarding its interpretation;
>
> (c) any relevant rules of international law applicable in the relations between the parties.
>
> 4. A special meaning shall be given to a term if it is established that the parties so intended."

8.21 Article 32 of the Vienna Convention further provides:

> "Recourse may be had to supplementary means of interpretation, including the preparatory work of the treaty and the circumstances of its conclusion, in order to confirm the meaning resulting from the application of Article 31, or to determine the meaning when the interpretation according to Article 31:
>
> (a) leaves the meaning ambiguous or obscure; or
>
> (b) leads to a result which is manifestly absurd or unreasonable."

8.22 We will follow these rules of interpretation in determining whether the tariff treatment of LAN equipment and multimedia PCs is in conformity with the tariff commitments contained in Schedule LXXX. The purpose of interpretation is, as is the case with any treaty text, to ascertain what a particular expression in the Schedule means.

8.23 The meaning of a particular expression in a tariff schedule cannot be determined in isolation from its context. It has to be interpreted in the context of Article II of GATT 1994 - a provision that gives the rationale for the specification of products and duty rates in tariff schedules in the first place: i.e., they constitute a binding commitment arising out of a negotiation. It should be noted in this regard that the protection of legitimate expectations in respect of tariff treatment of a bound item is one of the most important functions of Article II. The panel on *Oilseeds* stated as follows:

> "... The Panel considered that the main value of a tariff concession is that it provides an assurance of better market access through improved price competition. Contracting parties negotiate tariff concessions primarily to obtain that advantage. They must therefore be assumed to base their tariff negotiations on the expectation that the price effect of the tariff concessions will not be systematically offset. If no right of redress were given to them in such a case they would be reluctant to make tariff concessions and the General Agreement would no longer be useful as a legal framework for incorporating the results of trade negotiations..."[138]

The fact that the *Oilseeds* panel report concerns a non-violation complaint does not affect the validity of this reasoning in cases where an actual violation of tariff commitments is alleged. If anything, such a direct violation would involve a situation where expectations concerning tariff concessions were even more firmly grounded.

8.24 The importance of legitimate expectations in interpretation of tariff commitments can be confirmed by the text of Article II itself. Article II:5 provides as follows (emphasis added):

> "If any Member considers that a product is not receiving from another Member the treatment which the first Member *believes to have been contemplated* by a concession provided for in the appropriate Schedule annexed to this Agreement, it shall bring the matter directly to the attention of the other Member. If the latter agrees that the treatment *contemplated* was that claimed by the first Member, but declares that such treatment cannot be accorded because a court or other proper authority has ruled to the effect that the product involved cannot be classified under the tariff

[138] Panel Report on *European Economic Community - Payments and Subsidies Paid to Processors and Producers of Oilseeds and Related Animal-Feed Proteins*, adopted on 25 January 1990, BISD 37S/86, para. 148.

> laws of such Member so as to permit the treatment contemplated in this Agreement, the two Members, together with any other Members substantially interested, shall enter promptly into further negotiations with a view to a compensatory adjustment of the matter."

Although Article II:5 is a provision for the special bilateral procedure regarding tariff classification, not directly at issue in this case, the existence of this provision confirms that legitimate expectations are a vital element in the interpretation of Article II and tariff schedules.

8.25 This conclusion is also supported by the object and purpose of the WTO Agreement and those of GATT 1994. The security and predictability of "the reciprocal and mutually advantageous arrangements directed to the substantial reduction of tariffs and other barriers to trade"(expression common in the preambles to the two agreements) cannot be maintained without protection of such legitimate expectations. This is consistent with the principle of good faith interpretation under Article 31 of the Vienna Convention. It should be recalled that the panel report on *Underwear* stated as follows:

> "[T]he relevant provisions [of the Agreement on Textiles and Clothing] have to be interpreted in good faith. Based upon the wording, the context and the overall purpose of the Agreement, exporting Members can ... legitimately expect that market access and investments made would not be frustrated by importing Members taking improper recourse to such action."[139]

8.26 In our view, it may, as a matter of fact, be the case that in nearly all instances, the ordinary meaning of the terms of the actual description in a tariff schedule accurately reflects and exhausts the content of the legitimate expectations. It is clearly the case that most descriptions are to be treated with the utmost care to maintain their integrity precisely because, on their face, they normally constitute the most concrete, tangible and reliable evidence of commitments made. In our view, however, this cannot be the case *a priori* for all tariff commitments. It must remain possible, at least in principle, that parties have legitimately formed expectations based on other particular supplementary factors.

8.27 To deny this *a priori* would be to reduce the nature and meaning of commitments under Article II to a purely formal and mechanical task of noting descriptions in schedules. This would be to rob such commitments of the reality of the context in which they clearly occur in Article II.

---

[139] Panel Report on *United States - Restrictions on Imports of Cotton and Man-made Fibre Underwear*, adopted on 25 February 1997, WT/DS24/R, para. 7.20. See also Panel Report on *India - Patent Protection for Pharmaceutical and Agricultural Chemical Products*", WT/DS50/R, para. 7.18.

8.28 In interpreting Schedule LXXX, we will accordingly undertake *inter alia* an evaluation of what, as a matter of fact, the United States was entitled to expect legitimately regarding the actual tariff treatment of LAN equipment and multimedia PCs in the European Communities.

D. LAN Equipment

8.29 The United States claims that LAN equipment should have been accorded the tariff treatment of ADP machines or parts thereof under heading 84.71 or heading 84.73 in Schedule LXXX. The European Communities claims that its treatment of LAN equipment as telecommunication apparatus under heading 85.17 of Schedule LXXX is justified and that it is entitled to levy the rate of duty under that heading accordingly. Thus, we need to determine the proper interpretation of Schedule LXXX regarding LAN equipment. As noted earlier, the general question of where LAN equipment should be classified in a tariff nomenclature is beyond our mandate. Our finding is specific to obligations under Schedule LXXX, and should not be taken as anything going beyond that.

1 Textual Analysis

8.30 Following the rules of the Vienna Convention[140], we start from the textual analysis. Schedule LXXX does not specifically refer to LAN equipment. It generally refers to "automatic data processing machines and units thereof; magnetic or optical readers, machines for transcribing data onto data media in coded form and machines for processing such data, not elsewhere specified or included" under heading 84.71 and "parts and accessories of machines of heading No 8471"under heading 84.73. In view of the data processing capacities of LAN equipment, one might conclude that any type of LAN equipment is an ADP machine or part thereof. However, if one emphasizes the fact that LAN equipment is used for communication among various computer devices and the expression "not elsewhere specified", one could also argue that LAN equipment is an "electrical apparatus for line telephony or line telegraphy, including such apparatus for carrier current line systems" under heading 85.17.

8.31 Thus, for the purposes of Article II:1, it is impossible to determine whether LAN equipment should be regarded as an ADP machine purely on the basis of the ordinary meaning of the terms used in Schedule LXXX taken in isolation. However, as noted above, the meaning of the term "ADP machines" in this context may be determined in light of the legitimate expectations of an exporting Member.[141]

---

140 See paragraph 8.20.

141 See paragraphs 8.23-8.28.

2. *Actual Tariff Treatment and Legitimate Expectations*

8.32 The United States claims that it is entitled to tariff treatment of LAN equipment as ADP machines or parts thereof because customs authorities in the European Communities, particularly those in Ireland and the United Kingdom, actually treated LAN equipment that way when the tariff concession was being negotiated, thereby effectively creating legitimate expectations on the part of the United States that such tariff treatment would continue. The European Communities claims that the EC member States did not in fact treat these products uniformly during the Uruguay Round and therefore that the United States was not entitled to such expectations.

8.33 In addressing this issue, we consider it necessary (*a*) to weigh the evidence submitted by both parties regarding the actual tariff treatment of LAN equipment in the European Communities and, if the result supports the US claim, (*b*) to determine whether the actual tariff treatment entitles the United States to legitimate expectations in this regard.

(a) Evaluation of the Evidence of Actual Tariff Treatment

8.34 In the *Shirts and Blouses* case, the Appellate Body made the following observation:

> "[W]e find it difficult, indeed, to see how any system of judicial settlement could work if it incorporated the proposition that the mere assertion of a claim might amount to proof. It is, thus, hardly surprising that various international tribunals, including the International Court of Justice, have generally and consistently accepted and applied the rule that the party who asserts a fact, whether the claimant or the respondent, is responsible for providing proof thereof. Also, it is a generally-accepted canon of evidence in civil law, common law and, in fact, most jurisdictions, that the burden of proof rests upon the party, whether complaining or defending, who asserts the affirmative of a particular claim or defence. If that party adduces evidence sufficient to raise a presumption that what is claimed is true, the burden then shifts to the other party, who will fail unless it adduces sufficient evidence to rebut the presumption."[142]

8.35 Accordingly, we first examine evidence produced by the United States to determine whether it has successfully raised a presumption that its claim on the actual tariff treatment of LAN equipment in the European Communities is true.

---

[142] Appellate Body Report on *United States - Measure Affecting Imports of Woven Wool Shirts and Blouses from India*, adopted on 23 May 1997, WT/DS33/AB/R, DSR 1997:I, 323 at 337 (footnotes omitted).

8.36 To support its claim, the United States has submitted Binding Tariff Information (BTI) issued by Ireland[143] and letters from the UK Customs and Excise[144], which treated certain LAN equipment as ADP machines during the Uruguay Round. It has also produced letters from four of the leading US exporters of LAN equipment to Europe attesting to the fact that all of their LAN equipment exported to Ireland and the United Kingdom - which were their major market - between 1991 and 1994 had been treated as ADP machines.[145] The US industry appears to have been satisfied with this tariff treatment at that time, and did not voice any concerns in this regard to the US Government during the Uruguay Round.

8.37 Moreover, the BTIs submitted by the United States regarding other member States further support its position.[146] They indicate that even after the conclusion of the Uruguay Round tariff negotiations, customs authorities in Denmark, France and the Netherlands treated LAN equipment as ADP machines. In the case of France, a statement by a French customs official at a meeting of the European Commission's Customs Code Committee is also cited as support of this claim.[147] Although the United States cannot - and does not - claim that these BTIs formed the basis of its expectations because of the timing of their issuance, they lend supplementary support to the US claim on how LAN equipment was treated in the European Communities during the Uruguay Round in as much as there is no evidence to suggest that these BTIs were a particular departure from the prevailing practice in these member States.

8.38 We also note US export data showing that US exports of LAN equipment (classified under USX 847199 and 847330) to the European Communities continued to rise after the Uruguay Round, while EC import statistics, which formerly moved in the same direction as US export statistics, indicate a decline in the imports of "other ADP machines"(under CN 847199) from the United States and a simultaneous increase in the imports of telecommunication apparatus (under CN 851782) in 1995.[148] These statistics are aggregated at a level that makes it difficult to draw specific conclusions in respect of the tariff treatment of LAN equipment. This evidence does, however, indirectly support the US argument in as much as it is consistent with the effects that would be anticipated if there was a change in tariff treatment in the European Communities after the Uruguay Round.

8.39 In light of the evidence described in the preceding paragraphs, we conclude that the United States has adduced evidence sufficient to raise a presumption that its claim that LAN equipment was treated as ADP machines in the European Communities during the Uruguay Round is true.

---

143 Annex 4, Table 1.
144 Annex 4, Table 2.
145 Annex 4, Table 3. See also paragraph 5.44.
146 Annex 4, Table 1.
147 See paragraph 5.44.
148 Annex 7.

8.40 Following the Appellate Body report on *Shirts and Blouses*[149], the burden now shifts to the European Communities. To rebut the presumption raised by the United States, the European Communities has produced documents which indicate that LAN equipment had been treated as telecommunication apparatus by other customs authorities in the European Communities. In Germany, the customs authorities treated certain LAN equipment as telecommunication apparatus already in 1989, a practice upheld by the German Federal Tax Court (Bundesfinanzhof) in 1991.[150] The European Communities has also produced BTIs issued by the Dutch, French, German and UK customs authorities treating certain LAN equipment as telecommunication apparatus[151], although a close examination of these BTIs reveals that those from the Netherlands pertain to either multiplexers, which are outside the scope of our examination, or more generic networking equipment, which may or may not fall under the definition of LAN equipment used in this report.

8.41 The only direct counter-evidence against the US claim on practices in Ireland and the United Kingdom is a December 1993 BTI issued by the UK customs authority (HM Customs and Excise) to one of the US companies (CISCO), classifying one type of LAN equipment (routers) as telecommunication apparatus.[152] Since it became effective only a week or so before the conclusion of the Uruguay Round negotiations, it is not in our view sufficient to rebut the above presumption, which was raised by more extensive and general evidence, that LAN equipment was generally treated as ADP machines in Ireland and the United Kingdom during the Uruguay Round.

8.42 Regarding France, the European Communities has submitted conflicting BTIs (i.e., ones that classify LAN equipment as telecommunication apparatus) issued after the conclusion of the Uruguay Round. Thus, in light of our reasoning in paragraph 8.37, it would be reasonable to conclude at least that the practice was not uniform in France during the Uruguay Round.

8.43 Germany appears to have consistently treated LAN equipment as telecommunication apparatus. As noted above, a 1991 Bundesfinanzhof ruling af-

---

149 See paragraph 8.34.

150 See paragraph 5.46.

151 Annex 6, Table 1.

152 See paragraph 8.32. We do not consider other BTIs issued by the HM Customs and Excise submitted by the European Communities (Annex 6, Table 1) to be relevant because they became valid after the conclusion of substantive tariff negotiations of the Uruguay Round. In this connection, we find it noteworthy that the European Communities did not produce any British or Irish BTIs issued prior to December 1993 to support its case on this important issue. The European Communities suggests that the fact that American Electronics Association had scheduled a meeting with Commission officials on 25 February 1994 in order to discuss a number of issues including classification difference in member States with respect to a number of products including LAN interface is another indication of the non-uniform treatment of LAN equipment within the European Communities. See paragraph 5.29. However, in our view, the information was too vague and indirect to rebut the presumption mentioned above, even to the extent that it was unclear that the meeting had actually taken place.

firmed BTIs treating LAN equipment as telecommunication apparatus, although the BTIs involved in that case were issued to a non-US firm and could not have formed any basis for US expectations. In addition, the European Communities has submitted one German BTI, issued in 1992, treating LAN equipment as telecommunication apparatus.

8.44 In our view, the evidence produced by the European Communities does not rebut the presumption raised by the United States concerning the accuracy of its claim regarding the actual tariff treatment of LAN equipment during the Uruguay Round. The evidence concerning Ireland and the United Kingdom, which are the largest export market in the European Communities for the US industry, as well as the supplementary evidence concerning Denmark and the Netherlands, supports the US position, leaving Germany as the only member State with practices to the contrary.

(b) Legitimate Expectations

8.45 We now turn to the examination of whether the actual tariff treatment of LAN equipment entitles the United States to legitimate expectations in this regard sufficient to establish its claim of a violation of Article II of GATT 1994 by the European Communities. In our view, an exporting Member's legitimate expectations regarding tariff commitments are normally based, at a minimum, on the assumption that the actual tariff treatment accorded to a particular product at the time of the negotiation will be continued unless such treatment is manifestly anomalous or there is information readily available to the exporting Member that clearly indicates the contrary. The existence of such expectations in tariff negotiations can be seen in the fact that negotiators normally use actual trade data to calculate the effect of "requests" and "offers", and to evaluate the resulting tariff reductions in terms of trade-weighted average.[153] In other words, they work on the general assumption that the actual tariff treatment accorded to a particular product as traded is the relevant item for the purposes of negotiations.

8.46 In the present case, in view of the prevailing practice in the European Communities during the Uruguay Round, the United States would appear to have a legitimate expectation that LAN equipment would continue to be accorded tariff treatment as ADP machines in the European Communities. Certainly, such treatment could not be characterized as manifestly anomalous.[154] Was there information readily available to the United States that indicated that the actual tariff treatment of LAN equipment would not be continued?

---

[153] For instance, when the Ministers agreed in Montreal in 1988 on a "substantial reduction ... with a target amount for overall reductions at least as ambitious as that achieved by the formula participants in the Tokyo Round"(MTN.TNC/11), it was generally understood to mean more than 33 per cent reduction in trade-weighted average for industrial products. For how this figure was calculated, see General Agreement on Tariffs and Trade, *The Tokyo Round of Multilateral Trade Negotiations: Report by the Director-General of GATT* (Geneva, April 1979), p. 120.

[154] See paragraphs 8.30-8.31.

8.47 In this regard, the European Communities challenges the legitimacy of the United States' expectations by saying: "The US negotiators may find it difficult to admit now that their understanding of the tariff classification in the EC of the products they talk about now was erroneous; however, they only have themselves to blame. They should have come forward and requested clarification from the EC negotiators if they were not sure where these products should be classified in the EC especially since they themselves had reclassified these products only shortly beforehand".[155] There are two distinct issues in this argument: (i) Were the US negotiators required to clarify where LAN equipment was to be classified in the draft Schedule LXXX during the negotiations?; and (ii) Does the United States' own reclassification of LAN equipment from telecommunication apparatus to ADP machines affect the legitimacy of the United States' expectations? We examine these issues in turn.

(i) Requirement of Clarification

8.48 The European Communities argues that the United States should have clarified, during the negotiations, where LAN equipment would be classified. The question here is whether the exporting Member has any inherent obligation to seek clarification when it has been otherwise given a basis to expect that actual tariff treatment by the importing Member will be maintained.

8.49 In our view, to require exporting parties in negotiations to effectively work on the assumption that, absent a manifest anomaly, explicit and particular clarification should be sought at an item-by-item level would run fundamentally counter to the object and purpose of tariff negotiations (which in turn form the context for Article II and tariff schedules). On one level, it would both risk an erosion of the confidence upon which it is necessary for parties to rely in the conduct of tariff negotiations, as well as raising logistic difficulties which would make the actual management of them particularly onerous. More fundamentally, such a requirement would risk presumptively raising systemic doubt and uncertainty about the exact nature and scope of the actual tariff concessions themselves. Such an inherent tendency cannot be reconciled with one of the major objectives of the WTO, from which tariff negotiations pursuant to, *inter alia*, Articles XXVIII and XXVIII *bis* of GATT 1994 draw their purpose, viz: "reciprocal and mutually advantageous arrangements directed to the substantial reduction of tariffs"(an expression common to the preambles of the WTO Agreement and GATT 1994). Any interpretation of Article II which would be prone to have the practical effect of more generally facilitating the occasions upon which Members may apply a higher rate of duty and/or undermine the stability of concessions made (other than, of course, circumstances under which such action is explicitly provided for pursuant to relevant provisions of the WTO Agreement would run counter to this objective).

[155] See paragraph 5.33.

8.50 We also note in this context that a tariff commitment is an instrument in the hands of an importing Member which inherently serves the importing Member's "protection needs and its requirements for the purposes of tariff and trade negotiations".[156] The exporting party is well aware of that fact, and may therefore reasonably expect - absent something explicit to the contrary - that the importing party, in making a particular commitment has taken those needs and requirements already into account as matters over which it has competence and control. It is for this reason that it behooves the importing party, as the effective bearer of its rights and responsibilities, to correctly identify products and relevant duties in its tariff schedules, including such limitations or modifications as it intends to apply.

8.51 We consider that this reasoning is supported by past cases. In 1956, Germany complained that the Greek Government had increased the duty on gramophone records, which had been bound at the Annecy and Torquay rounds of tariff negotiations. The Group of Experts that examined the case stated as follows:

> "The Greek representative said that his Government had left unaltered the specific duty as bound in Schedule XXV on item 137, e, 3. What they had done was to impose a duty which, with surtax, amounted to 70 per cent *ad valorem* on 'long-playing' records (33 1/3 and 45 revolutions per minute). His Government explained this action on the grounds that such records did not exist at the time the Greek Government granted the above concession, that they contained a volume of recordings up to five times that of the old records, that they were lighter than conventional records, that they were made of different material, and that, therefore, as a new product, they were not covered by the item bound at Annecy and Torquay. The Greek representative further pointed out that countries which impose *ad valorem* duties on gramophone records were, because of the higher value of long-playing records, collecting substantially higher duties in monetary terms.
>
> ...
>
> "The Group agreed that the practice generally followed in classifying new products was to apply the tariff item, if one existed, that specified the products by name, or, if no such item existed, to assimilate the new products to existing

---

[156] Panel Report on *Japan - Tariff on Imports of Spruce, Pine, Fir (SPF) Dimension Lumber*, op cit., para. 5.9. Although this report affirms Japan's classification of particular items as a practice meeting these needs and requirements, the Panel Report on *Spain - Tariff Treatment of Unroasted Coffee*, op cit., - which found Spain's classification practice to be inconsistent with GATT 1947 on other grounds - states that such a practice is subject to the condition "that a reclassification subsequent to the making of a concession under the GATT would not be a violation of the basic commitment regarding that concession"(para. 4.4, footnote 1).

> items in accordance with the principles established by the national tariff legislation. It was noted that when this item was negotiated the parties concerned did not place any qualification upon the words 'gramophone record'.
>
> "The Group consequently reports to the CONTRACTING PARTIES its finding that 'long-playing' records (under 78 revolutions per minute) are covered by the description of item 137, e, 3 bound in Schedule XXV (Annecy and Torquay) and, therefore, the rate of duty to be applied to long-playing records is that bound in the schedules under that item. As the action taken by the Greek Government involves a modification in a bound rate, it is the opinion of the Group that the Greek Government should have resorted to the procedures provided in the Agreement for such modification."[157]

Despite the fact that "long-playing" records did not exist at the time of the Annecy or Torquay rounds, the group concluded that Greece was bound by its commitment on gramophone records because it did not place any qualification on the term "gramophone records" during the negotiations. The onus of clarifying (in this case "limiting") the scope of the tariff concession was put on the side of the importing Member.

8.52 The European Communities claims that the *Gramophone Records* case is not relevant to the present dispute because the case dealt with new products, while the US complaint in the present dispute is limited to products which already existed during the Uruguay Round.[158] We disagree. If the product had existed at the time of the negotiation, it would, if anything, have been easier for the importing Member to qualify the scope of its tariff commitments regarding that product, as it would not even have recourse to the argument that subsequent novelty was involved. Consequently, the reasoning regarding the requirement to respect the integrity of the commitment without qualification would seem to have even more force.

8.53 Similarly, in response to a Canadian claim that the European Communities had for the year 1984 opened an import quota for newsprint of only 500,000 tonnes instead of the bound quota of 1,500,000 tonnes as described in its tariff schedule and that this action was inconsistent with the European Communities' obligations under Article II of GATT 1947, the panel on *Newsprint* stated as follows:

> "The Panel could not share the argument advanced by the European Communities that their action did not constitute a change in their GATT tariff commitment. It noted that un-

---

157 *Greek Increase in Bound Duty*, complaint, op cit.

158 See paragraph 5.9.

> der long-standing GATT practice, even purely formal changes in the tariff schedule of a contracting party, which may not affect the GATT rights of other countries, such as the conversion of a specific to an *ad valorem* duty without an increase in the protective effect of the tariff rate in question, have been considered to require renegotiations. By the same token, the European Communities action would, in the Panel's view, have required the European Communities to conduct such negotiations. The Panel also noted that in granting the concession in 1973, the European Communities had not made it subject to any qualification or reservation in the sense of Article II:1(b) although at the time the concession was made, it was known that agreement had already been reached that the EFTA countries would obtain full duty-free access to the Community market for newsprint from 1 January 1984 onward. The Panel therefore found that although in the formal sense the European Communities had not modified its GATT concession, it had *in fact* changed its GATT commitment unilaterally, by limiting its duty-free tariff quota for m.f.n. suppliers for 1984 to 500,000 tonnes."[159]

8.54 In our view, the reasoning applied in these cases is consistent with that set forth in paragraphs 8.49 and 8.50 above. They confirm that the onus of clarifying tariff commitment is generally placed on the importing Member. In the absence of any such limitation by the importing Member, the benefits of the concession accrue to the exporting Member(s).

8.55 In light of the above, we find that the European Communities cannot place the burden of clarification on the United States in cases where it has created, through its own practice, the expectations regarding the continuation of the actual tariff treatment prevailing at the time of the tariff negotiations. It would not be reasonable to expect the US Government to seek clarification when it had not heard any complaints from its exporters, who were apparently satisfied with the current tariff treatment of LAN equipment in their major export market - Ireland and the United Kingdom. We have found no evidence to suggest that such treatment was manifestly anomalous or that there was information readily available that clearly indicated that the treatment would not be continued.

(ii) The United States' Own Reclassification

8.56 The European Communities further argues that since the United States itself had classified LAN equipment as telecommunication apparatus in its tariff

[159] Panel Report on *Newsprint*, op cit., para.50.

schedule until 1992, it could not have legitimately expected that the European Communities would treat LAN equipment as ADP machines.[160] It also argues that the difficulty of classifying LAN equipment was recognized in the negotiations of the North American Free Trade Agreement and that it was not until 1995 that Canada reclassified LAN equipment as ADP machines.[161] It further argues that Japan and Korea, which are third parties to this dispute, still classify some or all LAN equipment as telecommunication apparatus.[162]

8.57 Furthermore, the European Communities points out that it was not until April 1997 that the Harmonized System (HS) Committee of the World Customs Organization (WCO) decided on the classification of LAN equipment, indicating the difficulty of tariff classification of this product.[163]

8.58 We are not persuaded by these arguments. The subject matter of this dispute is the EC tariff schedule (Schedule LXXX). How the like or similar product is treated in the US tariff schedule (Schedule XX) or in any other Member's schedule is not relevant to the US expectations regarding the tariff treatment in its export market. Regarding the European Communities' argument on the difficulty of classification, we would recall that both parties are of the view that this is not a dispute about customs classification itself; rather it concerns the actual tariff treatment by customs authorities in the European Communities.

8.59 That being said, to the extent that the evolution of US classification practice has relevance at all, it fails, in our view, to support the European Communities' argument. Insofar as the United States and the US industry had been satisfied with the treatment of LAN equipment as ADP machines in the European Communities, the classification change by the United States in 1992 (from telecommunication apparatus to ADP machines) would have been perceived as a move in the right direction. Rather than giving any reasons for occasioning US uncertainty about the nature of actual tariff treatment of LAN equipment in the European Communities, it would, if anything, have signified that the United States had more reason than ever to believe that such actual tariff treatment would continue. Certainly, neither the US Government nor the US industry would have had any reason to be alarmed. Thus, we find that the United States' own reclassification of LAN equipment does not affect the legitimacy of the US expectations.

3. *Conclusion*

8.60 We find that the United States was entitled to legitimate expectations that LAN equipment would continue to be accorded tariff treatment as ADP machines in the European Communities, based on the actual tariff treatment during the Uruguay Round, particularly in Ireland and the United Kingdom (which were the

---

[160] See paragraph 5.26.
[161] See paragraph 5.33.
[162] See paragraph 5.35.
[163] See paragraph 5.12.

major export market for US products). We further find that the United States was not required to clarify the scope of the European Communities' tariff concessions on LAN equipment and that the United States' own reclassification of LAN equipment in 1992 was not relevant to the formation of its legitimate expectations regarding the European Communities' tariff treatment of the like or similar product.

8.61 It is clear from evidence that these legitimate expectations were frustrated by the subsequent change in the classification practice in the European Communities, including through the reclassification of LAN adapter cards under Regulation (EC) 1165/95.

8.62 We thus find that LAN equipment should have obtained the tariff treatment afforded to ADP machines in Schedule LXXX and that the European Communities has violated Article II:1 of GATT 1994 by failing to accord imports of LAN equipment from the United States treatment no less favourable than that provided for under heading 84.71 or heading 84.73, as the case may be, in Part I of Schedule LXXX.

E. Multimedia PCs

8.63 The United States claims that personal computers with multimedia capability should have been accorded the tariff treatment as ADP machines within the meaning of Schedule LXXX. The European Communities claims that the United States could not have had legitimate expectations that the European Communities would classify PCTVs or other multimedia equipment under tariff heading 84.71 and apply the corresponding duty rate.

1. Textual Analysis

8.64 Our starting point again is the textual analysis. We need not reproduce the definition of ADP machines under heading 84.71 in Schedule LXXX. We simply note that, as in the case of LAN equipment, certain types of multimedia PCs can be regarded, based on the ordinary meaning of the terms used in that Schedule, either as ADP machines under heading 84.71 or as television receivers under heading 85.28 depending on whether they are seen as "computers that can receive television signals" or as "television receivers that can also function as computers".[164] The textual analysis of Schedule LXXX alone does not lead to a clear solution of the problem.

---

[164] It should be emphasized once again that it is not our task to determine where multimedia PCs should be classified in a tariff nomenclature.

2. *Legitimate Expectations*

8.65 The United States claims that it is entitled to the legitimate expectations that multimedia PCs would be accorded the tariff treatment as ADP machines within the meaning of Schedule LXXX. We recall in this context the Appellate Body's observation regarding what amounts to proof.[165] We also note that the United States' assertion that "PCs with multimedia capability were treated as products under Chapter 84 during the Uruguay Round"[166] is not substantiated by any evidence as regards actual tariff treatment.[167] The only evidence produced by the United States in this regard is a judgement by a UK court on PCTVs, ruling that they are properly classified under heading 85.28 as television receivers.[168] We fail to see how this judgement supports the US position without any showing of the previous practices in the European Communities or in the United Kingdom. It is true that Regulation (EC) 1153/97 classifies all computers "capable of receiving and processing television, telecommunication, audio and video signals" under heading 84.71, but this regulation became effective in July 1997. Since the regulation was adopted in part to reflect a 1996 decision by the HS Committee of the WCO, it cannot be viewed as evidence of the EC practice during the Uruguay Round.

8.66 In summary, regarding multimedia PCs, the United States has failed to adduce evidence sufficient to raise a presumption that these products were in fact treated as ADP machines in the European Communities during the Uruguay Round. Thus, we are unable to decide the case on the basis of legitimate expectations as we did with respect to LAN equipment.

3. *Other Means of Interpretation*

8.67 The analysis of the context, object or purpose of Schedule LXXX, GATT 1994 or the WTO Agreement - apart from those relating to legitimate expectations - does not clarify the situation. Nor do we find any clear guidance in subsequent agreements or practices. Moreover, recourse to the supplementary means of treaty interpretation[169] is not helpful because neither party has produced sufficient evidence thereof. We are therefore unable to reach a positive conclusion

---

[165] See paragraph 8.34.

[166] See paragraph 5.66.

[167] Unlike the case of LAN equipment, the United States has not produced any evidence of record on actual tariff treatment, e.g., BTIs, customs rulings or actual invoices. Paragraphs 5.69 to 5.71 are the US replies to the following question by the Panel: "How do you respond to the EC argument that 'the United States did not produce any document showing that the EC did indeed classify all computers with multimedia capabilities under heading 84.71 during the Uruguay Round'? Do you have any specific documentation regarding the actual tariff treatment of computers with multimedia capabilities on importation during the period covered by the Uruguay Round?".

[168] Annex 3.

[169] See paragraph 8.21.

that multimedia PCs should have been treated as ADP machines within the meaning of Schedule LXXX.

8.68 In conclusion, based on the evidence submitted by the parties that is admissible under the terms of reference of this Panel, we do not find that the European Communities has violated Article II:1 of GATT 1994 regarding the tariff treatment of multimedia PCs.

F. Nullification or Impairment

8.69 We note the claim by the United States that the value of concessions accruing to the United States has been nullified or impaired by the application of the measures identified under item (a) through (f) of paragraph 8.5.

8.70 In view of our finding that the tariff treatment of LAN equipment by customs authorities in the European Communities violated Article II:1 of GATT 1994 (US claims under item (a) and (b) of paragraph 8.5), we find that it is not necessary to examine this additional claim with respect to LAN equipment, except to note that the infringement of GATT rules is considered *prima facie* to constitute a case of nullification or impairment under Article 3.8 of the DSU.

8.71 Regarding the tariff treatment of multimedia PCs, we note that we have not found a violation of GATT rules on the part of the European Communities. We also note that the United States has not attempted to establish nullification or impairment of the value of concessions accruing to it in respect of multimedia PCs, except through its claim on the violation of tariff bindings by the European Communities.

8.72 Finally, with respect to LAN equipment, since we find a violation of Article II:1 by the European Communities, it is unnecessary to rule on the US claims under item (d) and (f) of paragraph 8.5. With respect to multimedia PCs, we did not find any evidence of a violation (US claims under (c) and (e) of paragraph 8.5). Therefore, we do not find it necessary to make a specific finding on the request by the United States referred to in paragraph 8.15 regarding either product category.

IX. CONCLUSIONS

9.1 In light of the findings above, the Panel finds that the European Communities, by failing to accord imports of LAN equipment from the United States treatment no less favourable than that provided for under heading 84.71 or heading 84.73, as the case may be, in Part I of Schedule LXXX, acted inconsistently with the requirements of Article II:1 of GATT 1994.

9.2 The Panel recommends that the Dispute Settlement Body request the European Communities to bring its tariff treatment of LAN equipment into conformity with its obligations under GATT 1994.

ANNEX 1

Tariff Concessions contained in EC Schedule - LXXX relating to items under tariff headings 84.71, 84.73, 85.17, 85.21 and 85.28

Tariff item number	Description of products	Base rate of duty	Bound rate of duty	Initial negotiating right	Other duties and charges	Remarks
1	2	3	4	5	6	7
8471	Automatic data processing machines and units thereof; magnetic or optical readers, machines for transcribing data onto data media in coded form and machines for processing such data, not elsewhere specified or included:					
8471.10	-Analogue or hybrid automatic data processing machines:					
8471.10.10	--For use in civil aircraft	0.0	0.0			
8471.10.90	--Other	4.9	2.5			
8471.20	-Digital automatic data processing machines, containing in the same housing at least a central processing unit and an input and output unit, whether or not combined:					
8471.20.10	--For use in civil aircraft	0.0	0.0			
	--Other:					
8471.20.40	---With a random access memory (RAM) with a capacity not exceeding 64 kilobytes	4.9	2.5			
8471.20.50	---With a random access memory (RAM) with a capacity exceeding 64 kilobytes but not exceeding 256 kilobytes	4.9	2.5			
8471.20.60	---With a random access memory (RAM) with a capacity exceeding 256 kilobytes but not exceeding 512 kilobytes	4.9	2.5			
8471.20.90	---With a random access memory (RAM) with a capacity exceeding 512 kilobytes	4.9	2.5			

Tariff item number	Description of products	Base rate of duty	Bound rate of duty	Initial negotiating right	Other duties and charges	Remarks
1	2	3	4	5	6	7
	-Other:					
8471.91	--Digital processing units, whether or not presented with the rest of a system, which may contain in the same housing one or two of the following types of unit : storage units, input units, output units:					
8471.91.10	---For use in civil aircraft	0.0	0.0			
	---Other					
8471.91.40	----With a random access memory (RAM) with a capacity not exceeding 64 kilobytes	4.9	2.5			
8471.91.50	----With a random access memory (RAM) with a capacity exceeding 64 kilobytes but not exceeding 256 kilobytes	4.9	2.5			
8471.91.60	----With a random access memory (RAM) with a capacity exceeding 256 kilobytes but not exceeding 512 kilobytes	4.9	2.5			
8471.91.90	----With a random access memory (RAM) with a capacity exceeding 512 kilobytes	4.9	2.5			
8471.92	--Input or output units, whether or not presented with the rest of a system and whether or not containing storage units in the same housing:					
8471.92.10	---For use in civil aircraft	0.0	0.0			
8471.92.90	---Other	4.9	0.0			
8471.93	--Storage units, whether or not presented with the rest of a system:					
8471.93.10	---For use in civil aircraft	0.0	0.0			
	---Other:					
8471.93.40	----Central storage units	4.9	0.0			
	----Other:					
8471.93.50	----Disk storage units	4.9	0.0			
8471.93.60	----Magnetic tape storage units	4.9	0.0			

Tariff item number	Description of products	Base rate of duty	Bound rate of duty	Initial negotiating right	Other duties and charges	Remarks
1	2	3	4	5	6	7
8471.93.90	----Other	4.9	0.0			
8471.99	--Other:					
8471.99.10	---Peripheral units	4.9	0.0			
8471.99.30	---Punches, verifiers and calculators	4.9	0.0			
8471.99.90	---Other	4.9	0.0			
8473	Parts and accessories (other than covers, carrying cases and the like) suitable for use solely or principally with machines of headings Nos 8469 to 8472:					
8473.10.00	-Parts and accessories of the machines of heading No 8469:					
EX1-NEW	--Electronic assemblies	4.0	3.0			
EX2-NEW	--Other	4.0	0.0			
	-Parts and accessories of the machines of heading No 8470:					
8473.21.00	--Of the electronic calculating machines of subheading No 8470 10, 8470 21 or 8470 29:					
EX1-NEW	---Electronic assemblies	6.3	3.0			
EX2-NEW	---Other	6.3	0.0			
8473.29.00	--Other:					
EX1-NEW	---Electronic assemblies	4.0	3.0			
EX2-NEW	---Other	4.0	0.0			
8473.30.00	-Parts and accessories of the machines of heading No 8471:					
EX1-NEW	--Electronic assemblies	4.0	2.0			Concession to be implemented over 8 years
EX2-NEW	--Other	4.0	0.0			
8473.40.00	-Parts and accessories of the machines of heading No 8472:					

Tariff item number	Description of products	Base rate of duty	Bound rate of duty	Initial negotiating right	Other duties and charges	Remarks
1	2	3	4	5	6	7
EX1-NEW	--Electronic assemblies	4.0	3.0			
EX2-NEW	--Other	4.0	0.0			
8517	Electrical apparatus for line telephony or line telegraphy, including such apparatus for carrier-current line systems:					
8517.10.00	-Telephone sets	7.5	0.0			
8517.20.00	-Teleprinters	7.5	3.6			
8517.30.00	-Telephonic or telegraphic switching apparatus	7.5	3.6			
8517.40.00	-Other apparatus, for carrier-current line systems	4.6	3.6			
	-Other apparatus:					
8517.81	--Telephonic:					
8517.81.10	---Entry-phone systems	7.5	3.6			
8517.81.90	---Other	7.5	3.6			
8517.82.00	--Telegraphic	7.5	3.6			
8517.90	-Parts:					
8517.90.10	--Of apparatus of subheading 8517 40 00:					
EX1-NEW	---Electronics assemblies and sub-assemblies	4.6	3.0			
EX2-NEW	---Other	4.6	3.0			
	--Other:					
8517.90.91	---Of telephonic apparatus:					
EX1-NEW	----Electronics assemblies and sub-assemblies	7.5	3.0			
EX2-NEW	----Other	7.5	3.0			
8517.90.99	---Of telegraphic apparatus					
EX1-NEW	----Electronics assemblies and sub-assemblies	7.5	3.0			
EX2-NEW	----Other	7.5	3.0			
8521	Video recording or reproducing apparatus:					

Tariff item number	Description of products	Base rate of duty	Bound rate of duty	Initial negotiating right	Other duties and charges	Remarks
1	2	3	4	5	6	7
8521.10	-Magnetic tape-type:					
8521.10.10	--For use in civil aircraft	0.0	0.0			
	--Other:					
	---Of a width not exceeding 1,3 cm and allowing recording or reproduction at a tape speed not exceeding 50 mm per second:					
8521.10.31	----Within the same housing a built-in television camera	14.0	14.0			
8521.10.39	----Other	14.0	14.0			
8521.10.90	---Other	8.0	8.0			
8521.90.00	-Other	14.0	14.0			
8528	Television receivers (including video monitors and video projectors), whether or incorporating radio-broadcast receivers or sound or video recording of reproducing apparatus:					
8528.10	-Colour:					
	--Video recording or reproducing apparatus incorporating a video tuner:					
	---Using magnetic tape on reels or in cassettes:					
8528.10.11	----Of a width not exceeding 1,3 cm and allowing recording or reproduction at a tape speed not exceeding 50 mm per second	14.0	14.0			
8528.10.19	----Other	8.0	8.0			
8528.10.30	---Other	14.0	14.0			
8528.10.40	--Television projection equipment	14.0	14.0			
8528.10.50	--Apparatus incorporating a videophonic recorder or reproducer	14.0	14.0			
8528.10.60	--Video monitors	14.0	14.0			
	--Other:					
	---With integral tube, with a diagonal measurement of the screen:					
8528.10.71	----Not exceeding 42 cm	14.0	14.0			

Tariff item number	Description of products	Base rate of duty	Bound rate of duty	Initial negotiating right	Other duties and charges	Remarks
1	2	3	4	5	6	7
8528.10.73	----Exceeding 42 cm but not exceeding 52 cm	14.0	14.0			
8528.10.79	----Exceeding 52 cm	14.0	14.0			
	---Other:					
8528.10.91	----Video tuners	14.0	14.0			
8528.10.99	----Other	14.0	14.0			
8528.20	-Black and white or other monochrome:					
	--With integral tube:					
8528.20.10	---Video monitors	14.0	14.0			
	---Other, with a diagonal measurement of the screen:					
8528.20.71	----Not exceeding 42 cm	14.0	2.0			
8528.20.73	----Exceeding 42 cm but not exceeding 52 cm	14.0	2.0			
8528.20.79	----Exceeding 52 cm	14.0	2.0			
8528.20.90	--Other	14.0	2.0			

Source: European Communities - Schedule LXXX.

Note: "The tariff reductions agreed upon by each Member shall be implemented in five equal rate reductions, except as may be otherwise specified in a Member's Schedule. The first such reduction shall be made effective on the date of entry into force of the WTO Agreement, each successive reduction shall be made effective on 1 January of each of the following years, and the final rate shall become effective no later than the date four years after the date of entry into force of the WTO Agreement, except as may be otherwise specified in the Member's Schedule." (Marrakesh Protocol to the General Agreement on Tariffs and Trade 1994, paragraph 2)

ANNEX 2

Commission Regulation (EC) No. 1165/95 of 23 May 1995

concerning the classification of certain goods in the combined nomenclature

THE COMMISSION OF THE EUROPEAN COMMUNITIES,

Having regard to the Treaty establishing the European Community,

Having regard to Council Regulation (EEC) No. 2658/87[171] on the tariff and statistical nomenclature and on the Common Customs Tariff, as last amended by Commission Regulation (EC) No. 3115/94[172], and in particular Article 9,

Whereas in order to ensure uniform application of the combined nomenclature annexed to the said Regulation, it is necessary to adopt measures concerning the classification of the goods referred to in the Annex to this Regulation;

Whereas Regulation (EEC) No. 2658/87 has set down the general rules for the interpretation of the combined nomenclature and those rules also apply to any other nomenclature which is wholly or partly based on it or which adds any additional subdivision to it and which is established by specific Community provisions, with a view to the application of tariff and other measures relating to trade in goods;

Whereas, pursuant to the said general rules, the goods described in column 1 of the table annexed to the present Regulation must be classified under the appropriate CN codes indicated in column 2, by virtue of the reasons set out in column 3;

Whereas it is acceptance that binding tariff information issued by the customs authorities of Member States in respect of the classification of goods in the combined nomenclature and which do not conform to the rights established by this Regulation, can continue to be invoked, under the provisions in Article 12(6) of

[171] OJ No. L 256, 7/9/1987, p.1.
[172] OJ No. L 345, 31/12/94, p.1.

Council Regulation (EEC) No. 2913/92 establishing the Community Customs Code[173], for a period of three months by the holder;

Whereas the tariff and statistical nomenclature section of the Customs Code Committee has not delivered an opinion with the time limit set by its chairman as regards products Nos. 4 and 7 in the annexed table;

Whereas the measures provided for in this Regulation are in accordance with the opinion of the tariff and statistical nomenclature section of the Customs Code Committee as regards products Nos. 1, 3, 5 and 6 in the annexed table,

HAS ADOPTED THIS REGULATION:

Article 1

The goods described in column 1 of the annexed table are now classified within the combined nomenclature under the appropriate CN codes indicated in column 2 of the said table.

Article 2

Binding tariff information issued by the customs authorities of Member States which do not conform to the rights established by this Regulation can continue to be invoked under the provisions of Article 12(6) of Regulation (EEC) No. 2913/92 for a period of three months.

Article 3

This Regulation shall enter into force on the 21st day following its publication in the *Official Journal of the European Communities.*

This Regulation shall be binding in its entirety and directly applicable in all Member States.

Done at Brussels, 23 May 1995.

For the Commission
Mario MONTI
Member of the Commission

[173] OJ No. L 302, 19/10/92, p.1.

ANNEX

Description of goods	Classification CN code	Reason
(1)	(2)	(3)
1. An ornamental article (luminous fountain or "running tap"), put up unassembled in a packing for retail sale. Assembled, the various plastic components (a base about 15 cm. diameter, incorporating a lighting system and an electric motor with a power-supply cable, and equipped with a switch, three basins, various pipe connections, a tap, a small figure of a dancer, artificial flowers and foliage, etc.) form one or other of the articles depicted(*) (height between 30 cm. and 40 cm.) (*)See photograph	3926 40 00	Classification is determined by the provisions of General Rules 1 and 6 for the interpretation of the combined nomenclature and by the wording of CN codes 3926 and 3926 40 00
2. Slippers consisting of a textile upper and an outer sole of plastic (approximately one centimetre thick), the outside of which is entirely covered by a very thin layer of textile material, with poor wearing properties, stuck along the edges	6404 19 10	Classification is determined by the provisions of General Rules 1 and 6 for the interpretation of the combined nomenclature, note 4(b) to Chapter 64 and by the wording of CN codes 6404, 6404 19 and 6404 19 10
3. An automated cartridge system in a casing consisting, essentially, of: (a) one or more library storage modules (each containing cartridge storage cells and a microprocessor controlled robot and having one or more attached cartridge drive frames and control units); and (b) a library management unit with integral software (which acts as the link between the library storage modules and one or more central processing units). This system is specifically designed for the automatic loading, processing, storage and unloading of magnetic tape cartridges for automatic data processing purposes	8471 99 10	Classification is determined by the provisions of General Rules 1 and 6 for the interpretation of the combined nomenclature, by note 5B to Chapter 84 and by the wording of CN codes 8471, 8471 99 and 8471 99 10
4. An adapter card for incorporation in cable linked digital automatic data-processing (ADP) machines enabling the exchange of data over a local area network (LAN) without using a modem. With such a card, an ADP-machine can be used as an input-output device for another	8517 82 90	Classification is determined by the provisions of General Rules 1 and 6 for the interpretation of the combined nomenclature, by note 5 to Chapter 84 and by the wording of CN codes 8517, 8517 82 and

Description of goods	Classification CN code	Reason
(1)	(2)	(3)
machine or a central processing unit. The card constitutes a printed circuit of a size of about 10 x 21 cm. incorporating integrated circuits and active and passive components. It is fitted with a row of pin contacts corresponding to an expansion slot in the ADP-machine, with an attachment to the connection cable of the LAN and light emitting diodes (LEDs).		8517 82 90
5. A miniature electro-acoustic receiver (earphone) in a housing whose exterior dimensions do not exceed 7 x 7 x 5 mm. The receiver comprises a magnet, a coil and a diaphragm to receive electrical signals which cause the diaphragm to vibrate thus producing audible sound. The receiver may be used together with an amplifier as a hearing aid.	8518 30 90	Classification is determined by the provisions of General Rules 1 and 6 for the interpretation of the combined nomenclature, by note 2(a) to Chapter 90 and by the wording of CN codes 8518, 8518 30 and 8518 30 90
6. A laser copier comprising mainly a device for scanning (scanner), a digital image processing device and a printing device (laser printer), contained in a housing. The scanning device uses an optical system, consisting of a lamp, mirrors, lenses and photocells to scan the original image line by line. The copies are produced electrostatically via a drum on the laser printer using the indirect process. The laser copier has several additional features for altering the original image, e.g. reduction, enlargement, shading.	9009 12 00	Classification is determined by the provisions of General Rules 1 and 6 for the interpretation of the combined nomenclature and by the wording of CN codes 9009 and 9009 12 00
7. Little star and heart shapes in a variety of colours (red, green and shiny silver) and multicoloured granules, the size of pinheads, made from plastic film, and used to decorate e.g. a table on which food for a carnival celebration, children's party or Advent festivity is served. The decorative effect is achieved by sprinkling the products.	9505 90 00	Classification is determined by the provisions of General Rules 1 and 6 for the interpretation of the combined nomenclature and by the wording of CN codes 9505 and 9505 90 00

ANNEX 3

CUSTOMS DUTIES - classification - combined nomenclature - rules of interpretation - "PCTV" whether a composite machine with a "principal function" as an Automatic Data Processing Machine or composite goods given its "essential character" by the ADPM components so classified under heading 84.71 "ADPMs" or whether it fails to be classified by default under heading 85.28 "Television Receivers"- Council Reg. 2658/87 Annex 1, GIRs1.3(b)&(c)

LONDON TRIBUNAL CENTRE

INTERNATIONAL COMPUTERS LIMITED

Appellant

- and -

THE COMMISSIONERS OF CUSTOMS AND EXCISE

Respondents

Tribunal: MR. R.K. MILLER CB (Chairman)
MRS. S. SADEQUE M.Phil. MSc

Sitting in public at 15-19 Bedford Avenue, London WC1 on Thursday, 18 January and Friday, 19 January 1996

Mrs. P.A. Hamilton of Coopers and Lybrand for the Appellant

Mr. Hugh Davies, counsel instructed by the Solicitor for Customs and Excise for the respondents.

DECISION

This appeal by International Computers Ltd. ("ICL") is against a decision of the Commissioners on review as to the tariff classification for import customs duty of a machine known as the "PCTV". The machine has a full title "the Fujitsu ICL PCTV", Fujitsu being the major shareholder in ICL. It is an innovative product. The machine is both a multimedia personal computer and a full function colour television set, integrated within the same unit and using the same screen.

It is common ground that the machine fails to be classified in one of two headings. ICL contends that it should be classified under heading 84.71 of the Community Customs Code - "Automatic data processing machines", which carry a rate of duty on importation of 4.4 per cent. The Commissioners decided that it falls under heading 85.28 - "Television receivers", which carry a rate of duty on importation of 14 per cent. The dispute turns upon the way in which the rules governing how goods are to be classified are to be applied. ICL contends that the PCTV's "principal function" and/or its "essential character" is that of a personal computer. The Commissioners maintain that it is not possible to determine a principal function; so, presented with two tariff headings which equally merit consideration, one must classify the PCTV under that heading which occurs last in numerical order, namely 85.28 "Television receivers".

We heard oral evidence from Mr. Sidney Burton, Development Manager for the Advanced Technology Group of ICL, who designed the machine: Mr. Justin Matthew Houghton Clarke, Market Development Manager for consumer products within ICL; and Professor Robert Spence, Professor of Information Engineering at Imperial College. These witnesses were all called by Mrs. Hamilton, who presented the case for ICL. No witnesses were called on behalf of the Commissioners, who were represented by Mr. Hugh Davies. Mr. Burton demonstrated the machine in court. We were not, however, able to see it in operation as a TV because of the lack of a proper aerial on the tribunal's premises. Mrs. Hamilton also put before the tribunal a bundle of documents. It was not an agreed bundle but was used as a working bundle for both sides.

The goods to which the disputed decision refers were imported between 1 May and 31 July 1995 by Design to Distribution Ltd., a wholly owned subsidiary of ICL from Taiwan where the machines are manufactured.

ICL has designed a range of multimedia personal computers ("PCs") known as the Fujitsu Indiana range. Multimedia PCs are computer systems which can incorporate a number of media functions, such as CD-ROM, CD audio, PC generated sound, Joystick for games etc., in addition to the normal personal computer functions. The PCTV is part of that range and is an integrated single unit designed for use in the home. The finish of the unit is charcoal-grey to be more in keeping with, for example, normal Hi-Fi equipment and is intended to be used in a study or teenager's bedroom. It integrates a multimedia personal computer with a remote controlled television facility. It is thus a fully functioning PC and a fully functioning full screen analogue TV. It is supplied packaged in one box, which contains a Main Pack, with the PCTV system unit as the first item, and an Accessories Pack, of which the first item is the keyboard with built-in trackball (the equivalent of a "mouse").

The Accessories Pack also contains the PCTV software and Microsoft software, with their documentation packs, and the remote control and power cable.

It has a single power cable and, although the machine contains two power supplies, there is a single on/off switch. The PCTV, the very first time it is switched on and provided the keyboard is connected, turns on as a TV, the PC needing time to load. Thereafter the PC is fully capable from the time it is switched on.

The PCTV comes with a 66 MHz 486 DX2 processor 350 MB hard disk, 4 MB RAM, and double speed CD-ROM drive, integrated TV tuner with Teletext and Nicam Stereo, the integrated trackball on the keyboard, 14"SVGA display, 0.28mm dot pitch, Local bus graphics, 1 MB VRAM, 16-bit stereo sound; and software, MS DOS 6.22, Windows 3.11, MS Works CD, ICL The Den pre-installed and, on CD ROM, Wing Commander Privateer. MS Encarta, Putt Putt Joins Parade and PGA Tour Golf.

Both the PC and TV functions can be operated by the remote control unit. It is a normal remote control unit which can be used to change TV channels and to use Teletext. But it is unique in having an extra button which will operate the mouse using directional arrows and by being "clicked".

The ICL software applications can be accessed through "The Den" or by going instead direct to Windows. The Den is an ICL application consisting of a recognizable front end to Windows, to make it easier for novices to use the PCTV. Once the user is logged in he is presented with a graphic representation of a room full of familiar looking objects such as a CD player, games cupboard, clock, calendar and filing cabinet which act as "hotspots". By moving the cursor onto a hotspot a "prompt box" appears which explains the function. Clicking onto a "hotspot" activates the function.

The SoundStack is a comprehensive electronic CD player, recorder and mixer, for playing audio CDs, MIDI files and recording to hard disk.

The TV is automatically tuned in when the PCTV is switched on for the first time. Thereafter, it can be returned using the TV Channel controller. This software will automatically identify, name channels and place them in logical order. All cable and satellite channels can be picked up. Selected channels can be barred by parents so that access by unauthorized users is prevented until a password is entered.

The ICL application software also includes a "Live Mag" teletext "magazine" which stores selected teletext pages in an electronic file which are saved on the hard disk and updated automatically.

Since the pixels on a VGA screen are smaller and the degree of resolution required to display images generated by a PC even at the lowest VGA frequency is twice the frequency of 15,625 KHz fixed for all world wide TV standards, a television cathode ray tube is not physically capable of displaying the images generated by a PC nor is the television electronics capable of handling the PC display. But a PC cathode ray tube and electronics can have as a subset of its specification the necessary mode to allow the TV image to be displayed and with a picture quality which is sharper than on an equivalent portable TV.

Specifically, the PCTV has been designed as a standard Extended VGA monitor sub-system using a cathode ray tube and electronics to display all the common Extended VGA modes but with an additional 15.625 KHz mode for the display of images such as TV, VCR, Satellite and games controls. These TV style images are produced by a television card (a printed circuit board) using TV industry standard components to receive terrestrial broadcast signals or any composite video source and convert them to standard TV signals for the cathode ray tube electronics to display. Thus the monitor supports VGA resolutions up to 1024 x 768 pixels: the TV mode supports the 625 line/50 Hz PAL 1 and PAL B/G standards.

The audio design of the PCTV is a combination of the standard sound capabilities found in all multimedia PC's and which are normally achieved by adding a PC industry standard sound card containing those functions. This PC industry function has been incorporated into the PCTV by making the power amplifier part of the TV printed circuit board so that the TV related sounds can be routed through the common amplifier as well as the PC generated sounds. Hi Fi quality stereo sound is delivered through 12W Phillips Acoustic Horn Technology speakers, which are built into the system unit, in both PC and TV modes.

The machine does not contain a VCR. It has the capacity to play back signals from a VCR, although it might be more usual to use a larger screen TV for this, say the main household set in the sitting room. The TV facility on the PCTV being seen by ICL as providing a secondary TV set.

The imported value of the PCTV is 1500 US$ of which the TV printed circuit board represents a value of 120 US$.

The PCTV was designed to exploit a perceived market opportunity for personal computers specifically to be used in the home. It is not designed to be networked. It is targeted primarily at people in social categories A, B, and C, with school age children and also at other high income groups, e.g. students.

It is sold through a number of well known retail outlets, some of whom also sell TV sets, and through some retail buying chains. Shops display the PCTV with computers in that part of the shop and retail advertisements, for example in computer magazines, but also in other advertisements, include it with multi-media and other PCs.

ICL commissioned research from an independent research organization to find out who would be likely to buy a PCTV, where it would be used, who would make the decisions about buying it and how computer literate they were. The results were used in devising its advertising campaigns.

The marketing material and the guidance produced, for example for sales staff in the retail outlets, varies, as one would expect, in presenting the features and advantages of the PCTV to the particular audience at which that material is aimed. Consistently, however, it is presented as a fully integrated PC and TV, whereas sometimes it is the fully functional TV which is emphasized and at others it is its qualities as a multi-media PC which is put first.

In Professor Spence's opinion the PCTV in terms of its technical functionality is extremely rich. He identified those functions as including (a) programmability, (b) interactivity, (c) multi-modality (i.e. image, sound and text), (d) the storage of data and programs, (e) the representation of internally generated data, (f) the presentation of such data, (g) the performance, via a loudspeaker, of stored sound from a CD, (h) the presentation of externally generated data (i.e. the TV programmes). Of those technical functions, he said, only one can be described as a "TV set".

The cathode ray tube, which could well give the machine the appearance of being a TV set at first glance, simply takes data signals and displays them in graphical form. It does that equally for data created by the computer and data produced from the electronics which capture a broadcast signal and turn it into data that can be presented in sound and vision.

Professor Spence also examined the principal function of the PCTV in terms, as he put it, of its empowerment of human achievement in the cognitive and perceptual sense. In this he contrasted the passive role of the TV viewer and the interactive role offered by the ADP function of the PCTV. The one he described as being as a "simple, passive one-way experience" and the other a "rich, active and interactive experience", the difference between them being "staggering".

All this led him to the opinion that the principal function of the PCTV was its ADP function. That was also in his view its essential character, the essence of the machine being a personal computer notwithstanding its ability to present TV programmes.

The Combined Nomenclature, upon which the Community Customs Tariff is based, is reproduced in the annual revision of Annex 1 to Council Regulation (EEC) No. 2658/87 of 23rd July 1987 on the tariff and statistical nomenclature and on the Common Customs Tariff. Section 1 of Part 1 sets out under A the general rules for the interpretation of the combined nomenclature (the "GIRs"). The GIRs lay down the principles which govern the classification of goods in the combined nomenclature (or "CN").

Rule 1 states:

"The titles of sections, chapters and sub-chapters are provided for ease of reference only: for legal purposes, classification shall be determined according to the terms of headings and any relative section or chapter notes and, provided such headings or notes do not otherwise require, according to the following provisions:"

From this it appears that the titles of sections etc. have no legal bearing on classification, that must be determined according to the terms of the headings and any relevant section or chapter notes, and it is only where those headings or notes do not otherwise require - in other words they are paramount and thus the first consideration in determining classification - that classification may be determined, where appropriate, according to the provisions of the rules which follow.

Of those following rules, Rule 3 only was referred to in argument. Rule 3 states:

> "When by application of rule 2(b) or for any other reason, goods are *prima facie* classifiable under two or more headings, classification shall be effected as follows:
>
> > (a) The heading which provides the most specific description shall be preferred to headings providing a more general description. However, when two or more headings each refer to part only of the materials or substances contained in mixed or composite goods or to part only of the items in a set put up for retail sale, those headings are to be regarded as equally specific in relation to those goods, even if one of them gives a more complete or precise description of the goods.
> >
> > (b) Mixtures, composite goods consisting of different materials or made up of different components, and goods put up in sets for retail sale, which cannot be classified by reference to 3(a), shall be classified as if they consisted of the material or component which gives them their essential character in so far as this criterion is applicable.
> >
> > (c) When goods cannot be classified by reference to 3(a) or 3(b), they shall be classified under the heading which occurs last in numerical order among those which equally merit consideration."

It is common ground that the PCTV falls within Section XVI of the CN. It is also common ground that the applicable Section Note is Section Note 3 which states:

> "Unless the context otherwise requires, composite machines consisting of two or more machines fitted together to form a whole and other machines adapted for the purpose of performing two or more complementary or alternative functions are to be classified as if consisting only of that component or as being that machine which performs the principal function."

"Machine" for these purposes "means any machine, machinery, plant, equipment, apparatus or appliance cited in the headings of Chapter 84 or 85."- see Section Note 5.

Mrs. Hamilton for ICL submits that the PCTV is a "composite machine" and that its "principal function" is that of an Automatic Data Processing Machine ("ADPM") falling under heading No. 84.71.

Chapter Note 5 to Chapter 84 states -

"(A) For the purposes of heading No. 84.71, the expression "automatic data processing machines" means:

(a) Digital machines, capable of (1) storing the processing program or programs and at least the data immediately necessary for execution of the program; (2) being freely programmed in accordance with the requirements of the user; (3) performing arithmetical computations specified by the user; and, (4) executing, without human intervention, a processing program which requires them to modify their execution, by logical decision during the processing run;

(b) Analogue machines capable of simulating mathematical models and comprising at least: analogue elements, control elements and programming elements;

(c) Hybrid machines consisting of either a digital machine with analogue elements or an analogue machine with digital elements."

Mrs. Hamilton also referred to what are commonly called "HSENs", that is to say the Explanatory Notes of the Customs Co-operation Council. The "HS" or "Harmonized System", which is itself short for the International Convention on the Harmonized Commodity and Coding System, is administered under the auspices of the Customs Co-operation Council. As the recitals to Council Regulation (EEC) No. 2658/87 show, the European Community is a signatory to the Convention and the Combined Nomenclature of the Common Customs Tariff of the Community had to "be established on the basis of the Harmonized System".

That being the case, the HSENs, whilst not having legal force, nevertheless may be considered as a valuable aid to the interpretation of the provisions of the tariff although they may not alter their proper meaning. See the judgment of the European Court of Justice in *Develop Dr. Eisbein* v. *Hauptzollamt Stuttgart-West* Case C-35/93 (1993) ECR1-2655: in particular paragraph 21 of that judgment, and the decision of this tribunal in *Tretec UK Limited* v. *Customs and Excise Commissioners* (1995) Case No. C2. We gratefully accept and adopt the reasoning at paragraphs 24 to 28 of the decision with which we respectfully agree.

HSEN (V1) to Section XVI Note 3 states - (so far as is here relevant) -

"In general, multi-function machines are classified according to the principal function of the machine:

Multi-function machines are, for example, machine tools for working metal using interchangeable tools, which enable them to carry out different machining operations (e.g. milling, boring, lapping).

> Where it is not possible to determine the principal function, and where, as provided in Note 3 to the Section, the context does not otherwise require, it is necessary to apply General Interpretative Rule 3 (c): such is the case, for example, in respect of multi-function machines potentially classifiable in several of the headings 84.25 to 84.30, in several of the headings 84.58 to 84.63 or in several of the headings 84.69 to 84.72.
>
> Composite machines consisting of two or more machines or appliances of different kinds, fitted together to form a whole, consecutively or simultaneously performing separate functions which are generally complementary and are described in different headings of Section XVI, are also classified according to the principal function of the composite machine.
>
> The following are examples of such composite machines: printing machines with a subsidiary machine for holding the paper (heading 84.43); a cardboard box making machine combined with an auxiliary machine for printing a name or simple design (heading 84.41); industrial furnaces combined with lifting or handling machinery (heading 84.17 or 85.14); cigarette making machinery combined with subsidiary packaging machinery (Heading 84.78).
>
> For the purposes of the above provisions, machines of different kinds are taken to be fitted together to form a whole when incorporated one in the other or mounted one on the other; or mounted on a common base or frame or in a common housing.
>
> Assemblies of machines should not be taken to be fitted together to form a whole unless the machines are designed to be permanently attached either to each other or to a common base, frame, housing etc. This excludes assemblies which are of a temporary nature or are not normally built as a composite machine.....
>
> Note 3 to Section XVI need not be invoked when the composite machine is covered as such by a particular heading, for example, some types of air conditioning machines (heading 84.15).....

In Mrs. Hamilton's submission the principal function of the PCTV as a "composite machine" is as an Automatic Data Processing Machine. She contended that principal function can be deduced from the following areas: Design; Development Strategy; Manufacture; Cost; Marketing; Advertising; Retailing; Price; Packaging and presentation; Technical and active functionality.

Further and in the alternative she submitted that the PCTV is within the definition of "composite goods" in GIR 3(b). As will have been seen, where such goods cannot be classified by reference to GIR 3(a), GIR 3(b) lays down that they "shall be classified as if they consisted of the material or component which gives them their essential character in so far as this criterion is applicable". (emphasis added).

She relied upon HSEN (IX) to GIR 3(b). This states:

> "(IX) For the purposes of this Rule, composite goods made up of different components shall be taken to mean not only those in which the components are attached to each other to form a practically inseparable whole but also those with separate components, provided these components are adapted one to the other and are mutually complementary and that together they form a whole which would not normally be offered for sale in separate parts.
>
> Examples of the latter category of goods are:
>
> (1) Ashtrays consisting of a stand incorporating a removable ash bowl.
>
> (2) Household spice racks consisting of a specially designed frame (usually of wood) and an appropriate number of empty spice jars of suitable shape and size.
>
> As a general rule, the components of these composite goods are put up in a common packing".

The HSEN (VI) to GIR 3(b) says that this "second method" relates only to (i) Mixtures, (ii) Composite goods consisting of different materials, (iii) Composite goods consisting of different components, (iv) Goods put up in sets for retail sale. It applies only if Rule 3(a) fails.

HSEN (VII) to GIR 3(b) says that in all those cases the goods are to be classified as if they consisted of the material or component which gives them their essential character, insofar as this criterion is applicable.

HSEN (VIII) to GIR 3(b) then states:

> "The factor which determines essential character will vary as between different kinds of goods. It may, for example, be determined by the nature of the material or component, its bulk, quantity, weight or value, or, by the role of a constituent material in relation to the use of the goods".

Mrs. Hamilton submitted that the same evidence and criteria as she relied upon to establish the "principal function" of the PCTV were relevant and established that it was the ADPM component which gave it its "essential character".

Approaching the determination of the appropriate classification by that route, Section Note 3 to Section XVI requires the PCTV to be classified under 84.71 "Automatic Data Processing Machines" because, if Mrs. Hamilton is right, that is its "principal function". GIR 1 applies and that is an end of the matter. GIR 3 does not come into the picture because the terms of the headings and of the section note to Section XVI "do otherwise require" and they are paramount.

But, if it is not possible to determine its principal function as a composite machine, so that the PCTV is *prima facie* classifiable under two or more headings, one does go to GIR 3, and in particular GIR 3(b), and looks for the material or component which gives the PCTV as "composite goods" its essential character if that criterion *is* applicable.

It is only when that fails, and Mrs. Hamilton maintains that criterion is applicable and determines the classification of the PCTV as an ADPM, that GIR 3(c) can operate, as the Commissioners say that it has to be operated, to classify the PCTV under 85.28 "Television Receivers" as "the heading which occurs last in numerical order among those which equally merit consideration".

Mr. Davies put at the forefront of his submissions on behalf of the Commissioners that there are wider principles governing classification of goods identified in the case law of the European Court of Justice. First, there is the principle of legal certainty at the point of customs clearance. Thus "the preference is, in the interests of legal certainty and ease of verification, to have recourse to criteria for classification based on the objective characteristics and properties, as defined in the wording of the headings of the Common Customs Tariff and of the notes to the sections and chapters, which can be ascertained at the point of customs clearance"- paragraph 18 of the judgment in the *Develop Dr. Eisbein* case *(supra).* He also referred to the court's judgments in Case No. C-233/88 *Gifs Van de Kolk Douane Expediteur BV* v *Inspecteur der Invoerrechten en Accijnsen* (1990) ECR1-265; paras 12 and 16; and Case No. 200/84 *Erika Daiber* v. *Hauptzollamt Reutlingen* (1985) ECR 3363; para 13. Second, there is the objective of securing uniformity in the interpretation and application of the Harmonized System relating, in particular, to the application of the nomenclature. Mr. Davies pointed to the institutionalized and permanent mechanism set up to this end under the Brussels Convention (which continues under the Harmonized System) as explained in the Opinion of the Advocate General (Tesauro) in the *Van de Kolk* case *(supra)* at (1990) ECR-1 at pp. 273-5.

Mr. Davies submitted that there is no one heading which adequately classifies the PCTV. The classifications in the Tariff inevitably lag behind the advances in technology.

In his submission the route to the classification of the PCTV is through GIR 1 to the texts of the headings and relative section and chapter notes. ADPMs within heading 84.71 are narrowly defined; they do not equate with personal computers and, as the HSEN to that heading explains, that heading does not cover parts of the personal computer working in conjunction with an ADPM and having a specific function. Note 3 to Section XVI applies the principal function test both to "composite machines consisting of two or more machines fitted together to form a whole", the description contended for by the appellant, and "other machines adapted for the purpose of performing two or more alternative functions", as the Commissioners have regarded the PCTV. Either way classification is on the basis of treating the machine "as if consisting only of that component or as being that machine which performs the principal function".

Mr. Davies contended that it was not possible in relation to the PCTV to discern the component or machine which performs the principal function, that is to say a component or machine falling within a heading of the Tariff. The Commissioners on review had identified in relation to the PCTV four classifications in the Tariff based on function: 84.71 ADPMs; 85.19 "Other sound reproducing apparatus"; 85.21 "Video recording or reproducing apparatus"; and 85.28 "Television Receivers". None of these functions objectively considered could, in his submission, be said to be the principal one. The subjective tests put forward by Mrs. Hamilton are, in his view, manifestly undesirable: the proper approach to function is to determine what the machine does.

Where, as he maintained is the case with the PCTV, it is not possible to determine the principal function, HSEN (VI) to Section Note 3 explains that it is necessary to apply GIR 3(c), this being a case "where the context does not otherwise require". The HSEN does not alter the wording of the headings and notes but is entirely consistent with them in promoting certainty and consistency and uniformity in interpretation. The HSEN, which contains nothing to require a different approach for composite machines where it is not possible to determine a principal function, then makes the point of entry into GIR 3 specifically rule 3(c) - i.e. the last in the hierarchical structure of that rule which applies only if rules 3(a) and 3(b) fail in classification (see HSEN (1) to GIR 3) - and 3(c) provides for the machine to be classified under the heading which appears last in numerical order among those which equally merit consideration.

That provided a somewhat crude classification but one which had the merit of producing consistency and ease of verification.

If he was wrong on that, and GIR 3(b) did come into the picture, Mr. Davies observed that it is very difficult conceptually to think of determining that component which gives the PCTV as "composite goods" its "essential character" when, by definition, it has not been possible to determine the component which performs the principal function. But it was equally impossible to determine objectively what component gives the PCTV its "essential character". The PCTV is both a PC and a television set.

Mr. Davies introduced, by way of illustration of a similar result by the correct application of the rules, Commission Regulation (EEC) No. 754/94 of 30th March 1994 concerning the classification of certain goods in the combined nomenclature. That regulation, as shown by the recitals, was made having regard to Article 9 of Council Regulation (EEC) No. 2658/87 establishing the CN. It also recites that "... pursuant to the [general rules of interpretation set down in that Council Regulation], the goods described in the column 1 of the table annexed to the Present Regulation must be classified under the appropriate CN codes indicated in column 2, by virtue of the reasons set out in column 3".

Products 4 and 5 in the table are both classified under heading 85 21 90 00 "Video recording or reproducing apparatus, whether or not incorporating a video tuner", sub-heading "other" and for the following reasons:

> "Classification is determined by the provisions of General Rules 1, 3(c) and 6 for the interpretation of the combined nomenclature, Note 5 to Chapter 84 to the combined nomenclature as well as the texts of CN codes 85 21 and 85 21 90 00."
>
> General Rule 6 applies the rules in GIR 1 at sub-heading levels.

The description of product 4 refers to it as "A multi-media interactive system in a single housing ... capable of reproducing on a monitor, loudspeakers or headphones, audio, graphics text and video data recorded on compact disc". An infra-red remote control forms part of the system and through "the addition of other accessories (e.g. disk drive, keyboard and mouse) it may be used as a personal computer". The list of components shows a printed circuit board, including a digital processing unit (CPU, 1MB RAM and 512 KB ROM), a graphics component, a video component, a sound component with own CD audio unit, and a CD ROM.

The full description of product 5 is:

> "5. A CD interactive system in a single housing for the reproduction of digitally recorded pictures and sound for television by means of a laser optical reading system. It is supplied with a mouse and infra-red remote control unit.
>
> It contains a control unit that processes signals from the playing unit, from the remote control or from the mouse unit, to the television display and loudspeaker unit, enabling interaction with picture and sound".

The question for us to decide first is thus whether the PCTV can be classified under a heading in Section XVI of the Combined Nomenclature applying Section Note 3 because that heading describes the machine which performs the principal function. It seems to us that Mr. Davies was right to stress that one has to focus on the headings. Section Note 5, in defining the expression "machine" makes that abundantly clear. Also Chapter Note 5A, as Mr. Davies pointed out, defines an "ADPM" for the purpose of heading 84.71 in a very specific way; one cannot approach the question that we have to decide by, as it were, treating the PCTV as if what is not a TV is all an "ADPM" within heading 84.71. Whilst we accept that what Mr. Burton did was in his words to put a TV on top of a PC, it is misleading for our present purpose to refer to the PC element of the PCTV as if it equated with an "ADPM" as defined. This, as we see it, lessens the value of Professor Spence's evidence interesting though that contribution was.

Although there is a difference between the parties as to which limb it falls under, there is no dispute at this point in the argument that we have to look for that machine or component - that is to say component machine - of the PCTV which performs the principal function. The test is not so much what it is used for but what does it do.

In our judgement it is not possible in these terms and given the approach which we are constrained to adopt to determine the principal function of the PCTV. Although Mrs. Hamilton was right to point out that the cases in the European Court of Justice relied on by Mr. Davies show that there are limits to these principles, the objectives of legal certainty, uniformity of interpretation and ease of verification at the point of customs clearance are very important. Much of the matter relied upon by Mrs. Hamilton is in our opinion far too subjective to serve as criteria for determining what is a machine's principal function. The PCTV functions equally as a high quality TV and as a state of the art PC.

It is perhaps worth noting, although it does not form the basis for our decision, that HSEN (VI) to Section Note 3 in describing composite machines classified according to their principal function (and, agreeing with Mrs. Hamilton, in our judgement the PCTV is a "composite machine" and not an other, multi-function machine, for the purposes of Section Note 3) gives examples of where there is clearly a principal function for the composite machine and the function of the other machines within the composite machine are equally clearly auxiliary or subsidiary. Viewed objectively the TV function of the PCTV is not an auxiliary or subsidiary function of an ADPM.

It is also common ground that if it is not possible to determine the principal function one is thrown back into GIR 3. It is also common ground that GIR 3 provides a hierarchical approach and that the first sub-rule (a) does not apply. The dispute is as to the point of entry, GIR 3(b) or GIR 3(c). If one goes straight to 3(c), the Commissioners on the basis of our judgement so far have applied the correct classification.

Mr. Davies contends that the PCTV is a multi-function machine and that in explaining Section Note 3 HSEN (VI), as we understand the argument, shows that the terms of that Section Note require the point of entry to be GIR 3(c) and the conclusion must be the same even if the PCTV is to be regarded instead as being a composite machine.

We reject that argument. HSEN (VI) quite plainly is dealing with multi-function machines separately from composite machines. We have also determined that the PCTV is not a multi-function machine, by which is meant, in the terms of Section Note 3, "other"- that is in contrast to "composite machines consisting of two or more machines fitted together to form a whole"- "machines adapted for the purpose of performing two or more complementary functions". HSEN (VI) gives as examples of multi-function machines - "tools for working metal using interchangeable tools, which enable them to carry out different machinery operations (e.g. milling, boring, lapping)". It describes "composite machines" as "consisting of two or more machines or appliances of different kinds, fitted together to form a whole, consecutively or simultaneously performing separate functions, which are generally complementary and are described in different headings of Section XVI ...".

Making the necessary transition from mechanical machines as contemplated in the HSEN to the electronic machines before us, in our opinion a "composite machine" best describes the PCTV.

It also seems to us that Mrs. Hamilton was right to submit that the absence of a reference to GIR 3(c) in HSEN (VI) where it deals with composite machines is not accidental. The kind of multi-function machine contemplated, at least the kind of machine referred to in the example, seems to be one where it is very unlikely that it will be possible to determine a principal function let alone that machine which gives it its essential character. The latter may be possible in respect of a composite machine, although, as we have said, going by the examples it will be very much more likely to be able to determine a principal function. It is also, however, not difficult to see how in relation to the examples given of composite machines one could reasonably say that the machine performing the principal function also gives the machine its essential character.

We thus turn to GIR 3(b) which applies the "essential character" test "in so far as this criterion is applicable". We are prepared to accept that the PCTV can fairly be described as coming within the description "Composite goods consisting of different components" in HSEN (VI) to GIR 3(b) and as further explained in HSEN (IX) to that Rule (although the PCTV is a long way removed from the examples there given).

HSEN (VIII) to GIR 3(b) admits of a number of factors which may be relevant in determining the essential character of composite goods, some of which may well not assist in providing ease of verification but all of which are susceptible to objective evaluation. Although these factor admit, perhaps, more of the matters which Mrs. Hamilton relied upon, there is still force in Mr. Davies' submission that, when one has passed the point of being able to determine the component which performs the principal function of composite goods, in this case a composite machine, it is very difficult conceptually then to set about determining what component machine gives it its essential character.

For those reasons we doubt whether that criterion is applicable in classifying a machine such as the PCTV. But, even if it is, we are not persuaded, having carefully reviewed all the evidence, that it is the ADPM, as such, which gives the PCTV its essential character. It is, as Mr. Davies submitted, a new kind of hybrid machine which is both a PC and a TV, and neither gives it its essential character.

The appeal will accordingly be dismissed.

This does appear to be a case where the understandable desire of the importer to have goods classified as accurately as possible, preferably of course in a heading which relates to the item as a whole, comes into conflict with the objectives of the Harmonized System and Common Tariff in providing uniformity of interpretation, that conflict arising because rapid advances in technology with which the CN cannot keep pace produces new machines different in kind even if combining machines and functions which were historically separate.

The parties are at liberty to apply to the tribunal for a further deliberation if they are unable to agree about costs.

R.K. Miller CB

Chairman

ANNEX 4

SUMMARY TABLE OF EVIDENCE SUBMITTED BY THE UNITED STATES

TABLE 1

SUMMARY OF BTIS ISSUED BY EC MEMBER STATES

No.	*Member State*	*Compe-tent Customs Authority*	*Holder*	*Total no of BTIs*	*BTI reference number*	*Summarized Product Description*	*Date of Applica-tion*	*Date of start of validity*	*Classification*
	DEN-MARK	NA*	NA	4					
1.					DK 47068	Adapter unit to be installed in digital data processors (Standard PC) so that these will be able to exchange coded data through a local network and function as in- and output units for another connected PC or central unit	NA	30/11/94	8473.3010
2.					DK 47069	Adapter unit to be installed in digital data processors (Standard PC) so that these will be able to exchange coded data through a local network and function as in- and output units for another connected PC or central unit	NA	1/12/94	8473.3010
3.					DK 47070	Adapter unit to be installed in digital data processors (Standard PC) so that these will be able to exchange coded data through a local network and function as in- and output units for another connected PC or central unit.	NA	1/12/94	8473.3010

No.	*Member State*	*Competent Customs Authority*	*Holder*	*Total no of BTIs*	*BTI reference number*	*Summarized Product Description*	*Date of Application*	*Date of start of validity*	*Classification*
4.					DK 47071	Adapter unit to be installed in digital data processors (Standard PC) so that these will be able to exchange coded data through a local network and function as in- and output units for another connected PC or central unit.	NA	6/12/94	8473.3010
	FRANCE	Direction Générale des Douanes et Droits Indirects		8					
5.			NA		FR 16190199401777	Cartes modules électroniques destinées à être montées dans le châssis d'un concentrateur pour réseau ETHERNET.	16/8/94	20/9/94	8473.30109002
6.			NA		FR 16190199401776	Châssis de concentrateurs destiné à reçevoir des cartes modules électroniqes pour réseau ETHERNET.	16/8/94	20/9/94	8473 309000900
7.			NA		FR 16190199400755	Pont routeur permettant l'interconnexion de réseaux locaux d'entreprise (Ethernet, Token Ring, FFDI) qui utilisent des protocoles différents de commande de la liaison logique.	31/3/94	9/5/94	8471.9910.00
8.			NA		FR 16190199301442	Pont distant ETHERNET se présentant sous la forme d'un boîtier fermé incluant un logiciel interne.	24/9/93	21/10/93	8471 99 100000K

No.	*Member State*	*Compe-tent Customs Authority*	*Holder*	*Total no of BTIs*	*BTI reference number*	*Summarized Product Description*	*Date of Applica-tion*	*Date of start of validity*	*Classification*
9.			NA		FR 16190199500062	Unité périphérique d'adaptation se connectant directement sur le Réseau ETHERNET ou TOKEN RING, se présentant sous la forme d'un boîtier.	19/12/94	13/1/95	8471 99 100000K
10.			BT France SA		FR 16190199401349	Equipements destinés à servir de noeuds du réseau de la gamme tymnet. .	2/6/94	29/6/94	8471 99 100000K
11.			BT France SA		FR 16190199401911	Compresseur de données numériques permettant la transmission de la voix par paquet à haute vitesse en minimisant le côut des télécommunications.	9/9/94	23/12/94	8471 99 100000K
12.			BT France SA		FR 16190199401350	Equipements destinés à servir de noeuds du réseau de la gamme tymnet.	2/6/94	4/7/94	8471 99 100000K
	IRELAND	Irish Customs and Excise Branch	Cabletron Systems Ltd.	32			28/4/93	12/7/93	8471 99 10000
13.					IE 93N4-14-2310-01-05	Desktop Network (DNI) Interface Cards			
14.					IE 93N4-14-2310-02-05	Desktop Network (DNI) Interface Cards			
15.					IE 93N4-14-2310-03-05	Desktop Network (DNI) Interface Cards			
16.					IE 93N4-14-2313-01-05	Token Ring Standalone Passive Concentrator			
17.					IE 93N4-14-2313-02-05	Standalone Hubs			
18.					IE 93N4-14-2313-03-05	Multi Media Access Centre			

No.	*Member State*	*Compe-tent Customs Authority*	*Holder*	*Total no of BTIs*	*BTI reference number*	*Summarized Product Description*	*Date of Applica-tion*	*Date of start of validity*	*Classification*
19.					IE 93N4-14-2313-04-05	Standalone 24-port			
20.					IE 93N4-14-2313-05-05	Multi Media Access Centre Hubs			
21.					IE 93N4-14-2314-01-07	Ethernet-to-ethernet local bridges			
22.					IE 93N4-14-2314-02-07	Remote Bridge			
23.					IE 93N4-14-2314-03-07	Intelligent repeater Bridging Module			
24.					IE 93N4-14-2314-04-07	Ethernet Management Module			
25.					IE 93N4-14-2314-05-07	Multi-Protocol Router/Bridge (CRM-R)			
26.					IE 93N4-14-2314-06-07	Multi-Protocol Router/Bridge (CRM-L)			
27.					IE 93N4-14-2314-07-07	Local Talk to Ethernet Router/Repeater Module			
28.					IE 93N4-14-2315-01-03	Ethernet Local Repeater			
29.					IE 93N4-14-2315-02-03	Fibre Optic Repeater			
30.					IE 93N4-14-2315-03-03	Multiport Receivers			
31.					IE 93N4-14-2316-01-14	Intelligent Repeater Modules			
32.					IE 93N4-14-2316-02-14	Coaxial Repeater Module			
33.					IE 93N4-14-2316-03-14	Fibre Optic Modules			
34.					IE 93N4-14-2316-04-14	Twisted Pair Media Interface Modules			
35.					IE 93N4-14-2316-05-14	Media Interface Modules in a Local Area Network			
36.					IE 93N4-14-2316-06-14	Ethernet Terminal Server Modules			
37.					IE 93N4-14-2316-07-14	Multiport Transceiver Media Interface Module			
38.					IE 93N4-14-2316-08-14	Token Ring Management Module			
39.					IE 93N4-14-2316-09-14	Token Ring Media Interface Modules			
40.					IE 93N4-14-2316-10-14	Active Repeater Media Interface			

No.	*Member State*	*Compe-tent Customs Authority*	*Holder*	*Total no of BTIs*	*BTI reference number*	*Summarized Product Description*	*Date of Applica-tion*	*Date of start of validity*	*Classification*
						Modules			
41.					IE 93N4-14-2316-11-14	Token Ring Media Filter			
42.					IE 93N4-14-2316-12-14	Interface Modules			
43.					IE 93N4-14-2316-13-14	Concentrator Modules			
44.					IE 93N4-14-2316-14-14	Distributed Network Server Module			
	NETHER-LANDS	NA	NA	4					
45.					NL 51446	A 16-bits ISA bus Ethernet LAN adapter in the form of a computer built-in card.	NA	25/4/95	8473.3010
46.					NL 51447	A 16-bits ISA bus Ethernet LAN adapter in the form of a computer built-in card.	NA	25/4/95	8473.3010
47.					NL 51455	A LAN adapter card in the form of a computer built-in card	NA	25/4/95	8473.3010
48.					NL 51456	A 16-bits Arenet Ethernet LAN card in the form of a computer built-in card	NA	25/4/95	8473.3010

* Not available

TABLE 2

OTHER CLASSIFICATION DECISIONS BY EC MEMBER STATES

No.	*Member State*	*Competent Customs Authority*	*Directed towards*	*Form*	*Reference Number*	*Summarized Product Description*	*Date of Application*	*Classification*
	UNITED KINGDOM							
1.		HM Customs and Excise	NA	letter	Ref. TC11/92	LAN adapter cards	20/3/92	8471 99 10 900
2.		HM Customs and Excise	NA	letter	Ref. SO1/1358/92		28/7/93	
						22 types of Ethernet LAN boards		8473 3010 0 90
						12 types of token ring LAN boards		8473 301 0090
						6 types of repeaters imported in complete units		8471 99 10900
						5 types of repeaters imported in Board form		8473 301 0090
3.		HM Customs and Excise	NA	letter	Ref. CDO8/740/87		19/2/1988	
						Multiport repeater		8471 999 0090
						Local repeater		8471 999 0090

TABLE 3

OTHER TYPES OF EVIDENCE

No.	*Form*	*Place/Occasion*	*Date*	*Product Description*	*Classification*
1.	Belgium: Shipping Invoice	-	19/9/95	"onderdelen voor computers"	8473 3010
2.	France: Shipping Invoice	-	21/2/96	"accessoires ordinateurs"	8473.3010
3.	Statement by the representative of Sweden	57th meeting of the tariff and statistical nomenclature section of the Customs Code Committee	29-30/6/95	LAN equipment	Prior to accession, under tariff heading 84.71
4.	Statement by the representative of Finland	77th meeting of the tariff and statistical nomenclature section of the Customs Code Committee.	18/4 /96	LAN equipment	Prior to accession, under tariff heading 84.71
5.	Statement by the representative of France	57th meeting of the tariff and statistical nomenclature section of the Customs Code Committee	29-30/6/95	LAN bridges, routers, hubs, repeaters, media interface modules, and multimedia access centre	Tariff heading 84.71
6.	Letter from 3Com	Providing information requested by Director of Customs Affairs, USTR	8/7/97	LAN equipment and units thereof exported to UK between 1991 and 1994	Under tariff headings 84.71 and 84.73, respectively.
7.	Letter from Bay Networks	Providing information requested by Director of Customs Affairs, USTR	9/7/97	LAN equipment and units thereof exported to UK and Ireland since 1992.	Under tariff headings 84.71 and 84.73, respectively.
8.	Letter from Cisco Systems	Providing information requested by Director of Customs Affairs, USTR	9/7/97	LAN products exported during 1991 to 1994 to the UK and Ireland.	Under Chapter 84.

No.	*Form*	*Place/Occasion*	*Date*	*Product Description*	*Classification*
9.	Letter from Cabletron Systems	Providing information requested by Director of Customs Affairs, USTR	3/7/97	LAN products shipped during 1990 and 1994 to the UK and 1992 and 1994 to Ireland	Treated under tariff heading 84.71.
10.	European Court of Justice ruling (ECJ case C-11/93)	Siemens Nixdorf Informations system and the Hauptozollamt (principal customs office) Augsburg.	19/5/94	Colour Monitors	Ruled that colour monitors capable of accepting a signal only from the central processing unit of an automatic data-processing machine and not capable of reproducing a colour image from a composite video signal were to be classified under heading 8471 of the Combined Nomenclature of the Common Customs Tariff.

ANNEX 5

ITA CLASSIFICATION*

Network equipment in the ITA

Network equipment: Local Area Network (LAN) and Wide Area Network (WAN) apparatus, including those products dedicated for use solely or principally to permit the interconnection of automatic data processing machines and units thereof for a network that is used primarily for the sharing of resources such as central processor units, data storage devices and input or output units - including adaptors, hubs, in-line repeaters, converters, concentrators, bridges and routers, and printed circuit assemblies for physical incorporation into automatic data processing machines and units thereof.

Participant	Tariff Classification
Australia	847160, 847180, 847330, 85175010, 85175090
Canada	84711000, 84713000, 84714100, 84714910, 84714920, 84714931, 84714932, 84714933, 84714934, 84714935, 84714936, 84714939, 84714941, 84714942, 84714949, 84714951, 84714952, 84714959, 84714961, 84714969, 84714971, 84714972, 84714979, 84715000, 84716010, 84716021, 84716022, 84716023, 84716024, 84716025, 84716026, 84716029, 84716031, 84716032, 84716039, 84716050, 84716090, 84717010, 84717090, 84718010, 84718091, 84718099, 84719010, 84719090, 84733010, 84713021, 84713022, 84713023, 84713091, 84713099
Costa Rica	8473
Estonia	847150, 847160, 851750
EC	84715090, 84716090, 85175090
Hong Kong China	84718000
Iceland	847150, 847160, 847180, 847330, 851750
India	847190, 847330
Indonesia	847190
Japan	847180, 847330, 851750
Korea	851750
Macao	84715000, 84716000, 84718000, 84733000, 85175010, 85175020, 85175030, 85175090
Malaysia	ex847150000, ex847160000, ex847170000, ex847180000
New Zealand	847160, 847180, 847330, 851750
Norway	8471500, 8471600, 8471800, 8517800
Romania	84715090, 84716090, 85175090

Participant	Tariff Classification
Separate Customs Territory of Taiwan, Penghu, Kinmen & Matzo	84715000, 84716010, 84716020, 84716030, 84716090, 84718000, 84733010, 84733021, 84733029
Singapore	847150
Switzerland	85175000, 85178000, 85179010, 85179090
Thailand	847150, 847180
Turkey	84715090, 84716090, 85175090
USA	84718010, 84714960
Poland	847150900, 847160900, 851750900
Israel	84715090, 84716090, 85175000
Czech Republic	84715090, 84716090, 85175090
Slovak Republic	84715090, 84716090, 85175090
Panama	84719200, 84719300, 84719900, 84733000, 85044010, 85174000, 85366900, 85442000
Philippines	847110, 847130, 847141, 847149, 847150, 847160, 847170, 847180, 847190, 851750
El Salvador	84714900, 84718000

*Table submitted by the EC.

ANNEX 6

SUMMARY TABLE OF EVIDENCE SUBMITTED BY THE EC

TABLE 1

SUMMARY OF BTIs ISSUED BY EC MEMBER STATES

No.	*Member state*	*Competent Customs Authority*	*Holder*	*Total no of BTIs*	*BTI reference number*	*Summarized Product Description*	*Date of Application*	*Date of start of validity*	*Classification*
	FRANCE	Direction Générale des douanes et droits indirects.	NA*	3					
1.					FR 16190199401918	"Routeur d'accès dans les réseaux de type Ethernet permettant de diriger l'information vers des sites éloignés via le réseau public commuté, et vice-versa".	9/9/94	27/9/94 - 18/6/96	8517 4000 0009 S
2.					FR 16270199402539	"Routeur multiprotocole permettant d'interconnecter de réseaux ETHERNET ou IEEE 802.3."	3/10/94	28/11/94 - 18/6/96	8517 4000 0009 S

No.	*Member state*	*Competent Customs Authority*	*Holder*	*Total no of BTIs*	*BTI reference number*	*Summarized Product Description*	*Date of Application*	*Date of start of validity*	*Classification*
3.					FR 06190199102248	"Serveur de terminal multiprotocoles pour les échanges terminaux/ordinateur central."	1/10/91	3/2/92 - 12/3/96	8517 4000 9009 C
4.	GERMANY	Oberfinanz Direction Munchen	NA	1	DE/B/01242/92/02 01	Token ring adapter.	2/8/92	18/1/92	851782000000
	NETHER-LANDS	Belasting-dienst	NA	30					
5.					NL 199109209450089-0	Apparatus, capable of making multiple connections between different components of a computer network.	19/9/91	31/1/92 - 17/1/97	8517 8200 90000
6.					NL 199109209450091-0	Apparatus, capable of making multiple connections between different components of a computer network.	19/9/91	31/1/92 - 17/1/97	85178200 90000
7.					NL 199109209450115-0	Apparatus, capable of making multiple connections between different components of a computer network.	19/9/91	31/1/92 - 17/1/97	85178200 90000

No.	*Member state*	*Competent Customs Authority*	*Holder*	*Total no of BTIs*	*BTI reference number*	*Summarized Product Description*	*Date of Application*	*Date of start of validity*	*Classification*
8.					NL 199109209450114-0	Apparatus, capable of making multiple connections between different components of a computer network.	19/9/91	31/1/92 - 17/1/97	85178200 90000
9.					NL199109209450090-0	Apparatus, capable of making multiple connections between different components of a computer network.	19/9/91	31/1/92 - 17/1/97	85178200 90000
10.					NL 199109209450089-0	Apparatus, capable of making multiple connections between different components of a computer network.	19/9/91	31/1/92 - 17/1/97	85178200 90000
11.					NL 199109209450113-0	Apparatus, capable of making multiple connections between different components of a computer network.	19/9/91	31/1/92 - 17/1/97	85178200 90000
12.					NL 199204239450098-0	Apparatus in a separate housing intended to amplify or to transform signals on certain points of a network.	23/4/92	7/9/92 - 17/1/97	85178200 90000

No.	*Member state*	*Competent Customs Authority*	*Holder*	*Total no of BTIs*	*BTI reference number*	*Summarized Product Description*	*Date of Application*	*Date of start of validity*	*Classification*
13.					NL 199204239450099-0	Apparatus in a separate housing intended to inter-connect sub-networks into one network or to increase the effective scope of a network.	23/4/92	7/9/92 - 17/1/97	85178200 90000
14.					NL 199109209450092-0	Apparatus, capable of making multiple connec-tions between different components of a computer network.	19/9/91	31/1/92 - 17/1/97	85178200 90000
15.					NL 199307219450116-0	Apparatus (integrated switching system) capable of making multiple con-nections between different components of a com-puter-network and be-tween networks.	6/7/93	7/9/93 - 17/1/97	85178290
16.					NL 199307219450115-0	Apparatus (integrated switching system) capable of making multiple con-nections between different components of a com-puter-network and be-tween networks.	6/7/93	7/9/93 - 17/1/97	85178290

No.	*Member state*	*Competent Customs Authority*	*Holder*	*Total no of BTIs*	*BTI reference number*	*Summarized Product Description*	*Date of Application*	*Date of start of validity*	*Classification*
17.					NL 199307219450114-0	Apparatus capable of making multiple connections between different components of a computer-network and between networks.	6/7/93	7/9/93 - 17/1/97	85178290
18.					NL 199307219450113-0	Apparatus (x 25 data communication network system) intended to make multiple connections between different components of a computer network.	6/7/93	7/9/93 - 17/1/97	85178290
19.					NL 199307249450123-0	Electronic multiplex apparatus in a housing.	14/7/93	23/11/93 - 17/1/97	8517829000000
20.					NL 199307249450122-0	Electronic apparatus consisting of a system housing, power supply, a processor card and three connection cards for ethernet or token ring connections.	14/7/93	23/11/93 - 17/1/97	8517829000000
21.					NL 199307249450121-0	Electronic apparatus consisting of a system housing, power supply, a processor card and a connection card.	14/7/93	23/11/93 - 17/1/97	8517829000000

No.	*Member state*	*Competent Customs Authority*	*Holder*	*Total no of BTIs*	*BTI reference number*	*Summarized Product Description*	*Date of Application*	*Date of start of validity*	*Classification*
22.					NL 199307249450120-0	Electronic apparatus consisting of a system housing, power supply, connection card, for token ring and FDDI.	14/7/93	23/11/93 - 17/1/97	8517829000000
23.					NL 199307249450119-0	Network steering unit.	14/7/93	6/12/93 -	8517829000000
24.					NL 199302089450020-0	Apparatus in a separate housing intended to amplify or to transform signals on a certain points of a network.	8/2/93	19/2/93 - 17/7/97	8517829000000
25.					NL199302089450040-0	Apparatus capable of making multiple connections between different components of a computer network.	8/2/93	19/2/93 - 17/7/97	8517829000000
26.					NL 199302089450039-0	Apparatus capable of making multiple connections between different components of a computer network.	8/2/93	19/2/93 - 17/7/97	8517829000000
27.					NL 199302089450038-0	Apparatus capable of making multiple connections between different components of a computer network.	8/2/93	19/2/93 - 17/7/97	8517829000000

No.	*Member state*	*Competent Customs Authority*	*Holder*	*Total no of BTIs*	*BTI reference number*	*Summarized Product Description*	*Date of Application*	*Date of start of validity*	*Classification*
28.					NL 199302089450037-0	Apparatus capable of making multiple connections between different components of a computer network.	8/2/93	19/2/93 - 17/7/97	8517829000000
29.					NL 199302089450036-0	Apparatus capable of making multiple connections between different components of a computer network.	8/2/93	19/2/93 - 17/7/97	8517829000000
30.					NL 199302089450035-0	Apparatus capable of making multiple connections between different components of a computer network.	8/2/93	19/2/93 - 17/7/97	8517829000000
31.					NL 199302089450034-0	Apparatus capable of making multiple connections between different components of a computer network.	8/2/93	19/2/93 - 17/7/97	8517829000000
32.					NL 199302089450021-0	Apparatus in a separate housing intended to interconnect sub-networks into one network or to increase the effective scope of a network	8/2/93	19/2/93 - 17/7/97	8517829000000
33.					NL 199308069450129-0	Network steering unit to steer from 4 to 8 channels.	5/8/93	3/1/94 - 17/1/97	8517829

No.	*Member state*	*Competent Customs Authority*	*Holder*	*Total no of BTIs*	*BTI reference number*	*Summarized Product Description*	*Date of Application*	*Date of start of validity*	*Classification*
34.					NL 199308069450128-0	Network steering unit to support a maximum of a 4 LAN/WAN interfaces	5/8/93	3/1/94 - 17/1/97	85178290
	UNITED KINGDOM	HM Customs and Excise	NA	10					
35.					UK 57112	ILAN. A universal router that provides internet-working between LANs and wide area networks (WANs)	24/11/93	17/2/94 - 21/2/96	8517 8290 000
36.					UK 57127	Microcom bridge router 6000 series.	27/1/94	17/2/94 - 21/2/96	8517 8290 000
37.					UK 57128	Microannex NCSs.	4/2/94	17/2/94 - 16/2/96	8517 8290 000
38.					UK 57141	Access/one remote multi-protocol bridge/router.	7/12/93	18/2/94 - 16/2/96	8517 8290 000
39.					UK 57142	ASM 6301 Access/one remote ethernet bridge.	7/12/93	18/2/94 - 16/2/96	8517 8290 000
40.					UK 57110	Crossbow FX 6600. This is a network cabling hub that supports up to 14 LANs	24/11/93	17/2/94 - 21/2/96	8517 8290 000
41.					UK 55711	CISCO routers	11/10/93	6/12/93 - 16/2/96	8517 8290 000
42.					UK 55700	Intelligent Network Processors	15/10/93	6/12/93 - 16/2/96	8517 8290 000

No.	*Member state*	*Competent Customs Authority*	*Holder*	*Total no of BTIs*	*BTI reference number*	*Summarized Product Description*	*Date of Application*	*Date of start of validity*	*Classification*
43.					UK 55704	Modulus series. This is a family of data communication products. This has a variety of products which include multiplexers, processors, bridges, pads etc	15/10/93	6/12/93 - 16/2/96	8517 8290 000
44.					UK 57108	Magnum 100 - Multprotocol time-division multiplexer.	24/11/93	17/2/94 - 21/2/96	8517 8290 000

* Not available.

TABLE 2

OTHER CLASSIFICATION DECISIONS BY EC MEMBER STATES

No.	*Member State*	*Competent Customs Authority*	*Directed Towards*	*Form*	*Reference Number*	*Summarized Product Description*	*Date of Application*	*Classification*
1.	GERMANY	Bundesfinanzhof	Transtec	Judgement	NA	Multiplexers, bridge, server and three different repeaters	17/9/91	85.17

ANNEX 7

TRADE DATA*

Heading	UR Base	1994	1995	1996
CN 851782	57,175	337,605	494,853	not available
CN 847199	1,244,068	1,385,569	731,533	not available
CN 847330	2,848,716	3,602,702	3,464,127	not available
USX 847199	417,696	1,071,967	1,407,577	4,361,160
USX 851782	15,825	24,189	51,962	568,463
USX 847330	4,308,369	5,126,879	6,592,151	6,810,744

Notes:

(1) Full year EU import data are not released until late in the following year. Some member States are slow in reporting such data to EUROSTAT.

(2) Headings 847199 and 851782 do not exist in the 1996 revision to the Harmonized System. Products previously entering under heading 847199 now enter under 847180, 847190 or 847149; products that previously entered under heading 851782 now enter under 851721, 851750 and 851780. The figures cited above for US exports in 847199 and 851782 represent the total of the new headings.

* Table submitted by the United States.

EUROPEAN COMMUNITIES - MEASURES AFFECTING THE IMPORTATION OF CERTAIN POULTRY PRODUCTS

Report of the Appellate Body

WT/DS69/AB/R

Adopted by the Dispute Settlement Body on 23 July 1998

Brazil, *Appellant/Appellee*	Present:
European Communities, *Appellant/ Appellee*	Bacchus, Presiding Member
Thailand and the United States, *Third Participants*	El-Naggar, Member
	Feliciano, Member

TABLE OF CONTENTS

I. INTRODUCTION

1. Brazil and the European Communities appeal from certain issues of law and legal interpretations in the Panel Report, *European Communities - Measures Affecting the Importation of Certain Poultry Products*.[1] The Panel was established to consider a complaint by Brazil regarding the EC regime for the importation of certain frozen poultry meat products falling within Common Nomenclature ("CN") categories 0207 14 10, 0207 14 50 and 0207 14 70 (formerly CN

[1] WT/DS69/R, 12 March 1998.

categories 0207 41 10, 0207 41 41 and 0207 41 71), and the implementation by the European Communities of the tariff-rate quota in these products agreed in negotiations between Brazil and the European Communities.

2. The relevant factual aspects of this dispute are set out in the Panel Report, in particular, at paragraphs 8-12. On 19 June 1992, the CONTRACTING PARTIES authorized the European Communities to enter into negotiations with interested contracting parties under Article XXVIII of the GATT 1947, following adoption of the panel report on *European Economic Community - Payments and Subsidies Paid to Processors and Producers of Oilseeds and Related Animal-feed Proteins*[2] ("*EEC - Oilseeds*"). The European Communities entered into negotiations with Brazil, as well as nine other contracting parties. The negotiations with Brazil terminated in July 1993, and the parties signed Agreed Minutes on 31 January 1994. The bilateral agreement set out in these Agreed Minutes (the "Oilseeds Agreement") provided, *inter alia*, for a duty-free global annual tariff-rate quota of 15,500 tonnes for frozen poultry meat under CN categories 0207 41 10, 0207 41 41 and 0207 41 71. The tariff-rate quota was opened as from 1 January 1994 by Council Regulation 774/94[3] ("Regulation 774/94") of 29 March 1994. Commission Regulation 1431/94[4] ("Regulation 1431/94") of 22 June 1994 sets out detailed rules for the application of Regulation 774/94, and stipulates, in Article 1, that all imports under the tariff-rate quota for the relevant poultry meat products are subject to the presentation of an import licence. There are no licensing requirements for out-of-quota imports of these products.

3. Schedule LXXX of the European Communities[5] ("Schedule LXXX") provides for a duty-free tariff-rate quota for up to 15,500 tonnes of frozen poultry meat in Part I - Most Favoured Nation Tariff, Section I - Agricultural Products, Section I - B - Tariff Quotas, with out-of-quota base duty rates of 1,600 ECU/tonne, 940 ECU/tonne and 1,575 ECU/tonne, respectively. The European Communities reserved the right in Schedule LXXX to introduce an additional duty on out-of-quota imports of the relevant poultry meat if the conditions for imposition of the "Special Safeguard" in Article 5 of the *Agreement on Agriculture* were satisfied. Council Regulation 2777/75[6] ("Regulation 2777/75") of 29 October 1975, as amended by Council Regulation 3290/94[7] ("Regulation 3290/94") of 22 December 1994, contains the general rule for the application of the additional safeguard duties in Article 5 of the *Agreement on Agriculture*. Article 5.3 of this regulation states:

---

2 Adopted 25 January 1990, BISD 37S/86; and DS28/R, 31 March 1992.

3 Official Journal No. L 91, 8 April 1994, p. 1.

4 Official Journal No. L 156, 23 June 1994, p. 9.

5 Schedule LXXX of the European Communities, *Final Act Embodying the Uruguay Round of Multilateral Trade Negotiations*, done at Marrakesh, 15 April 1994.

6 Official Journal No. L 282, 1 November 1975, p. 77.

7 Official Journal No. L 349, 31 December 1994, p. 105.

> The import prices to be taken into consideration for imposing an additional import duty shall be determined on the basis of the cif import prices of the consignment in question.

Commission Regulation 1484/95[8] ("Regulation 1484/95") of 28 June 1995 contains the detailed rules pertaining to such special safeguard, and provides that, unless the imports of frozen poultry meat are unlikely to disturb the EC internal market, an additional duty will be levied if the import price falls below a trigger price set out in Annex II of the Regulation. The import price is either the "representative price" or, upon the request of the importer, the c.i.f. price, if this price is higher than the applicable representative price. The "representative price" is to be determined by taking into account: (i) "prices on third country markets"; (ii) "free-at-Community-frontier offer prices"; and (iii) "prices at the various stages of marketing in the Community for imported products".[9] If the c.i.f. price of the shipment is used, the importer must provide to the competent authorities the documents enumerated in Article 3 of Regulation 1484/95, that is: the purchasing contract (or any other equivalent document), the insurance contract, the invoice, the certificate of origin (where applicable), the transport contract, and, in the case of sea transport, the bill of lading.

4. The Panel Report was circulated to the Members of the World Trade Organization (the "WTO") on 12 March 1998. The Panel reached the following conclusions:

> 294. In light of our findings in Section B and C above, we conclude that Brazil has not demonstrated that the EC has failed to implement and administer the poultry TRQ in line with its obligations under the WTO agreements.
>
> 295. In light of our findings in Section D above, we conclude that Brazil has not demonstrated that the EC has failed to implement the TRQ in accordance with Article XIII of GATT.
>
> 296. In light of our findings in Section E above, we conclude that Brazil has not demonstrated that the EC has failed to implement the TRQ in accordance with Articles 1 and 3 of the Licensing Agreement, except on the point that the EC has failed to notify the necessary information regarding the poultry TRQ to the WTO Committee on Import Licensing under Article 1.4(a) of the Licensing Agreement.
>
> 297. In light of our findings in Section F, G and H above, we conclude that Brazil has not demonstrated that the EC has failed to comply with the provisions of Articles X, II

8 Official Journal No. L 145, 29 June 1995, p. 47.

9 Regulation 1484/95, Article 2.

> and III of GATT in respect of the implementation and administration of the poultry TRQ.
>
> 298. In light of our findings in Section I above, we conclude that the EC has failed to comply with the provisions of Article 5.1(b) of the Agreement on Agriculture regarding the imports of the poultry products outside the TRQ.[10]

and made the following recommendation:

> We recommend that the Dispute Settlement Body request the EC to bring the measures found in this report to be inconsistent with the Licensing Agreement and the Agreement on Agriculture into conformity with its obligations under those agreements.[11]

5. On 29 April 1998, Brazil notified the Dispute Settlement Body ("DSB") of its decision to appeal certain issues of law covered in the Panel Report and certain legal interpretations developed by the Panel, pursuant to paragraph 4 of Article 16 of the *Understanding on Rules and Procedures Governing the Settlement of Disputes* (the "DSU"), and filed a notice of appeal[12] with the Appellate Body pursuant to Rule 20 of the *Working Procedures for Appellate Review* (the "*Working Procedures*"). On 11 May 1998, Brazil filed an appellant's submission.[13] On 14 May 1998, the European Communities filed its own appellant's submission.[14] On 25 May 1998, both the European Communities[15] and Brazil filed appellee's submissions.[16] On the same day, Thailand and the United States filed separate third participants' submissions.[17]

6. The oral hearing in the appeal was held on 9 June 1998. The participants and third participants presented oral arguments and responded to questions put to them by the Members of the Division hearing the appeal. The participants and third participants also gave oral concluding statements. At the request of the Members of the Division, the participants and third participants submitted, on 12 June 1998, written post-hearing memoranda on particular issues relating to the appeal. The participants submitted their respective written replies to these post-hearing memoranda on 15 June 1998.

---

[10] Panel Report, paras. 294-298.

[11] Panel Report, para. 299.

[12] WT/DS69/4, 29 April 1998.

[13] Pursuant to Rule 21(1) of the *Working Procedures.*

[14] Pursuant to Rule 23(1) of the *Working Procedures.*

[15] Pursuant to Rule 22 of the *Working Procedures.*

[16] Pursuant to Rule 23(3) of the *Working Procedures.*

[17] Pursuant to Rule 24 of the *Working Procedures.*

II. ARGUMENTS OF THE PARTICIPANTS AND THIRD PARTICIPANTS

A. *Brazil - Appellant*

1. *The Oilseeds Agreement*

7. Brazil asserts that the Panel failed to apply the customary rules of interpretation of public international law properly to the Oilseeds Agreement, as required by Article 3.2 of the DSU. Brazil maintains that in limiting its examination of the Oilseeds Agreement to the "relevant parts" of the Oilseeds Agreement, the Panel failed to examine all of the terms and provisions of the Oilseeds Agreement in accordance with Article 31 of the *Vienna Convention on the Law of Treaties*[18] (the "*Vienna Convention*"), including, in particular, how many parties there were to the agreement, the structure of the agreement, the content of the different sections and the declared intention of the parties upon seeking authorization from the CONTRACTING PARTIES to negotiate.

8. With respect to the ordinary meaning to be given to all the terms of the Oilseeds Agreement, Brazil states that nothing in the text of the Oilseeds Agreement limits or diminishes the exclusive nature of that Agreement. Brazil contends that the Panel failed to interpret the Oilseeds Agreement in good faith, and instead interpreted Article XXVIII of the GATT without taking the Oilseeds Agreement appropriately into account. Brazil argues that the Panel examined the object and purpose of Article XXVIII of the GATT but not the object and purpose of the Oilseeds Agreement itself. According to Brazil, the Panel should have examined what was, in fact, agreed between the parties in the Oilseeds Agreement and, in particular, the reasons the parties had entered into that Agreement and also its compensatory nature. Therefore, in the Brazilian view, the proper analysis of the Oilseeds Agreement between Brazil and the European Communities required an examination of all the parts of that Agreement as well as the different bilateral oilseeds agreements that the European Communities had reached with different negotiating Members.

9. In the alternative, Brazil argues that the Panel erred in law in not examining the ordinary meaning of the "relevant parts" of the Oilseeds Agreement in the light of their context. Brazil stresses that the European Communities had specifically chosen to negotiate with Brazil separately from the other parties to be compensated so that variable solutions on compensation, rather than a common most-favoured-nation ("MFN") solution, could be reached.

---

18 Done at Vienna, 23 May 1969, 1155 U.N.T.S. 33; 8 International Legal Materials 679.

2. *Article XXVIII of the GATT*

10. Brazil asserts that the Panel failed to apply to Article XXVIII of the GATT properly the customary rules of interpretation of public international law, as required by Article 3.2 of the DSU. According to Brazil, under the terms of Article 31 of the *Vienna Convention*, the Panel should have examined: what was agreed between the parties; whether what was agreed between the parties is legally possible within the terms of Article XXVIII of the GATT; and finally, if it found that the specific agreement was not compatible with other GATT provisions (Articles I and XIII), what the consequences of such incompatibility would be. Rather than adopting this step-by-step approach, the Panel only examined the question as to whether Articles I and XIII of the GATT 1994 apply to Article XXVIII tariff-rate quotas or whether Article XXVIII of the GATT can give rise to country-specific provisions.

11. In the view of Brazil, Article XXVIII of the GATT is a *lex specialis* providing for bilateral solutions within a multilateral framework and maintaining a balance between bilateral and multilateral rights and obligations. There is nothing in Article XXVIII of the GATT that prevents two contracting parties from making an agreement on a country-specific package of compensatory measures, although, at the same time, nothing requires that compensation must be country-specific. Brazil argues that Article XXVIII allows certain defined contracting parties to negotiate and agree. And it provides that other contracting parties have the right to ensure that such an agreement does not prejudice their own rights. In relation to the tariff-rate quota for frozen poultry meat, Brazil points out that no Member objected to the specific agreement reached between the principal negotiating parties. Therefore, all Members must be deemed to have agreed to the solution reached between Brazil and the European Communities.

12. In Brazil's view, Article XXVIII of the GATT can be an exception to the MFN rule contained in Article I of the GATT 1994 if the parties negotiating the agreement so choose and if the other contracting parties do not object. The European Communities and Brazil had agreed on a country-specific tariff-rate quota and did not provide that the MFN principle should apply to that tariff-rate quota. Brazil argues that the Panel erred in law in finding that an element in compensation for the withdrawal of an MFN concession must be MFN. According to Brazil, the opening of a country-specific tariff-rate quota for frozen poultry meat by the European Communities does not impact negatively on the trade interests of other Members. That quota is not therefore something to which the MFN principle necessarily applies.

3. *Article XIII of the GATT 1994*

13. Brazil claims that the Panel erred in finding that there was no evidence of an agreement between the European Communities and Brazil on the allocation of the tariff-rate quota to Brazil. The Panel based its finding on supplementary evidence, that is, certain letters from Brazil to the EC Commission, and failed to analyze the main supporting evidence of an agreement - the Oilseeds Agreement

itself. Brazil argues that, by not interpreting the Oilseeds Agreement at all, the Panel failed to examine all of the evidence before it.

14. According to Brazil, the Panel also erred in law in its analysis of the participation of non-Members in tariff-rate quotas allocated within the terms of Article XIII of the GATT 1994. Brazil states that the relevant issue is whether or not a non-Member can be unilaterally allowed to participate in a compensatory tariff-rate quota, especially in a situation where there is considerable over-quota trade open to that non-Member. It is clear from the text of Article XIII of the GATT 1994, particularly Article XIII:2 and Article XIII:2(d), that the allocation of quota shares is always intended for Members. In footnote 140 of the Panel Report, the Panel reads paragraph 7.75 of the panel reports in *European Communities - Regime for the Importation, Sale and Distribution of Bananas*[19] ("*EC - Bananas*") only partially. According to Brazil, when the panel in *EC - Bananas* quoted the phrase "all suppliers other than Members with a substantial interest in supplying the product", it referred exclusively to all suppliers that are Members with no substantial interest in supplying the product. The Panel appeared to be mandating the inclusion of non-Members, thereby expanding the wording of Article XIII of the GATT 1994, which merely limits the non-discrimination rule as between Members.

15. Brazil submits that the Panel involved itself in a fundamental contradiction on Article XIII of the GATT 1994. On the one hand, the Panel pointed out that the exclusion of non-Members would not be contrary to Article XIII:2 and that Members are free to choose; but, on the other hand, the Panel found that, if non-Members are excluded, the purposes of Article XIII are not achieved. Brazil notes that if the presence of non-Members is necessary for purposes of approximating the shares in the absence of the restriction, then non-Members need to be included in the allocation of the tariff-rate quota. They should be treated like Members. This constitutes a violation of the *WTO Agreement*, which is an international treaty laying down contractual obligations and not *erga omnes* obligations. According to Brazil, the only valid resolution of this contradiction is to interpret Article XIII of the GATT 1994 so as to prevent Members from allocating shares within the tariff-rate quota to non-Members. In Brazil's view, the origin and nature of the tariff-rate quota need to be considered, and the Panel erred in concluding that the compensatory nature of the tariff-rate quota opened under the terms of Article XXVIII of the GATT was not to be considered and that Article XIII of the GATT 1994 was simply a general provision.

4. *Article X of the GATT 1994*

16. Brazil alleges that the Panel erroneously assessed measures of general application under Article X of the GATT 1994. Brazil maintains that any meas-

[19] Adopted 25 September 1997, WT/DS27/R/ECU, WT/DS27/R/GTM, WT/DS27/R/HND, WT/DS27/R/MEX, and WT/DS27/R/USA.

ure of general application will always have to be applied to specific cases. Therefore, a panel cannot dismiss a claim of inconsistency with Article X of the GATT 1994 merely because the impact of the inconsistency is felt by individual traders in individual situations. The generally applicable regulations of the European Communities under review do not allow Brazilian traders to know whether the rules relating to in-quota or out-of-quota trade will be applicable to a particular shipment of frozen poultry meat. The object of Article X of the GATT 1994 is to ensure that traders can become familiar with the applicable trade rules. According to Brazil, mere publication of the rules is not sufficient to ensure familiarity and predictability. The rules must be drafted and administered in a reasonable way. According to Brazil, the Panel should have applied the principle of legal certainty to its examination of Article X of the GATT 1994 and its application to trade in frozen poultry meat.

17. Brazil submits that EC laws should allow traders to know which set of conditions is applicable (the in-quota or the out-of-quota system) in a particular case. There is a general need to draft clear general rules that will allow traders to distinguish between two systems that may be applicable in a given case. The Panel assumed that Brazil was arguing for transparency in each specific licence or shipment. The lack of clarity and transparency in the general rules and in their administration inevitably impact upon specific shipments and licences.

5. *Agreement on Import Licensing Procedures*

18. To Brazil, the *Agreement on Import Licensing Procedures* (the "*Licensing Agreement*") applies to both in-quota and out-of-quota trade in frozen poultry meat from Brazil to the European Communities, and, in Brazil's view, the Panel erred in interpreting Article 3.2 of the *Licensing Agreement* as applicable only to in-quota trade. Brazil argues that the Panel failed to give an objective statement of reasons for this particular conclusion, and that there is nothing in the text of the *Licensing Agreement* to justify the Panel's findings. In the view of Brazil, nothing in the text or context of Articles 1.2 and 3.2 of the *Licensing Agreement* limits exclusively to in-quota trade the requirement that licensing systems for tariff-rate quotas be "implemented ... with a view to preventing trade distortions".

19. The Panel, in examining whether there had been trade distortions in out-of-quota trade, dismissed the evidence submitted by Brazil on its falling market share. This evidence relates to Brazil's claim that the licensing system distorts total trade. According to Brazil, in holding that an increase in exports demonstrated that the decline in the percentage share in total trade was, first, not relevant and, second, not due to a violation of the *Licensing Agreement*, the Panel failed to address the real issue, which is, whether the fall in the market share was caused by the introduction of the licensing system. Brazil believes that it established a *prima facie* case of distortion of trade and that the burden of proof had shifted to the European Communities to show why the licensing system was not distorting trade. The Panel did not address this matter.

20. According to Brazil, the administration by the European Communities of the tariff-rate quota for frozen poultry meat does not comply with the requirements of fairness, equity and proportionality expressed in Article 1.2, and in the preamble, to the *Licensing Agreement*. Brazil argues that the European Communities allows speculation in licences and the proliferation of traders. Allowing speculation is unfair and distorts trade. It is also "disproportionate". The Panel failed to examine whether speculation was affecting trade relations between Brazilian exporters and EC importers with the subsequent reduction in Brazil's market share. Brazil maintains that the Panel should also have examined the changes to the licensing rules, licence entitlement based on export performance, and the issuance of licences in non-economic quantities in the light of the requirement not to distort trade. Allowing the volume covered by individual licences to fall to below 5.5 tonnes is "disproportionate". The Panel places an unusual emphasis on the fact that the tariff-rate quota licences were fully utilized. According to Brazil, there has been full utilization of the licences because an economic benefit accrues to the holder of the licence when the privilege to import is exercised. The licences can be fully utilized even if the rules on administering the licences are "disproportionate" and unreasonable.

21. Brazil maintains that the Panel incorrectly restricted Brazil's claims concerning transparency under the *Licensing Agreement* to an analysis of Article 3.5(a) of the *Licensing Agreement*. The administration of import licences in such a way that the exporter does not know what trade rules apply is, Brazil insists, a breach of the fundamental objective of the *Licensing Agreement*. Brazil made a comprehensive claim before the Panel relating to the violation of "the general principle of transparency" in the administration of the licensing procedures "as laid down in the Preamble and which underpin" the *Licensing Agreement*. The Panel did not address this claim.

6. Article 11 of the DSU

22. Brazil asserts also that the Panel did not fulfil the duties incumbent upon it under Article 11 of the DSU. Although Brazil acknowledges that Article 11 of the DSU should not be interpreted so as to limit the scope of any investigation a panel might wish to make or to limit what a panel considers will assist the DSB in making recommendations, Brazil maintains nonetheless that the wide discretion to examine issues of concern should not disguise a failure of a panel to fulfil the requirement to make an objective assessment of the matter before it. Nor, when a panel chooses to examine issues of principle, should it be allowed the discretion not to examine evidence of the practice of Members in relation to those principles.

23. Brazil also contends that the Panel did not address a series of arguments put forward by Brazil in relation to both GATT law and the practice of the Members: first, the similarities between Articles XXVIII and XXIV of the GATT that lead Brazil to question why the MFN principle in Article I of the GATT 1994 must always apply in relation to Article XXVIII, but not necessarily so in relation

to Article XXIV; second, the flexible nature of Article XXVIII of the GATT, which permits bilateral agreements and the opening of bilateral concessions subject to the review of all Members; and, third, the text of Article XXVIII of the GATT, which allows the establishment of country-specific tariff-rate quotas when other Members do not object.

24. The Panel failed in its obligation to the DSB to examine the practice of the Members. The Panel erred in law in considering that the practice of the Members does not show the possibility of departing from the MFN principle in the case of tariff-rate quotas resulting from Article XXVIII of the GATT. According to Brazil, Article XXVIII of the GATT, in and of itself, cannot be used by the Panel as an evidence to show that the Oilseeds Agreement signed between the European Communities and Brazil could not give rise to country-specific tariff-rate quotas.

25. Brazil submits that panels, and the Appellate Body, do not have the competence, within the terms of the DSU, to limit or change the clear terms of agreements made between two Members to which the other Members do not object. The MFN principle is not absolute; there are exceptions. If the Members have determined that the tariff-rate quota for frozen poultry meat is an exception, then a panel must respect that determination of the Members. If, on the other hand, a panel does find that an agreement is void, it must examine the consequences of such a void agreement. The Panel did not examine this matter.

B. European Communities - Appellee

1. The Oilseeds Agreement

26. In the view of the European Communities, the Panel reasonably and correctly performed its task of interpreting the Oilseeds Agreement in the proper manner, by applying the principles established in Article 31 of the *Vienna Convention*. First, the Panel identified the relevant part of the agreement in dispute. Second, when addressing the "ordinary meaning" of the relevant terms of the Oilseeds Agreement, the Panel analyzed the arguments of both parties to conclude that "[various arguments made by Brazil] ... do not constitute conclusive evidence to the effect that the particular terms used in the Oilseeds Agreement must be read in the way claimed by Brazil". Third, the Panel also concluded that the context of the terms "global annual tariff quota" does not give any additional guidance for the purpose of determining a particular interpretation of the terms involved. Fourth, the Panel analyzed the object and purpose of the Oilseeds Agreement, which could not be assessed without determining the object and purpose of the procedure set out in Article XXVIII of the GATT. According to the European Communities, such an analysis is necessary in particular to consider the inter-relationship between this provision and Article I of the GATT 1994. The conclusion of the Panel that there is no provision in the WTO Agreements which allows departure from the MFN principle in the case of tariff-rate quotas resulting from Article XXVIII negotiations removed any reasonable need to address

the subordinate issue of the object and purpose of the specific procedure under Article XXVIII that was concluded with the Oilseeds Agreement.

2. *Article XXVIII of the GATT*

27. The European Communities maintains that the Panel findings on the interpretation of Article XXVIII of the GATT are correct, and that the arguments put forward by the Panel to demonstrate that Article XXVIII of the GATT does not waive Members' obligations with respect to the MFN clauses contained in Articles I and XIII of the GATT 1994 are extensively reasoned.

28. In the view of the European Communities, Article XXVIII is *lex generalis* insofar as it provides the normal procedural framework to be used by any Member in order legally to modify, change or withdraw, totally or partially, one of its concessions. Brazil is "wrong" to suggest that there is nothing in Article XXVIII of the GATT that prevents two contracting parties from agreeing on a country-specific package of compensatory measures. The European Communities argues that the terms of Article XXVIII:2, read in their context and in the light of its object and purpose, do not support Brazil's claims with respect to the Oilseeds Agreement. The agreement resulting from the Article XXVIII oilseeds negotiations and the poultry meat tariff concessions resulting from the *Marrakesh Agreement Establishing the World Trade Organization*[20] (the "*WTO Agreement*") had the same objective. The fact that the oilseeds negotiations and the Uruguay Round negotiations were initiated for partially different reasons cannot affect these conclusions. The negotiating history of Article XXVIII of the GATT confirms that Articles I and XIII of the GATT 1994 must be respected when achieving an agreement in the framework of compensatory adjustment negotiations. The fact that the Article XXVIII negotiating process occurs on a bilateral basis cannot change this.

3. *Article XIII of the GATT 1994*

29. The European Communities argues that Brazil's claim concerning the existence of an agreement between the European Communities and Brazil on the allocation of the tariff-rate quota for frozen poultry meat should be rejected. The Panel's conclusions, drawn from the examination of the letters sent by Brazil to the European Communities, are logical and fully reasoned and relate to questions of fact. Thus, Brazil's complaints in this respect appear totally unjustified and cannot properly be the subject of this appeal. According to the European Communities, the fact that the European Communities did not answer these letters officially is further evidence of the lack of explicit (or even implicit) agreement with Brazil on this issue.

---

[20] Done at Marrakesh, 15 April 1994.

30. The European Communities states furthermore that the Panel correctly interpreted Article XIII:2(d) of the GATT 1994 and that Brazil's appeal of the Panel's finding that Article XIII does not oblige Members to include or exclude non-Members therefore should be rejected. The EC position that Article XIII of the GATT 1994 operates only as a positive obligation to provide MFN treatment to Members when allocating tariff-rate quota shares is based on both the terms of Article XIII:2 and on its objective. An allocation of a share of a tariff-rate quota has been considered to be an advantage by the Appellate Body in *EC - Bananas*[21] to such an extent that the basic principle of non-discrimination applies strictly when allocating shares of a tariff-rate quota, including for Members not having a substantial interest. Thus, by assigning a share of the tariff-rate quota to all substantially interested Members, including Brazil, the European Communities has provided Brazil with the best possible (and legally sound) situation in the trade of frozen poultry meat within the tariff-rate quota.

31. The European Communities insists that while there is a general obligation to treat on an MFN basis any Member with respect to advantages granted even to a non-Member, there is no provision in the *WTO Agreement* forbidding Members from providing market access to non-Members on an MFN basis. Moreover, Brazil's claim that the European Communities should exclude any non-Member supplying country from the allocation of the tariff-rate quota would inevitably entail an increase in its share of the tariff-rate quota. This is an "unjustified" request in the light of the chapeau of Article XIII:2 of the GATT 1994. Market access to the residual part of a tariff-rate quota is a matter that cannot harm in any manner the trade interests of Members having a substantial interest if their shares have been correctly allocated in accordance with the relevant provisions of Article XIII. According to the European Communities, this is the case for Brazil with respect to the allocation of the duty-free tariff-rate quota concerning frozen poultry meat, and therefore Brazil's position that Article XIII of the GATT 1994 is for the benefit of Members only is incorrect.

32. The European Communities maintains that the text of Article XIII:2(d) of the GATT 1994 is clear: a quota must be allocated among "supplying countries". However, the rights and obligations attached to the allocation between supplying countries having a substantial interest apply only to "contracting parties". Thus, only substantial suppliers who are Members can claim participation in an agreed distribution or can expect a share in case the importing Member proceeds to an allocation. According to the terms of Article XIII, the shares to be allocated to the substantial suppliers/Members can be calculated as "proportions ... of the total quantity or value of imports of the products". The European Communities insists that it applied the provisions of Article XIII:2(d) to the tariff-rate quota for frozen poultry meat: "the allocation has been effected only with respect to Mem-

[21] Brazil refers to Appellate Body Report, *EC - Bananas*, adopted 25 September 1997, WT/DS27/AB/R, paras. 161 and 162.

bers having a substantial interest on the basis of proportions of imports into the EC during a previous representative period of three years". Non-Member participation has been limited to the "others" category.

4. *Article X of the GATT 1994*

33. The European Communities submits that the Panel's approach in interpreting "measures of general application" in Article X of the GATT 1994 was correct. Article X requires that the general terms and conditions of trade regulation be transparent so that operators are aware of the conditions applying to commerce. Application of Article X in the manner suggested by Brazil would be impossible to implement in practice and would require that Members manage completely the terms and conditions of trade. With respect to out-of-quota trade, the European Communities demonstrated, to the satisfaction of the Panel, as a matter of fact, that it has fully complied with the requirements of Article X. By arguing that the Panel mischaracterized its claim under Article X, Brazil is seeking to refine and re-organize its arguments. Brazil also raises an additional argument that the Panel erred in law by failing to apply the principle of legal certainty. According to the European Communities, the approach followed by Brazil is contrary to the provisions of Article 17.6 of the DSU, and therefore those of Brazil's submissions that amount to either a re-characterization of its arguments or to new arguments not submitted to the Panel should be dismissed as inadmissible.

5. *Agreement on Import Licensing Procedures*

34. The European Communities contends that the Panel correctly restricted the application of the *Licensing Agreement* to in-quota trade. This ruling is not only consistent with the text of the Agreement, but also it is the logical consequence of the Panel's ruling on Article X of the GATT 1994. Articles 1.2 and 3.2 of the *Licensing Agreement* make it clear that the trade restriction is clearly linked to the effects flowing from the restriction imposed.

35. The European Communities submits that Brazil has been unable to demonstrate any trade distorting effects of the administration of the tariff-rate quota for frozen poultry meat, on either in-quota or out-of-quota trade. Brazil's submissions concerning falling market share and burden of proof amount to a request to the Appellate Body not to correct an error of law by the Panel but rather to re-investigate and re-assess the factual questions before the Panel. These submissions do not fall within the proper scope of the appellate process. Brazil seeks to advance before the Appellate Body "re-worked arguments" on transparency, equity and proportionality, thereby re-introducing its arguments on speculation and economic quantities that were considered and dismissed by the Panel. This constitutes an "abuse" by Brazil of the appellate process.

6. *Article 11 of the DSU*

36. The European Communities agrees with the Panel that Article XXVIII of the GATT does not waive Members' obligations with respect to the MFN clauses contained in Articles I and XIII of the GATT 1994. In the context of the tariff-rate quota for frozen poultry meat, the issue of the relations between Article XXIV and Article XXVIII was a "side-issue". Although paragraphs 4 and 5 of Article XXIV provide a legal basis for an exception to Article I of the GATT 1994, these relate to the actual creation of a customs union. The Oilseeds Agreement did not involve the creation of a customs union or a free-trade area. The Panel was therefore fully justified in not addressing that specific argument. According to the European Communities, Brazil confuses the legal nature of a particular tariff treatment granted through an Article XXVIII procedure, that is based on the MFN, with the economic effects of that particular tariff treatment. Article XXVIII is a procedural, rather than a substantive, provision and no Article XXVIII negotiation in which the European Communities was involved was concluded with a non-MFN agreement.

37. With respect to the practice of Members in Article XXVIII negotiations, the European Communities asserts that Brazil has not shown the existence of a "concordant, common and consistent" practice of non-MFN Article XXVIII agreements. Brazil's argument that Articles I and XIII do not necessarily apply to tariff-rate quotas opened as a result of compensation negotiations under Article XXVIII of the GATT, is not supported either by the text of the *WTO Agreement* or past GATT practice. The *WTO Agreement* entered into force after the conclusion of the Oilseeds Agreement. At the time of the negotiation of the Oilseeds Agreement, the practice of the GATT contracting parties, including panels, was squarely within the MFN interpretation of concessions. Moreover, as found by the Panel, the Oilseeds Agreement was incorporated into Schedule LXXX, whose poultry meat tariff concession is also undisputedly a MFN tariff commitment. Finally, the Oilseeds Agreement was "undoubtedly aimed at (partially) replacing MFN concessions in Oilseeds".

C. *European Communities - Appellant*

1. *Relationship between Schedule LXXX and the Oilseeds Agreement*

38. The European Communities is satisfied with the conclusion reached in the Panel Report on the relationship between the Oilseeds Agreement and Schedule LXXX, but submits that the Panel should have followed a different line of legal reasoning to reach that conclusion. According to the European Communities, the relationship between the bilateral Oilseeds Agreement and the later Schedule LXXX should be examined on the basis of Article 59.1, or, in the alternative, Article 30.3, of the *Vienna Convention*. The Panel did not draw the logical conclusions from its finding in paragraph 206 of the Panel Report that Articles 59.1 and 30.3 of the *Vienna Convention* are customary rules of interpretation of public

international law. Rather than applying Article 3.2 of the DSU and the *Vienna Convention*, the Panel referred to the panel report in *EEC - Oilseeds*, which predates the entry into force of the DSU and which is therefore "irrelevant" in this case because it was decided in the context of a non-violation case.

39. The undisputed evidence before the Panel showed that the results of the bilateral Oilseeds Agreement were incorporated into the final stages of the negotiations of Schedule LXXX and eventually agreed and ratified by all parties, including Brazil. This was a "conscious act" of the two parties in order to clarify their mutual obligations. In the meantime, the European Communities had autonomously put into force the tariff-rate quota as an MFN market access opportunity. The fact that the EC Schedule applicable at the time did not provide for any tariff treatment for frozen poultry meat other than variable levies should not be overlooked.

40. In the present case, the European Communities asserts that only one alternative is logically possible: either the Oilseeds Agreement and Schedule LXXX are identical in their content, or they are not. If they are identical, then the principle laid down in Article 59.1 of the *Vienna Convention* must be applicable because, in the specific context of the WTO, Brazil and the European Communities intended that the matter should be governed by the later treaty, which introduced the tariff-rate quota as a new element of tariff binding within the framework of the EC Schedule. If they are not identical, the earlier Oilseeds Agreement was changed by the later Schedule LXXX with the assent and the active participation of all parties, including Brazil. Thus, the rule established by Article 30.3 of the *Vienna Convention* must be applicable, and the Oilseeds Agreement can only be applied to the extent that its provisions are compatible with those of the later treaty, namely, Schedule LXXX. And, in the view of the European Communities, there cannot be any doubt that a new tariff-rate quota negotiated during the Uruguay Round was meant to be applied on an MFN basis.

2. *Agreement on Agriculture*

41. The European Communities contends that contrary to the legal interpretation applied by the majority of the Panel, the phrase "on the basis of the c.i.f. import price" in Article 5.1(b) of the *Agreement on Agriculture* refers to the cost of the product plus insurance and freight charges and does not include the duties payable.

42. Article 5.1(b) refers to the price at which imports "may enter" the customs territory. This wording confirms that the price in issue is that which is calculated at the moment a shipment arrives and before its entry on to the EC market, at which point taxes and duties become payable. The Panel incorrectly assumed that the words "the price at which imports of that product may enter the customs territory" and the words "market entry price" are equivalent. The phrase "on the basis of" in Article 5.1(b) means "founded on". The authors of the *Agreement on Agriculture* selected the c.i.f. price as the principal parameter for the application of the special safeguard. The Panel's statement in paragraph 278 of the Panel

Report that "the market entry price is something that has to be constructed using the c.i.f. price as one of the parameters" incorrectly presupposes that the c.i.f. price is always the basis for the calculation of the duties to be included in the notion of "market entry price". Duties upon importation of frozen poultry meat into the European Communities are not *ad valorem* but, rather, fixed duties that are calculated on the basis of the quantities imported and not on the basis of the c.i.f. price. The European Communities maintains that the Panel's "restrictive" reading of Article 5.1(b) does not take account of the proper context of that provision, in particular, footnote 2 to Article 5.1(b) and Article 5.5, and disregards the fact that the system applying the special safeguard clause is separate and parallel to the tariffication scheme applied under Article 4.2 of the *Agreement on Agriculture*.

43. Moreover, the European Communities states, the Panel disregarded the broader context of the border protection measures in the agricultural sector that existed before the Uruguay Round and their conversion into ordinary customs duties. The special safeguard provision exists to ensure that unknown or unpredictable factors that would cause c.i.f. prices of imports to drop below the level taken as a reference point during the Uruguay Round negotiations, could not fundamentally alter the internal market prices and the domestic price support system. This is in line with the results of tariffication as embodied in the schedules. It is for this reason that Articles 5.1 and 5.5 of the *Agreement on Agriculture* provide for calculation of the additional duty "on the basis of the c.i.f. price". If this basis is altered, then the entire result of the Uruguay Round is modified. The result of the majority of the Panel's interpretation is, as the dissenting member noted, that where a specific duty is payable and this is higher than the trigger price, the trigger price can never be exceeded. With respect to "subsequent practice" in Article 31.3(b) of the *Vienna Convention*, the European Communities understands that the practice of other Members is not to include customs duties in the calculation under Article 5.1(b). A document used in the WTO technical assistance training courses confirms this approach.

44. Should the Appellate Body reverse the Panel's findings relating to Article 5.1(b) of the *Agreement on Agriculture*, the European Communities submits that the Appellate Body should dismiss Brazil's requests that issues relating to Articles 5.5 and 4.2 of that Agreement be taken up. These issues were not appealed in accordance with the rules on the scope of an appeal in Article 16.4 of the DSU and in Rules 20.2(d) and 21.2(b)(i) of the *Working Procedures.* For reasons of due process, consistency and fair treatment among all Members, the European Communities argues that the Appellate Body should not depart from the "strict" interpretation of these provisions adopted in *EC - Bananas*. In respect of the reason given by the Division in the course of the oral hearing, "i.e. that 'due process considerations' justified an additional exchange of written memoranda" between the participants, the European Communities wonders whether it would be compatible with the DSU to incorporate other due process considerations that are not included in the DSU, any other covered agreement, or the *Working Procedures.* Any specific procedures adopted pursuant to Rule 16.1 of the *Working Proce-*

dures must be consistent with the DSU, the other covered agreements and the *Working Procedures* themselves.

45. According to the European Communities, in practice, there is no need for the Appellate Body to address in this case the theoretical issue raised by Brazil of whether the application by a panel of the principle of judicial economy would allow departure from the explicit provisions of Article 16.4 of the DSU and Rule 20 of the *Working Procedures.* The Panel made a finding in paragraph 286 with respect to Article 5 of the *Agreement on Agriculture* and Article X of the GATT 1994, that Brazil "had not specified the manner in which the EC has violated these provisions". Brazil did not appeal from this finding, and the European Communities cannot be required to suffer the consequences of an appellant's failure to define properly the scope of its appeal.

46. According to the European Communities, Brazil's claim under Article 4.2 of the *Agreement on Agriculture* was vague and was not supported by factual or legal arguments. The purpose of the appellate process is not to allow Members to correct or re-plead arguments that were barely sketched out in the panel procedure and which, with hindsight, may be expanded, refined or improved. Brazil should not be allowed to abuse the appellate procedure by invoking non-existent reasons of "due process" when Brazil did not properly make its case clear during the panel procedure. In any event, the Panel's findings on Articles 5.5 and 4.2 are not logically or legally linked with the issues concerning the interpretation of Article 5.1(b) of the *Agreement on Agriculture*, and the Panel erred in creating a link among these provisions that is non-existent in fact and law.

47. In the view of the European Communities, a determination as to whether the representative price violates Articles 5.5 and 4.2 of the *Agreement on Agriculture* requires a finding of fact centered on the examination of EC legislation. Examination of EC legislation is not an interpretation of legislation as such: it is a judgment as to whether or not the European Communities, in applying its law, is acting in conformity with its WTO obligations. The Appellate Body cannot address issues of fact and is bound by the determinations of fact made during the panel procedure. Brazil itself admits that the Appellate Body would have to address issues of fact in order to decide these questions. The European Communities submits that certain assertions by Brazil relating to the document submitted by the European Communities to the Panel on 21 November 1997 misrepresent the reality of the panel procedure. The European Communities also states that Brazil breached the confidentiality requirements of the panel procedure.

48. According to the European Communities, Brazil acknowledges that the EC rules on the application of the special safeguard provision are in line with the provisions of Article 5 of the *Agreement on Agriculture*. Thus, Brazil has formally accepted that its complaint concerning Article 5.5 of the *Agreement on Agriculture* is unfounded in law and should be dismissed.

49. The European Communities observes further that the *Agreement on Agriculture* does not impose a pre-determined system of calculating the "c.i.f. price of

the shipment expressed in terms of the domestic currency." Thus, the fact that a representative price system is not explicitly provided in the *Agreement on Agriculture* does not imply that the use of such a system automatically constitutes a violation of Article 5. The representative price is based on two main regulations. First, Regulation 3290/94, which implements the agreements concluded during the Uruguay Round in the agricultural sector, amends Regulation 2777/75. The revised version of Article 5.3 of Regulation 2777/75 lays down the general rule for the application of the special safeguard additional duties as provided for in Article 5 of the *Agreement on Agriculture*. Second, the detailed rules for the application of this provision are found in Regulation 1484/95. The European Communities states that Article 3 of that Regulation shows that "any importer is completely free to follow an approach based on a shipment by shipment basis if he so wishes", as indicated by Article 5 of the *Agreement on Agriculture*. The apparent limitation of this entitlement to situations in which the c.i.f. import price is higher than the applicable representative price is not in violation of the *Agreement on Agriculture*. It represents, in fact, a substantial benefit for the importer: if the c.i.f. price is lower than the representative price, then the additional duty to be paid is higher.

50. The European Communities states that the representative price, which is an average c.i.f. price, is determined at regular intervals in order to keep the system up-to-date. Availability of recourse to the different sources set out in Article 2.1 of Regulation 1484/95 is designed to ensure that the average c.i.f. price arrived at for a given country of origin "is truly representative". For the poultry products in question, the representative price is, in general, calculated on the basis of free-at-frontier offer prices transmitted by the EC member states, either from usual monthly import statistics or from *ad hoc* price recording of such date by importers. Thus, the European Communities is, in fact, using the free-at-frontier price. The representative price is a means of boosting trade by reducing bureaucracy and paperwork.

51. According to the European Communities, the representative price does not impose penalties on, or create deterrents for, the importer. According to Article 3.2 of Regulation 1484/95, the importer is given four months from the date of acceptance of the declaration of release for free circulation to provide the necessary proof that the c.i.f. import price is higher than the representative price. If no such proof is provided, then the security is withheld. This security amounts exactly to the additional duty calculated on the basis of the representative price plus interest as from the date of release of the goods into free circulation. The evidence requested of the operators in order to establish the c.i.f. price of a specific shipment consists of normal and customary commercial documents for the shipment of the products. The representative price is "more transparent" than the determination of the c.i.f. price on a shipment-by-shipment basis. It is a "more stable and less variable system" than the shipment-by-shipment approach explicitly mentioned in Article 5.5 of the *Agreement on Agriculture*. It provides operators with published c.i.f. prices that are regularly updated, but are applied only after

they have been published. There is, according to the European Communities, no relation between the representative price and a variable levy.

D. Brazil - Appellee

1. Relationship between Schedule LXXX and the Oilseeds Agreement

52. Brazil argues that the Panel reached the correct conclusions on the applicability of Articles 59.1 and 30.3 of the *Vienna Convention*. Article 59 of the *Vienna Convention* is not applicable to the present situation because the Oilseeds Agreement was incorporated into the *WTO Agreement*, and therefore the intention was that the matter be governed by the *WTO Agreement*, in the light of the Oilseeds Agreement. The intention of the parties was to incorporate the Oilseeds Agreement into the *WTO Agreement*. This confirms the relevance of the Oilseeds Agreement in understanding Schedule LXXX. According to Brazil, this is a question of the continuation of a valid agreement that was not terminated and was specifically incorporated into the later agreement intact and without amendment. For this reason, there was no provision in the Oilseeds Agreement relating to its termination, or denunciation or withdrawal. The Oilseeds Agreement remains a valid agreement between Brazil and the European Communities, is incorporated into the *WTO Agreement* and, therefore, remains the basis for the interpretation of the tariff-rate quota for frozen poultry meat.

53. Brazil states that the European Communities showed its intention to continue to be bound by the terms of the earlier Oilseeds Agreement by specifically incorporating the earlier agreement into the later *WTO Agreement*. The matter is therefore governed by the *WTO Agreement* as incorporating the Oilseeds Agreement, which is compatible with the *WTO Agreement*. Country-specific tariff-rate quotas are compatible with the *WTO Agreement* and with Members' Schedules, and Members provide for country-specific tariff-rate quotas in their Schedules.

54. According to Brazil, the European Communities misreads Article 59 of the *Vienna Convention* by limiting its application to only one element of the subsequent treaty, its Schedule, rather than referring to the *WTO Agreement* as a whole. Members intend that their relations should be governed by the *WTO Agreement* read in the light of earlier agreements reached between Members. The Oilseeds Agreement may be considered part of the GATT 1994, as a protocol or certification relating to tariff concessions within the meaning of paragraph 1(b)(i) of the language in Annex 1A incorporating the GATT 1994 into the *WTO Agreement*.

55. Article 30.3 of the *Vienna Convention* is not applicable in this case because the country-specific aspects of the incorporated Oilseeds Agreement are fully compatible with the *WTO Agreement*. The incorporation of the Oilseeds Agreement into the *WTO Agreement* did not change the terms of the earlier agreement.

56. Brazil argues that if the tariff-rate quotas for frozen poultry meat in the Oilseeds Agreement and the *WTO Agreement* are identical, and if the Oilseeds Agreement was incorporated into Schedule LXXX, then, on the basis of Article 30.2 of the *Vienna Convention*, the tariff-rate quota in Schedule LXXX is the same as the tariff-rate quota in the Oilseeds Agreement and is therefore subject to the conditions set out in the Oilseeds Agreement. If the tariff-rate quotas in the Oilseeds Agreement and the *WTO Agreement* are not identical, and if the Schedule LXXX tariff-rate quota is a new tariff-rate quota negotiated within the terms of the Uruguay Round, then the European Communities would be in breach of its obligations under the Oilseeds Agreement, Article XXVIII of the GATT and Article 26 of the *Vienna Convention*.

57. According to Brazil, customary international law cautions against the application of one legal maxim for the interpretation of treaties to the exclusion of others. Acceptance of the EC arguments on Articles 59 and 30.3 of the *Vienna Convention* would give undue weight to the legal maxim *lex posterior derogat prior* on the issue of the succession of treaties relating to the same subject-matter. To ignore the relevance of the Oilseeds Agreement would undermine the security and predictability in the multilateral trading system and the fundamental principle of legal certainty. The European Communities "did not perform its obligations to Brazil in good faith".

2. *Agreement on Agriculture*

58. In the view of Brazil, the Panel reached the correct conclusion on the interpretation of Article 5.1(b) of the *Agreement on Agriculture*. The special safeguard provision is an exception to the requirement set out in Article 4.2 of that Agreement. Contrary to the EC argument, the system applying the special safeguard clause is not separate and parallel to the tariffication process under Article 4.2. The provisions are linked. Special safeguards are dependent on the implementation of tariffication. The reduction in tariffs over time may, in certain circumstances, increase the need for the introduction of special safeguards, but this does not necessarily make the two processes a different set of rights and obligations.

59. According to Brazil, the "price at which a product may enter the customs territory" is the duty-paid price and this market entry price, while "determined on the basis of" the c.i.f. price, is not the c.i.f. price itself. Payment of any applicable customs duty is a *sine qua non* of customs clearance. Brazil agrees with the finding of the Panel that, for present purposes, the words "market entry price" and the "price at which a product may enter the customs territory" are equivalent. Article 5.1(b) requires that the c.i.f. price is the price from which the calculation of the market entry price begins, but the market entry price is not the same as, but is "based on", the c.i.f. price.

60. Brazil stresses that Members were free to fix an appropriate "reference price"(or trigger price) which was only, in general, to be based on the average c.i.f. unit value. Members had a certain discretion in fixing the reference price.

The fact that some Members may now be in a situation where use of the special safeguard is unlikely in relation to a limited number of products because of the level of the reference price which they have set and the level of tariff they have negotiated, is not material to the proper interpretation of the text of Article 5.

61. Brazil asserts that if the Appellate Body reverses the findings of the Panel on Article 5.1(b) of the *Agreement on Agriculture*, then the question will remain whether or not the European Communities has complied with the other provisions of Article 5, in particular Article 5.5, or with Article 4.2, and that the Appellate Body must consider the proper procedure to be followed with regard to the finding of a panel on the basis of judicial economy. Because the Panel did not examine the substance of the claims under Articles 5.5 or 4.2 of the *Agreement on Agriculture*, there were no issues of law to be appealed by Brazil. According to Brazil, the very act of appeal of a panel's finding must open the possibility for the appellee to address, not only the grounds of appeals raised by the appellant, but also those issues of law and of fact that become germane as a consequence of the examination of those grounds. This would be "in line with" the doctrine of due process, to consider otherwise would be to defeat the doctrine of judicial economy. Should the Appellate Body reverse the findings of the Panel on Article 5.1(b), Brazil considers that the Appellate Body should also address the question of the substantive issues raised by Brazil so as not to diminish Brazil's rights in relation to dispute settlement. Brazil considers that the best approach is the approach adopted in previous appeals, and that Rule 16 of the *Working Procedures* allows such an approach. The problem in this case only arises if a finding is cross-appealed (without the benefit of a notice of appeal) and if that finding is reversed.

62. Brazil maintains that nothing in Article 5 of the *Agreement on Agriculture* permits a Member to introduce a representative price system. According to Brazil, the representative price mechanism distorts the implementation by the European Communities of Article 5 and results in the application of additional duties in a manner incompatible with that Article. Even though Regulation 1484/95 gives importers of out-of-quota frozen poultry meat two options for establishing the c.i.f. price of any one shipment, the representative c.i.f. price nevertheless determines the conditions for the import of frozen poultry meat into the European Communities. This is so because, upon importation, the European Communities requires immediate payment of the additional duty calculated on the basis of the representative price. If the importer elects to establish the actual c.i.f. price, payment of a security of the same value as the additional duty is required. This security must be pre-paid, and it is forfeited unless the trader can comply with the proofs required under Article 3.1 of Regulation 1484/95.

63. According to Brazil, the information provided by the European Communities to the Panel on the use by traders of all origins of the option to prove the actual c.i.f. price was inadequate and lacked transparency. Because of the complexities of the system, the use of the representative price is the rule and not the exception. The European Communities did not provide information to the Panel on how precisely the representative price is calculated in practice. Although the

representative price is supposed to be representative of an average c.i.f. price of all shipments from any one origin, there is no element in its calculation that refers to the value of the product at the EC frontier or to the value of the product on world markets. To comply with Article 5 of the *Agreement on Agriculture*, the European Communities is obliged to use the actual world price or free-at-frontier price. Brazil argues that as an exception to Article 4.2 of the *Agreement on Agriculture*, Article 5 must be construed narrowly. The representative price is not the c.i.f. price, nor is it representative of the c.i.f. price of any one shipment. Therefore, the representative price mechanism is not provided for, nor in compliance with, Article 5 of the *Agreement on Agriculture*. Brazil did not have an opportunity to comment on the EC submission to the Panel of 21 November 1997 concerning the calculation by the European Communities of the representative price, other than in a letter responding to the EC protest that Brazil breached confidentiality with respect to these documents, and in the comments on the interim report.

64. Brazil contends that, because the additional duty or bond that is payable on the basis of the EC representative price varies regularly depending on the published representative price, it is equivalent to a variable levy. This form of border protection measure is prohibited under Article 4.2 of the *Agreement on Agriculture*. Additional duties under Article 5.1(b) should be allowed to rise and fall on the basis of the shipment-by-shipment c.i.f. price changes.

E. Arguments by the Third Participants

1. Thailand

65. Thailand is of the view that a Member is free to conclude any bilateral agreement with any country. However, if the agreement has any effect on the rights and obligations of Members, all the provisions of general application of the *WTO Agreement*, including Articles I, III and XIII of the GATT 1994, must apply. Thailand agrees with the Panel's findings in paragraphs 213, 216 and 218 of the Panel Report. Allocation of any tariff-rate quota is governed by, and must be consistent with, Article XIII:2(d) of the GATT 1994. Insofar as the allocation of tariff-rate quotas to Members is concerned, Thailand agrees with the Panel's finding in paragraph 232 of the Panel Report that "Article XIII is a general provision regarding the non-discriminatory administration of import restrictions applicable to any TRQs regardless of their origin."

66. Thailand disagrees with the Panel's conclusion in paragraph 262 of the Panel Report that the tariff-rate quota for frozen poultry meat is fully utilized. Because the import licensing regime of the European Communities is operating in such a way that exporters do not know whether the transactions involved are within or outside the tariff-rate quota, and thus cannot take that factor into account when making the transactions, Thailand maintains it cannot be said that the tariff-rate quota is fully utilized. Once a tariff-rate quota is allocated, it must be administered in a manner that enables Members to "utilize fully the share of any

such total quantity or value which has been allotted" to them in accordance with Article XIII:2(d) of the GATT 1994. No conditions or formalities may be imposed that would prevent such full utilization. This is a substantive provision that Thailand understands to be applicable not only with respect to the total quantity or total value *per se*, but also in respect of the full benefits derived from the tariff-rate quotas, including the full enjoyment of the in-quota tariff rate.

67. Thailand agrees with the Panel's finding in paragraph 278 of the Panel Report that the "ordinary meaning of the phrase 'the price at which imports may enter the customs territory of the member granting the concession' would include payment of applicable duties" and in paragraph 282 of the Panel Report that "the EC has not invoked the special safeguard provision with respect to poultry in accordance with Article 5.1(b)." Thailand, however, disagrees with the Panel's exercise of judicial economy concerning Article 5.5 of the *Agreement on Agriculture* and argues that the Panel should have examined the consistency of the representative price with Article 5.1(b). In Thailand's opinion, the representative price is not in conformity with Article 5.1(b), which requires that the market entry price must be calculated on the basis of the c.i.f. import price of the shipment concerned alone. To the extent that the representative price is used in place of the c.i.f. import price for comparison with the trigger price for the purpose of setting additional duties to be paid as special safeguard duties, it is also inconsistent with Article 5.5 of the *Agreement on Agriculture*, which requires that the comparison be made only between the c.i.f. import price and the trigger price. Because the representative price is calculated on the basis of an average of a variety of prices, including internal market prices that are not c.i.f. prices within the meaning of Article 5.1(b), the representative price is thus functioning in such a way as to stabilize the price of the product concerned in the same fashion as the former EC regime of variable import levies.

2. *United States*

68. The United States supports the conclusion of the Panel that Brazil is not entitled to an allocation of the entire in-quota quantity of the tariff-rate quota for frozen poultry meat. The United States maintains that Brazil has failed to demonstrate that the EC allocation of this tariff-rate quota is inconsistent with the obligations of the European Communities under Articles XIII and XXVIII of the GATT, or that Brazil is otherwise entitled to the entire in-quota quantity of this tariff-rate quota. Brazil is incorrect to argue that as no Member objected, all Members must be deemed to have agreed to the solution agreed between Brazil and the European Communities. According to the United States, Brazil misunderstands the purpose of a notice withdrawing concessions under Article XXVIII of the GATT. Failure to have recourse under Article XXVIII:3 of the GATT can hardly be perceived as "agreement" of all Members, since not all Members have a right to such recourse. Brazil also errs in claiming that the opening of a country-specific tariff-rate quota for frozen poultry meat by the European Communities does not give rise to a negative impact on the trade interests of other Mem-

bers. A country-specific tariff-rate quota increases a trade opportunity for one Member, which receives a benefit relative to other Members.

69. The United States believes that the Panel correctly found in paragraph 230 of the Panel Report that there is "nothing in Article XIII that obligates Members to calculate tariff quota shares on the basis of imports from Members only", and, consequently, that it was consistent with Article XIII of the GATT 1994 for the European Communities to allow non-Members access to the tariff-rate quota. The obligations in Article XIII with respect to the treatment of Members when allocating a tariff-rate quota in no way imply that non-Members must be excluded from access to the in-quota quantity of a tariff-rate quota. The Panel correctly defined the issue before it as whether the European Communities is required to exclude non-Members from the basis of the calculation of tariff quota shares.

70. The United States supports the Panel's conclusion in paragraph 269 of the Panel Report that licences granted to a specific company or tariffs applied to a specific shipment would not be considered measures of "general application" within the scope of Article X of the GATT 1994. Moreover, the United States agrees with the EC view that Brazil's request to have each shipper informed of whether a shipment would be in-quota or out-of-quota could be impossible to implement in practice and is not required by Article X of the GATT 1994.

71. To the extent that the Panel's statement in paragraph 249 of the Panel Report that "[t]he Licensing Agreement, as applied to this particular case, only relates to in-quota trade" could be read to require that the "effects" referred to in Article 3.2 of the *Licensing Agreement* are limited to effects on in-quota imports, the United States supports the appeal of Brazil that the Panel's reasoning should be modified. The United States also supports Brazil's appeal with respect to the Panel's reliance on "full utilization" of the in-quota quantity as being dispositive of whether or not there is a breach of Article 3.2 of the *Licensing Agreement*. To the extent that the Panel's reasoning may be read to imply that full utilization of a quota allocation would preclude a finding of trade distortion, the United States supports the appeal of Brazil that the Panel's reasoning should be modified.

72. According to the United States, the Appellate Body should reject the EC appeal concerning the application of Articles 30.3 and 59.1 of the *Vienna Convention*. The approach advocated by the European Communities is based on the erroneous assumption that the agreement between the European Communities and Brazil - whether reflected in the bilateral Oilseeds Agreement or in Schedule LXXX - is dispositive in this case. According to the United States, it is not the bilateral agreement between the European Communities and Brazil which is at issue; rather, the question is whether the current allocation by the European Communities of its tariff-rate quota is in accordance with its obligations under Articles XIII and XXVIII of the GATT. The Oilseeds Agreement is not a "covered agreement" under the DSU. The Panel correctly set forth the role of the Oilseeds Agreement in its analysis in paragraph 202 of the Panel Report. The Panel's conclusion that the provisions of the Oilseeds Agreement did not provide for Brazil to receive the entire amount of the tariff-rate quota for frozen poultry meat

renders moot much of the EC argument on this point. Article XXVIII of the GATT could not justify a quota allocation inconsistent with Article XIII, even had that allocation been implemented in accordance with the terms of the Oilseeds Agreement.

73. With respect to Article 5.1(b) of the *Agreement on Agriculture*, the United States supports the position of the European Communities and believes that the Panel erred in interpreting the phrase "the price at which imports of that product may enter the customs territory of the Member granting the concession" to mean the price including the payment of applicable duties.

74. According to the United States, the *Working Procedures* do not appear to address the situation where a successful cross-appeal under Rule 23 would require that other issues raised in the panel proceeding be addressed by the Appellate Body in order to resolve the dispute. However, the United States notes that where a procedural question arises that is not covered by the *Working Procedures*, Rule 16.1 of the *Working Procedures* permits a Division to adopt an appropriate procedure for the purposes of a particular appeal. In this case, Brazil should not be denied relief to which it might otherwise be entitled simply because it did not appeal issues that only became relevant in light of the EC cross-appeal. However, the United States adds that for the purpose of making legal findings on Brazil's claims relating to additional duties, the Appellate Body should make legal findings based only on the Panel's factual findings or on facts submitted by the parties that were uncontested at the panel stage, and not on facts presented by a party for the first time on appeal.

75. The United States maintains that the EC representative price is inconsistent with Article 5.5 of the *Agreement on Agriculture*, as it appears to bear no relationship to the price of the individual shipment it is intended to represent. The United States agrees with Brazil that the burdens imposed by the European Communities, and its use of a penalty provision, create an effective deterrent to traders seeking to have additional duties calculated on a shipment-by-shipment basis. In the view of the United States, these facts undermine the EC claim that the use of a representative price is optional and help to explain the low rate at which traders are requesting shipment-by-shipment calculation of additional duties. With respect to Brazil's claim under Article 4.2 of the *Agreement on Agriculture*, the United States wishes to express caution as to whether the changes in the special safeguard duty as applied by the European Communities are such as to render it a "variable levy" within the meaning of that provision. By its nature, the amount of additional duties calculated under Article 5.5 could vary from shipment to shipment, so some variation must be permitted under the *Agreement on Agriculture*.

III. ISSUES RAISED IN THIS APPEAL

76. The following legal issues were raised by the appellants in this appeal:

(a) Whether the Panel erred in its interpretation of the relationship between Schedule LXXX and the Oilseeds Agreement;

(b) Whether the Panel erred in finding that the tariff-rate quota for frozen poultry meat in Schedule LXXX was not exclusively for the benefit of Brazil and that no agreement existed between Brazil and the European Communities on the allocation of the tariff-rate quota within the meaning of Article XIII:2(d) of the GATT 1994;

(c) Whether a tariff-rate quota resulting from negotiations under Article XXVIII of the GATT 1947 must be administered in a non-discriminatory manner consistent with Article XIII of the GATT 1994;

(d) Whether the Panel erred in its interpretation of Article XIII of the GATT 1994 with respect to the rights and obligations of Members in relation to non-Members in the administration of tariff-rate quotas;

(e) Whether the Panel erred in its application of Article X of the GATT 1994, and, in particular, in its assessment of measures "of general application" in this case;

(f) Whether the Panel erred: in finding that the *Licensing Agreement* applies only to in-quota trade in this case; in finding that there was no trade distortion within the meaning of Articles 1.2 and 3.2 of the *Licensing Agreement*; and in not examining Brazil's claim concerning a general principle of transparency underlying the *Licensing Agreement*;

(g) Whether the Panel acted inconsistently with Article 11 of the DSU in not examining certain arguments made by Brazil relating to GATT/WTO law and practice; and

(h) Whether the Panel erred in finding that the "price at which imports of [a] product may enter the customs territory of the Member granting the concession, as determined on the basis of the c.i.f. import price of the shipment concerned" in Article 5.1(b) of the *Agreement on Agriculture* is the c.i.f. price *plus* ordinary customs duties.

IV. RELATIONSHIP BETWEEN SCHEDULE LXXX AND THE OILSEEDS AGREEMENT

77. With respect to the relationship between the Oilseeds Agreement and Schedule LXXX in this case, the Panel found, *inter alia*:

> ... in the present case, the Oilseeds Agreement was negotiated within the framework of Article XXVIII of GATT. Insofar as the content of the Oilseeds Agreement is incorpo-

> rated into Schedule LXXX - a point not disputed by the parties - there is a close connection between the two.[22]

The Panel also stated:

> ... the Oilseeds Agreement was concluded within the context of Article XXVIII negotiations. Under ordinary circumstances, the resulting modification of the EC tariff schedule would have been certified by the Director-General pursuant to the 1980 procedure for modification and rectification of schedules. However, as the conclusion of the Oilseeds Agreement coincided with the substantive conclusion of tariff negotiations in the Uruguay Round, this procedure was not strictly followed. The EC directly incorporated the substance of the Oilseeds Agreement into its then-current tariff schedule, effective 1 January 1994, and also into Schedule LXXX at the conclusion of the Uruguay Round negotiations. This procedural anomaly, in our view, does not affect the legal characterization of the Oilseeds Agreement as a bilateral agreement concluded within the context of Article XXVIII negotiations, as is evidenced by the fact that the negotiations leading to its conclusion were authorized by the CONTRACTING PARTIES.[23]

The Panel asserted that it would:

> ... proceed to the examination of the Oilseeds Agreement to the extent relevant to the determination of the EC's obligations under the WTO agreements vis-à-vis Brazil.[24]

78. Although the European Communities is satisfied with the practical result of the Panel Report on this point, the European Communities argues that the Panel erred in its interpretation of the relationship between Schedule LXXX and the Oilseeds Agreement.[25] The Panel did not accept the argument of the European Communities that Schedule LXXX superseded and terminated the Oilseeds Agreement because the *WTO Agreement* was a later treaty relating to the same subject-matter in accordance with Article 59.1 of the *Vienna Convention*, or that the Oilseeds Agreement only applies to the extent compatible with Schedule LXXX in accordance with Article 30.3 of the *Vienna Convention*. The Panel stated:

> ... we cannot summarily dismiss the significance of the Oilseeds Agreement in the interpretation of Schedule LXXX

---

22 Panel Report, para. 201.
23 Panel Report, para. 204.
24 Panel Report, para. 202.
25 EC appellant's submission, para. 33.

> by recourse to the public international law principles embodied in the Vienna Convention.[26]

79. In our view, it is not necessary to have recourse to either Article 59.1 or Article 30.3 of the *Vienna Convention*, because the text of the *WTO Agreement* and the legal arrangements governing the transition from the GATT 1947 to the WTO resolve the issue of the relationship between Schedule LXXX and the Oilseeds Agreement in this case. Schedule LXXX is annexed to the *Marrakesh Protocol to the General Agreement on Tariffs and Trade 1994* (the "*Marrakesh Protocol*"), and is an integral part of the GATT 1994.[27] As such, it forms part of the multilateral obligations under the *WTO Agreement*. The Oilseeds Agreement, in contrast, is a bilateral agreement negotiated by the European Communities and Brazil under Article XXVIII of the GATT 1947, as part of the resolution of the dispute in *EEC - Oilseeds*.[28] As such, the Oilseeds Agreement is not a "covered agreement" within the meaning of Articles 1 and 2 of the DSU. Nor is the Oilseeds Agreement part of the multilateral obligations accepted by Brazil and the European Communities pursuant to the *WTO Agreement*, which came into effect on 1 January 1995. The Oilseeds Agreement is not cited in any Annex to the *WTO Agreement*. Although the provisions of certain legal instruments that entered into force under the GATT 1947 were made part of the GATT 1994 pursuant to the language in Annex 1A incorporating the GATT 1994 into the *WTO Agreement*[29], the Oilseeds Agreement is not one of those legal instruments.

80. Furthermore, the Oilseeds Agreement does not constitute part of the "decisions, procedures and customary practices followed by the CONTRACTING PARTIES to GATT 1947"by which the WTO "shall be guided" under Article XVI:1 of the *WTO Agreement*. These "decisions, procedures and customary practices" include only those taken or followed by the CONTRACTING PARTIES to the GATT 1947 acting *jointly*.

81. It is Schedule LXXX, rather than the Oilseeds Agreement, which contains the relevant obligations of the European Communities under the *WTO Agreement*. Therefore, it is Schedule LXXX, rather than the Oilseeds Agreement, which forms the legal basis for this dispute and which must be interpreted in accordance with "customary rules of interpretation of public international law" under Article 3.2 of the DSU.

82. In *European Communities - Customs Classification of Certain Computer Equipment*, we made the following general statement on the interpretation of concessions in a Member's Schedule:

---

26 Panel Report, para. 207.

27 Article II:7 of the GATT 1994.

28 Adopted 25 January 1990, BISD 37S/86; and DS28/R, 31 March 1992.

29 Those legal instruments are described in paragraph 1(b) of that incorporating language as including certain protocols and certifications relating to tariff concessions, certain protocols of accession, certain decisions on waivers granted under Article XXV of the GATT 1947, and "other decisions of the CONTRACTING PARTIES to GATT 1947".

> A Schedule is made an integral part of the GATT 1994 by Article II:7 of the GATT 1994. Therefore, the concessions provided for in that Schedule are part of the terms of the treaty. As such, the only rules which may be applied in interpreting the meaning of a concession are the general rules of treaty interpretation set out in the *Vienna Convention.*[30]

83. We recognize that the Oilseeds Agreement was negotiated within the framework of Article XXVIII of the GATT 1947 with the authorization of the CONTRACTING PARTIES and that both parties agree that the substance of the Oilseeds Agreement was the basis for the 15,500 tonne tariff-rate quota for frozen poultry meat that became a concession of the European Communities in the Uruguay Round set forth in Schedule LXXX. Therefore, in our view, the Oilseeds Agreement may serve as a *supplementary means* of interpretation of Schedule LXXX pursuant to Article 32 of the *Vienna Convention*, as it is part of the historical background of the concessions of the European Communities for frozen poultry meat.

84. The Panel accepts that the Oilseeds Agreement can be useful in interpreting the EC concession on frozen poultry meat in Schedule LXXX.[31] In paragraph 202, the Panel states "we proceed to the examination of the Oilseeds Agreement to the extent relevant to *the determination of the EC's obligations under the WTO agreements* vis-à-vis Brazil". (emphasis added) In paragraph 207, the Panel states, "we cannot summarily dismiss the significance of the Oilseeds Agreement *in the interpretation of Schedule LXXX* by recourse to the public international law principles embodied in the Vienna Convention". (emphasis added)

85. We find no reversible error in the Panel's treatment of the relationship between Schedule LXXX and the Oilseeds Agreement.

V. THE TARIFF-RATE QUOTA IN SCHEDULE LXXX

86. Three legal issues are raised with respect to the tariff-rate quota for frozen poultry meat in Schedule LXXX:

(a) Whether the tariff-rate quota of 15,500 tonnes for frozen poultry meat specified in Schedule LXXX is allocated exclusively for the benefit of Brazil, and whether an agreement existed between Brazil and the European Communities on the allocation of the tariff-rate quota within the meaning of Article XIII:2(d) of the GATT 1994;

(b) Whether a tariff-rate quota resulting from negotiations under Article XXVIII of the GATT 1947 must be administered in a non-

---

[30] Adopted 22 June 1998, WT/DS62/AB/R, WT/DS67/AB/R, WT/DS68/AB/R, para. 84.

[31] Panel Report, paras. 202 and 207.

discriminatory manner consistent with Article XIII of the GATT 1994; and

(c) Whether the trade of non-Members should be taken into account in calculating tariff-rate quota shares under Article XIII of the GATT 1994.

A. *The Exclusive or Non-exclusive Character of the Tariff-Rate Quota for Frozen Poultry Meat in Schedule LXXX*

87. With respect to the tariff-rate quota for frozen poultry meat of 15,500 tonnes specified in Schedule LXXX, the Panel found, *inter alia*:

> To sum up our findings in this section, we find no proof (either in the text or in the object and purpose of the Oilseeds Agreement) in support of the Brazilian claim that the poultry TRQ opened as the result of the Oilseeds Agreement was intended to be a country-specific tariff quota with Brazil being the sole beneficiary. In other words, we find that the European Communities is bound, on an MFN basis, by its tariff commitments for frozen poultry meat.[32]

88. Brazil argues that the Panel erred in finding that the tariff-rate quota for frozen poultry meat was not allocated exclusively to Brazil, and in finding that there was no explicit agreement between Brazil and the European Communities to this effect within the meaning of Article XIII:2(d) of the GATT 1994.[33] Brazil contends further that the Panel erred in limiting its examination of the Oilseeds Agreement to the "relevant parts" of that Agreement, and in failing to examine all the provisions of the Oilseeds Agreement in accordance with Article 31 of the Vienna Convention.[34]

89. As we stated previously, it is Schedule LXXX, rather than the Oilseeds Agreement, that is the relevant WTO obligation in this dispute and that must therefore be interpreted in accordance with "customary rules of interpretation of public international law" under Article 3.2 of the DSU.

90. Part I (Most-Favoured-Nation-Tariff), Section I (Agricultural Products), Section I-B (Tariff Quotas) of Schedule LXXX provides a duty-free quota of 15,500 tonnes of frozen poultry meat falling within CN subheadings 0207 41 10, 0207 41 41 and 0207 41 71. There are no "other terms and conditions" specified relating to this tariff-rate quota in Schedule LXXX, and, in particular, there is no reference to the Oilseeds Agreement and no mention that the tariff-rate quota is exclusively reserved for exports from Brazil. The fact that the tariff-rate quota for frozen poultry meat appears in Part I under the heading "Most-Favoured-Nation

---

32 Panel Report, para. 218.

33 Brazil's appellant's submission, paras. 80-84.

34 Brazil's appellant's submission, paras. 17 and 21.

Tariff" and that there are no other terms or conditions specified in Schedule LXXX concerning that concession would suggest, on the basis of the ordinary meaning of the terms, that the tariff-rate quota for frozen poultry meat was intended to be allocated on an MFN basis.

91. This view is confirmed by an examination of the relevant provisions of the Oilseeds Agreement as a supplementary means of interpretation of the concessions made by the European Communities in Schedule LXXX. A footnote in the Oilseeds Agreement states:

> Duty exemption shall be applicable for cuts falling within subheadings 0207.41.10, 0207.41.41 and 0207.41.71 within the limits of a *global annual tariff quota* of 15.500 tonnes to be granted by the competent Community authorities. (emphasis added)

92. The Oilseeds Agreement uses the term "global annual tariff quota" in describing the 15,500 tonnes. Although we agree with the Panel that this term is "non-legal", nevertheless, this is a term well-understood in GATT/WTO practice to mean a tariff-rate quota that is to be administered on a non-discriminatory basis pursuant to Article XIII of the GATT 1994. As early as the Havana Conference in 1947, it was pointed out during discussions on the provision that later became Article XIII of the GATT that "*global quotas* not allocated among supplying countries might sometimes operate in a manner unduly favourable to those countries best able for any reason to take prompt advantage of the *global quotas* at the opening of the quota period".[35] (emphasis added) We also refer to the statement in *Panel on Newsprint*:

> In examining the EEC Regulation 3684/83, the Panel found that it did not in fact constitute a change in the administration or management of the tariff quota from a *global quota* system to a system of country shares, as had been asserted by the EC.[36] (emphasis added)

In both cases, the term "global quota" was used in contrast with quotas allocated on a country-specific basis. In the light of this, and in the absence of any persuasive evidence to the contrary, we cannot construe the term "global annual tariff quota" as used in the Oilseeds Agreement to mean a country-specific quota allocated exclusively to Brazil.[37]

---

[35] Reports of Committees and Principal Sub-Committees: ICITO I/8, Geneva, September 1948, p. 91, para. 28, cited in GATT, *Analytical Index: Guide to GATT Law and Practice* (1995), Vol. I, p. 400.

[36] Adopted 20 November 1984, BISD 31S/114, para. 51.

[37] See Jackson, J., *World Trade and the Law of GATT* (Bobbs-Merrill, 1969), p. 232. See also, for example, the *Dictionary of Trade Policy Terms* (Centre for International Economic Studies, 1998), and the *Dictionary of International Trade* (World Trade Press, 1998).

93. We proceed next to an examination of Brazil's claim that the Panel erred in finding that there was no evidence of an agreement between Brazil and the European Communities on the allocation of the tariff-rate quota for frozen poultry meat within the meaning of Article XIII:2(d) of the GATT 1994. To conform to Article XIII:2(d), all other Members having a "substantial interest" in supplying the product concerned would have to agree. That is not the case here. As the European Communities did not seek an agreement with Thailand, the other contracting party having a substantial interest in the supply of frozen poultry meat to the European Communities at that time, the Oilseeds Agreement cannot be considered an agreement within the meaning of Article XIII:2(d) of the GATT 1994.

94. We understand Brazil to argue that the bilateral character of the Oilseeds Agreement implies, in itself, that the tariff-rate quota for frozen poultry meat is for Brazil's exclusive benefit and should not be extended to others who are not parties to that Agreement. The bilateral character of the Oilseeds Agreement does not, by itself, constitute evidence of a common intent that the tariff-rate quota was for the exclusive benefit of Brazil. We agree with the Panel that:

> … most tariff concessions are negotiated bilaterally, but the results of the negotiations are extended on a multilateral basis. The fact that the tariff-rate quota for frozen poultry meat was opened as a result of bilateral negotiations between the EC and Brazil does not mean that the EC was obligated to accord the benefit exclusively to Brazil.[38]

95. Therefore, we uphold the Panel's finding in paragraph 218 of the Panel Report that there is no adequate proof to support Brazil's claim that the tariff-rate quota for frozen poultry meat set forth in Schedule LXXX was intended to be a country-specific tariff-rate quota with Brazil as the sole beneficiary. We also agree with the Panel that there is no evidence that an agreement, explicit or otherwise, existed between Brazil and the European Communities concerning the allocation of the tariff-rate quota for frozen poultry meat within the meaning of Article XIII:2(d) of the GATT 1994.[39]

B. *Article XIII of the GATT 1994*

96. The Panel found that:

> … there is no provision in the WTO agreements that allows departure from the MFN principle in the case of TRQs resulting from Article XXVIII negotiations. Nor is there any decision of the CONTRACTING PARTIES or of the Min-

[38] Panel Report, para. 216.
[39] Panel Report, para. 227.

> isterial Conference/General Council, or any adopted panel or Appellate Body report that permits such departure.[40]

97. Brazil argues that the MFN principle in Articles I and XIII of the GATT 1994 does not necessarily apply to tariff-rate quotas resulting from compensation negotiations under Article XXVIII of the GATT.[41] According to Brazil, because the purpose of the Oilseeds Agreement was to compensate Brazil for the modification of EC concessions on oilseeds, Brazil is entitled to benefit exclusively from the modified concession. In Brazil's view, the European Communities failed to respect the balance between the withdrawal of a concession and the offering of compensation in another product.[42]

98. In *United States - Restrictions on Imports of Sugar*[43], the panel stated that Article II of the GATT permits contracting parties to incorporate into their Schedules acts yielding rights under the GATT, but not acts *diminishing* obligations under that Agreement. In our view, this is particularly so with respect to the principle of non-discrimination in Articles I and XIII of the GATT 1994. In *EC - Bananas*, we confirmed the principle that a Member may yield rights but not diminish its obligations and concluded that it is equally valid for the market access concessions and commitments for agricultural products contained in the Schedules annexed to the GATT 1994.[44] The ordinary meaning of the term "concessions" suggests that a Member may yield or waive some of its own rights and grant benefits to other Members, but that it cannot unilaterally diminish its own obligations. This interpretation is confirmed by paragraph 3 of the *Marrakesh Protocol*, which provides:

> The implementation of the concessions and commitments contained in the schedules annexed to this Protocol shall, upon request, be subject to multilateral examination by the Members. This would be *without prejudice to the rights and obligations of Members under Agreements in Annex 1A of the WTO Agreement*. (emphasis added)

99. Therefore, the concessions contained in Schedule LXXX pertaining to the tariff-rate quota for frozen poultry meat must be consistent with Articles I and XIII of the GATT 1994.

100. Brazil argues that the Oilseeds Agreement was negotiated under Article XXVIII to compensate Brazil for the impairment of benefits from the oilseeds concession. According to Brazil, there is an element of specificity about compensation, which explains and justifies possible departure from the principle of non-

[40] Panel Report, para. 213.

[41] Brazil's appellant's submission, para. 46.

[42] Brazil's appellant's submission, paras. 47-55.

[43] Adopted 22 June 1989, BISD 36S/331, para. 5.2.

[44] Adopted 25 September 1997, WT/DS27/AB/R, para. 154.

discrimination.[45] In support of this interpretation, Brazil refers to compensation under Article XXIV:6 of the GATT. In Brazil's view, no distinction should be made, either in procedure or in intention, between compensation negotiated under Articles XXIV:6 and XXVIII of the GATT. In practice, Brazil maintains, there are examples of both country-specific and non-discriminatory tariff-rate quotas offered and implemented by the European Communities as compensation under Article XXIV:6 of the GATT. There is no reason, Brazil argues, why the same principle should not apply to compensation under Article XXVIII of the GATT.[46] We do not accept this argument. We see nothing in Article XXVIII to suggest that compensation negotiated within its framework may be exempt from compliance with the non-discrimination principle inscribed in Articles I and XIII of the GATT 1994. As the Panel observed, this interpretation is, furthermore, supported by the negotiating history of Article XXVIII. Regarding the provision which eventually became Article XXVIII:3, the Chairman of the Tariff Agreements Committee at Geneva in 1947, concluded:

> It was agreed that there was no intention to interfere in any way with the operation of the most-favoured-nation clause. This Article is headed "Modification of Schedules". It refers throughout to concessions negotiated under paragraph 1 of Article II, the Schedules, and there is no reference to Article I, which is the Most-Favoured-Nation Clause. Therefore, I think the intent is clear: that in no way should this Article interfere with the operation of the Most-Favoured-Nation Clause.[47]

Although this statement refers specifically to the MFN clause in Article I of the GATT, logic requires that it applies equally to the non-discriminatory administration of quotas and tariff-rate quotas under Article XIII of the GATT 1994.

101. We agree with the Panel that:

> If a preferential treatment of a particular trading partner not elsewhere justified is permitted under the pretext of "compensatory adjustment" under Article XXVIII:2, it would create a serious loophole in the multilateral trading system. Such a result would fundamentally alter the overall balance of concessions Article XXVIII is designed to achieve.[48]

102. For these reasons, we uphold the Panel's finding in paragraph 213 of the Panel Report that a tariff-rate quota which resulted from negotiations under Article XXVIII of the GATT 1947, and which was incorporated into a Member's

---

45 Brazil's appellant's submission, paras. 46 and 51.

46 Brazil's appellant's submission, para. 59.

47 EPCT/TAC/PV/18, p. 46; see Panel Report, para. 217.

48 Panel Report, para. 215.

Uruguay Round Schedule, must be administered in a non-discriminatory manner consistent with Article XIII of the GATT 1994.

C. *Treatment of Non-Members under Article XIII of the GATT 1994*

103. According to the Panel, there is nothing in Article XIII of the GATT 1994 that obligates Members to calculate tariff-rate quota shares on the basis of imports from Members only.[49] In the Panel's view, if the purpose of using past trade performance is to approximate the shares of Members in the absence of the restrictions, as required under the chapeau of Article XIII:2, exclusion of a non-Member, particularly if it is an efficient supplier, would not serve that purpose.[50] Accordingly, the Panel found:

> ... the EC has not acted inconsistently with Article XIII of GATT by calculating Brazil's tariff quota share based on the total quantity of imports, including those from non-Members.[51]

104. Brazil submits that under Article XIII:2(d) of the GATT 1994 non-Members have no right to participate in a tariff-rate quota, and that a Member opening a tariff-rate quota has no right unilaterally to allow such participation.[52] In Brazil's view, the Panel has expanded the wording of Article XIII of the GATT 1994 by allowing the inclusion of non-Members in a tariff-rate quota.[53]

105. We note that the finding of the Panel on this point is limited to one issue, namely, whether trade of non-Members may be taken into account in the calculation of shares in a tariff-rate quota. This finding is narrower than the scope of Brazil's argument before the Panel, which was concerned with other issues related to the rights and obligations of Members in relation to non-Members under Article XIII, and particularly the participation of a non-Member in the "others" category of a tariff-rate quota. The Panel's finding is also narrower than the scope of Brazil's appeal, which is concerned with the rights and obligations of Members in relation to non-Members in the administration of tariff-rate quotas under Article XIII.

106. We agree with the Panel that the calculation of shares must be based on the total imports of the product in question - whether those imports originate from Members or non-Members. Otherwise, it would not be possible to comply with the requirement in the chapeau of Article XIII:2 that:

---

[49] Panel Report, para. 230.
[50] Panel Report, para. 230.
[51] Panel Report, para. 233.
[52] Brazil's appellant's submission, para. 89.
[53] Brazil's appellant's submission, para. 95.

> In applying import restrictions to any product, Members shall aim at a distribution of trade in such product approaching as closely as possible the shares which the various Members might be expected to obtain in the absence of such restrictions … .

107. This leaves unanswered two issues that were raised by Brazil before the Panel and also in both Brazil's notice of appeal and Brazil's appellant's submission, namely, the *allocation* of tariff-rate quota shares to a non-Member, and the *participation of non-Members in the "others" category* of a tariff-rate quota. With respect to these two issues, we are mindful of our mandate under Article 17.6 of the DSU to limit appeals "to issues of law covered in the panel report and legal interpretations developed by the panel". Also, we are mindful of Article 17.13 of the DSU, which states, "The Appellate Body may uphold, modify or reverse the legal findings and conclusions of the panel." With these constraints in mind, we note that there is no finding by the Panel or legal interpretation developed by the Panel on either of these two issues. It is true that in footnote 140 of the Panel Report, the Panel states that paragraph 7.75 of the *EC - Bananas* panel reports and "particularly the use of the phrase 'all suppliers other than Members with a substantial interest in supplying the product' … indicates that the *Banana III* panel did not take the view that allocation of quota shares to non-Members under Article XIII:2(d) was not permitted". We do not consider this comment made in a footnote by the Panel to be either a "legal interpretation developed by the panel" within the meaning of Article 17.6 of the DSU or a "legal finding" or "conclusion" that the Appellate Body may "uphold, modify or reverse" under Article 17.13 of the DSU. It is undisputed in this case that there is no *allocation* of a country-specific share in the tariff-rate quota to a non-Member. There is, therefore, no finding nor any "legal interpretation developed by the panel" that may be the subject of an appeal of which the Appellate Body may take cognizance.

108. Therefore, we uphold the finding of the Panel in paragraph 233 of the Panel Report that the European Communities has not acted inconsistently with Article XIII of the GATT 1994 by calculating Brazil's tariff-rate quota share based on the total quantity of imports, including those from non-Members.

VI. ARTICLE X OF THE GATT 1994

109. Article X of the GATT 1994 states, in relevant part:

> 1. Laws, regulations, judicial decisions and administrative rulings of general application, made effective by any Member ... shall be published promptly in such a manner as to enable governments and traders to become acquainted with them ...
>
> ...

> 3. (*a*) Each Member shall administer in a uniform, impartial and reasonable manner all its laws, regulations, decisions and rulings of the kind described in paragraph 1 of this Article.

110. With respect to Article X, the Panel found:

> ... that Article X is applicable only to laws, regulations, judicial decisions and administrative rulings "of general application"... licences issued to a specific company or applied to a specific shipment cannot be considered to be a measure "of general application". In the present case, the information which Brazil claims the EC should have made available concerns a specific shipment, which is outside the scope of Article X of GATT.
>
> In view of the fact that the EC has demonstrated that it has complied with the obligation of publication of the regulations under Article X regarding the licensing rules of general application, without further evidence and argument in support of Brazil's position regarding how Article X is violated, we dismiss Brazil's claim on this point.[54]

111. Article X:1 of the GATT 1994 makes it clear that Article X does not deal with specific transactions, but rather with rules "of general application".[55] It is clear to us that the EC rules pertaining to import licensing set out in Regulation 1431/94 are rules "of general application". The Panel found that with respect to these rules of general application, the European Communities had complied with its publication obligations under Article X.[56] Brazil does not appeal this finding.

112. Brazil, however, argues that the Panel erred in law in assessing measures of general application in Article X of the GATT 1994 and that the Panel also misinterpreted Brazil's submissions relating to Article X. According to Brazil, the generally applicable rules of the European Communities relating to imports of frozen poultry meat do not allow Brazilian traders to know whether a particular shipment will be subject to the rules governing in-quota trade or to rules relating to out-of-quota trade, and Brazil maintains that this is a violation of Article X.[57]

113. The approach to Article X of the GATT 1994 advocated by Brazil would require that a Member specify in advance the precise treatment to be accorded to each individual shipment of frozen poultry meat into the European Communities. Although it is true, as Brazil contends, that any measure of general application will always have to be applied in specific cases, nevertheless, the particular

---

54 Panel Report, paras. 269-270.
55 Panel Report, para. 269.
56 Panel Report, para. 270.
57 Brazil's appellant's submission, paras. 105 and 114.

treatment accorded to each individual shipment cannot be considered a measure "of general application" within the meaning of Article X. The Panel cited the following passage from the panel report in *United States - Restrictions on Imports of Cotton and Man-made Fibre Underwear*:

> The mere fact that the restraint at issue was an administrative order does not prevent us from concluding that the restraint was a measure of general application. Nor does the fact that it was a country-specific measure exclude the possibility of it being a measure of general application. If, for instance, the restraint was addressed to a specific company or applied to a specific shipment, it would not have qualified as a measure of general application. However, to the extent that the restraint affects an unidentified number of economic operators, including domestic and foreign producers, we find it to be a measure of general application.[58]

We agree with the Panel that "conversely, licences issued to a specific company or applied to a specific shipment cannot be considered to be a measure 'of general application'"[59] within the meaning of Article X.

114. It is inherent in the nature of a tariff-rate quota that imports over the threshold quantity specified in the rules of general application will not benefit from the terms of the tariff-rate quota. Within the framework of the rules of general application that establish the terms of the tariff-rate quota for frozen poultry meat, the detailed arrangements concerning the importation of a particular shipment of frozen poultry into the European Communities are made primarily among private operators. These arrangements will determine whether a particular shipment falls within or outside the tariff-rate quota, and will consequently determine whether the rules relating to in-quota trade or those relating to out-of-quota trade will apply to a given shipment. These arrangements among private operators have been generally left to them by the government of the Member concerned. Article X of the GATT 1994 does not impose an obligation on Member governments to ensure that exporters are continuously notified by importers as to the treatment particular impending shipments will receive in relation to a tariff-rate quota.

115. Article X relates to the *publication* and *administration* of "laws, regulations, judicial decisions and administrative rulings of general application", rather than to the *substantive content* of such measures. In *EC - Bananas*, we stated:

---

[58] Adopted 25 February 1997, WT/DS24/R, para. 7.65. In that case, we agreed with the panel's finding that the safeguard measure restraint imposed by the United States was "a measure of general application" within the contemplation of Article X:2 of the GATT 1994. See Appellate Body Report, *United States - Restrictions on Imports of Cotton and Man-made Fibre Underwear*, adopted 25 February 1997, WT/DS24/AB/R, DSR 1997:I, 11 at 29.

[59] Panel Report, para. 269.

> The text of Article X:3(a) clearly indicates that the requirements of "uniformity, impartiality and reasonableness" do not apply to the laws, regulations, decisions and rulings *themselves*, but rather to the *administration* of those laws, regulations, decisions and rulings. The context of Article X:3(a) within Article X, which is entitled "Publication and Administration of Trade Regulations", and a reading of the other paragraphs of Article X, make it clear that Article X applies to the *administration* of laws, regulations, decisions and rulings. To the extent that the laws, regulations, decisions and rulings themselves are discriminatory, they can be examined for their consistency with the relevant provisions of the GATT 1994.[60]

Thus, to the extent that Brazil's appeal relates to the *substantive content* of the EC rules themselves, and not to their *publication* or *administration*, that appeal falls outside the scope of Article X of the GATT 1994.[61] The WTO-consistency of such substantive content must be determined by reference to provisions of the covered agreements other than Article X of the GATT 1994.

116. For these reasons, we uphold the Panel's finding in paragraph 269 of the Panel Report that "the information which Brazil claims the EC should have made available concerns a specific shipment, which is outside the scope of Article X of GATT".

VII. AGREEMENT ON IMPORT LICENSING PROCEDURES

117. Three issues are raised by Brazil with respect to the *Licensing Agreement*:

(a) Whether the Panel erred in interpreting Articles 1.2 and 3.2 of the *Licensing Agreement* so as to restrict the scope of application of that Agreement, in this case, to in-quota trade;

(b) Whether the Panel erred in finding that there was no trade distortion in this case within the meaning of Articles 1.2 and 3.2 of the *Licensing Agreement*; and

(c) Whether the Panel erred in failing to examine the general claim made by Brazil concerning the violation of a principle of transparency set out in the preamble to, and underlying, the *Licensing Agreement.*

118. Article 1.2 of the *Licensing Agreement* states:

> Members shall ensure that the administrative procedures used to implement import licensing regimes are in

60 Adopted 25 September 1997, WT/DS27/AB/R, para. 200.

61 We note that the issue of the *comprehensibility* of the EC measure does not arise in this case.

> conformity with the relevant provisions of GATT 1994 including its annexes and protocols, as interpreted by this Agreement, *with a view to preventing trade distortions that may arise from an inappropriate operation of those procedures*, taking into account the economic development purposes and financial and trade needs of developing country Members. (emphasis added)

Article 3.2 of the *Licensing Agreement* provides:

> Non-automatic licensing shall *not* have *trade-restrictive or -distortive effects on imports additional to those caused by the imposition of the restriction*. Non-automatic licensing procedures shall correspond in scope and duration to the measure they are used to implement, and shall be no more administratively burdensome than absolutely necessary to administer the measure. (emphasis added)

119. With respect to the *Licensing Agreement*, the Panel found, in relevant part:

> In examining these claims, we first note that Brazil's reference to the percentage share relates to its total exports of poultry products to the EC market, the majority of which consists of over-quota (duty paid) trade. *The Licensing Agreement, as applied to this particular case, only relates to in-quota trade*. Second, the licences issued to imports from Brazil are *fully utilized*, which strongly suggests that *any trade-distortive effects of the operation of the licensing rules have been overcome by exporters*. Third, the total volume of poultry exports from Brazil has generally been increasing ... . Therefore, *we fail to understand the relevance of the decline in the percentage share in total trade to a violation of the Licensing Agreement*. Thus, based on the evidence presented by Brazil regarding its percentage share of the EC poultry market, *we do not find that the EC has acted inconsistently with Articles 1.2 and 3.2 of the Licensing Agreement.*[62] (emphasis added)

A. *Scope of Application*

120. Brazil maintains that there is nothing in the text or context of Articles 1.2 and 3.2 of the *Licensing Agreement* that limits to in-quota trade the requirement in Article 1.2 that licensing systems be implemented "with a view to preventing

---

[62] Panel Report, para. 249.

trade distortions" or the prohibition in Article 3.2 of additional trade-restrictive or trade-distortive effects.[63]

121. The preamble to the *Licensing Agreement* stresses that the Agreement aims at ensuring that import licensing procedures "are not utilized in a manner contrary to the principles and obligations of GATT 1994"and are "implemented in a transparent and predictable manner". Moreover, Articles 1.2 and 3.2 make it clear that the *Licensing Agreement* is also concerned, with, among other things, preventing trade distortions that may be caused by licensing procedures. It follows that wherever an import licensing regime is applied, these requirements must be observed. The requirement to prevent trade distortion found in Articles 1.2 and 3.2 of the *Licensing Agreement* refers to *any* trade distortion that may be caused by the introduction or operation of licensing procedures, and is not necessarily limited to that part of trade to which the licensing procedures themselves apply. There may be situations where the operation of licensing procedures, in fact, have restrictive or distortive effects on that part of trade that is not strictly subject to those procedures.

122. In the case before us, the licensing procedure established in Article 1 of Regulation 1431/94 applies, by its terms, only to in-quota trade in frozen poultry meat.[64] No licensing is required by Regulation 1431/94 for out-of-quota trade in frozen poultry meat. To the extent that the Panel intended merely to reflect the fairly obvious fact that this licensing procedure applies only to in-quota trade, we uphold the finding of the Panel that "[t]he Licensing Agreement, as applied to this particular case, only relates to in-quota trade".[65]

B. Trade Distortion

123. Brazil maintains that the Panel failed to address or examine properly certain evidence, including evidence concerning Brazil's falling share of the EC poultry market, and did not examine whether this falling market share was caused by the introduction of the EC licensing procedures for the tariff-rate quota for frozen poultry meat.[66]

124. The Panel stated that it "fail[ed] to understand the relevance of the decline in the percentage share in total trade to a violation of the Licensing Agreement."[67] The Panel then concluded that, "based on the evidence presented by Brazil regarding its percentage share of the EC poultry market, we do not find

---

[63] Brazil's appellant's submission, para. 140.

[64] Article 1 of Regulation 1431/94 states: "All imports into the Community under [the tariff-rate quota] ... shall be subject to the presentation of an import licence."

[65] Panel Report, para. 249.

[66] Brazil's appellant's submission, paras. 143-150.

[67] Panel Report, para. 249.

that the EC has acted inconsistently with Articles 1.2 and 3.2 of the Licensing Agreement."[68]

125. Under Regulation 1431/94, Brazil's share in the EC tariff-rate quota for frozen poultry meat is 7,100 tonnes out of the total tariff-rate quota of 15,500 tonnes.[69] This share is equal to approximately 45 per cent of the tariff-rate quota. This is the same as Brazil's percentage share of the total exports of frozen poultry meat to the European Communities during the reference period of the preceding three years. In addition, the Panel noted, licences issued by the European Communities for imports of frozen poultry meat from Brazil have been fully utilized.[70] This means that Brazil's percentage share in the tariff-rate quota has remained at the same level as Brazil's share in the total trade over the relevant period. Moreover, the absolute volume of exports of frozen poultry meat by Brazil in the total exports of this product to the European Communities has been rising since the imposition of the tariff-rate quota for frozen poultry meat.[71]

126. Brazil has not, in our view, clearly explained, either before the Panel or before us, how the licensing procedure *caused* the decline in market share. Brazil has not offered any persuasive evidence that its falling market share could, in this particular case - with a constant percentage share of the tariff-rate quota, full utilization of the tariff-rate quota and a growing total volume of exports - be viewed as constituting trade distortion attributable to the licensing procedure. In other words, Brazil has not proven a violation of the prohibition of trade distortion in Articles 1.2 and 3.2 of the *Licensing Agreement* by the European Communities.

127. Brazil argues that the Panel did not consider a number of other arguments in its examination of the existence of trade distortion: that licences have been apportioned in non-economic quantities; that there have been frequent changes to the licensing rules; that licence entitlement has been based on export performance; and that there has been speculation in licences.[72] These arguments, however, do not address the problem of establishing a causal relationship between imposition of the EC licensing procedure and the claimed trade distortion. Even if conceded *arguendo*, these arguments do not provide proof of the essential element of causation.

128. For these reasons, we uphold the finding of the Panel that Brazil has not established that the European Communities has acted inconsistently with either Article 1.2 or Article 3.2 of the *Licensing Agreement*.[73]

---

68 Panel Report, para. 249.

69 Regulation 1431/94, Annex I.

70 Panel Report, para. 249.

71 Panel Report, para. 249 and Annex I.

72 Brazil's appellant's submission, paras. 151-160. We note that these facts *were* considered by the Panel in the context of other alleged violations of the *Licensing Agreement*, but *not* in the context of trade distortion within the meaning of Articles 1.2 and 3.2 of the *Licensing Agreement*.

73 Panel Report, para. 249.

C. *Transparency*

129. Brazil's notice of appeal contained no reference to a general issue of transparency in relation to the *Licensing Agreement*. However, Brazil argued in its appellant's submission that the Panel erred in restricting Brazil's "comprehensive claim in relation to a violation of the general principle of transparency underlying the Licensing Agreement"[74] to an analysis of Article 3.5(a) of the *Licensing Agreement*. The contention of Brazil is that "the administration of import licenses in such a way that the exporter does not know what trade rules apply is a breach of the fundamental objective of the Licensing Agreement."[75]

130. Brazil argued before the Panel that "underlying the Licensing Agreement was the principle of transparency."[76] Brazil submitted, in particular, that the European Communities was obliged under either Article 3.5(a)(iii) or (iv) of the *Licensing Agreement* to provide complete and relevant information on the distribution of licences among supplying countries and statistics on volumes and values. According to Brazil, the European Communities failed to fulfil this obligation.[77] The Panel found that Brazil had not demonstrated that the European Communities had violated either Article 3.5(a)(iii) or (iv) of the *Licensing Agreement.*[78] In the light of the existence of express provisions in Article 3.5(a) of the *Licensing Agreement* relating to transparency on which the Panel did in fact make findings, we do not believe that the Panel erred by refraining from examining Brazil's "comprehensive" claim relating to a general principle of transparency purportedly underlying the *Licensing Agreement*.

VIII. ARTICLE 11 OF THE DSU

131. Article 11 of the DSU states in part:

> The function of panels is to assist the DSB in discharging its responsibilities under this Understanding and the covered agreements. Accordingly, a panel should make an objective assessment of the matter before it, including an objective assessment of the facts of the case and the applicability of and conformity with the relevant covered agreements, and make such other findings as will assist the DSB in making the recommendations or in giving the rulings provided for in the covered agreements.

132. Brazil maintains that the Panel did not make "an objective assessment of the matter before it", as required by Article 11 of the DSU, because the Panel

---

74 Brazil's appellant's submission, para. 161.
75 Brazil's appellant's submission, para. 163.
76 Panel Report, para. 105.
77 Panel Report, para. 107.
78 Panel Report, para. 265.

allegedly failed to consider a series of arguments put forward by Brazil relating to GATT/WTO law and practice. These arguments were: "first, the similarities between Article XXIV and XXVIII: second, the flexible nature of Article XXVIII that permits bilateral agreements and the opening of bilateral concessions subject to the review of all Members: [and] third, the text of Article XXVIII, which allows the possibility of country-specific solutions when other contracting parties do not object."[79]

133. An allegation that a panel has failed to conduct the "objective assessment of the matter before it" required by Article 11 of the DSU is a very serious allegation. Such an allegation goes to the very core of the integrity of the WTO dispute settlement process itself. In *EC Measures Concerning Meat and Meat Products* (*Hormones*), in relation to the requirement in Article 11 of the DSU that a panel "make an objective assessment of the facts of the case", we stated:

> Clearly, not every error in the appreciation of the evidence (although it may give rise to a question of law) may be characterized as a failure to make an objective assessment of the facts. ... The duty to make an objective assessment of the facts is, among other things, an obligation to consider the evidence presented to a panel and to make factual findings on the basis of that evidence. The deliberate disregard of, or refusal to consider, the evidence submitted to a panel is incompatible with a panel's duty to make an objective assessment of the facts. The wilful distortion or misrepresentation of the evidence put before a panel is similarly inconsistent with an objective assessment of the facts. "Disregard" and "distortion" and "misrepresentation" of the evidence, in their ordinary signification in judicial and quasi-judicial processes, imply not simply an error of judgment in the appreciation of evidence but rather an *egregious error that calls into question the good faith of a panel.* A claim that a panel disregarded or distorted the evidence submitted to it is, in effect, a claim that the panel, to a greater or lesser degree, denied the party submitting the evidence fundamental fairness, or what in many jurisdictions is known as due process of law or natural justice.[80] (emphasis added)

Subsequently, in *Argentina - Measures Affecting Imports of Footwear, Textiles, Apparel and Other Items*[81], we found that the panel there had not committed an abuse of discretion amounting to a failure to render "an objective assessment of the matter before it", as mandated by Article 11.

---

79 Brazil's appellant's submission, para. 58.

80 Adopted 13 February 1998, WT/DS26/AB/R, WT/DS48/AB/R, para. 133.

81 Adopted 22 April 1998, WT/DS56/AB/R, paras. 81 and 86.

134. The same is true here. The alleged failures imputed to the Panel by Brazil do not approach the level of gravity required for a claim under Article 11 of the DSU to prevail.

135. We note, furthermore, that Brazil's appeal under Article 11 of the DSU relates, in effect, to the judicial economy exercised by the Panel in its consideration of a number of arguments in support of the various claims that Brazil submitted to the Panel. Brazil argues that the Panel, in effect, abused its discretion in not addressing in the Panel Report a series of arguments Brazil made in relation to GATT/WTO law and practice. In *United States - Measure Affecting Imports of Woven Wool Shirts and Blouses from India*, we stated that nothing in Article 11 "or in previous GATT practice *requires* a panel to examine *all* legal claims made by the complaining party", and that "[a] panel need only address those claims which must be addressed in order to resolve the matter in issue in the dispute."[82] Just as a panel has the discretion to address only those *claims* which must be addressed in order to dispose of the matter at issue in a dispute, so too does a panel have the discretion to address only those *arguments* it deems necessary to resolve a particular claim. So long as it is clear in a panel report that a panel has reasonably considered a claim, the fact that a particular argument relating to that claim is not specifically addressed in the "Findings" section of a panel report will not, in and of itself, lead to the conclusion that that panel has failed to make the "objective assessment of the matter before it" required by Article 11 of the DSU.

136. For these reasons, we conclude that the Panel did not fail to make the "objective assessment of the matter before it" required by Article 11 of the DSU.

IX. AGREEMENT ON AGRICULTURE

A. *Article 5.1(b)*

137. Article 5.1 of the *Agreement on Agriculture* provides, in relevant part, as follows:

> 1. Notwithstanding the provisions of paragraph 1(b) of Article II of GATT 1994, any Member may take recourse to the provisions of paragraphs 4 and 5 below in connection with the importation of an agricultural product, in respect of which measures referred to in paragraph 2 of Article 4 of this Agreement have been converted into an ordinary customs duty and which is designated in its Schedule with the symbol "SSG" as being the subject of a concession in respect of which the provisions of this Article may be invoked, if:
>
> ...

[82] Adopted 23 May 1997, WT/DS33/AB/R, DSR 1997:I, 323 at 339.

> (b) the price at which imports of that product may enter the customs territory of the Member granting the concession, as determined on the basis of the c.i.f. import price of the shipment concerned expressed in terms of its domestic currency, falls below a trigger price equal to the average 1986 to 1988 reference price[2] for the product concerned.
>
> [2] The reference price used to invoke the provisions of this subparagraph shall, in general, be the average c.i.f. unit value of the product concerned, or otherwise shall be an appropriate price in terms of the quality of the product and its stage of processing. It shall, following its initial use, be publicly specified and available to the extent necessary to allow other Members to assess the additional duty that may be levied.

138. With respect to "the price at which imports of that product may enter the customs territory of the Member granting the concession, as determined on the basis of the c.i.f. import price of the shipment concerned" in Article 5.1(b) of the *Agreement on Agriculture*, the Panel found that,

> ... the ordinary meaning of the terms used in Article 5.1(b) would appear to support the interpretation advanced by Brazil, i.e. that the market entry price must include duties paid.[83]

and that,

> The object and purpose of Article 5.1(b) is to provide additional protection against significant decline in import prices during the implementation period of the Agreement on Agriculture after all agricultural products have been "tariffied" under Article 4.2. By its nature, it has to address a situation that has occurred after the tariffication process. If the market entry price is equated with the c.i.f. import price, and then compared with the trigger price calculated using the c.i.f. price only, it would disregard the effect of protection granted by high duties resulting from tariffication. Thus, although the drafting of Article 5.1(b) is not a model of clarity, in light of the object and purpose of that subparagraph, it would be appropriate to interpret the market entry price under Article 5.1(b) to include duties paid.[84]

[83] Panel Report, para. 278.

[84] Panel Report, para. 281.

139. On this basis, the majority of the Panel concluded that "the EC has not invoked the special safeguard provision with respect to the poultry products in question in accordance with Article 5.1(b)."[85]

140. In contrast, one member of the Panel was "of the view that Article 5 of the Agreement on Agriculture requires an importing Member to calculate the relevant import price within the meaning of Article 5.1(b) on the basis of the c.i.f. import price only."[86]

141. Brazil, as the exporting Member, endorses the Panel's finding that the relevant import price in Article 5.1(b) of the *Agreement on Agriculture* is the c.i.f. price *plus* ordinary customs duties. This is not surprising. This would limit the instances in which the European Communities could impose additional safeguard duties. In contrast, the European Communities, as the importing Member, is of the view that the relevant import price in Article 5.1(b) is the c.i.f. price *without* ordinary customs duties. This view increases the opportunities for an importing Member to impose additional safeguard duties.

142. The legal issue raised in this appeal concerns the proper interpretation of the phrase, "the price at which imports of that product may enter the customs territory of the Member granting the concession, *as determined on the basis of the c.i.f. import price of the shipment concerned*"(emphasis added) in Article 5.1(b) of the *Agreement on Agriculture*. Specifically, the issue is whether the special safeguard mechanism in Article 5.1(b) is triggered when the c.i.f. price, or when the c.i.f. price *plus* ordinary customs duties, falls below the reference or trigger price.

143. The practical significance of this issue can be illustrated with the following hypothetical example. This dispute has no practical significance if both the c.i.f. import price and the c.i.f. import price plus customs duties fall above or below the trigger price. If both prices are above the trigger price, then additional duties cannot be imposed. And, if both prices fall below the trigger price, then additional duties may be imposed regardless of which definition of the relevant import price is adopted. However, the practical significance of this dispute becomes apparent whenever the trigger price falls between the other two prices, that is, when the trigger price is greater than the c.i.f. import price but smaller than the c.i.f. import price plus customs duties. To illustrate:

c.i.f. import price plus customs duties	=	1,200
trigger price	=	1,000
c.i.f. import price	=	800

In this example, if the relevant price is defined as the c.i.f. import price plus customs duties, additional duties may not be imposed since the relevant price is well above the trigger price. If, on the other hand, it is defined as the c.i.f. import price

85 Panel Report, para. 282.
86 Panel Report, para. 292.

only (that is, without customs duties), additional duties may be imposed because the relevant price is below the trigger price. Thus, to adopt one definition, rather than another, will determine whether or not an importing Member may impose additional safeguard duties.

144. In examining this issue, we begin with the text of Article 5.1(b) which refers to: "the price at which imports of that product *may enter the customs territory* of the Member granting the concession ...". (emphasis added) In interpreting this provision, the majority of the Panel uses the concept of "market entry price". However, this phrase is not found in the text of Article 5.1(b). Yet, the Panel states as follows:

> Thus, the ordinary meaning of the terms used in Article 5.1(b) would appear to support the interpretation advanced by Brazil, i.e. *that the market entry price must include duties paid.*[87] (emphasis added)

Again, in paragraph 281 of the Panel Report, the Panel states that "If *the market entry price* is equated with the c.i.f. import price ... ." (emphasis added) In fact, this section of the Panel Report is entitled: "*Market entry price* and the c.i.f. price". (emphasis added)

145. The relevant import price in Article 5.1(b) is described as "the price at which imports of that product *may enter the customs territory* of the Member granting the concession, as determined on the basis of the c.i.f. import price of the shipment concerned". It is noteworthy that the drafters of the *Agreement on Agriculture* chose to use as the relevant import price the entry price into the *customs territory*, rather than the entry price into the *domestic market*. This suggests that they had in mind the point of time *just before* the entry of the product concerned into the customs territory, and certainly before entry into the domestic market, of the importing Member. The ordinary meaning of these terms in Article 5.1(b) supports the view that the "price at which that product may enter the customs territory" of the importing Member should be construed to mean just that - the price at which the product may enter the *customs territory*, not the price at which the product may enter the *domestic market* of the importing Member. And that price is a price that does not include customs duties and internal charges. It is upon entry of a product into the customs territory, but before the product enters the domestic market, that the obligation to pay customs duties and internal charges accrues.

146. Article 5.1(b) also states that the relevant import price is to be "as determined *on the basis of* the c.i.f. import price of the shipment concerned". (emphasis added) The Panel interprets this phrase to mean "that the market entry price is something that has to be constructed using the c.i.f. price as one of the parameters."[88] We disagree. In the light of our construction of the preceding phrase "the

---

87 Panel Report, para. 278.

88 Panel Report, para. 278.

price at which imports of the product may enter the customs territory of the Member granting the concession", we conclude that the phrase "as determined *on the basis of* the c.i.f. import price of the shipment concerned" in Article 5.1(b) refers simply to the c.i.f. price without customs duties and taxes. There is no definition of the term "c.i.f. import price" in the *Agreement on Agriculture* or in any of the other covered agreements. However, in customary usage in international trade, the c.i.f. import price does not include any taxes, customs duties, or other charges that may be imposed on a product by a Member upon entry into its customs territory.[89] We think it significant also that ordinary customs duties are not mentioned as a component of the relevant import price in the text of Article 5.1(b). Article 5.1(b) does not state that the relevant import price is "the c.i.f. price plus ordinary customs duties". Accordingly, to read the inclusion of customs duties into the definition of the c.i.f. import price in Article 5.1(b) would require us to read words into the text of that provision that simply are not there.

147. This reading of the text of Article 5.1(b) is supported by our reading of the context of that provision in accordance with Article 31 of the *Vienna Convention*, which specifies that the ordinary meaning of the terms of a treaty should be interpreted in their context.

148. We look first to the rest of Article 5.1. In considering when additional special safeguard duties under Article 5.1(b) may be imposed, the relevant import price must be compared with a trigger price. According to Article 5.1(b), this trigger price is "equal to the average 1986 to 1988 reference price for the product concerned". Footnote 2 to Article 5.1(b) states:

> The reference price used to invoke the provisions of this subparagraph shall, in general, be the average c.i.f. unit value of the product concerned, or otherwise shall be an appropriate price in terms of the quality of the product and its stage of processing. It shall, following its initial use, be publicly specified and available to the extent necessary to allow other Members to assess the additional duty that may be levied.

149. Thus, the reference price with which the relevant price is compared under Article 5.1 does *not* include ordinary customs duties. It is simply the average c.i.f. import price of the product concerned during the reference period, 1986-1988. Given this definition of the reference price, it could not have been the intention of the drafters to compare a c.i.f. price exclusive of customs duties for the reference period with a c.i.f. price inclusive of such duties today.

---

[89] We note that the *Incoterms 1990* of the International Chamber of Commerce explains what the acronym "c.i.f." means "cost, insurance and freight", but does not give a definition of "c.i.f. import price". However, according to customary usage in international trade, c.i.f. import price, or simply c.i.f. price, is equal to the price of the product in the exporting country plus additional costs, insurance and freight to the importing country. This definition may also be inferred from paragraph 2 of the *Attachment to Annex 5 of the Agreement on Agriculture*.

150. Paragraph 5 of Article 5 is also part of the context of Article 5.1(b). This provision establishes a link between the amount of the additional duty to be imposed and the difference between the c.i.f. import price of the shipment and the trigger price. According to the schedule contained in paragraph 5, when the difference between the c.i.f. import price of the shipment and the trigger price is not greater than 10 per cent, no additional duty shall be imposed. When the difference is greater than 10 per cent, additional duties may be imposed. The amount of the additional safeguard duties increases as the difference in the two prices increases. We see no reference in paragraph 5 to "c.i.f. import price *plus* ordinary customs duties". The price used to determine when the special safeguard may be triggered and the price used to calculate the amount of the additional duties must be one and the same.

151. Certain anomalies would arise from the interpretation adopted by the majority of the Panel. One of these anomalies was cited in the opinion of the dissenting member of the Panel.[90] If tariffication of non-tariff barriers on a certain product took the form of specific duties that were greater than the trigger price, then an importing Member may never be able to invoke Article 5.1(b). The truth of this observation is evident from the fact that the c.i.f. import price plus customs duties may never fall below the trigger price. This consequence is not limited to the case of specific duties that exceed the trigger price. It could also occur in cases where tariffication takes the form of *ad valorem* duties. We know that tariffication has resulted in tariffs which are, in a large number of cases, very high. The probability is strong, therefore, that the *ad valorem* duties could exceed the percentage decrease in the c.i.f. import price by a substantial margin. In such cases, the decrease in the c.i.f. price would have to be very deep before the relevant import price would fall below the trigger price. Thus, the provisions of Article 5.1(b) would not be operational in many cases. It is doubtful that this was intended by the drafters of the "Special Safeguard Provisions".

152. Another anomaly that would arise from defining the relevant import price as the c.i.f. import price *plus* ordinary customs duties would be that the right of Members to invoke the provisions of Article 5.1(b) would depend on the level of tariffs resulting from tariffication. Faced with a certain decline in the c.i.f. price - say, 20 per cent - some Members would find themselves in a situation where they could not invoke the price safeguard; others would have the right to do so. The first category would comprise those Members with a relatively high level of tariffied duties; the second would be those with a relatively moderate level. Thus, the rights of Members would ultimately depend on the level of their tariffied duties. It is doubtful, too, that this was intended by the drafters of the "Special Safeguard Provisions".

153. For the foregoing reasons, we interpret the "price at which the product concerned may enter the customs territory of the Member granting the conces-

---

[90] Panel Report, para. 291.

sion, as determined on the basis of the c.i.f. import price" in Article 5.1(b) as the c.i.f. import price not including ordinary customs duties. Accordingly, we reverse the finding of the Panel in paragraph 282 of the Panel Report.

B. Article 5.5

154. As noted above, the Panel found that the European Communities has acted inconsistently with Article 5.1(b) of the *Agreement on Agriculture*. In consequence, the Panel chose not to make a finding under Article 5.5 of the *Agreement on Agriculture*. The Panel stated:

> We note that Brazil's argument on this point appears to address the issue of whether the EC has followed its own regulations concerning the operation of special safeguards. To the extent that Brazil's claim is directed to the appropriateness of the special safeguard mechanism within the EC, we are unable to find any violation of the WTO rules. Although Brazil refers to Article 5 of the Agreement on Agriculture and Article X:3 of GATT, it has not specified in what manner the EC has violated these provisions. In any event, since we have already found a violation of Article 5.1(b) by the EC, for the sake of judicial economy, we do not examine this claim any further.[91]

This paragraph of the Panel Report can only be interpreted to mean that the Panel did not make a finding on the consistency of the EC measure with Article 5.5. The Panel acted within its discretion in choosing to exercise judicial economy in this manner.[92]

155. Brazil did not include a claim relating to Article 5.5 of the *Agreement on Agriculture* in its notice of appeal. Nor did Brazil claim in its appellant's submission that the Panel erred in failing to make a finding relating to Article 5.5. The European Communities later filed an appellant's submission of its own appealing the Panel's finding on Article 5.1(b) of the *Agreement on Agriculture*. Brazil then argued in reply in its appellee's submission that if we reversed the Panel's finding on Article 5.1(b), it would then be necessary for us to address the issues arising under Articles 5.5 and 4.2 of the *Agreement on Agriculture*. Having decided to reverse the Panel's finding relating to Article 5.1(b), we turn now to these additional issues.

156. We are aware of the provisions of Article 17 of the DSU that state our jurisdiction and our mandate. Article 17.6 of the DSU provides: "An appeal shall be limited to issues of law covered in the panel report and legal interpretations

---

[91] Panel Report, para. 286.

[92] We refer to our decision in *United States - Measure Affecting Imports of Woven Wool Shirts and Blouses from India*, WT/DS33/AB/R, adopted 23 May 1997, DSR 1997:I, 323 at 339.

developed by the panel". Article 17.13 of the DSU states: "The Appellate Body may uphold, modify or reverse the legal findings and conclusions of the panel." In certain appeals, however, the reversal of a panel's finding on a legal issue may require us to make a finding on a legal issue which was not addressed by the panel. This occurred, for example, in the appeals in *United States - Standards for Reformulated and Conventional Gasoline*[93] and in *Canada - Certain Measures Concerning Periodicals*.[94] And, in this appeal, as we have reversed the Panel's finding on Article 5.1(b), we believe we should complete our analysis of the c.i.f. import price by making a finding with respect to the consistency of the EC regulation with Article 5.5, which was not addressed by the Panel for reasons of judicial economy.

157. Looking at Article 5 of the *Agreement on Agriculture* as a whole, it is clear that the provisions of Article 5.1(b) and Article 5.5 are closely linked. Together, these provisions establish the precise conditions for imposing additional duties under the price-triggered special safeguards mechanism that is established by Article 5. Article 5.1(b) determines when the price-triggered special safeguard mechanism may be activated so that additional duties may be imposed. Article 5.5 determines the method by which such additional duties will be calculated.

158. Article 5.5 of the *Agreement on Agriculture* reads:

> The additional duty imposed under subparagraph 1(b) *shall* be set according to the following schedule:
>
> (a) if the difference between the c.i.f. import price of the shipment expressed in terms of the domestic currency (hereinafter referred to as the "import price") and the trigger price as defined under that subparagraph is less than or equal to 10 per cent of the trigger price, no additional duty shall be imposed;
>
> (b) if the difference between the import price and the trigger price (hereinafter referred to as the "difference") is greater than 10 per cent but less than or equal to 40 per cent of the trigger price, the additional duty shall equal 30 per cent of the amount by which the difference exceeds 10 per cent;
>
> (c) if the difference is greater than 40 per cent but less than or equal to 60 per cent of the trigger price, the additional duty shall equal 50 per cent of the amount by which the difference exceeds 40 per cent, plus the additional duty allowed under (b);

[93] Adopted 20 May 1996, WT/DS2/AB/R, DSR 1996:I, 3 at 14-27.
[94] Adopted 30 July 1997, WT/DS31/AB/R, DSR 1997:I, 449 at 467-468.

(d) if the difference is greater than 60 per cent but less than or equal to 75 per cent, the additional duty shall equal 70 per cent of the amount by which the difference exceeds 60 per cent of the trigger price, plus the additional duties allowed under (b) and (c);

(e) if the difference is greater than 75 per cent of the trigger price, the additional duty shall equal 90 per cent of the amount by which the difference exceeds 75 per cent, plus the additional duties allowed under (b), (c) and (d). (emphasis added)

159. The legal issue raised with respect to Article 5.5 is whether it is permissible for the importing Member to offer the importer a choice between the use of the c.i.f. price of the shipment as provided in Article 5.5, and another method of calculation which departs from this principle. In this case, the alternative method consists of the "representative price" provided in Regulation 1484/95.

160. Regulation 2777/75, the Council regulation, contains the general rule for the application of the additional "special safeguard" duties provided for in Article 5 of the *Agreement on Agriculture*. Article 5.3 of Regulation 2777/75 states:

> The import prices to be taken into consideration for imposing an additional import duty shall be determined on the basis of the cif import prices of the consignment in question.

161. However, what is really at issue here is Regulation 1484/95, the Commission regulation, which sets forth in detail the EC system for calculating the additional duties on shipments of frozen poultry meat to be imposed as a "special safeguard" over and above the ordinary customs duties. Regulation 1484/95 provides for two methods of calculating these additional duties.

162. The first method is explained in Article 3.1 of Regulation 1484/95, which provides: "At the request of the importer the additional duty may be established on the basis of the cif import price of the consignment in question, if this price is higher than the applicable representative price … ." According to Article 3.1, "the application of the cif price of the consignment in question for establishing the additional duty is subject to the presentation by the interested party to the competent authorities of the importing Member State of at least the following proofs: the purchasing contract, or any other equivalent document, the insurance contract, the invoice, the certificate of origin (where applicable), the transport contract, and, in the case of sea transport, the bill of lading".[95] An importer requesting that this method be followed must lodge a security "equal to the amount of the additional duty which he would have paid if the calculation of the additional duty had been made on the basis of the representative price applicable to

[95] Regulation 1484/95, Article 3.1.

the product in question"[96], for the goods to be released immediately for free circulation within the European Communities.

163. The second method is explained in Article 3.3 of Regulation 1484/95, which provides that in the absence of a request by the importer to calculate the additional duties on the basis of the c.i.f. import price of the consignment in question, "the import price of the consignment in question to be taken into consideration for imposing an additional duty shall be the representative price referred to in Article 2(1)"of the regulation. According to Article 2.1 of Regulation 1484/95, the EC Commission determines at regular intervals the "representative prices" of frozen poultry meat, "taking into account in particular: the prices on third country markets, free-at-Community frontier offer prices, and prices at the various stages of marketing in the Community for imported products."

164. To determine whether the two methods specified in the EC measure are consistent with the obligations of the European Communities under Article 5.5 of the *Agreement on Agriculture*, we must turn first to an examination of the text of Article 5.5. The chapeau of Article 5.5 states: "The additional duty imposed under subparagraph 1(b) *shall* be set according to the following schedule ... ". (emphasis added) According to the schedule in Article 5.5, the additional safeguard duty is calculated as a certain percentage of the difference between the c.i.f. import price and the trigger price. This percentage increases with the increases in that difference.

165. In our view, the ordinary meaning of the text of Article 5.5 is clear. The chapeau of Article 5.5 clearly states that the schedule in the body of that provision is mandatory. The word used in the chapeau is "shall", not "may". There is no qualifying language, and there is no language that permits any method other than that set out in the schedule in Article 5.5 as a basis for the calculation of additional duties. Likewise, Article 5.5 clearly identifies the *c.i.f. import price of the shipment* as the sole element to be compared with the trigger price in the calculation of the additional duties. Article 5.5 stipulates that the amount of additional duties "*shall* be set" on the basis of the comparison of *the c.i.f. import price of the shipment* concerned with the trigger price. Thus, the ordinary meaning of the *c.i.f. import price of the shipment* is precisely that: the c.i.f. import price *of the shipment*. Unlike the trigger price with which it is compared, the c.i.f. import price is not described in the text of Article 5 of the *Agreement on Agriculture* as an average price during a certain period of time. It is simply *the c.i.f. import price of the shipment*, that is, the actual price of an actual shipment. There is no authority in the text of Article 5.5 for a Member to use any alternative to the c.i.f. import price, shipment-by-shipment, in the calculation of the additional duties imposed under this special safeguard mechanism.

166. The context of Article 5.5 supports this conclusion. The context of Article 5.5 includes both Article 5.1(b) and Article 4.2 of the *Agreement on Agriculture*.

---

96 Regulation 1484/95, Article 3.2.

As noted previously, Articles 5.1(b) and 5.5 are inextricably linked. We have already concluded that the relevant import price in Article 5.1(b) is the c.i.f. import price of the shipment. Under Article 5.1(b), this price must be compared to the trigger price to determine whether the special safeguard mechanism is activated. Both the import price and the trigger price mentioned in Article 5.1(b) are also the very same import price and trigger price, respectively, that are mentioned in Article 5.5. If the relevant import price that is compared to the trigger price to determine whether the safeguard mechanism in Article 5.1(b) is activated is *the c.i.f. import price of the shipment*, then logic dictates that *the c.i.f. import price of the shipment* that is used to set the amount of those additional duties under Article 5.5 cannot be anything else.

167. We note that the safeguard mechanism in Article 5 of the *Agreement on Agriculture* is described as "special". The reason for this description is that it is a unique mechanism compared with safeguard provisions in Article XIX of the GATT 1994, the *Agreement on Safeguards*, and in Article 6 of the *Agreement on Textiles and Clothing*. It is not conditional upon a test of injury as it is the case with other safeguard provisions; it can be automatically activated when there is a certain surge in the volume of imports (Article 5.1(a)) or a certain drop in the price of the product (Article 5.1(b)). For this reason, it should not be invoked except in accordance with, and within the confines of, the strict requirements of Article 5. One of these requirements is that the relevant import price to be compared with the trigger price for the purpose of establishing the amount of the additional duties under Article 5.5 must be the *c.i.f. import price of the shipment*. To read the text of Article 5.5 as permitting the use of any price other than the c.i.f. import price, shipment-by-shipment, would not be consistent with the *special* character of this provision.

168. Therefore, neither the text nor the context of Article 5.5 of the *Agreement on Agriculture* permits us to conclude that the additional duties imposed under the special safeguard mechanism in Article 5 of the *Agreement on Agriculture* may be established by any method other than a comparison of the *c.i.f. price of the shipment* with the trigger price.

169. With this conclusion in mind, we turn again to the two methods employed in the EC measure. With respect to the first method, it will be recalled that Article 3.1 of Regulation 1484/95 permits the additional duties to be calculated, at the request of the importer, on the basis of "the c.i.f. price of the consignment" in question. To the extent that this method uses the c.i.f. price of the shipment to calculate the amount of the additional duties, it is consistent with Article 5.5 of the *Agreement on Agriculture*. We note, however, that this method is only available at the request of the importer and also is only available if the price established by this method is higher than the applicable representative price. Otherwise, the alternative method, which does not use the c.i.f. price of the shipment, is used. This means that the actual c.i.f. price of the consignment is not used in all cases. To this extent, this method is not consistent with Article 5.5 of the *Agreement on Agriculture*.

170. With respect to the second method, it will be recalled that Article 3.3 of Regulation 1484/95 provides for the calculation of additional duties by reference to the "representative price". As pointed out previously, the basic characteristic of the "representative price" is that it is an average of three elements over a certain period of time. The "representative price" may be more advantageous for exporters of frozen poultry meat to the European Communities, "a useful and transparent tool for importers to reduce bureaucracy",[97] conducive to the avoidance of fraud or other irregularities in the pricing of imports of frozen poultry meat,[98] "a means of boosting trade by dramatically reducing bureaucracy and paperwork",[99] and a method that the importer is "completely free" to choose.[100] We offer no views on any of these possible justifications for, or consequences of, the EC "representative price". We need not do so. For, whatever the "representative price" may or may not be, it is clear on the face of the regulation that the "representative price" is *not* calculated on a shipment-by-shipment basis and, therefore, it is not the c.i.f. price *of the shipment* concerned. Article 3.1 of Regulation 1484/95 states that: "At the request of the importer the additional duty may be established on the basis of the cif import price of the consignment in question, *if this price is higher than the applicable representative price* ... ."(emphasis added) If the representative price can be lower or higher than the c.i.f. price of the shipment concerned, then it obviously will not always be the same as the c.i.f. price *of the shipment*. For this reason, and because we hold that calculation of the additional "special safeguard" duties on the basis of the c.i.f. price *of the shipment* is mandatory, we conclude that the use of the "representative price" is inconsistent with Article 5.5 of the *Agreement on Agriculture*.

171. To the extent that Regulation 1484/95 allows for the calculation of the additional duties under Article 5 of the *Agreement on Agriculture* on a basis other than the c.i.f. price *of the shipment* concerned, it is inconsistent with the obligations of the European Communities under Article 5.5 of the *Agreement on Agriculture*. Therefore, the "representative price" method in Regulation 1484/95 is not consistent with Article 5.5 of the *Agreement on Agriculture*. Having made this determination, it is not necessary for us to proceed to examine whether the EC measure is consistent with Article 4.2 of the *Agreement on Agriculture*.

X. FINDINGS AND CONCLUSIONS

172. For the reasons set out in this Report, the Appellate Body:

(a) finds no reversible error in the interpretation by the Panel of the relationship between Schedule LXXX and the Oilseeds Agreement;

---

[97] EC post-hearing reply memorandum, para. 16.

[98] EC post-hearing reply memorandum, para. 15.

[99] EC post-hearing reply memorandum, para. 11.

[100] EC post-hearing reply memorandum, para. 11.

(b) upholds the Panel's findings that the European Communities is bound, on a non-discriminatory basis, by its tariff commitments for frozen poultry meat, and that no agreement existed between Brazil and the European Communities on the allocation of the tariff-rate quota for frozen poultry meat within the meaning of Article XIII:2(d) of the GATT 1994;

(c) upholds the Panel's finding that a tariff rate-quota resulting from negotiations under Article XXVIII of the GATT 1947 must be administered in a non-discriminatory manner consistent with Article XIII of the GATT 1994;

(d) upholds the Panel's finding that the European Communities has not acted inconsistently with Article XIII of the GATT 1994 in calculating Brazil's tariff-rate quota share based on the total quantity of imports, including those from non-Members;

(e) upholds the Panel's finding relating to Article X of the GATT 1994;

(f) upholds the Panel's findings relating to Articles 1.2 and 3.2 of the *Licensing Agreement*;

(g) concludes that the Panel did not act inconsistently with Article 11 of the DSU in not examining certain arguments made by Brazil relating to GATT/WTO law and practice;

(h) reverses the finding of the Panel that the European Communities has acted inconsistently with Article 5.1(b) of the *Agreement on Agriculture* by invoking the safeguard mechanism when the c.i.f. import price, not including ordinary customs duties, falls below the trigger price; and

(i) concludes that the representative price used in certain cases by the European Communities in calculating the additional safeguard duties is inconsistent with Article 5.5 of the *Agreement on Agriculture*.

173. The Appellate Body *recommends* that the DSB request that the European Communities bring its measures found in this Report, and in the Panel Report as modified by this Report, to be inconsistent with the *Agreement on Agriculture* and the *Licensing Agreement* into conformity with its obligations under those agreements.

EUROPEAN COMMUNITIES - MEASURES AFFECTING THE IMPORTATION OF CERTAIN POULTRY PRODUCTS

Report of the Panel
WT/DS69/R

Adopted by the Dispute Settlement Body on 23 July 1998 as modified by the Appellate Body Report

TABLE OF CONTENTS

Page

Page

I. INTRODUCTION

1. On 24 February 1997, Brazil requested consultations with the European Communities ("the Community" or the "EC") pursuant to Article 4 of the Understanding on Rules and Procedures governing the Settlement of Disputes ("DSU"), Article XXIII of the General Agreement on Tariffs and Trade 1994 ("GATT") and Article 6 of the Agreement on Import Licensing Procedures ("Licensing Agreement"), regarding the EC regime for the importation of certain poultry products (CN codes 0207 41 10, 0207 41 41 and 0207 41 71) and the implementation by the EC of the tariff rate quota in these products agreed in negotiations between Brazil and the EC under Article XXVIII of GATT (WT/DS69/1).

2. Consultations were held on 11 April and 21 May 1997. As they did not result in a mutually satisfactory solution of the matter, Brazil, in a communication dated 12 June 1997, requested the establishment of a panel to examine this matter in light of the GATT, the Licensing Agreement and the Agreement on Agriculture (WT/DS69/2).

3. The Dispute Settlement Body ("DSB"), at its meeting on 30 July 1997, established a panel with standard terms of reference in accordance with Article 6 of the DSU (WT/DS69/3). Thailand and the United States reserved their third party rights to make a submission and to be heard by the Panel in accordance with Article 10 of the DSU.

Terms of Reference

4. The following standard terms of reference applied to the work of the Panel:

> "To examine, in the light of the relevant provisions of the covered agreements cited by Brazil in document WT/DS69/2, the matter referred to the DSB by Brazil in that document and to make such findings as will assist the DSB in making the recommendations or in giving the rulings provided for in those agreements."

Panel Composition

5. The parties to the dispute agreed on 11 August 1997 to the following composition of the Panel:

Chairman: Mr. Wilhelm Meier

Members: Mr. Peter May

Ms. Magda Shahin

6. The Panel met with the parties on 29-30 October and on 18 November 1997 and with third parties on 30 October 1997.

7. The Panel submitted its interim report to the parties of the dispute on 23 January 1998 and the final report on 12 February 1998.

II. FACTUAL ASPECTS

Background

8. Following the completion of the panel on the *European Economic Community - Payments and Subsidies Paid to Processors and Producers of Oilseeds and Related Animal-feed Proteins* ("Oilseeds panel")[1], the EC was authorized by the GATT CONTRACTING PARTIES on 19 June 1992 to enter into negotiations under Article XXVIII of GATT - Modification of Schedules - with interested contracting parties. Such negotiations were entered into with Brazil as well as with nine other contracting parties.[2] The negotiations with Brazil were terminated in July 1993 and the Agreed Minutes were signed by both parties on 31 January 1994.

9. The Agreement set out in the Agreed Minutes between Brazil and the EC resulting from negotiations pursuant to Article XXVIII, modified concessions in EC's Schedule LXXX concerning oilseeds, adding *inter alia* a new, duty-free, global tariff rate quota (TRQ) of 15,500 tonnes on frozen poultry meat under CN sub-headings 0207 41 10, 0207 41 41 and 0207 41 71. The poultry meat TRQ was also free from variable levies. Tariff quotas were also established for meat of turkey and beef. The tariff rate quotas were opened as from 1 January 1994 by

1 Panel Report adopted on 25 January 1990, BISD 37S/86 and DS28/R, dated 31 March 1992.

2 Argentina, Canada, Hungary, India, Pakistan, Poland, Sweden, the United States and Uruguay.

Council Regulation (EC) No 774/94, dated 29 March 1994. Those concerning frozen poultry meat were contained in Article 3 which stated that "... an annual quota of 15,500 tonnes is hereby opened for poultry meat falling within CN codes 0207 41 10, 0207 41 41 and 0207 41 71." Rules for adjustment of the volumes and other conditions of the tariff quotas were also provided for (Article 8). Regulation 774/94 was amended in September 1995 by Regulation 2198/95 to take account of the Agreement on Agriculture resulting from the Uruguay Round negotiations.

Current EC Schedule LXXX

10. The current EC Schedule LXXX (Part I - Most Favoured Nation Tariff, Section I -Agricultural Products, Section I B - Tariff Quotas) provided for a duty-free tariff quota up to 15,500 tonnes of poultry meat[3] while the out-quota base duty rate was 1,600 ECU/tonne, 940 ECU/tonne and 1,575 ECU/tonne, respectively. The new decreasing bound out-of-quota rates replaced the variable levy that constituted the EC commitment under its previous Schedule as modified by the Article XXVIII Oilseeds negotiations. There were no licensing requirements for out-of-quota imports of frozen poultry meat.

Licensing Requirements for the Poultry TRQ

11. Council Regulation 774/94 opened, *inter alia*, a tariff quota for an annual volume of 15,500 tonnes for the relevant poultry meat products and provided that detailed rules for the application of the Regulation should be adopted in accordance with the procedures in Article 27 of Regulation 805/68 or in the corresponding Articles of other Regulations on the common organization of the markets concerned. Such detailed rules were subsequently set out in Commission Regulation 1431/94, dated 22 June 1994. Article 1 of Regulation 1431/94 provided that all imports under the tariff quotas for the relevant poultry meat products were subject "to the presentation of an import licence." 25 per cent of the quantity of the quota was allocated for each quarter of the year, save for 1994 when 50 per cent was allocated for each half of the year. Applicants for import licences had to be natural or legal persons who, at the time applications were submitted, had imported not less than 100 tonnes (product weight) of products falling within CN codes 0207 14 10, 0207 14 50 and 0207 14 70 in each of the two previous calendar years[4] whether in-quota or out-of-quota product. Licence applications and licences should show the country of origin. Applicants had to lodge a security. Licences were not transferable.[5] If applications exceeded the volume available for the quarter, the Commission fixed "a single percentage of

---

3 HS 0207 14 10, 0207 14 50 and 0207 14 70.

4 Article 3 of Regulation 1431/94 as amended by Regulation 958/96.

5 Article 5 of Regulation 1431/94.

acceptance for the quantities applied for". If this percentage was less than 5 per cent, the Commission was authorized not to award those quantities in which case the security was released (Article 4.4 of Regulation 1431/94).

Special Safeguards for out-of-Quota Volumes of Frozen Poultry Meat

12. The EC Schedule for out-of-quota frozen poultry meat reserved the right to introduce an additional duty (special safeguards) on imports of such meat if the conditions of Article 5 of the Agreement on Agriculture were fulfilled. The EC rules pertaining to special safeguards for out-of-quota poultry meat were contained in Regulation 1484/95, dated 28 June 1995, and provided that, unless the poultry imports were unlikely to disturb the EC internal market, an additional duty would be levied if the import price fell below a specific trigger price[6] set out in Annex II of Regulation 1484/95 for each product. The import price to be taken into account "should be checked against the representative prices on the world market or on the Community import market for the products in question;" (recital 7 of Regulation 1484/95). Such representative prices were to be determined taking into account in particular (i) the prices on third country markets; (ii) free-at-frontier offer prices; and (iii) prices at the various stages of marketing in the EC for imported products.[7] Recital 8 provided that the importer could choose a different basis from the representative price[8] for the calculation of the additional duty. Article 3 allowed for the possibility, at the request of the importer, to establish the additional duty on the basis of the c.i.f. price, if this price was higher than the applicable representative price. If the importer had chosen to use the c.i.f. price, he would have to provide to the competent authorities (i) the purchasing contract (or equivalent document); (ii) the insurance contract; (iii) the invoice; (iv) the certificate of origin; (v) the transport contract; and (vi) the bill of lading (where applicable).[9]

III. MAIN ARGUMENTS[*]

General

13. The complaint examined by the Panel was related to the EC's measures governing the importation of poultry meat falling within CN codes 0207 14 10, 0207 14 50 and 0207 14 70 (formerly 0207 41 10, 0207 41 41 and 0207 41 71).

---

6 ECU 333.5, 235.7 and 316.6, respectively, for CN 0207 41 10, 0207 41 41, 0207 41 71, respectively.

7 Article 2 of 1484/95.

8 The representative prices were set out in Annex 1 to Regulation 1484/95. An example of a calculation of the additional duty was supplied to the Panel, by the EC, on a confidential basis. See paragraphs 191 and 192.

9 Article 3 of Regulation 1484/95.

* Note that footnotes in this and the following chapter are those of the parties.

14. **Brazil** requested the Panel to find

(a) that the EC had failed to implement and administer the compensation TRQ in certain poultry meat products in line with the bilateral agreement reached with Brazil within the context of Article XXVIII:4 of GATT;

(b) that the provisions of Articles I and XIII of GATT did not necessarily apply to compensation TRQs;

(c) in the alternative, that the EC had failed to implement the TRQ in accordance with Article XIII, since the EC did not follow the allocation procedures contained in Article XIII;

(d) that the EC had failed to comply with the provisions of Articles 1 and 3 of the Agreement on Import Licensing in the administration of the import licences;

(e) that the licensing system did not comply with the transparency provisions of Article X and the specific provisions of Articles II and III of GATT;

(f) that the licensing system did not comply with the specific provisions of Articles II and III of GATT;

(g) that the EC had failed to comply with the provisions of Articles 4 and 5 of the Agreement on Agriculture in the implementation of the special safeguards that apply for trade in poultry meat outside the TRQ.

15. In the view of Brazil, such infringements of the covered Agreements implied the nullification or impairment of benefits accruing to Brazil. Accordingly, Brazil asked the Panel to recommend that the EC bring its measures into conformity with its obligations under the GATT, the Agreement on Import Licensing Procedures and the Agreement on Agriculture.

16. The **EC** requested the Panel to dismiss the claims advanced by Brazil either as inadmissible or unfounded. In particular, the Panel should find

(a) that there had been no breach by the EC of Articles XXVIII, XIII, X, II and III of GATT, Articles 4 and 5 of the Agreement on Agriculture and Articles 1 and 3 of the Agreement on Import Licensing Procedures; and

(b) that, consequently, there had been no nullification or impairment of Brazil's rights under the WTO.

Article XXVIII:4 of GATT

(i) General

17. Quoting paragraph 4(b) of Article XXVIII and its reference to paragraph 3(b), **Brazil** submitted that there was a balance in Article XXVIII between the recognition of the individual needs of Members and the global need to maintain

an overall balance of concessions within a multilateral framework. In Brazil's opinion, there was nothing in the Article which prevented two Members from agreeing on a country-specific package of compensatory measures. Nor was there anything which mandated that compensation should be country-specific. Article XXVIII maintained a fine balance between these two possibilities. It allowed certain defined Members to negotiate and agree. Then it provided that other Members which might be dissatisfied with the agreement or which might wish to benefit from the agreement should have the right to ensure that the agreement did not prejudice their own rights and obligations. A time limit was placed on this right so as to promote legal certainty of the bilateral agreement within the multilateral framework. In this particular case, the EC created a series of distinct bilateral agreements, each with a distinct package of country-specific compensatory measures. These agreements were accepted by the other Members and had to stand within the multilateral system as country-specific agreements. No Member notified its intention to the CONTRACTING PARTIES to withdraw equivalent concessions.

18. The **EC** submitted that the purpose of the procedure under Article XXVIII was to ensure that the "security and predictability of GATT tariff bindings, a principle which constituted a central obligation in the system of the General Agreement", was preserved, in accordance with the provisions of Article II. In recognizing that the procedure under Article XXVIII had been successfully completed, the CONTRACTING PARTIES accepted that the EC Schedules of concessions had been modified with their agreement and represented the new tariff commitments of the EC for the products concerned. The EC noted that no GATT contracting party objected to the revised Schedule within the three month period set out in the Decision of the CONTRACTING PARTIES of 26 March 1980. On the contrary, they had all agreed by 30 March 1994 to a new EC Schedule of commitments, as a result of the Uruguay Round, which included the outcome of Article XXVIII Oilseeds negotiations with respect to the frozen poultry meat.

19. **Brazil** submitted that the question of the compatibility with the General Agreement of bilateral agreements concluded outside, as opposed to within, the framework of the GATT was considered at the nineteenth Session of the CONTRACTING PARTIES in 1961. Referring to a note by the Executive Secretary[10], and while disagreeing that there were no provisions within the GATT itself for bilateral agreements, Brazil agreed with the view that there was no provision in the GATT for bilateral agreements between contracting parties and non-

[10] "The General Agreement contains no provisions dealing specifically with the use of bilateral agreements. If a Contracting Party concludes a bilateral agreement with another contracting party or a government not party to the GATT, what is relevant for the General Agreement is the effect on the trade of other Contracting Parties of any measures affecting trade which that Government takes to make effective the provisions of the bilateral agreement ... it is therefore necessary to know the nature of the quota obligation provided for in the bilateral agreement and details of any measures affecting imports which are taken for the fulfilment of the bilateral obligation."

contracting parties. The Executive Secretary was concerned with the effect of bilateral agreements on other contracting parties. This concern was, in the view of Brazil, addressed in the multilateral aspects of Article XXVIII. However, in relation to the Executive Secretary's concerns, Brazil submitted that the opening of a country-specific frozen chicken TRQ by the Community did not give rise to a negative impact on the trade interests of other Members. There was considerable over-quota trade and this trade continued and would continue whether or not a TRQ had been opened. A country-specific TRQ merely increased a trade opportunity for one Member but did not preclude or diminish continued trading on an MFN basis for all Members.

20. The **EC** submitted that Article XXVIII of GATT was not a substantive provision but provided only the procedural requirements by which a Member could legally modify, change or withdraw, totally or partially, one of its concessions. These changes were justified by commercial considerations or by the creation of a customs union. In the latter case, Article XXIV:6 referred explicitly "to the procedures set forth in Article XXVIII", thus underlining again the procedural nature of that provision. Under Article XXVIII, there was no obligation to *reach* an agreement but there was an obligation to *seek* an agreement, in particular with Members having a particular trade interest. Detailed rules to be respected in order to ensure the participation of those Members were provided in the Understanding on the interpretation of Article XXVIII of the General Agreement on Tariffs and Trade 1994 which was annexed to the GATT 1994. Further guidelines were detailed in the Decision of the GATT CONTRACTING PARTIES adopted on 10 November 1980. The EC argued that Brazil had not complained, either during the consultations or in its request for the establishment of the Panel or, finally, in its written and oral interventions before this Panel, of any violation by the EC of the procedural requirements set out in that provision. It had signed an agreement with the EC on 31 January 1994, thus acknowledging that the procedures had been fully respected to the satisfaction of the two parties concerned. Any subsequent later complaint with respect to the procedure followed in order to reach that agreement was clearly "estopped" by now. Brazil could not therefore claim today, three years after the conclusion of that procedure, that a violation of Article XXVIII had occurred. Moreover, no evidence had been provided to support such a claim by Brazil. The negotiating history of Article XXVIII indicated that the GATT CONTRACTING PARTIES had expressed their views to the effect that no violation of the non-discrimination principle through an Article XXVIII procedure was possible. The EC believed that this was still the case.

21. **Brazil** argued that there was no obligation to conclude an agreement under Article XXVIII but Brazil and the EC did reach an agreement. And this agreement reflected the specification of the general rights and obligations. The EC could withdraw concessions, without the fear of counter withdrawals, on condition that it opened up other concessions. Brazil had agreed to forego its right to counter withdraw. These rights and obligations were directly applicable by reason of Article XXVIII. The CONTRACTING PARTIES authorized these specifications of the Article XXVIII rights and no contracting party had objected to

the agreements reached within Article XXVIII. Under the terms of Article XXVIII:3(b), contracting parties which were not party to the negotiations were free within six months of the conclusion of negotiations, to withdraw substantially equivalent concessions if they were not satisfied with the bilateral country-specific agreements between the Members principally concerned. No contracting party took such action so therefore it could be concluded that all the contracting parties were satisfied. Brazil submitted, moreover, that in order to determine the nature of the EC's current commitments to Brazil within the WTO, this Panel had to look at the Oilseeds Agreement. The dispute between Brazil and the EC did not relate to whether the EC was complying with its Schedule but whether the EC's Schedule reflected the commitments made by the EC to Brazil following the Oilseeds negotiations.[11] Brazil maintained that a commitment had been made, within the terms of Article XXVIII of GATT, to open a *country-specific* TRQ of 15,500 tonnes of frozen chicken. The EC maintained, Brazil argued, that a commitment had been made to open such a TRQ but on an MFN basis. Brazil believed that the difference between the parties could only be resolved by the Panel by reference to the Oilseeds Agreement itself and by reference to the implementation of the other TRQs opened as part of that agreement.

(ii) Modifications of Schedules

22. The **EC** submitted that the purpose of the procedure under Article XXVIII was to ensure that the "security and predictability of GATT tariff bindings, a principle which constituted a central obligation in the system of the General Agreement"[12], was preserved, in accordance with the provisions of Article II. In recognizing that the procedure under Article XXVIII had been successfully completed, the CONTRACTING PARTIES accepted that the EC Schedules of concessions had been modified with their agreement and represented the new tariff commitments of the EC for the products concerned. The EC explained that the EC Schedule[13] provided, as a result of the Uruguay Round negotiations with respect to the three products at issue in this dispute[14] for a duty-free tariff quota up to 15,500 tonnes for the frozen poultry meat[15] while the out-quota base duty rate was 1,600 ECU/tonne, 940 ECU/tonne and 1,575 ECU/tonne, respectively. The duty-free in-quota rate after the Uruguay Round negotiations corresponded exactly to the results of the Article XXVIII Oilseeds negotiations. However, market

[11] These commitments were contained in the Oilseeds Agreement.

[12] Panel Report on *Newsprint*, adopted 20 November 1984, BISD 31S/114, 131-133, paragraph 52.

[13] LXXX, Part I - Most Favoured Nation Tariff, Section I - Agricultural Products, Section I B - Tariff Quotas.

[14] Which had been indicated under the tariff number 0207 41 10, 0207 41 41 and 0207 41 71 and were presently indicated under the tariff lines 0207 14 10, 0207 14 50 and 0207 14 70.

[15] Schedule CXL after the Article XXIV:6 negotiations following the most recent EC enlargement will not entail any modification of the concessions of the EC in this respect.

access for the frozen poultry meat was the subject of further negotiation as a result of the tariffication exercise that consisted in the introduction of out-quota decreasing bound rates. The new decreasing bound rates had replaced the variable levy that constituted the EC commitment under its previous Schedule as modified by the Article XXVIII Oilseeds negotiations. Thus, there was a series of modifications to the EC GATT Schedule of commitments with respect to the frozen poultry meat all of which were effected with the active support and agreement of all the other Members (GATT contracting parties at the time), including Brazil. In summary, first, the EC Schedule was modified as a result of the conclusion of the Article XXVIII Oilseeds Agreement. Secondly, it was then renegotiated and modified as a result of the Uruguay Round.

23. **Brazil** replied that during the time in which the Oilseeds Agreement determined the EC's obligations to Brazil, the EC had commitments under Article XXVIII of GATT which were not reflected in its Schedule. If the EC had not changed its Schedule so as to reflect the opening of a 15,500 TRQ (whatever its nature) could a Member not have asked a dispute settlement panel to ensure that the EC's Schedule did reflect the commitments it had made? Thus, a closer examination of the EC's two agreements argument, giving rise to "successive modifications", revealed, according to Brazil that (i) the EC did not twice modify its country schedule; (ii) the EC had commitments under Article XXVIII that were not reflected in its Schedule; and (iii) whatever those commitments were, the EC did not offer security and predictability to WTO Members.

24. The **EC,** recalling a passage in the recent *Banana III* panel report[16], submitted that it seemed indisputable that the tariff rates specified in the EC's Uruguay Round Schedule, including the TRQs, were the valid EC tariff bindings in respect of frozen poultry meat. No declaration which would amount to a reservation or any belated after thought could affect the validity and the effects of the voluntary acceptance by Brazil of the results of the Uruguay Round negotiation.

25. As concerns the question of entering a reservation because the country-specific nature of a TRQ was not apparent from the Schedule, **Brazil** observed that no reservations were permissible to the Marrakesh Agreement which established the WTO.[17] Secondly, as had been established by the Appellate Body[18], the presence of a reservation was not a prerequisite for the challenge by a Member of another Member's schedule.

16 "it was for all prospective members of the WTO to decide whether they would accept the new agreements [resulting from the Uruguay Round], including the new bindings proposed by other participants. Under Article XVI:5 of the WTO Agreement, reservations are not permitted, except to the extent provided for in a WTO agreement; there is no such provision in GATT 1994. In this regard, we recognize the importance of not undermining the stability and predictability of tariff bindings"(paragraph 7.139 of WT/DS27R/GTM).

17 Article 19 of the Vienna Convention specifically recognized that a reservation was only allowable if it was not prohibited by the Treaty.

18 Appellate Body Report on *European Communities - Regime for the Importation, Sale and Distribution of Bananas*, adopted on 25 September 1997, WT/DS27/AB/R.

(iii) The Vienna Convention on the Law of Treaties

(a) Article 59(1)[19] of the Vienna Convention

26. The EC submitted its analysis was confirmed by the application to this case of the customary rules of interpretation of public international law. In applying Article 3.2 of the DSU, a number of recent WTO dispute settlement decisions[20] had indicated that certain provisions of the Vienna Convention on the Law of Treaties (Vienna Convention) had attained the status of rules of customary or general international law. This had been specifically indicated for Article 31 and 32 of the Vienna Convention. The EC was of the view that that was also the case for Articles 59(1) and 30(3). These provisions were the expression of the general international law principle concerning the succession of legal acts having an identical binding force between the same parties.[21] Citing Article 59(1) of the Vienna Convention[22], the EC submitted that in the case in dispute, the two parties, EC and Brazil, were not only parties to the bilateral agreement concluding the Article XXVIII Oilseeds negotiations under the GATT but also to the later Marrakesh agreement encompassing the results of the Uruguay Round. Both agreements related, *inter alia*, to the tariff levels for frozen poultry products at issue in this dispute. Both Brazil and the EC ratified the Marrakesh Agreement which contained the agreed new set of rules with respect, *inter alia*, to the tariff treatment of the frozen poultry meat. The rule under Article 59(1) solved the issue of the coexistence of the two agreements in this case by considering that the Article XXVIII Oilseeds Agreement was no longer applicable. The EC was therefore of the view that the modified EC Schedule which resulted from the Uruguay Round negotiations had replaced the earlier Article XXVIII Oilseeds Agreement. It was no longer possible for Brazil to allege a violation by the EC of the Article XXVIII Oilseeds Agreement and there was no violation by the EC of the existing commitments under the EC Schedule LXXX. As a subsidiary argument, the EC recalled briefly that in any event, Article 30(3) of the Vienna Convention would not allow any different conclusion: "When all the parties to the

---

[19] Article 59(1) (entitled "Termination or suspension of the operation of a treaty implied by conclusion of a later treaty") provided that:
"1. A treaty shall be considered as terminated if all the parties to it conclude a later treaty relating to the same subject matter and

(a) it appears from the later treaty or is otherwise established that the parties intended that the matter should be governed by that treaty; (...)

(b) the provisions of the later treaty are so far incompatible with those of the earlier one that the two treaties are not capable of being applied at the same time.

2. The earlier treaty shall be considered as only suspended in operation if it appears from the later treaty or is otherwise established that such was the intention of the parties."

[20] Appellate Body Report on *United States - Standards for Reformulated and Conventional Gasoline*, WT/DS2/AB/R; Appellate Body Report on *Japan - Taxes on Alcoholic Beverages*, WT/DS8/AB/R; Panel Report on *European Communities - Regime for the Importation, Sale and Distribution of Bananas*, adopted on 25 September 1997, WT/DS27/R, para.7.272.

[21] The same principle was reflected also in Article 39, 40(2) and 54(b) of the Vienna Convention.

[22] For text of Article 59(1), see footnote above.

earlier treaty are parties also to a later treaty but the earlier treaty is not terminated or suspended in operation under Article 59, the earlier treaty applies to the extent that its provisions are compatible with those of the later treaty".

27. Brazil submitted that the EC had not shown that the conditions of Article 59(1)(a) and (b) had been fulfilled in relation to the Article XXVIII negotiations. Brazil considered, however, that Brazil had shown that there was no incompatibility between Part I of the Uruguay Round schedules, and in particular the EC schedule, with country-specific TRQs. It was clear from the EC schedule that country-specific TRQs were provided for. Secondly, the EC accepted that country-specific provisions were compatible with the WTO Agreements. Thus, incompatibility could not be the ground for the automatic termination of the commitments agreed to under Article XXVIII. Nor had the EC shown that it was the clear intention of the parties that the matter of compensation be governed by the later treaty and not by the terms of the earlier agreement. The EC had itself observed that the earlier agreement had been "incorporated" into the later agreement. The ordinary meaning of the word "incorporation" did not include the idea of "modification". Incorporation meant, according to Brazil, that the terms of the first agreement were incorporated as they stood into the second agreement. Thus, the EC's Article XXVIII commitment was incorporated into the Uruguay Round agreement. Brazil concluded therefore that, if Article 59 was found to be declaratory of customary international law, the EC had not shown that the earlier agreement had been terminated or suspended by operation of Article 59.

28. The EC replied that Article 59(1)(a) of the Vienna Convention was fully relevant to this case. Brazil had disregarded that Article 59(1) provided, under (a) and (b), for two hypotheses which were separate and alternative. Contrary to what Brazil seemed to suggest, the EC was of the opinion that the text of Article 59(1) did not require cumulation of these two hypotheses.

(b) Article 30(3) of the Vienna Convention

29. Citing Article 30(3) of the Vienna Convention[23], the EC submitted that the Article XXVIII Oilseeds Agreement between the EC and Brazil modified the EC Schedule as of 1 January 1994. The Uruguay Round agreement then entered into force on 1 January 1995 and became applicable for agricultural products on 1 July 1995. This treaty covered *inter alia* the same subject matter (the EC concessions on the frozen poultry meat) among the same contracting parties as the earlier treaty (Brazil and the EC). EC believed that there was no disagreement between Brazil and the EC on the content of the current concessions by the EC with respect to the frozen poultry meat. Neither party contested that a duty-free tariff quota had been established, there was no disagreement on the decreasing duties applicable to the out-quota imports bound as a result of the Uruguay Round ne-

---

[23] See paragraph 26.

gotiations, neither was there disagreement on the size of the TRQ. The revised EC Schedule which incorporated the Article XXVIII Oilseeds Agreement with respect to frozen poultry meat, the EC said, had been replaced, as from 1 January 1995, by the EC Schedule of commitments resulting from the Uruguay Round consistently with Article 59(1) of the Vienna Convention. Reference to the earlier Article XXVIII Oilseeds Agreement was therefore no longer relevant. In any event, in application of Article 30(3) of the Vienna Convention, should the Panel reach any different conclusion (contrary to the EC's submissions) and in particular that the Article XXVIII Oilseeds Agreement was not applicable on a MFN basis and was still relevant, then it could be applicable only to the extent it was compatible with the EC's later Schedule resulting from the Uruguay Round which was a MFN TRQ. Both these lines of argument led to the inevitable conclusion that the EC frozen poultry meat TRQ was applicable on a MFN basis.

30. Referring to Article 30(3) of the Vienna Convention and to paragraph 1(b) of GATT 1994[24], Brazil submitted that the EC agreed that a tariff concession had been given, and had entered into force, prior to the entry into force of the WTO agreements and that this concession was based on the Article XXVIII of GATT negotiations with Brazil. By the terms of the WTO Agreement itself, that prior concession was incorporated into the EC's GATT 1994 Article II Schedule. The specific concession had to be incorporated and not modified. If the EC had failed to incorporate the TRQ agreed with Brazil and opened on the basis of an Article XXVIII Agreement, it could not use that failure to claim that the TRQ included in the Schedule was a modification of the original concession. This Panel should uphold Brazil's claim in respect of the EC's failure to incorporate the agreed concession. Secondly, Brazil reiterated, the provision of a country-specific concession to Brazil was not incompatible, as required by the terms of Article 30(3) of the Vienna Convention cited above by the EC, with the terms of the Uruguay Round Agreement. Brazil argued that the EC's and other Members' schedules provided a significant number of examples of country-specific TRQs. In any event, the EC itself accepted that Article XXIV of GATT and Article IX of WTO gave rise to such commitments so that they therefore were not incompatible with the terms of the second treaty. Brazil concluded, therefore, that the EC had not demonstrated incompatibility of the provisions of the earlier treaty with the terms of the later treaty within the terms of Article 30(3) of the Vienna Convention.

---

[24] "(b) the provisions of the legal instruments set forth below that have entered into force under the GATT 1947 before the date of entry into force of the WTO Agreement:

(i) protocols and certifications relating to tariff concessions; ..."

(c) Article 31 of the Vienna Convention

31. Referring to the general rule of interpretation laid down in Article 31 of the Vienna Convention[25], the EC submitted that, together with the context, the interpreter should also take into account "any subsequent agreement between the parties regarding the ... application of its provisions" and "any relevant rules of international law applicable in the relations between the parties"(Article 31(3)(c)). Thus, the EC considered that the term "global" should be given its ordinary meaning in its context and in the light of its object and purpose. Irrespective of the philological meaning of the term "global", Brazil could not disregard the fact that the Article XXVIII Oilseeds negotiations were undertaken in the framework of the GATT. The object and purpose of the negotiations was to re-establish the balance of rights and obligations, following the Oilseeds panel report, within the scope of the GATT and in particular its Articles I and II. The EC found it difficult to conceive of a violation of Articles I and II of GATT that would be more obvious and indefensible than a discrimination on the duty applied upon importation of (like) products based on the origin of those products.[26] The EC noted that during the discussions of the provisions which became the present Article XXVIII, in the Tariff Agreement Committee at Geneva in 1947, the Chairman in summing up the discussions concerning the possibility of withdrawing concessions, stated: "... Therefore, the intent is clear: that in no way should this Article interfere with the operation of the Most-Favoured-Nation clause".[27] The EC also noted that this statement was made in the context of retaliatory trade measures against a unilateral modification or reduction by a Member of its own concessions. The same considerations must apply *a fortiori* to the *agreed* modification of a Member's Schedule as a result of *authorized* Article XXVIII:4 negotiations.

32. Brazil observed that the principle of good faith was a fundamental element in interpreting, understanding and implementing agreements. Interpreting agreements in good faith meant that all parties had to interpret the clear intention of the parties to the agreement and not read the agreement in a way that would lead to an unreasonable or absurd interpretation. In the opinion of Brazil, the ordinary meaning of the Brazil/EC Oilseeds Agreement was clear. Within the context of Article XXVIII of GATT, Brazil had agreed that it would not object to the EC withdrawing certain concessions on the condition that, in return, the EC would open a new compensatory concession specifically for Brazil. The agreement was made within the framework of Article XXVIII which ensured that all Members

---

[25] "A treaty shall be interpreted in good faith in accordance with the ordinary meaning to be given to the terms of the treaty in their context and in the light of its object and purpose."

[26] The recent Appellate Body Report in the *Banana III* dispute stated in paragraph 190 "the essence of the non-discrimination obligations is that like products should be treated equally, irrespective of their origin".

[27] Analytical Index of the GATT, Article XXVIII - Modification of the Schedules, Volume 2, 1995 ed., page 947.

which had an interest would not be prejudiced. In the opinion of Brazil, no other Member was so prejudiced. Brazil claimed that the EC had agreed in writing, and within the multilateral GATT framework, a country-specific compensation package with Brazil. It was Brazil's opinion that the EC had not respected this package. Moreover, Brazil said, Article 26 of the Vienna Convention set out one of the fundamental principles of law, of whatever nature, namely "*pacta sunt servanda*", providing that "Every treaty in force is binding upon the parties to it and must be performed by them in good faith". In the opinion of Brazil, the EC had not implemented in good faith the agreement with Brazil.

33. The EC replied that Articles I and XIII of GATT were also clear provisions of a treaty that was binding upon Brazil: did Brazil suggest that the principle "*pacta servanda sunt*" authorized Brazil to breach those other clear international obligations? It was the EC's view that this theory was deprived of any legal and logical foundation in international law and in the WTO system. The EC had fully complied with its international obligations under both the general provisions of the GATT and the specific commitments of the Article XXVIII Oilseeds Agreement: the EC opened as from 1 January 1994 an MFN frozen poultry meat TRQ and Brazil obtained immediate access to a share of that tariff quota which corresponded to its share of the overall EC imports.

(iv) Incorporation

34. Brazil argued that the Community did not administer the TRQ as a country-specific TRQ in the period from January 1994 to July 1995. Moreover, the frozen chicken TRQ had been agreed within the terms of bilateral Article XXVIII negotiations and the multilateral checks and balances that were provided for in that Article. It was distinct from agreements reached within the context of multilateral negotiations. The bilateral Oilseeds Agreement made no mention of the Uruguay Round. Nor did it leave the Community the unilateral right to amend the agreement and change the nature of the concession in line with other bilateral Oilseeds agreements.[28] Brazil did not agree that the Article XXVIII country-specific commitments were changed by reason of their incorporation into the Uruguay Round. The fact that the incorporation was unilaterally made under the heading "minimum access" did not act so as to modify the commitment. Nor did the inclusion of the TRQ within the schedule act so as to diminish the commitment. If the commitments were country-specific before the Uruguay Round, they remained country-specific after the Uruguay Round.

35. The EC submitted that Brazil had not contested the legal analysis made by the EC. The legal issue here was not whether the Article XXVIII Oilseeds Agreement had been "incorporated" in the Uruguay Round but, more fundamentally, what the current obligations of the EC under the GATT were with respect

---

28 Argentina, Poland and Sweden.

to frozen poultry meat. The Vienna Convention gave a clear and convincing answer to this problem: the Uruguay Round EC Schedule was the only relevant obligation of the EC in this respect. This obligation had been undertaken in full respect of Articles I and XIII of GATT. Brazil had not advanced any argument to the contrary. The EC insisted that, in accordance with Article 3.2 of the DSU, Article 59(1) or, in the alternative, Article 30(3) in connection with Article 31 of the Vienna Convention, should be used by the Panel to solve this dispute.

36. Brazil replied that the rights and obligations of Members of the WTO should be determined on the basis of the clear and precise terms of the WTO Agreements and, where necessary, the dispute settlement mechanism, in clarifying the provisions of those rights and obligations, should do so in accordance with customary rules of interpretation of public international law.[29] In interpreting the scope of Article 3.2 of the DSU, the Appellate Body[30] had found that parts of the Vienna Convention, in particular Articles 31 and 32, had attained the status of customary international law.

(v) MFN and Article XXVIII

37. Brazil noted that the structure of Article XXVIII was such that it both distinguished between Members and allowed them a certain flexibility in reaching bilateral agreements, subject to the review of all Members. The object of the negotiations was to ensure that the general level of trade was maintained but there was no requirement in Article XXVIII that the trade to be maintained by means of compensation in other products had to be on an MFN basis. Brazil argued that Article XXVIII could be an exception to the MFN rule contained in Article I if the parties negotiating the agreement so chose and the other Members did not object. It was Brazil's view that the EC and Brazil had chosen to make the TRQs country-specific and chosen that the MFN principle should not apply. Nor was there anything, in Brazil's opinion, in the nature or text of Article I of GATT which made it automatically applicable to compensation agreements. Citing Article I of GATT, Brazil submitted that a measure given in compensation was based on the granting of restitution, not on the giving of an advantage, favour or privilege. Nor was compensation an immunity. For these reasons, Article I did not apply to compensation TRQs agreed within the framework of Article XXVIII:4. In conclusion, Brazil argued, Article XXVIII was a lex specialis in that it provided for bilateral solutions within a multilateral framework. Article XXVIII:4 negotiations were initially conducted with those specific Members who were primarily concerned. It was only when a bilateral agreement was reached that a limited number of Members who had a substantial interest gained rights. The

[29] See Article 3.2 of the DSU.

[30] Appellate Body Report on *United States - Standards for Reformulated and Conventional Gasoline*, WT/DS2/AB/R and Appellate Body Report on *Japan - Taxes on Alcoholic Beverages*, WT/DS8/AB/R.

rights of these parties were limited in time. Finally, all contracting parties under Article XXVIII had the right to intervene to ensure the reasonableness of the parties, in the absence of agreement.

38. The **EC** submitted that Brazil's claims concerning the MFN nature of the EC frozen poultry meat TRQ could not be considered in the context of a violation of Article XXVIII since that provision only contained procedural obligations. This was a rather belated complaint concerning the content of a Schedule that was negotiated during the Uruguay Round and not about the procedures followed in order to revise the EC Schedule that was applicable before the current Uruguay Round Schedule was negotiated. Brazil had ratified the Uruguay Round agreements and was an original Member of the WTO within the terms of Article XI of the WTO Agreement. It could not request now the re-opening of the tariff negotiations with the EC through a dispute settlement procedure. Brazil could not request either, in the opinion of the EC, that the Panel re-do the Article XXVIII negotiations which were concluded in 1993. This would be clearly outside the terms of reference of this Panel. Moreover, it would amount, in practice, to requesting the Panel to substitute itself for the GATT CONTRACTING PARTIES by replacing their judgement on whether offers and counter-offers were "adequate" and in considering the "value" of the different elements of the Oilseeds package which went far beyond the frozen poultry meat. The EC considered that this action by the Panel would clearly breach Article 3.2 of the DSU and would not assist the DSB in discharging its responsibilities in accordance with Article 11 of the DSU. The EC submitted that Brazil confused the legal nature of a particular tariff treatment granted through the procedures foreseen in Article XXVIII - which was based on the MFN clause - with the economic effects of that particular tariff treatment.

39. **Brazil** submitted that the parties agreed that there were exceptions to the MFN principle within the terms of the GATT Articles. It could also be seen from the practice of the Members that exceptions to the MFN principle were common and that these exceptions were included in the schedules under the parts dealing with MFN commitments. Members' schedules were public documents and formed an integral part of the GATT (and were thus within the standard terms of reference). The schedules did not show, however, from where the country-specific commitments flowed. In practice, they flowed, in the opinion of Brazil, from Articles XXIV and XXVIII of GATT and from other bilateral agreements. It was, therefore, perfectly reasonable for Brazil to consider, on the basis of the provisions of GATT and of Members practice, that the EC had committed itself to opening a country-specific TRQ in Brazil's favour. Brazil claimed that the EC's principal arguments did not address the issue of country-specific commitments but were based on fundamental GATT/WTO principles and the succession of international agreements within the terms of the Vienna Convention. The first question to be addressed, according to Brazil, was the extent to which MFN was an overriding principle in the GATT and the extent to which exceptions were allowable. Brazil considered that it had shown that the procedure to be followed in Article XXIV was the same as in Article XXVIII. Brazil had also shown that

the object of both Articles was the same, namely the need to compensate contracting parties for changes to the schedules. Under Article XXIV the change to the schedule came about by reason of the formation of a customs union while the changes under Article XXVIII were made for other reasons. In both situations, the changes were unilateral by the Member making the change, which in turn gave rights to other Members either to agree to the changes and accept compensation or to counter-withdraw equivalent concessions.

(vi) Principle of Non-Discrimination

40. **Brazil** claimed that the EC had unilaterally decided that instead of a TRQ as compensation of 15,500 tonnes, it should be 7,100 tonnes. The arbitrariness of this decision and its consequences were inconsistent with the principle of non-discrimination. This general principle of law underlay the GATT/WTO Agreements. It was also a fundamental principle of international law and thus should be applied by the Panel under Article 3.2 of the DSU. The MFN principle was not to be confused with the concept of discrimination. According to Brazil, these two concepts were distinct in their meaning. Within the global balance of the GATT, including Articles I and XXVIII, Brazil and the EC had sought to achieve a non-discriminatory balance. The balance was between the withdrawal of an advantage and the offering of compensation in another product. If the EC failed to respect the agreement which fixed that balance, it was discriminating against Brazil so as to deny Brazil its rights within the multilateral system. In the opinion of Brazil, Regulation 1431/94[31] discriminated to the extent that it allocated the frozen chicken TRQ among other Members that were not entitled to compensation under Article XXVIII and consequently had not concluded bilateral agreements with the EC or were not even contracting parties to the GATT or Members of the WTO.

41. The **EC** replied that the purpose and object of the negotiations under Article XXVIII could *not* have been, as Brazil claimed, to achieve a result that would constitute a fundamental violation of the basic principle of non-discrimination among Members, which was one of the founding elements of the entire GATT (and now WTO) system. As to Brazil's assertion that a difference existed between the principle of non-discrimination and the MFN principle, the EC could theoretically accept that the general principle of non-discrimination could encompass situations going beyond the mere application of the MFN principle. The EC could nevertheless not accept the consequence implied in Brazil's approach that the implementation of the MFN principle could correspond to a violation of the principle of non-discrimination. This was absurd and should be clearly rejected by the Panel. (See also paragraphs 62 and 60.)

[31] Commission Regulation 1431/94 of 22 June 1994. O.J. L 156/9 of 23.6.1994.

(vii) The EC's Uruguay Round Schedule - Minimum Access

42. **Brazil** submitted that if the TRQ in the EC's Schedule was a minimum access TRQ, then the Community had failed to include the Brazilian Article XXVIII TRQ in its Schedule. The Community subsequently amended its schedule in line with the commitments it had undertaken within the context of the Uruguay Round but these changes were the result of a different series of commitments and were distinct in law. The Community Schedule appeared therefore to be inconsistent with its obligations under Article XXVIII. It was understood between the parties that the EC would submit to the GATT the changes to its Schedule at the same time as it would submit its Uruguay Round changes. When the EC submitted a Schedule with a frozen chicken TRQ of 15,500 tonnes, Brazil presumed that this TRQ referred to the TRQ agreed to be specifically for Brazil.

43. At the same time as the Article XXVIII procedures were being completed, the **EC** replied, the Uruguay Round was also coming to an end. In a letter signed by Ambassador Tran Van Thinh on 14 December 1993, the EC requested Mr. P. Sutherland, Director-General of the GATT, to distribute a revised version of the EC draft lists of commitments together with supporting tables, in order to establish final commitments. In that letter, an "Information Note Concerning the EC Offer on Agriculture" was included. That Information Note indicated the content of the tables attached thereto. For Table 3 - Minimum Access - the following was specifically indicated:

- *"the agreement on oilseeds negotiated under Article XXVIII has been incorporated*
- *tariff quotas, including in-quota tariff rates, agreed in bilateral negotiations have been incorporated."*

Finally, the table "Agricultural Negotiations: List of Commitments - Market access: EC - Lists Relating to Minimum Access" provided for a zero per cent TRQ for tariff items 0207 41 10, 0207 41 41 and 0207 41 71 up to 15,500 tonnes. The letter was distributed to all GATT CONTRACTING PARTIES. In the meantime, the revised Schedule was applied by the EC as from 1 January 1994. Within the three-month period set out in the Decision of the CONTRACTING PARTIES of 26 March 1980, no GATT CONTRACTING PARTY objected to the revised Schedule. On the contrary, they had all agreed by 30 March 1994 to a new EC Schedule of commitments, as a result of the Uruguay Round, which included the Article XXVIII Oilseeds Agreement results with respect to the frozen poultry meat.

44. Thus, the EC claimed, the formal notification to the GATT of a separate revised Schedule LXXX of the EC had been carried out: *all* GATT contracting parties were thus aware of the results of the Article XXVIII Oilseeds negotiations and of the intentions of the EC. The results of the Article XXVIII Oilseeds negotiations were therefore an *integral* part of the Uruguay Round formal negotiations. This procedure was considered correct and accepted by *all* the interested Members. It was therefore not correct to affirm, that the complainant was not aware of the interpretation to be given to the Article XXVIII Oilseeds Agreement

with respect to the poultry meat TRQ, or of the content of the Oilseeds agreements entered into with the other primarily concerned and substantially interested GATT contracting parties and that no notification had been provided to the GATT. The EC claimed that Brazil was fully informed on all these matters.

45. **Brazil** considered that it had no reason to understand from the text of the Community's Schedule and from the fact that the changes to the Schedule would be included in the Uruguay Round changes and that the Article XXVIII negotiations were taking place against the background of the Uruguay Round negotiations, that the country-specific chicken TRQ was a minimum access TRQ. It was settled GATT and WTO law, Brazil argued, that a schedule could not take precedence over underlying GATT/WTO obligations. The *Sugar* panel and the *Banana III* report[32] (as confirmed by the Appellate Body) provided that inclusion or exclusion of a measure in a schedule could not justify inconsistencies in that schedule with requirements of generally applicable GATT/WTO rules. The fact that the EC excluded from (or failed to include in) its Schedule a TRQ agreed for Brazil, meant that the EC was in clear breach of the basic compensatory rule in Article XXVIII:4. The EC did not compensate Brazil as it was obliged to do, and had agreed to do. Brazil submitted that the key to determining the EC's current commitments to Brazil was not restricted to an examination of the EC's Schedule. A Member could and did have commitments beyond the strict terms of its schedule.

(viii) Protection of Legitimate Expectations

46. **Brazil** submitted that the benefits accruing to Brazil under the GATT included the protection of the expectation that prevailed in July 1993, when the new concessions were agreed, that Brazil would be fully compensated. Brazil had had a reasonable expectation that the value of the concession agreed would not be nullified or impaired by the subsequent introduction of a lesser TRQ for the products concerned.[33] Brazil also had a legitimate expectation that the EC would not attempt to change the country-specific nature of the TRQ when Brazil agreed that the changes would be made at the time the EC submitted its Uruguay Round schedule. Brazil was entitled to expect that the EC would implement the Oilseeds Agreement TRQ in a manner compatible with the terms and objectives of the Agreed Minutes. Brazil signed the bilateral agreement because the compensation package addressed its specific concerns.

47. The **EC** replied that this Panel was not concerned with a non-violation case under Article XXIII:1(b) of GATT. The notion of "legitimate expectations" was developed only in the framework of such cases and, therefore, it was not

---

[32] Panel Report on *United States - Restrictions on Imports of Sugar*, adopted on 22 June 1989, BISD 36S/331, paragraph 58. Panel Report on *Banana III, op. cit.*, (WT/DS27/R/USA), page 360. Appellate Body Report on *Banana III, op. cit.*

[33] *Ibid.*

relevant here. The EC considered also that Article II:5 was irrelevant in the present context: that provision was, like Article XXVIII, a procedural one since it provided for the possibility to enter negotiations. It was evident, the EC believed, that none of the conditions set out in that provision were fulfilled here and Article II:5 should not be considered relevant for the resolution of the issues raised in this case.

(ix) The Implementation of the Frozen Chicken TRQ

48. **Brazil** submitted that since the EC had ratified the Oilseeds Agreement in Council Decision 87/94 of 20 December 1993, it considered the agreement to be distinct from other agreements (and not part of the Uruguay Round agreement). The frozen chicken TRQ was opened by Council Regulation 774/94 and allocated among supplying countries by Commission Regulation 1431/94. According to the recitals to 774/94 the purpose of opening the frozen chicken TRQ (as well as the other TRQs provided for in the Regulation) was to comply with the Article XXVIII commitments which required that the TRQ be opened by 1 January 1994. There was no reference to any other GATT commitments to be met. It was clear therefore, in the opinion of Brazil, that the EC considered that it was fulfilling its commitments under Article XXVIII only.

49. The **EC** replied that the negotiations between Brazil and the EC further to the Article XXVIII:4 procedure resulted in an agreement in the form of Agreed Minutes in July 1993, formally concluded by the EC institutions on 20 December 1993 and formally signed by both parties on 31 January 1994. The Agreement was published in the Official Journal of the EC on 18 February 1994. On the same date, a number of parallel agreements signed with other primarily concerned and substantially interested GATT contracting parties[34] was published. Whilst the content of those agreements varied, they were identical to the extent that they stated that an agreement had been reached in negotiations under Article XXVIII:4 of GATT concerning the elimination of the impairment of the tariff concessions as recommended by the panel report on *EEC - Payments and Subsidies paid to Processors and Producers of Oilseeds and Related Animal-Feed Proteins*. By 17 February 1994 at the latest, therefore, the EC argued, *all* the primarily concerned and substantially interested GATT contracting parties had acknowledged that the procedure under Article XXVIII:4 which had been authorized on 19 June 1992, had been successfully completed.

50. With respect to the question of whether the rights of other Members could be diminished by a finding that a schedule submitted as part of a multilateral negotiating process did not reflect the full range of that Member's commitments, **Brazil** was of the view that this question should be examined in respect of the conclusion of the Article XXVIII negotiations. The EC had stated that it had no-

---

[34] Argentina, Canada, Poland, Sweden and Uruguay.

tified the CONTRACTING PARTIES of the conclusion of the Article XXVIII negotiations at the latest on 17 February 1994. Under the terms of Article XXVIII, contracting parties who were not parties to the negotiations were free (under the terms of Article XXVIII:3(b)), within six months of the conclusion of negotiations, to withdraw substantially equivalent concessions if they were not satisfied with the bilateral country-specific agreements between the Members principally concerned. No contracting party took such action. Therefore, Brazil concluded that all contracting parties were satisfied.

(x) Compensation

51. **Brazil** submitted that the importance of compensation as an element of the multilateral system was apparent from the ranking of GATT/WTO remedies in the case of nullification or impairment. The preferred remedy in the case of a finding of nullification or impairment was the changing of the GATT/WTO inconsistent provisions. The second remedy was the granting of compensatory concessions and the third was the withdrawal of concessions. According to Brazil, "compensation" was a broad concept not specifically defined in the GATT/WTO. Its objective was to ensure that the same level of reciprocal trade was maintained in favour of the Member with a principal supplying interest. Brazil was of the view that compensation had an element of specificity about it. It was not, therefore, something to which the MFN principle necessarily applied. The drafters of Article XXVIII did not consider it to be so as they allowed for bilateral negotiations within its framework. Brazil argued that compensation was usually in the form of a concession to increase market access (or trade) in another product. Where the compensation was in the form of a lower tariff, the intention of the Member was clearly to grant it on an MFN basis. Where the concession was granted in the form of a TRQ, in the opinion of Brazil, the intention of the Member was to ensure the same level of reciprocal trade between the two negotiating parties. The question of the allocation of the TRQ was a separate issue to be agreed between the parties.

52. Brazil submitted that the compensation package was not built upon an exact compensation figure. The value had never been clearly defined by the parties and was not deemed necessary for the purpose of concluding the bilateral negotiations. In the case of the Article XXVIII:4 negotiations between Brazil and the EC, a choice was made to avoid the difficulties created by the calculation of an exact amount of total compensation. Therefore, Brazil accepted the EC's proposal to conduct the negotiations by working from a list of offers which included the frozen chicken TRQ, and not from an exact or fixed compensation value. Negotiation resulted in the agreed final offers. Brazil submitted that the Panel should only take into consideration that there was now an agreed compensation package made up of different elements, that the 15,500 tonnes TRQ in frozen chicken was part of that package and that it should have been allocated to Brazil.

53. The **EC** recalled that the EC and Brazil reached an agreement in accordance with Article XXVIII, which was accepted by both parties. Whether each of

the parties negotiated and obtained certain concessions on the basis of a specific value which they attributed to such concessions was not only irrelevant once the negotiating process was completed, but was also not necessarily capable of being reduced to a straightforward calculation. The agreement reached was the consequence of a GATT panel's finding that the EC's support system for oilseeds had the effect of reducing the value of the tariff concessions granted by the Community in 1962 and the agreed outcome of the negotiations not only comprised new tariff concessions on certain products including frozen poultry meat products (to which the EC did not at the time apply fixed tariffs, but variable levies), but also modifications to the EC's internal regime on oilseeds. As concerns the frozen poultry meat TRQ, the Brazilian allocation of the TRQ (7,100 tonnes) corresponded to Brazil's share of the overall imports of those frozen poultry meat products at the time of the negotiations.

54. Referring to Article XIX:3 and Article XXIII:2 of GATT which, according to Brazil, both authorized country-specific compensation, **Brazil** argued that there was very little guidance in the reports of previous panels or of the Appellate Body on which to base the justification that agreements within the terms of Article XXIV:6 were an exception to the general MFN rule. It had been accepted that, by nature, these compensatory agreements had to be country-specific as the rights of specific Members had been diminished by the creation of custom unions. No distinction could be made either in procedure or in intention between the compensation agreements under Articles XXIV and those of XXVIII. In practice, Brazil continued, there were examples of both country-specific and MFN TRQs offered and implemented by the EC as compensation under Article XXIV:6 of GATT. Those considered to be *erga omnes* or MFN were usually stated to be so by means of the letters "MFN" or the words "*erga omnes*" in brackets after the TRQ.[35] There were also examples of country-specific TRQs.[36] The GATT therefore recognized a number of exceptions to the MFN rule. These exceptions were provided for in both the text of the GATT and practised by the Members. They were also well recognized by academic writers.[37]

55. The **EC** indicated that, in its view, the agreement resulting from the Article XXVIII Oilseeds negotiations and the Uruguay Round agreement had the same objective albeit a (partially) different purpose. They both pursued the objective of ensuring a particular (reduced) tariff rate for frozen poultry meat as compared to the normal bound duty rate applicable to imports into the EC. They both also pursued the objective of ensuring that tariff treatment was bound in the

---

35 See for example Agreement between the United States and the EC published in O.J. L 098 of 10 April 1987 as well as Council Decision 95/592 of 22 December 1995.

36 See for example Council Decision 95/592 of 22.12.95 and published in O.J. L 334 of 30.12.95.

37 Merciai (Patricio Merciai, Safeguard Measures in GATT, 15 Journal of World Trade Law (1981)) stated that it was standard practice that country-specific trade benefits were the result of negotiations to avoid retaliatory action under Article XIX:3 or XXIII:2. Bronckers (Marco Bronckers, Selective Safeguard Measures in Multilateral Trade Relations, TM Asser Instituut, (1995)) stated that this compensation needed not be administered on an MFN basis.

EC Schedule of commitments. In the EC's view, since they both were undertaken in the framework of the GATT, they both had also the objective of complying with the general principles of non-discrimination as set out in Articles I and XIII of GATT. Otherwise, they would have violated the general principle of customary public international law *pacta servanda sunt*. However, the EC continued, the two negotiations were initiated for partially different reasons: the earlier Article XXVIII negotiations were justified by the limited purpose of ensuring compensation after the Oilseeds panel while the later Uruguay Round agreements had a much wider purpose of ensuring an overall balance of concessions between Members where tariff concessions in certain products could balance (or "compensate") tariff concessions for other products.[38] Thus, in order to create a new level of reciprocal commitments, the later negotiations incorporated the results of the earlier more limited negotiation which had been reflected in the revised EC Schedule.[39] However, the EC Schedule resulting from the Uruguay Round negotiations maintained unaltered the level of tariff treatment agreed in the Article XXVIII Oilseeds negotiations with respect to the frozen poultry meat TRQ. "Compensation" could therefore not change the legal reality under the WTO covered agreements: the EC was bound, on a MFN basis, by its current Schedule of commitments for the tariff treatment of frozen poultry meat which was the result of the Uruguay Round. The application of the principles of the Vienna Convention, and in particular Articles 59(1), 30(3) and 31, fully supported this view. (See also paragraphs 146 and 150).

(xi) Interpretation of "Global"

56. **Brazil** submitted that there was one word in the Agreed Minutes, i.e. "global", which required special consideration as the Community had placed great emphasis on this word in bilateral consultations prior to the commencement of the dispute settlement procedure. In the view of Brazil, the word "global" had no fixed or established meaning in GATT law or practice. It was not equivalent to the words "*erga omnes*" or to "MFN". These words had distinct meanings and were available for use should the parties to an agreement wish to use them in the sense that they had. The parties to the Agreed Minutes did not wish to use these words, according to Brazil, and therefore did not do so. The word global, Brazil continued, had been used in relation to all the TRQs which were opened by the

---

38 This was clearly expressed for instance in paragraph 4 of the Marrakesh Protocol to the General Agreement on Tariffs and Trade 1994. It was apparent from that provision that the EC could have been theoretically entitled to withhold or withdraw the frozen poultry meat concession in the event that Brazil's Schedule had not yet become a schedule to GATT 1994. However, paragraph 4 of the Marrakesh protocol was further evidence of the fact that the CONTRACTING PARTIES to the Uruguay Round considered the new agreements as a new set of rules and commitments replacing earlier concessions (such as the ones resulting from Article XXVIII Oilseeds negotiation), which was fully in accordance with Article 59.1 of the Vienna Convention.

39 As indicated expressly in Ambassador Tran Van Thinh's letter on 14 December 1993, annexed to the EC's first written submission.

Community in all the Oilseeds agreements, except the maize TRQ opened for Argentina. The maize TRQ was the only one encompassing only one tariff line, so there was no need to use the word "global" to cover a variety of tariff lines. In relation to the Brazil-EC Agreement the word "global" was used in respect of all three TRQs. When the EC opened the quotas by means of Council Regulation 774/94, it accumulated the three Hilton beef TRQs provided for in three of the agreements, and allocated the quota among those countries, but did not accumulate the three frozen chicken TRQs in a like manner. Both TRQs were described as being "global". "Global" was not therefore equivalent to the MFN principle. Brazil observed that the use of the word "global" in the Agreed Minutes did not prevent the Community from interpreting the Agreed Minutes in such a way so as not to open the TRQ on an "*erga omnes*" basis. The TRQ was allocated, albeit incorrectly and inconsistently with the Oilseeds Agreement, among certain supplying countries by Commission Regulation 1431/94. "Global" was not therefore to be read as meaning *erga omnes*.

57. The only element of disagreement, the **EC** said, resided in the claim by Brazil that the 15,500 tonnes TRQ should be reserved only for Brazil. Brazil's claims in this respect rested on a reading of the word "global"[40] of the Article XXVIII Oilseeds Agreement which was different from the normal meaning, understood by the EC to be equivalent to "general", "universal", "comprehensive", "catch-all" or, in WTO terms, MFN or *erga omnes*. According to Brazil's interpretation, that word meant that the EC was committing itself only vis-à-vis Brazil for a quantity that globally encompassed the frozen poultry meat. The EC was firmly of the view that this interpretation had no value for the following reasons. An interpretation in good faith of the word "global" in the light of the object and purpose of a negotiation under Article XXVIII *could not* mean, EC argued, anything else than "*erga omnes*" or "MFN". This was indeed the manner in which the EC had immediately and consistently implemented its agreement with Brazil, together with all the other parallel agreements concluded with other GATT contracting parties in the context of the Oilseeds case settlement.[41] Moreover, Brazil could not have disregarded the interpretation of the word "global" as meaning "MFN" that resulted from the practice of the management of the TRQ and from the EC Schedule as they were formally used in the context of the Uruguay Round final negotiations and verification process. The fact that Brazil and the EC (together with all the other WTO Members), by ratifying the Marrakesh Agreement, agreed to the EC Schedule with respect to the *MFN* TRQ concerning the frozen poultry meat could certainly be defined as a "subsequent agreement between the parties regarding the ... application of its provisions". The EC did not admit, even

40 To be found in the text of the Agreed Minutes of Article XXVIII Oilseeds Agreement between the EC and Brazil, in particular in the Annex, part D - new concessions, footnote No. 2.

41 Brazil indicated in this respect that the EC had created some country-specific TRQs for other products. The EC denied this allegation with force. All products negotiated under Article XXVIII, including those mentioned by Brazil, were provided duty treatment on an MFN basis.

for the sake of argument, that an ambiguity existed with regard to the interpretation of the word "global" at the moment of the signature of the Article XXVIII Agreement in January 1994. In any event, the alleged ambiguity could not reasonably persist after the *agreed* conclusions of the Uruguay Round negotiations. Should the Panel consider, *quod non*, that the word "global" in the earlier treaty meant country-specific, then the EC submitted that there would be a clear conflict between the provisions in the earlier treaty and the EC MFN Schedule in the later treaty. In application of Article 30(3) of the Vienna Convention, the former could therefore continue to apply *only* "to the extent of their compatibility with the later treaty". This necessarily meant that the duty-free poultry TRQ, which continued to exist, necessarily had to be applied on an *erga omnes* basis.

58. **Brazil** further submitted that it was obvious from references to the word "global" in the GATT academic literature that the word did not mean MFN or *erga omnes*. In the Handbook of GATT[42], reference was made to the establishment of a global quota in the head note to the *Chilean Apples* case[43] but in the text of the commentary reference was being made to the "total amount of permitted imports". Furthermore, in the Analytical Index of the GATT[44] reference was made to "global quotas for leather".[45] It was clear from this case that reference was being made to the total amount of imports under all the quotas which were, in practice, country-specific. Brazil argued that in the present context the word "global" should be read in its ordinary sense in light of its objective and purpose and in good faith. A global annual tariff quota of 15,500 tonnes made up of three product classifications was referring to the fact that three different products were bundled within the same global TRQ volume. Thus, within the "global" TRQ of 15,500 tonnes there was to be no subdivision between the different products. In conclusion, therefore, the text of the Brazil-EC Oilseeds Agreement was clear and precise. There was no special meaning to be given to any terms used in the Agreement. Not to interpret the Agreement in its ordinary sense would lead to results that were manifestly absurd or unreasonable.

Article XIII of GATT

59. In the view of **Brazil**, Article XIII did not apply to compensatory, country-specific TRQs which had their origins in Article XXVIII, unless the parties agreed that the TRQ should be MFN. Brazil argued that the reason Article XIII did not apply to the allocation of the frozen chicken TRQ was that it was a TRQ

---

[42] Handbook of WTO/GATT Dispute Settlement, ed. Pierre Pescatore, William Davey and Andreas Lowenfeld, New York, Transnational Publishers, Inc., 1995, at CS 43/2 and CS 43/3.

[43] Panel Report on *EEC - Restrictions on Imports of Dessert Apples*, adopted on 10 November 1980, BISD 275/98.

[44] GATT, Analytical Index: Guide to GATT Law and Practice, updated 6th edition (1995) page 298.

[45] Panel Report on *Japanese Measures on Imports of Leather*, adopted on 6 November 1979, BISD 26S/320.

agreed within the context of a bilateral agreement negotiated between Brazil and the EC under Article XXVIII with the specific purpose of compensating Brazil for the modification or withdrawal of a concession. Referring to the observation of a previous panel that Article XIII was "basically a provision relating to the administration of restrictions authorized as exceptions to one of the most basic GATT provisions - the general ban on quotas and other non-tariff restrictions contained in Article XI"[46], Brazil argued that the frozen chicken TRQ was not a restriction on trade prohibited by Article XI of GATT. There was considerable trade in poultry products into the Community over and above the volume of the TRQ. The TRQ was compensation for the withdrawal of a concession. It provided for market access at a tariff rate lower than that generally applicable with the purpose of compensating one Member for a loss elsewhere. Brazil noted that the Appellate Body had recently ruled that Article XIII applied to TRQs.[47] In the view of Brazil, this did not mean that Article XIII applied automatically to all TRQs. It did not necessarily apply to country-specific TRQs.

60. The **EC** argued that it had demonstrated that any country-specific tariff advantage (like a country-specific, reduced-rate or duty-free TRQ), bound as a result of a re-scheduling negotiation under Article XXVIII would be contrary to Article I:1 of GATT and could not be justified either by reference to Article XXIV of GATT or by any decision under Article IX of the WTO Agreement. The EC failed therefore to see how, in the absence of any legal justification under those Articles the "basic principle of non-discrimination" would not apply to the allocation of any TRQ established as a result of an Article XXVIII negotiation. The quoted paragraph of the *Banana III* Appellate Body report, albeit limited to the particular issue of Members not having a substantial interest that was specific to that case, clearly indicated, in the view of the EC, that this was indeed the case.

61. **Brazil** submitted that, to the extent that country-specific quotas existed in Members' schedules, Article XIII did not apply. It would be illogical, in the view of Brazil, to apply Article XIII in such a situation. The EC Schedule provided for a series of country-specific agricultural TRQs, all of which were included in "Part I Most-Favoured-Nation Tariff, Section I - B Tariff Quotas". Brazil considered that the EC was not consistent in its arguments in relation to Article XIII as evidenced by its practice in relation to other TRQs in its Schedule. Article XIII was not applied by Members to country-specific TRQs, and as the frozen chicken TRQ was specific to Brazil, Article XIII did not apply. However, if this Panel was to consider that Article XIII did apply to the frozen chicken TRQ, as an alternate plea Brazil claimed the EC had not complied with the terms of Article XIII.

---

[46] The Panel Report on *Banana III*, *op. cit.*, page 344.

[47] The Appellate Body Report on *Banana III*, *op. cit.*

62. The **EC** replied that the recent Appellate Body report in the *Banana III* dispute[48] addressed the issue of the applicability of the "basic principle of non-discrimination" to Members not having a substantial interest. The Appellate Body stated in particular "when this principle of non-discrimination is applied to the allocation of tariff quota shares to Members not having a substantial interest, it is clear that a Member cannot, whether by agreement or by assignment, allocate tariff quota shares to some Members not having a substantial interest while not allocating shares to other Members who likewise do not have a substantial interest. To do so is clearly inconsistent with the requirement in Article XIII:1".

63. Referring to paragraph 1 and paragraph 2(d) of Article XIII, **Brazil** noted that Article XIII provided that a TRQ could be allocated among supplying countries in one of two, mutually exclusive, ways, i.e. (i) by agreement; or, in the absence of agreement, (ii) by allocation on the basis of past supply performance during a specific reference period, due account being taken of special factors. Brazil considered that there was a clear prioritization between these two options. The first option was to reach agreement with Members having a substantial interest. Only in the absence of agreement could a Member allot the shares on the basis of past performance.

(i) By Agreement

64. **Brazil** held the view that the EC had reached an agreement with Brazil in 1993 on the allocation of the full TRQ to Brazil. There had been no change to that agreement and Brazil had made its views known to the Community prior to the country allocation of the TRQ in June 1994. No other Member did seek an agreement with the EC on the allocation of the TRQ. Frozen chickens were the subject of agreement with other Members negotiating with the EC on Oilseeds compensation. However, Brazil was of the view that neither Argentina nor Poland had a real interest in supplying frozen chicken to the Community. Brazil had consistently maintained that there was an agreement on the full allocation of the frozen chicken TRQ exclusively to Brazil. The EC had failed to respect this agreement.

65. The **EC** replied that the EC and Brazil had agreed, *inter alia* - firstly in January 1994 and later at the end of the Uruguay Round negotiations - on the principle of an *erga omnes* TRQ up to 15,500 tonnes for the three poultry products concerned with this dispute. They had also agreed on the level of duties that should be applied within that TRQ (duty-free tariff treatment). By contrast, they did not agree - either in January 1994 or at the conclusion of the Uruguay Round negotiation or at any later moment - on the allocation of the TRQ. Therefore, the EC had decided autonomously, in accordance with the rules of Article XIII:2(d), to assign to the Members having a substantial interest in supplying the product

[48] The Appellate Body Report on *Banana III*, *op. cit*, paragraph 159 to 163.

concerned a share of the TRQ with the aim to achieving "a distribution of trade in such product[s] approaching as closely as possible the shares which the various contracting parties might be expected to obtain in the absence of such restriction".[49]

(ii) By Allocation on the Basis of Past Performance

66. **Brazil** argued that the EC appeared to have applied the second method for the allocation of a TRQ set out in Article XIII. Brazil noted that the past performance method required that the TRQ be allocated among supplying countries based on their past supply performance during a specific reference period, due account being taken of special trade factors. It was understood that the EC chose the period 1991-1993 as the reference period. On that basis, three categories of origins were created: Brazil, Thailand and others. The size of the "others" category reflected, according to Brazil, the percentage of EC imports of frozen chicken from China. It was designed to facilitate the continuation of this trade (until imports were stopped because of phytosanitary problems). China filled most of the "others" category. By this method the Community granted a non-Member access to a TRQ which was designed to compensate GATT Members only.

67. Brazil's assumption was incorrect, **EC** replied: Article XIII:2(d), first sentence, clearly referred to "supplying countries" in general. It used the expression "contracting parties" only with respect to "contracting parties having a substantial interest in supplying the product concerned" with which an agreement could be sought or to which a share could be autonomously allotted by the importing Member. The EC had complied to the letter with these requirements. The total amount of the TRQ, the EC submitted, was allocated in accordance with the quantities shown in Annex 1 of Regulation 1431/94 and in compliance with the provisions of Article XIII of GATT. The quantities allocated to Groups 1 (Brazil) and 2 (Thailand) were specific to those countries since licences carried with them an obligation to import from those countries (Article 1 of Commission Regulation 997/97). Licences for Group 3 countries were not country-specific but they could not be used in respect of products originating in Brazil or Thailand (Commission Regulation 1514/97). Licences for all groups of countries were allocated on a quarterly basis in accordance with the procedures set out in Article 4 of Regulation 1431/94 which provided for the fixing of a single percentage of acceptance of the quantities applied for. There was no allocation on a "first-come, first-served" basis.

68. **Brazil** submitted that the *Banana III* panel examined the concept of an "others" category in the allocation of TRQs. The panel considered that this type of category had a value in allowing new trade patterns to develop. It also consid-

[49] Article XIII:2, first sentence.

ered that country allocations of TRQs needed to be reviewed on the accession of new Members to the WTO. However, Brazil argued, the EC could not unilaterally grant to non-WTO members the right to participate in a compensatory TRQ. Nor could the EC operate a TRQ allocation system which allowed a non-WTO member to participate by default. The WTO was a system for the benefit of Members who had chosen to be bound by its obligations. In addition, Brazil continued, the EC allowed Members with other privileged market access to partake of the TRQ. This practice was declared to be inconsistent with the GATT in the *Newsprint* panel.[50] The East European countries which had association agreements with the EC had all been allocated privileged access to the EC market in chicken products. By allowing these countries to participate in the TRQ, the EC was reducing the benefit to other Members. In conclusion, Brazil said, the EC had used Article XIII to avoid its commitments under the Article XXVIII Oilseeds Agreement with Brazil. Secondly, the Community had misinterpreted the terms of Article XIII and, finally, the EC had denied Brazil compensation within the global balance of benefits that had existed prior to the Article XXVIII negotiations.

69. The **EC** noted that the allocation of a share of a TRQ had been considered an advantage by the recent Appellate Body report in the *Banana III* dispute[51] to such an extent that the "basic principle of non-discrimination" applied strictly when allocating shares of a TRQ, including for Members *not* having a substantial interest. By assigning a share of the TRQ to all substantially interested Members, including Brazil, the EC had therefore provided the complainant with the best possible (and legally sound) situation in the trade of the poultry products within the TRQ. The EC had made use of the most recent statistics available at the time of the negotiations (1991-1993) to elaborate the "previous representative period" required under Article XIII:2(d) and had followed a criterion[52] that was considered correct by the recent *Banana III* panel.[53] That panel had also accepted (and the point was not overturned by the Appellate Body) the creation of a residual category "others" "for *all suppliers* other than Members with a substantial interest in supplying the product".[54] (emphasis added)

70. **Brazil** considered that if the TRQ was given in compensation to Members, the EC could not justify the administration of the TRQ in such a way that non-Members benefited whether that administration was justified under Article XIII or not. The proper question was not only whether non-Members came within the terms of Article XIII, which they clearly did not, but the extent to which non-

[50] Panel Report on *Newsprint, op. cit.*; paragraph 55 of the findings and conclusions: "Imports which are already duty-free, due to a preferential agreement, cannot by their very nature participate in an MFN duty-free quota".

[51] Appellate Body Report on *Banana III, op. cit.*, paragraphs 161 and 162.

[52] The average of the last three full years of trade in the product concerned for which reliable official statistics are available at the time of the negotiation.

[53] Paragraph 7.83.

[54] Paragraph 7.75.

Members could benefit from compensation at all. It was within the context of the examination of the nature of compensation that the Panel should examine the administration of the TRQ. If the EC was permitted to offer WTO-specific compensation to non-WTO members, Brazil continued, it had diminished that compensation whether it was "MFN" compensation or not. Even if it was MFN (which Brazil denied), it remained compensation to WTO Members. It was not a TRQ which could be administered so that non-WTO members benefited. Finally, the EC had erred in applying Article XIII by allowing Members with privileged access in the same products to benefit from the compensation TRQ.

71. The **EC** considered that the text of Article XIII:2(d) was clear: when proceeding to the allocation of a TRQ, there was an obligation to allocate a share to *Members* having a substantial interest and this was what the EC did, *inter alia*, with Brazil. By contrast, there was *no* obligation to discriminate against non-Members of the WTO in their access to the TRQ in the residual category under "others". The EC maintained that while there was a general principle to treat on an MFN basis any Member with respect to advantages granted even to a non-Member, there was no provision in the WTO forbidding the Members from providing market access to non-Members on an MFN basis. Moreover, Brazil's claim that the EC should exclude any non-Member-supplying country from the allocation of the TRQ would inevitably entail an increase of its share of the tariff quota. This was, in the view of the EC, an unjustified request in the light of the *chapeau* of Article XIII:2: Brazil would then obtain a significantly higher share of imports than it "might be expected to obtain in the absence of such restriction", thus violating the provision it allegedly wished to see applied by the EC. The EC also noted that what market access to the residual part of a TRQ and to whom it was given by the importing country following the allocation amongst the substantially interested Members, was a matter that could not harm in any manner the trade interests of Members having a substantial interest, if their shares had been correctly allocated in accordance with the relevant provisions of Article XIII. This was certainly the case for Brazil with respect to the allocation of the duty-free TRQ concerning the frozen poultry meat.

The Agreement on Import Licensing Procedures[55]

72. **Brazil** submitted that there had been some debate on the extent to which the Licensing Agreement applied to TRQs. This debate had been to a large measure resolved in the findings of the *Banana III* panel according to which the Licensing Agreement did apply to TRQs. The Community had chosen to operate a non-automatic licensing system within the terms of Article 3 of the Licensing Agreement. The EC poultry licensing system was therefore subject to the disciplines set out in Articles 1 and 3 of the Licensing Agreement and to the principles of transparency and certainty which underlay the Agreement. Article 1.3 of the

[55] Hereafter the Licensing Agreement.

Licensing Agreement provided that Members had to ensure that the administrative procedures used to implement licensing regimes were not operated inappropriately so as to give rise to trade distortions. This general prohibition, Brazil argued, was repeated and amplified in Article 3.2 which provided that non-automatic licensing should not have trade restrictive or distortive effects on imports additional to those caused by the imposition of the restriction. The licensing procedures set out in Commission Regulation 1431/94, as amended, for administering the frozen chicken TRQ did not, in the opinion of Brazil, meet the strict requirements of the Licensing Agreement and in fact distorted trade within the TRQ. As will also be seen below, the licensing system operated as to distort non-quota trade.

73. The **EC** replied that in its *Banana III* report[56], the Appellate Body had clarified the nature of the obligations imposed on the Members by the Licensing Agreement. In particular, the Appellate Body had stated that the Licensing Agreement pertained to the *application* and *administration* of import licensing procedures, and required that this application and administration be "neutral ... fair and equitable".[57] The Appellate Body continued: "As a matter of fact, none of the provisions of the Licensing Agreement concerns import licensing *rules*, per se. As is made clear by the title of the Licensing Agreement, it concerns import licensing *procedures*. The preamble of the Licensing Agreement indicates clearly that this agreement relates to import licensing procedures and their administration, not to import licensing rules. Article 1.1 of the Licensing Agreement defines its scope as the administrative procedures used for the operation of import licensing regimes".[58] In the light of this clarification, it was clear to the EC that the only issue before the Panel in this case was whether the EC's licensing regime for the TRQ complied with the administrative procedures set out in the Licensing Agreement.

74. **Brazil** submitted that the Appellate Body report on *Banana III*[59] made clear that the Licensing Agreement required that the "application and administration (of licensing rules) be neutral ... fair and equitable". The Appellate Body found that this terminology was equivalent to the terms of Article X:3(a) of GATT which provided that rules be "neutral in application and administered in a fair and equitable manner". These were substantive obligations which had to be respected by Members. Secondly, the Appellate Body had ruled that subsequent panels should examine the context in which particular findings of previous panels or the Appellate Body were made.[60] The object of the Appellate Body in *Ba-*

---

56 Appellate Body Report on *Banana III, op. cit.*

57 *Ibid*, paragraph 197.

58 *Ibid.*

59 *Ibid*, paragraphs 192 to 198.

60 As the Appellate Body stated in *United States - Measures Affecting Imports of Woven Wool Shirts and Blouses from India* (Shirts and Blouses): "Given the explicit aim of dispute settlement that permeates the DSU, we do not consider that Article 3.2 of the DSU is meant to encourage either panels or the Appellate Body to 'make law' by clarifying existing provisions of the WTO Agreement

nana III was to determine the extent to which the EC was entitled to design different licensing rules for the same product from different origins. The Appellate Body found that different rules could apply to the same product from different origins. On the reasoning of the Appellate Body in *Shirts and Blouses* it was open to this Panel, in the view of Brazil, to find that the provisions of the Licensing Agreement, mentioned in paragraph 75 below, were mandatory and that the EC had failed to comply with these provisions.

75. Brazil submitted further that the Licensing Agreement had extensive provisions to guide panels in the interpretation of what was neutral, fair and equitable in the administration of licensing procedures. These included the requirements: not to distort trade (Article 1.3); that licences be allocated on the basis of import performance (Article 3.5(j)); that traders and their governments should be able to become familiar with the licensing procedures (Articles 1.4, 3.3, 3.5(b), 3.5(c) and 3.5(d)); that nothing should hinder the full utilization of licences (Article 3.5(j)); that licences be issued in economic quantities (Article 3.5(i)); and that provision be made for newcomers (Article 3.5(j)). If these provisions of the Licensing Agreement were not mandatory then, it appeared to Brazil, they should still be taken into consideration by panels when determining what was the nature of the obligation of neutrality, fairness, equality, impartiality and uniformity in the administration of the licensing procedures. Brazil maintained that the EC had not complied with the Licensing Agreement whether or not it was considered that the substantive provisions contained therein were mandatory or were instances of uniformity, fairness and neutrality.

(i) Notification

76. **Brazil** submitted that Article 1.4 of the Licensing Agreement provided that all the rules and regulations had to be published and the place of publication notified to the WTO Committee on Import Licensing in such a manner that governments and traders could become familiar with them. Articles 1.4, 3.3, 3.5(b), 3.5(c), 3.5(d) made repeated reference to the need for traders to become acquainted with the terms and conditions of licensing procedures. The EC appeared to have failed to comply with the terms of the Licensing Agreement and had not notified to the Committee on Import Licensing the sources in which EC licensing provisions were published and the specific import licensing rules for frozen chicken products. The Community had, however, published the licensing procedures in the Official Journal of the EC and thus, it could be said, had allowed governments and traders to become familiar with them. Brazil maintained, however, that the constant and contradictory amending of the regulations was such as to nullify the requirements of transparency set out in Article 3.3 of the Licensing Agreement.

---

outside the context of resolving a particular dispute. A panel need only address those claims which must be addressed in order to resolve the matter in issue in the dispute."

77. The **EC** submitted that in the *Banana III* report, the Appellate Body had confirmed that import licensing procedures for tariff quotas fell within the scope of application of the Licensing Agreement.[61] The EC observed in this respect that notification was a procedural, rather than a substantive, requirement and since the question of whether the Licensing Agreement applied to TRQs had only been clear as from the date of the Appellate Body's decision in the *Banana III* case, the mere fact of non-notification of the licensing regime at issue in this case could not be considered to render this regime illegal in any way. All details relating to the licensing system had been published in the Official Journal of the European Communities in all official languages, including Portuguese, thus ensuring transparency and that both governments and traders were aware of the requirements of the regime.

78. **Brazil** submitted that the object of notification was that governments and traders should become familiar with the rules and procedures governing imports. Non-notification invalidated the underlying objective of transparency in the Licensing Agreement. Notification in the Official Journal or Gazette did not satisfy the transparency requirement. Governments and traders of a Member could not be expected to read, on a regular basis, the official publications of all Members just in case a new provision in relation to trade was published. Notification to the WTO removed this need and ensured that governments and their traders did become familiar with the import rules and procedures. Notification was a substantive obligation which the EC had failed to satisfy.

79. The **EC** replied that Brazil had fully utilized its allocation under the frozen poultry meat TRQ during its period of application. The licensing procedures at issue in this Panel related only to the management of the TRQ. There was no evidence whatsoever that a distortion or reduction of trade in the products at issue had been caused by operation of the import licensing system. The evidence was rather to the contrary: the licensing system had never prevented the Brazilian poultry products from fully exploiting the tariff reduction under the TRQ. Moreover, even if the market (in- and out-quota) was taken as a whole, volumes of Brazilian imports in frozen poultry meat had steadily increased during the period of application of the TRQ. Brazil's submissions appeared to be based on a misunderstanding of the transparency provision of the Licensing Agreement. What was important, EC said, and as was clear from the text of Article 1.4, was that licensing procedures were *published*. Moreover, the EC had notified to the WTO the administration of all its agricultural tariff quotas including the frozen poultry meat TRQ.[62]

[61] Appellate Body Report on *Banana III, op. cit.*, paragraph 195.
[62] See documents G/AG/N/EEC/1, G/AG/N/EEC/3 and G/AG/N/EEC/3/Corr.1.

(ii) Changes to the Licensing Rules

80. **Brazil** submitted that the EC had changed the licensing rules and procedures at least seven times, making it difficult for governments and traders to become familiar with the rules. The changes themselves were evidence of a lack of certainty and transparency in the EC's licensing procedures. In addition, the changing rules only acted to confuse traders. Brazil observed that not all the changes had been for the purpose of the elimination of speculation. Those changes that had addressed the issue of speculation had not resulted in its elimination. The combination of these two considerations was that the changes in the licensing rules did not allow traders and their governments to become familiar with them as required by the Licensing Agreement.

81. The **EC** replied that if the EC were to have changed the system and *not* published the changes effected, this would have led to lack of transparency in the system. But that the changes, of themselves, created lack of transparency, the EC had difficulties in understanding. Moreover, there was nothing in the Licensing Agreement which said that import licensing procedures could not be changed. Brazil would have been the first to complain if the system had remained identical during the entire period of the TRQ and the Community could have been accused of not taking account of the realities of the commercial situation. The Community noted, furthermore, that the "100 tonnes rule" had in fact not been changed since 1 June 1996. The changes in market access conditions effected by the Commission were designed to ensure a reasonable distribution of licences amongst an ever increasing number of applicants. The changes made to these criteria were necessary to ensure the proper functioning of the licensing system and, as was clear from the motivation given in the various Regulations, were necessary to take account of experience gained in the operation of the regime.

(iii) Distortion of Trade

82. **Brazil** asserted that its percentage share in the EC market had been falling since the introduction of the TRQ in 1994.[63] Prior to the opening of the TRQ, Brazil had a fairly constant market share of 45 per cent to 47 per cent. In 1993, Brazil's percentage market share was 45.6 per cent. After the opening of the TRQ, in 1994, Brazil's total market share (made up of both quota and non-quota trade) fell to 42.5 per cent; in 1995 it fell further to 36.2 per cent and in 1996 to 33.2 per cent. Brazil considered that the fall in overall market share, made up of both in-quota and out-quota product, was evidence of the distortion of trade resulting from the introduction of the TRQ contrary to the provision of Article 1.2 of the Licensing Agreement. In normal trading circumstances, Brazil would have been expected to increase market share as a result of the introduction of the TRQ.

---

[63] Brazil confirms the Panel's understanding that the statistics provided refer both to TRQ and non-TRQ trade in the products under consideration.

This did not occur. Brazil considered that the principal cause of the fall in market share was the disturbance in trading relations which had been built up over time. Brazil was not arguing that only traditional importers should be entitled to benefit, nor was Brazil suggesting what the appropriate number of importers should be. Brazil argued that the administration of the TRQ had resulted in speculation and in a sharp decline in its market share. The cause in the decline in market share was not competition from competing supplying countries. The statistics showed that, in 1993, despite the marked increase in exports from China, Brazil maintained its market share. The statistics also showed that there was no correlation between the fall in Brazil's market share and an increase in market share of any one other source.

83. The **EC** replied that Brazil had not contested the EC's evidence that there had been full utilization of the TRQ. Despite the decrease in market share of Brazil, the overall volumes of imports from Brazil had increased (from 21,493 to 28,701 tonnes). Brazil had not explained how it considered that the overall market share was relevant to trade within the TRQ. It appeared itself to concede that factors such as the competitivity of Brazilian exports vis-à-vis other exporters were relevant to overall market share. The EC had noted that another relevant factor was the harmonization of veterinary standards within the Community which had contributed to the opening up of the Community market to imported products (imports had almost doubled over the period 1992-1997). The EC submitted that Brazil had not demonstrated a *prima facie* case. Its allegations regarding distortions of trade were vague and unsubstantiated. There had been full use of the TRQ and volumes of trade had increased.

84. **Brazil** submitted that Members were required, under Article 1.2 of the Licensing Agreement, to ensure that the administrative procedures were in conformity with the relevant provisions of GATT 1994 so that trade distortions, arising from the inappropriate operation of the import licensing procedures, did not occur. This appeared to be a mandatory requirement that distortions to trade be avoided. The requirement not to distort trade was not limited to trade within the TRQ. It applied to all trade, whether within the TRQ or outside it. Article 3.2 provided that non-automatic licensing "shall not have trade-restrictive or -distortive effects on imports additional to those caused by the imposition of the restriction". The word "shall" was not "should" or "might" or "best efforts". By means of the word "shall", the Agreement set out an obligation which had to be respected.

85. The **EC** submitted that during the period of application of the TRQ, Brazil's exports of poultry products into the EC had increased substantially. In the EC's view, Brazil had failed to discharge the burden of proof incumbent on it to show that the procedures used in the application of the TRQ had caused distortions of trade. The statistics which Brazil claimed constituted *prima facie* evidence appeared to relate to its overall market share rather than to imports within the TRQ. The EC considered that these statistics could not constitute probative evidence in demonstrating that the licensing procedures for the TRQ had been responsible for what Brazil alleged were distortions in trade. The TRQ had been

fully utilized, hence the licensing procedures had not affected the possibility for Brazilian traders to benefit completely from the advantageous conditions provided under the TRQ. Trade outside the TRQ was not subject to any licensing procedures. During the period of application of the TRQ, the overall volume of imports from Brazil into the Community had increased. As Brazil itself appeared to concede, increases in market share could be due to other factors unrelated to the TRQ. Thus, decreases in market share could also be attributable to other factors including the overall competitivity of Brazilian imports and harmonization of veterinary standards within the EC which had contributed to the opening up of the Community market to imports from third countries.

(iv) Licence Entitlement Based on Export Performance

86. Article 1.3 of the Licensing Agreement provided that the procedures should be administered in a neutral, fair and equitable manner. It could not be said, **Brazil** argued, that the EC's allocation of import licences on the basis of export performance was neutral and fair. It automatically biased the licensing system in favour of Community traders and producers who were exporters. The terms of Article 3.5(j) and the underlying intent of the Licensing Agreement were that licence entitlement should be based on import performance and not on export performance. The very inclusion of exports as a criteria for licence entitlement was a *de facto* and *de jure* breach of the provisions of the Licensing Agreement.

87. The **EC** recalled that the Licensing Agreement applied only in respect of the procedures and not the *rules* applied to licensing systems. The EC argued that the question of whether a licensing system functioned through import or export licences constituted a rule relating to the operation of the system and not a procedure relating to its administration. Hence, this issue was not regulated by the Licensing Agreement, which contained no provisions detailing the criteria to be applied to the operation and functioning of licensing systems. The EC would note, in any event, that as a matter of fact, export performance was only taken into account for the period from 26 June 1994 to 1 June 1995.[64] In consequence, the EC argued, this claim should be dismissed as inadmissible, firstly because it fell outside the scope of application of the Licensing Agreement, and secondly because it related to a situation which as a matter of fact no longer existed and therefore there could be no nullification or impairment of any of Brazil's rights under the WTO. There were, according to the EC, no continuing effects of the previous use of export performance. Eligibility was based only on import performance.

88. In the event that the Panel were to consider, contrary to the primary submission of the EC on this point, that Brazil's claim was admissible, in the view of the EC, Article 1.3 of the Licensing Agreement stated no more than that rules for

[64] As from the adoption of Regulation No. 1244/95 on 1 June 1995, the criterion of export performance no longer applied.

import licensing should be neutral in application and administered in a fair and equitable manner. It was not possible, as Brazil asserted, to discern from the plain wording of Article 1.3, read in the light of the objective and purpose of the Licensing Agreement, that *any* inclusion of criteria relating to export automatically biased the system in favour of importers. The only relevant provision in the Licensing Agreement, in the view of the EC, was Article 3.5(j) which stipulated that Members should "consider the import performance of the applicant" and "in this regard, consideration should be given as to whether licences issued to applicants in the past have been fully utilized". Hence, the requirement to take account of import performance was linked to the need to ensure full utilization of licences issued. The EC had adapted its administration of the licensing system on a number of occasions in order to fulfil this requirement. Furthermore, Article 3.5(j) did not stipulate that licence entitlement should be based only on import performance and that any criterion relating to export was precluded. That provision simply required that Members should "*consider* the import performance of the applicant". Article 3 of Commission Regulation 1431/94 fulfilled this requirement in that it stipulated that import performance should be taken into account.

89. **Brazil** maintained that during the time that rules in relation to exports were in force there was distortion and because licences were allocated on the basis of past performance, those distortions carried forward into the present (see also paragraph 153).

90. The **EC** replied that there were no continuing effects of the previous use of export performance. Eligibility was based only on import performance and so the EC failed to see how the previous inclusion of export performance could have any continuing effects.

(v) Speculation in Licences

91. **Brazil** noted that the third subparagraph of Article 5 of Commission Regulation 1431/94 provided that licences should not be transferable. This requirement was to ensure that licences were only used by those to whom licences were allocated and to avoid speculation. Article 3.5(j) of the Licensing Agreement required that licences issued be fully utilized. According to Brazil, speculation in licences discouraged their full utilization in contradiction of the requirement in Article 3.5(h) of the Licensing Agreement. When licences became the object of trade in themselves, it was not certain that they would be used to effect import. A speculative market gave rise to its own rules and logic and in these circumstances licences could be used to disrupt the behaviour of competitor importers or could be bought up by EC exporters who produced on the domestic market so as to protect the market. Most importantly, Brazil argued, the rapid movement of licences among importers and non-importers (i.e. EC exporters who had never imported from Brazil) made it impossible for Brazilian exporters to make contact with, and effect sales to, importers, so as to effect trade and ensure that there was full utilization of the licences. Finally, Article 3.5(j) provided that in allocating licences, Members should consider the import performance of the

applicants. This obligation did not only refer to making licence entitlements dependant on past import performance but also to ensuring that licences issued in the past to applicants had been fully utilized. The EC had not shown that all licences had in fact been used.

92. The **EC** submitted that the above-mentioned provisions were exhortatory in nature and did *not* impose mandatory requirements: Article 3.5(h) said Members "*shall not discourage* full utilization of quotas" and Article 3.5(j) that Members should "*give consideration*" to whether licences issued in the past have been *fully utilized* during a representative period". As a matter of *commercial* reality, it would be impossible for a Member to control the behaviour of economic operators so as to *ensure* full utilization of licences granted. Moreover, as mentioned above, the legal reality was, the EC asserted, that commitments exchanged under the WTO agreements related to conditions of competition for trade and to market access opportunities and *not* to volumes of trade. The EC stressed that Article 5 of Regulation 1431/94 stipulated that licences were not transferable with a view to avoiding speculation in licences. The EC had done nothing to discourage the full utilization of licences; indeed Brazil's claims as regards utilization of the quota appeared to be entirely unfounded since according to the statistics available to the Commission, the TRQ had in fact been fully utilized (see Annex II). Brazil had been informed of this during the consultations. Regulation 1431/94 had been modified on a number of occasions to take account of experience gained in the operation of the licensing system. This demonstrated that the system was subject to constant monitoring and adaptation, if necessary, to ensure that it operated in a fair and equitable manner and to fulfil the obligations imposed under Article 3.5(h) and (j) of the Licensing Agreement. Moreover, the EC submitted, no responsibility of the EC could be incurred as a result of the alleged action of private companies or bodies that had no direct or indirect relation or connection with the EC authorities. The EC confirmed, and this was not contested by the complainant, that there were no legal requirements imposing charges or duties additional to those which were bound in the EC Schedule of commitments.

93. **Brazil** submitted that the EC had not shown that the quota had been filled in all of 1994 and in the first quarter of 1996. The EC did not provide this information during consultations. Speculation in licences distorted patterns of trade. Established trading relationships could not be maintained. Furthermore, exporters would not know whether or not they had trading relations with serious or non-serious importers.

94. The **EC** replied that the Community's information gathering and processing of statistics had been improved during the operation of the TRQ. However, in 1994, Member States did not supply a breakdown of utilization of the quota by country of origin. For the first quarter of 1996, the data was lost because of internal data bank problems.

95. **Brazil** submitted that there was speculation in licences and that the value of a licence was between 2.30 and 3 DM per kilo. The speculation in licences had not stopped even with the changes to the rules. More and more operators were

applying for licences. This both decreased the licence volume and increased the speculation. Brazil had set out the average number of importers in each quarter in 1997. Similar analysis revealed that the average number of importers in 1996 was 181, and for 1995 was 187. It was clear that the number of importers was increasing and thus the rate of speculation.

96. The **EC** replied that because there had been an increase in the number of importers this did not mean, *ipso facto*, that speculation had increased. There had been an across-the-board increase in the number of importers in the frozen poultry meat market. This was due to the Community's enlargement and the fact that importers had established legally separate subsidiary companies.

(vi) Economic Quantities

97. Referring to Article 3.5(h) which provided that Members should not discourage the full utilization of quotas, and in particular to Article 3.5(i) which stated that Members had to take into account the desirability of issuing licences in economic quantities, **Brazil** considered that the allocation of licences such that each applicant received a licence allowing imports of about 5 tonnes could not be considered to be an economic quantity. Article 3.5(i) did not mandate that licences always had to be issued in economic quantities but it recognized the desirability that they should be so. Article 3.5(i) should be read within the context of the requirement that the licensing system should not distort trade. If a licence was for an uneconomic quantity it became difficult and uneconomic for exporters to make sales especially from distant supplier countries. Moreover, the economic consequences for an importer not to utilize the licence were not severe.[65]

98. The **EC** replied, as mentioned above, that the licensing system had been constantly modified in order to ensure that licences were allocated on the basis of economic quantities amongst what had been an ever increasing number of importers. Amongst the 200 "serious" importers, the Commission had made efforts to ensure that there was a minimum distribution of 5 per cent of the quantity requested. The EC submitted that the reality that the quota had been fully utilized provided corroboration of the fact that the level of security required (ECU 500 per tonne, or 38 per cent of the duty payable) was sufficient to ensure full use of the licences granted. The quarterly average licence quantity for imports from Brazil under the TRQ in 1997 was 5.6 tonnes. This resulted from the fact that the maximum quantity an operator could apply for in accordance with Article 3 of Regulation 1431/94 was 10 per cent of the quarterly volume (1,775 tonnes) and the average attribution percentage as published every quarter was 3.17 per cent. On the basis of these figures 315 importers applied for licences in 1997. As could be seen from the table in ANNEX II the licence quantity for 1997 was not representative of the licence quantities for the period of application of the TRQ. Two

65 ECU 50 per 100 kg.

hundred was the number of importers in the Community when the TRQ was established. The Community had already observed above that the number of importers over the period of the TRQ had increased.

99. **Brazil** replied that importers did not get a minimum of 5 per cent of the quantity requested. Commission Regulation EC No 2120/97[66] of 28 October 1997, set the percentage figure for the acceptance of licence applications for the fourth quarter of 1997, the Annex of which provided that only 3.24 per cent of the licence applications for Brazil had been accepted, a figure which did not amount "a minimum distribution of 5 per cent of the quantity requested". (The figure for the third quarter 1997 was 3.13 per cent, 3.13 per cent for the second quarter and 3.19 per cent for the first quarter.) Brazil maintained that the licence volume of 5,751 tonnes was uneconomic. Trade in frozen chickens between Brazil and the EC was by container ship. Containers were either 20 or 40 foot which held 16-18 tonnes or 26-28 tonnes, respectively. The cost of shipping 5.5 tonnes per tonne alone in a container was US$320 while the cost per tonne of shipping a full container was US$115. It was therefore uneconomic to ship at US$320 a tonne. In addition, an importer had to show imports of 100 tonnes in a previous two year representative period for eligibility for licences. An importer who wished to import from Brazil only was not in a position to obtain entitlement on the basis of TRQ imports alone but had to import from other sources or over the quota. In each quarter there were, on average, 315 licences issued to, on average, 315 importers. Thus, if the EC considered that there were 200 "serious" importers, there were, on average, 115 non-"serious" importers. Brazil did not understand what the EC meant by the word "serious" in relation to the importers. Did this mean that the EC accepted that, on average, 115 importers were applying for licences for the purposes of trade in licences as opposed to imports from Brazil?

100. The **EC** submitted that the quarterly average licence quantity for imports from Brazil under the TRQ in 1997 was 5.6 tonnes. This resulted from the fact that the maximum quantity an operator could apply for in accordance with Article 3 of Regulation 1431/94 was 10 per cent of the quarterly volume (1,775 tonnes), and the average attribution percentage as published every quarter was 3.17 per cent. On the basis of these figures 315 importers applied for licences in 1997. Moreover, the Community considered that since the quota had been fully utilized there was no evidence to suggest that the licence quantities were uneconomic or that importers had, as a result of the licence quantity, been deterred from making use of the advantages in trading conditions offered under the TRQ. Article 3.5 (i) of the Licensing Agreement stated that Members "should *take into account* the desirability of issuing licences for products in economic quantities"(emphasis added). This was, however, merely one factor to be taken into account in ensuring that the licensing procedure was administered, in accordance with Article 1.3, in a neutral, fair and equitable manner. Consideration

66 L 295/21, published in the Official Journal of 29 October 1997.

should also be given to the factors enumerated in Article 3.5(j), in particular, the need to "give consideration" to ensuring a reasonable distribution of licences to new importers. The EC was, furthermore, of the view that the size of consignments of poultry was irrelevant. There was nothing in the Licensing Agreement which supported Brazil's suggestion that the volume of a licence should be determined by reference to the method of transportation of a product. Moreover, since a licence could be used for part of a consignment and needed not cover the consignment in its entirety, average consignment size was of no relevance when considering the use made of the TRQ. The EC understood that the companies of Brazilian origin which had, in Brazil's words, "a traditional presence on the EC market" were in fact the most important exporters of poultry meat products. As already explained elsewhere, the number of importers in the Community had increased mainly because of the enlargement of the Community and the establishment by traditional importers of legally separate subsidiary companies.

(vii) Newcomers

101. **Brazil** submitted that there were no provisions in the EC rules in relation to newcomers. Article 3.5(j) of the Licensing Agreement provided, however, that consideration should be given to ensuring that there was a reasonable distribution of licences to newcomers. The absence of the newcomer provision meant that Brazilian exporters could not begin importing by establishing themselves in the Community and qualifying as new importers.

102. The **EC** replied that the TRQ was not restricted only to traditional importers who had imported from Brazil. The requirements imposed relating to quantities imported over a two calendar year period were designed to ensure a balance between access to the TRQ for all importers and the need to issue licences in economic quantities. The EC argued that there was no incompatibility with the provisions of Article 3.5(j) of the Licensing Agreement. The number of importers had increased over the period of application of the TRQ. Furthermore, according to evidence available to the Commission, contrary to the assertion made by Brazil, most of the important Brazilian exporters had, in fact, established sales offices in the EC from which they too applied for import licences.

103. **Brazil** responded that not many Brazilian exporters had become EC importers, contrary to the EC assertions. Only two companies of Brazilian origin had, in association with EC companies, a traditional presence in the EC market. The allocation of import licences on the basis of past performance meant that it was not economic for Brazilian exporters to establish themselves in the EC for the purposes of importing and applying for licences.

104. The **EC** retorted that it was a matter of mathematical impossibility, to expect that the licence quantities could be increased without reducing the number of importers who had access to the TRQ. The requirements imposed in respect of access to the TRQ were designed to ensure a balance between access to the TRQ for all importers and the need to issue licences in economic quantities. If the rules were to be adjusted so that the licence quantity were to be the size of a container

as Brazil asserted (16-18 tonnes or 26-28 tonnes) this would have the effect of rendering it impossible to ensure "a reasonable distribution of licences to new importers" as required by Article 3(5)(j) of the Licensing Agreement.

(viii) Transparency

105. **Brazil** argued that underlying the Licensing Agreement was the principle of transparency. The publication provisions in Articles 1.4 and 3.2 along with the consultation and information provisions in Articles 1.4 and 3.5 were specific instances of this right of transparency. Under the licensing and trade monitoring system in place for frozen chicken, it had not been possible for the EC, let alone Brazil, to determine definitively whether or not there were distortions of trade due to the operation of the licensing system. However, there was *prima facie* evidence of such distortion and the EC had done nothing to address the issues raised by Brazil in this regard. The inability to determine which consignments were being imported within or outside the TRQ and the failure of the EC to confirm to Brazil that that part of the TRQ which had been allocated to Brazil had in fact been fulfilled meant, in the opinion of Brazil, that the EC was not administering the licensing system in a transparent manner.

106. The **EC** replied that the claim that there was "*prima facie* evidence" of trade distortion was entirely unsubstantiated and failed to meet the standards of evidence determined by the Appellate Body as set out below. This claim should therefore be rejected as inadmissible by the Panel. With respect to Brazil's claims that the EC had not complied with the Licensing Agreement's provisions on transparency in respect of the changes made to the criteria relating to licence entitlement, the EC submitted that the changes in market access conditions effected by the Commission were designed to ensure a reasonable distribution of licences amongst a number of applicants who had serious intentions of importing poultry products into the EC. As Brazil itself noted, full details of the licensing procedures, including the criteria used in their application, had been published in the Official Journal of the European Communities. In consequence, transparency in the criteria applied for the allocation of licences had been assured. The changes made to these criteria were necessary to ensure the proper functioning of the system and as was clear from the motivation given in the various Regulations were necessary to take account of experience gained in the operation of the regime.

107. **Brazil** submitted that the EC was obliged under Article 3.5(a)(iii) and (iv) of the Licensing Agreement to provide complete and relevant information on the distribution of licences among supplying countries and statistics on volumes and values. In the view of Brazil, the EC had failed to do so. In addition, the transparency provisions underlying the Licensing Agreement were not respected by the EC. Exporters did not know what trade measures were applicable in respect of any one consignment of frozen chicken sent to the EC. For exports within the TRQ, no duties or additional duties were payable. For exports outside the TRQ full bound duties were payable and in addition the imports were subject to price

safeguards. Price safeguards could result in additional duties if the exporter did not maintain a c.i.f. price at the Community frontier. The licensing system was administered in such a way that the exporter did not know what trade rules applied in breach of the fundamental objective of the Licensing Agreement.[67] It was imperative that the licensing system be administered in a transparent manner such that exporters were not inhibited in achieving full market access and prices.

108. The **EC** replied that the requirement to supply statistics was subject to a request from a WTO Member. The EC had produced the relevant information when requested to do so. Moreover, the EC's system was by its very nature transparent. The figures relating both to the allocation of the quota and the percentage of the licence applications granted had been published. In consequence, as Brazil's submissions to the panel had amply demonstrated, it was very well able to determine the distribution of licences and their volumes.

(ix) Compensation

109. **Brazil** submitted that compensation should serve to re-establish the original overall balance of concessions. It did so by providing for an improvement in the conditions of competition under which the product in question could be sold on the importing market. This could be achieved either through improved price concession[68] or - in the case of a TRQ - through the concession of a financial benefit to the exporters. If there was no improvement in the conditions of competition and the financial benefits failed to materialize, then it could be considered that no compensation had in fact been provided. Moreover, Brazil considered that it was in the nature of a zero tariff compensatory-TRQ, that the Member entitled to benefit from the TRQ should be allowed to compete on an equal footing with local producers in the importing market. This meant that the exporters had to be able to benefit from the competitive conditions prevailing on the import market. The price obtainable on the import market was one such benefit. So the exporter had to be able to obtain that price. Lack of transparency of the TRQ had, however, the effect that the exporter could not obtain that price. If the cost of production on the exporting market was less than the average cost of production in the importing market, this was a benefit that should be available to the exporter. Any administration of the TRQ which attempted to prevent the exporter

---

[67] The Licensing Agreement provided in its Preamble:

"Convinced that import licensing, particularly non-automatic import licensing, should be implemented in a transparent and predictable manner;

"Desiring to simplify, and bring transparency to, the administrative procedures and practices used in international trade, and to ensure the fair and equitable application and administration of such procedures and practices;"

[68] Panel Report on *European Economic Community - Payments and Subsidies Paid to Processors and Producers of Oilseeds and Related Animal-feed Proteins*, adopted on 25 January 1990, BISD 37S/86, paragraph 148.

from benefiting from the cost advantages that he had was, in the opinion of Brazil, a denial of the compensation which the TRQ was designed to create.

110. The **EC** replied that without any clear reference to a relevant provision of the Licensing Agreement or indeed any other WTO provision, the EC found it difficult to reply to a vague assertion concerning "no compensation" and therefore simply recalled that the provisions of the General Agreement had been consistently interpreted as provisions establishing conditions of competition. Consequently, the commitments exchanged in such negotiations were "commitments on conditions of competition" for trade, not on volumes of trade.[69] Brazil's assertions were, in the opinion of the EC, contrary to this basic principle to the extent that they required that the exporter had to be able to obtain a particular price on the market of the importing country.

111. In conclusion, **Brazil** argued, the combination of all these elements had the effect of undermining the objectives of the Licensing Agreement, in particular the requirements as to transparency, non-distortion of trade and that the licensing system be the least burdensome possible. It was this combination of inconsistencies alongside the individual inconsistencies which had a negative effect on trade both within and outside the TRQ and which impeded the achievements of the principles underlying the Agreement on Agriculture.

(x) Burden of Proof

112. The **EC** underlined the need for Brazil, in making its various allegations, to demonstrate at least a *prima facie* infringement of the cited provisions of the Licensing Agreement. As the Appellate Body stated in its report on *Shirts and Blouses*, "a party claiming a violation of a provision of the WTO Agreement must assert *and prove* its claim"(emphasis added).[70] It was thus for the party asserting a violation of a WTO obligation to put forward evidence and legal arguments sufficient to demonstrate its claim. In respect of a number of the claims made in relation to the operation of the licensing regime at issue in this case, the EC was of the view that Brazil had failed to adduce any, or at least any sufficient evidence, that there had been a violation of the obligations of the EC under the Licensing Agreement. Some of Brazil's claims amounted to little more than unsubstantiated assertions.

113. Recalling Article 3.8 of the DSU[71], **Brazil** replied that the Appellate Body report on the *Shirts and Blouses* had stated that "In the context of the

[69] See, for example, *Ibid,* paragraphs 150-151.

[70] See section IV of the Appellate Body Report on *Shirts and Blouses, op. cit.*

[71] "In cases where there is an infringement of the obligations assumed under a covered agreement, the action is considered *prima facie* to constitute a case of nullification or impairment. This means that there is normally a presumption that a breach of the rules has an adverse impact on other Members parties to that covered agreement, and in such cases, it shall be up to the Member against whom the complaint has been brought to rebut the charge."

GATT 1994 and the WTO Agreement, precisely how much and precisely what kind of evidence will be required to establish such a presumption will necessarily vary from measure to measure, provision to provision and case to case." Brazil considered that it had met the standard of proof that was necessary to sustain its claims. The EC had not addressed the facts that had been put before this Panel and had not indicated how Brazil had failed to meet the burden of proof standard. Quoting the findings of the Appellate Body in *Shirts and Blouses*[72], Brazil was of the opinion that it had adduced evidence of fact and of law that the EC had not complied with its obligations under the WTO Agreement. Brazil considered that it had established a *prima facie* case. Brazil believed that the weight of the evidence adduced was such that it had passed the threshold at which the burden of proof shifted to the EC. It was now up to the EC to rebut this evidence. Brazil was not in a position to adduce all the factual evidence in this case and, in particular, in relation to licence usage, the methods used to determine the representative price or the representative price itself. These were facts which only the EC could provide and the EC had, in the opinion of Brazil, failed to provide them. Brazil considered that, by not addressing the issues of fact established by Brazil, and by not presenting, to Brazil or to the Panel, those issues of fact which only the EC could provide, the EC was not fulfilling its role in establishing the facts of this dispute.

114. In the **EC**'s view Brazil had failed to discharge the burden of proof incumbent on it to show that the procedures used in the application of the TRQ had caused distortions of trade. Brazil was not able to submit sufficient factual evidence because that evidence did not exist.

The Agreement on Agriculture

(i) Article 4

115. **Brazil** submitted that the Agreement on Agriculture constrained WTO Members to binding commitments in agricultural products for market access, domestic support and export competition, as well as to agreeing on sanitary and phytosanitary issues. Referring to the market access provisions contained in Arti-

---

[72] "Also, it is a generally accepted canon of evidence in civil law, common law and in fact, most jurisdictions, that the burden of proof rests upon the party, whether complaining or defending, who asserts the affirmative of a particular claim or defence. If that party adduces evidence sufficient to raise a presumption that what is claimed is true, the burden then shifts to the other party, who will fail unless it adduces sufficient evidence to rebut the presumption." The Appellate Body further stated that "We agree with the Panel that it, therefore, was up to India to put forward evidence and legal argument sufficient to demonstrate that the transitional safeguard action by the United States was inconsistent with the obligations assumed by the United States under Articles 2 and 6 of the ATC. India did so in this case. And, with India having done so, the onus then shifted to the United States to bring forward evidence and argument to disprove the claim."

cle 4.2[73] and its footnote[74], Brazil argued that Article 4 was a comprehensive prohibition against the maintenance of any type of border protection measures other than tariffs. It was the embodiment of the principle of tariffication and was one of the pillars of the Agreement. However, the text of Article 4 provided for two exceptions to the general prohibition, i.e. the "special treatment clause"(Annex 5) and "the special safeguard clause"(Article 5). As exceptions to the general rule, Brazil pointed out, both "clauses" had to be interpreted strictly. Brazil made two distinct claims in relation to price safeguards. Firstly, that the terms of Article 5.1(b) of the Agreement on Agriculture required an examination of the price at which the product entered the EC's customs territory; and secondly, that the representative price was incompatible with Article 5.

(ii) Article 5: Safeguards

116. **Brazil** was of the view that special safeguards could not be used in all cases. The EC had, however, retained the possibility of introducing special safeguards for poultry and in particular for the three specific frozen chicken products which were the subject of this complaint. Brazil noted that the EC had invoked the special price safeguards for frozen chickens as of the date of its implementation of the Uruguay Round agricultural provisions on 1 July 1995. In the opinion of Brazil, it had done so in breach of the strict provisions of Article 5 of the Agreement on Agriculture. The maintenance of this variable additional duty for frozen chicken by the Community was therefore a breach of the obligation to remove all variable levies in compliance with Article 4.

117. The **EC** replied that Article 5 was a *special safeguard provision* applying to agricultural products. Citing Article 21.1 of the Agreement of Agriculture[75], the EC recalled that the Appellate Body in applying that Article in the *Banana III* report stated that: "the provisions of GATT 1994 apply to market access commitments concerning agricultural products, except to the extent that the Agreement on Agriculture contains specific provisions dealing specifically with the same subject matter".[76] The EC was of the view that there could be no doubt that Article 5 could be considered to constitute a "specific provision" dealing specifically with safeguards in the agricultural sector. In consequence, it formed a complete, self-contained code for the rules to be followed for special agricultural

---

[73] "Members shall not maintain, resort to, or revert to any measures of the kind which have been required to be converted into ordinary customs duties, except as otherwise provided for in Article 5 and Annex 5."

[74] "These measures include quantitative import restrictions, variable import levies, minimum import prices, discretionary import licensing, non-tariff measures maintained through state trading enterprises, voluntary export restraints, and similar border measures other than ordinary customs duties, whether or not the measures are maintained under country-specific derogations form the provisions of GATT 1947 ..."

[75] "The provisions of GATT 1994 and of other Multilateral Trade Agreements ... shall apply subject to the provisions of this Agreement."

[76] Appellate Body Report on *Banana III, op. cit.*, paragraph 204.

safeguards which might be necessary as a result of tariffication. The EC was of the view that it had applied correctly the special safeguards provisions under Article 5. Brazil's claims in this respect, related, in particular, to the definition of the c.i.f. price and the alleged obligation of showing injury prior to the implementation of the SSG, amounted in substance to a re-writing of that Agreement which was clearly beyond the powers and the terms of reference of this Panel.

118. **Brazil** submitted that Article 5 allowed for the imposition of an additional customs duty, over and above the bound customs duty (or tariffied duty), when a "trigger" price or a "trigger" volume was reached for the product in question.[77] The use of the special safeguards required two preconditions which were set out in the first part of subparagraph 1, i.e. "tariffication"(or the conversion into ordinary customs duties of non-tariff border measures) of the products to which the special safeguard was to apply; and the designation of the product in question with the symbol "SSG" in the Member's schedule. If these two preconditions were met, Brazil said, a Member could invoke the special safeguard clause. Brazil noted that the EC had notified to the Committee on Agriculture that it maintained a price safeguard in respect of frozen chicken parts.

(a) The Price Safeguard

119. Referring to subparagraphs (a) and (b) of paragraph 5 of Article 5[78] of the Agreement on Agriculture, **Brazil** argued that it was clear from the structure of Article 5(1) that the provisions of paragraph 5 could only be invoked if the conditions set out in paragraph 1 and, in addition, the conditions of subparagraph 1(b), were met. To satisfy the conditions for the application of subparagraph 1(b), it was necessary to determine the price at which the product entered the customs territory of the Member invoking the safeguard. However, Brazil claimed that the Community had not introduced a system for measuring the price at which the product entered the Community market. It merely measured the c.i.f.

---

[77] (a) "the volume of imports of that product entering the customs territory of the Member granting the concession during any year exceeds a trigger level which relates to the existing market access opportunity as set out in paragraph 4; or, but not concurrently:

(b) the price at which imports of that products may enter the customs territory of the Member granting the concession, as determined on the basis of the c.i.f. import price of the shipment concerned expressed in terms of its domestic currency, falls below a trigger price equal to the average 1986-1988 reference price for the product concerned."

[78] "The additional duty imposed under subparagraph 1(b) shall be set according to the following schedule:

(a) if the difference between the c.i.f. import price of the shipment in expressed in terms of the domestic currency (hereinafter referred to as the "import price") and the trigger price as defined under that subparagraph is less than or equal to 10 per cent of the trigger price, no additional duty shall be imposed;

(b) if the difference between the import price and the trigger price (hereinafter referred to as the "difference") is greater than 10 per cent but less than or equal to 40 per cent of the trigger price, the additional duty shall equal 30 per cent of the amount by which the difference exceeds 10 per cent;"

price and should that price fall below the trigger price it imposed an additional duty.

120. The **EC** replied that Brazil's assertion that Article 5 of the Agreement on Agriculture stipulated that the price of a product had to be measured "after" the product had entered the market was clearly contradicted by the text of Article 5.1(b) which referred to the price at which imports "*may* enter" the customs territory. The EC submitted that the figures presented by Brazil, and which were intended to show a decline in the volume of imports into the EC, were not representative of the entire period over which the special safeguard was applied. The special safeguard had been applied since 1 July 1995. In 1995 the total volume of imports was 53,067 tonnes and this figure increased to 86,501 tonnes in 1996. These statistics showed that there had been an upward trend in imports.

(b) C.i.f. Prices

121. **Brazil** submitted that the whole phrase "determined on the basis of the c.i.f. import price" in Article 5 needed to be examined by the Panel, not only the letters c.i.f. This price was not the c.i.f. price itself; it was something more than the c.i.f. price, it was "the price at which imports of that product may enter the customs territory of the Member granting the concession". The c.i.f. price was the price at the frontier prior to entry or otherwise the free at frontier price which the EC referred to in Article 2 of Regulation 1484/95.[79] The price (as determined on the basis of the c.i.f. price but not the c.i.f. price itself) at which the product could enter the customs territory was the c.i.f. price plus the bound duty. This was, according to Brazil, the clear meaning of the text. Brazil did not share the view that as the trigger price was based on the c.i.f. unit value of the product concerned the comparative price for the purposes of Article 5(1)(b) had to be the c.i.f. price. A market entry price determined on the basis of the c.i.f. price allowed for fair comparison if the non-c.i.f. element was the fixed and bound tariff in the Schedule.

122. The **EC** replied that Brazil's claim as regards the interpretation to be given to "on the basis of the c.i.f. price" was not supported by the text which in the Community's view clearly and unambiguously stated precisely the opposite of what Brazil asserted. The EC considered that Brazil's assertion undermined entirely the plain meaning of the words used by the authors of the Agreement. There was nothing in the Agreement on Agriculture to suggest that the parties intended that the "c.i.f. import price" should have any special meaning in this context. Therefore, the EC submitted, the Panel should give the phrase "on the basis of the c.i.f. import price" its normal meaning, i.e. cost of the product plus insurance and freight charges. Further support could be drawn from the manner in which Article 5(1)(b) was structured and the fact that it envisaged that the cal-

[79] Official Journal L 145/47 of 29 June 1995.

culation would take place prior to the entry of the product onto the Community market. The EC argued that "on the basis of" meant "founded on"[80] and in consequence the purpose of the authors of the Agreement in using this terminology was that the c.i.f. price should be the principal reference point. The EC had not deviated from this standard. Brazil's suggestion of the market entry price on the contrary bore no relation to, and indeed constituted a substantial deviation from, the standard set in Article 5. Brazil appeared to be advocating a re-writing by the Panel of the Agreement on Agriculture.

123. Moreover, the EC indicated that Article 5.1(b) of the Agreement on Agriculture referred to the price at which imports "may enter" the customs territory. This wording confirmed that the price at issue was that which was calculated at the moment a shipment arrived prior to its entry on to the Community market, at which point taxes and duties become payable. Moreover, footnote 2 to Article 5.1(b) stated that the reference price to be used to invoke the provision of that subparagraph "shall, in general be the average c.i.f. unit value of the product concerned". This confirmed the Community's interpretation of the wording of Article 5.1(b). Any other interpretation rendered nonsensical the comparison between the import price and the trigger price since the comparison would not be one of like with like.

124. **Brazil** submitted that the negotiating history of the special safeguard mechanism in Article 5 showed that it was to be used when the tariffied duty under the tariffication principles was insufficient to protect the domestic market. If, in exceptional circumstances, this new tariff was insufficient to protect markets that were once protected by variable levies, then price safeguards were applicable. The protection of the market was not an abstract concept.

125. The **EC** replied that Brazil had put before the Panel extracts from the negotiating history of the Agriculture Agreement. Since, however, the plain wording of the Agreement was clear, the negotiating history was, in the opinion of the EC, of little relevance to the Panel's deliberations on this issue.[81]

(c) Injury Requirement

126. **Brazil** submitted that the text of Article 5(1)(b) gave no exact measure of what the market entry price was. It provided that it was to be determined "on the basis of the c.i.f. import price". In the opinion of Brazil, it was clearly not the c.i.f. price itself. Nor was it the customs value of the product in question. It was something more. The whole purpose of the special safeguard provisions was to protect Members' markets. However, there had to be a measure of injury before

[80] The Oxford English Dictionary entry for "basis" reads: "foundation, main or determining principle or ingredient; starting-point for discussion".

[81] Article 31 of the Vienna Convention which set out fundamental canons of treaty interpretation and which had now been referred to in several Appellate Body reports above, provided that the words of the treaty form the foundation of the interpretative process.

any safeguard measure could be taken. The Community not only did not measure a market entry price but also it had no mechanisms for examining the effects on the Community market. The Community had thus failed to show one of the essential preconditions for the application of the special safeguard measure. It applied, in the view of Brazil, the additional duty in the absence of an examination of possible harm to the Community market.

127. The **EC** replied that a safeguard element was already encompassed in the trigger price mechanism under Article 5 of the Agreement on Agriculture and that there was therefore no need for a separate demonstration of injury. In other words, once the c.i.f. price fell below the trigger price there was *ipso facto* a disruptive effect on domestic production. In the opinion of the EC, this was clear from Article 5.1 which provided that the designation "SSG" could be used *either* where "the volume of products ... exceeds a trigger level" *or* where "the price at which imports of that product may enter the customs territory of the member granting the concession ... falls below a trigger price equal to the average 1986 to 1988 reference price for the product concerned". There was no provision in Article 5 which introduced a *further* requirement that the country imposing the SSG demonstrate the nature and extent of the disruptive effect on its domestic market.[82] The EC recalled that, as mentioned above, the "*special* safeguard provision" dealt specifically with agricultural products. If the authors of the agreement had intended that the additional hurdle of a demonstration of further injury should be included, they would surely have inserted this in the text of the Agreement. The EC underlined that under Article 3.2 of the DSU, the objective of a dispute settlement procedure was to clarify the existing provisions of the covered agreements and not to add to existing obligations provided for in those agreements. Brazil's claim infringed this basic principle.

128. **Brazil** did not agree with the EC's view that there was no need to demonstrate injury to trigger the price safeguard mechanism. Nor that, if the c.i.f. price fell below the trigger price, there was "*ipso facto*" a disruptive effect on domestic production. In the opinion of Brazil, injury or damage to the market had to be shown. The EC had not done so. The drafters of the text of Article 5.1(b), Brazil submitted, did not consider it necessary to define the price at which the product entered the customs territory other than to state that it should be "determined on the basis of the c.i.f. price". Entry to the customs territory of a Member required the payment of all taxes and the completion of all administrative requirements. The market entry price was therefore the c.i.f. price plus the bound tariff provided for in the Member's schedule. The failure to measure this market entry price or to make this price the determinant for triggering the application of an

[82] It could be said that an "additional" requirement flowed from Article 5(7) which stated that Members undertook not to invoke Article 5(1)(b) when imports were declining but the EC noted that Members only undertook to do this "as far as practicable" and that in any event no evidence had been put forward to suggest that imports were doing anything else than increasing or remaining constant.

additional duty was, in the opinion of Brazil, a fundamental breach of Article 5. It meant that the additional duty was not a "safeguard" in the ordinary meaning of that word. It was a c.i.f. price maintenance system and was independent of any safeguard element. The additional duties which the EC applied to frozen chicken products were therefore outside the scope of the exception to the basic prohibition on variable levies. There was no other exception to the prohibition on variable levies to which the EC could have recourse. Thus, the additional levies were, in the opinion of Brazil, a clear breach of Article 4.

129. Brazil submitted that there was nothing in the negotiating history of the special safeguard provisions to justify the imposition of additional duties based on the need to maintain a c.i.f. entry price. The special safeguard provisions were designed to protect markets against possible disturbances as a result of tariffication. The volume safeguards were not designed to protect the Community market from volume surges in deliveries to the Community frontier but only from volume surges of imports onto the market. In the same way, the price safeguards were not designed to maintain the world market price or even the c.i.f. price but to keep the price on the Community market from falling below a certain level. Brazil believed that this understanding of the terms of Article 5 was in line with the overall scope of the Agreement on Agriculture and the history of the negotiation of the Agreement. Brazil submitted that the concern of the negotiators of the Agreement on Agriculture had been to find a mechanism that would deal with the problem of possible import surges or excessive world price movements once tariffication had been completed and gradual tariff reductions had commenced. It was considered that tariff increases might be allowable in these special circumstances (thus the term special safeguard clause) and "would remain in force only as long as the conditions which led to their implementation remained in place".[83]

130. The intent of the negotiators, according to Brazil, was to "sweeten the pill" of tariffication. Should the price safeguard be triggered, the additional duty would be based on differences between the c.i.f. import price and the trigger price. However, Brazil believed that this additional duty was only to be triggered if there was a danger to domestic production or the domestic market. The negotiators agreed that the price at which the whole mechanism would be triggered was the price at which the product "entered the customs territory"(and not "arrived at the port of entry"). In the opinion of Brazil the negotiators of the special safeguard clauses were concerned with safeguarding markets, not merely maintaining c.i.f. prices. The EC appeared to have misunderstood this fundamental objective of the clause which should only come into play when the tariffs resulting from tariffication proved insufficient to safeguard a market in the case of exchange rate or world market price fluctuations.

131. The **EC** replied that it was not necessary for the Panel to consider the negotiating history of Article 5. Even if this were to be taken into account, it pro-

[83] MTN/GNG/NG5/W/194.

vided no support for Brazil's arguments since it confirmed that the text of Article 5 reflected fully the intentions of the authors of the treaty.

(d) The Representative Price

132. **Brazil** submitted that the Community had not complied with its own interpretation of the price safeguard mechanism. The Community had introduced a mechanism for measuring the c.i.f. price so as to verify whether an additional duty was payable. This mechanism, known as the representative price, was set out in Article 2(1) of Commission Regulation 1484/95. For the purposes of the application or not of an additional levy, an importer could choose to establish the actual c.i.f. price of the consignment in question or, in the alternative, could pay an additional duty based on the representative price. If the importer had chosen to establish the actual c.i.f. price, then a bond equal to the additional duty was payable just as if the consignment price was the representative price. In practice, Brazil understood that all traders had chosen not to establish the actual consignment c.i.f. price as the requirements and timing made it practically impossible to establish.

133. The **EC** stressed that the representative price was an average price which provided a facility to operators, should they decide to avail themselves of it. The figures which were taken into account in determining the representative price were average c.i.f. prices. There was no requirement, either in law or in fact, that the representative price mechanism had to be used and operators were free to opt for the actual c.i.f. import price. The documents which had to be supplied by importers as evidence of the actual c.i.f. price were documents which were normally available. The importer had a period of one month from the date of sale of the products in question, subject to a limit of four months from the date of acceptance of the declaration of release for free circulation, to supply the relevant documentation. This time limit could be extended on the basis of a duly substantiated request of the importer (Article 3 of Regulation 1484/95).

134. **Brazil** submitted that the representative price was calculated on the basis of three elements set out in Article 2(1) of Commission Regulation 1484/95, namely external market prices, internal market prices and prices adjusted for quality. Brazil was, however, of the opinion that the method of calculation of the additional duty was not transparent. This, in itself, was a breach of the underlying GATT/WTO principle of transparency. In addition, the Community could not take an internal market price as the determinant for the external c.i.f. price. There was nothing in Article 5 or elsewhere in the Agreement on Agriculture which justified the use of internal market prices to determine external c.i.f. prices. Finally, the Community had failed to indicate how the quality element provided for in its examination of the internal market price was to be factored. Brazil concluded therefore that the EC had implemented the special price safeguard in a manner such that it functioned as a variable levy in breach of Article 4 and in a way that did not bring it within the exception to Article 4 of the Agreement on Agriculture provided for in Article 5.1(b). There was nothing in the text of Arti-

cle 5, or in the object or purpose of the special safeguard provisions, or in the negotiating history of the provision, that could justify the measures that the EC had introduced on the basis of Article 5.

135. The **EC** replied that the representative price was based on prices on the world market and on the Community market, i.e. both were taken into account in the calculation according to Article 2 of Regulation 1484/95. The representative price was published in the Official Journal and was therefore known to traders. Article 2 of Regulation 1484/95 required Member States to supply regularly statistics relating to Article 5 of Regulation 1484/95 so that the representative price could be adjusted, if necessary. This representative price was an average c.i.f. price which excluded taxes and duties and was therefore a valid comparative price. This mechanism constituted an opportunity afforded to importers, should they choose to avail themselves of it, to reduce the formalities to be completed by them by avoiding a shipment by shipment approach which was more burdensome and was thus more favourable than the shipment by shipment approach advocated by Article 5 of the Agreement on Agriculture.

136. **Brazil** submitted that if no importer could comply with the procedures necessary to prove the shipment by shipment c.i.f. price, then it was clear that the EC had not met its obligations under Article 5 to measure c.i.f. prices on a shipment by shipment basis. One of the reasons why importers did not use the shipment by shipment approach was that if they failed to satisfy the Community as to the actual c.i.f. price, the bond payable on import was forfeited. In addition to the bond, the importer had to pay interest. The importer was, therefore, penalized for trying to establish the shipment by shipment c.i.f. price. Article 5 of the Agreement on Agriculture did not provide for a c.i.f. price "policing" mechanism. Therefore, this mechanism of itself was not compatible with the provisions of Article 5. This was particularly the case as a duty was payable on the basis of the representative price either in the form of a bond or in the form of the duty itself. Moreover, the representative price was not the c.i.f. price. Article 2 of Regulation 1484/95 provided that the representative price be based on three elements, one of which was the domestic price. This was not the c.i.f. price and no provision was made in the regulations for extrapolating the c.i.f. price from the domestic price. The result of these inconsistencies, Brazil said, was that the additional duty was always, as a matter of fact and practice, payable and that traders were not given a reasonable opportunity to maintain their prices and thus avoid the imposition of the penalty duty. This was, in the opinion of Brazil, a clear breach both of the terms of Article 5 of the Agreement on Agriculture itself and Article X:3(a) of the GATT. Finally, Brazil observed, at the time the price safeguard was introduced by the EC, in July 1995, the volume of imports was declining. Article 5.7 of the Agreement on Agriculture provided that Members undertook, as far as practicable, not to take recourse to price safeguards when the volume of imports was declining.

137. As Brazil noted in its submission, the **EC** submitted, importers were not prevented from adopting a shipment by shipment approach. Under Article 3 of Regulation 1484/95 they could request that the additional duty be established on

the basis of the c.i.f. import price if this price was higher than the applicable representative price. Hence, if importers so desired they were free to establish the individual c.i.f. price of their consignment and to request that the additional duty be determined on that basis. In either case, all the elements to be taken into account were specified and the calculation was clear and fully transparent. The EC also observed that Brazil advanced no evidence of any reduction in the competitive opportunities open to Brazilian products as a consequence of the administration of the additional duties pursuant to the SSG.

138. **Brazil** submitted that if an importer chose to use the shipment by shipment approach under Community law, that importer was required to pay a bond equal to the amount of the additional duty. This bond was redeemable if certain conditions were met. Article 3 of Regulation 1484/95 set out what those conditions were. It was Brazil's understanding that no importers made use of this facility as the procedure was too burdensome. Brazil was not in a position to prove this assertion as the information was not available to Brazil. However, the EC had recognized, according to Brazil, that the procedure could be burdensome and therefore it had provided importers with the opportunity of using the representative price.

139. The **EC** replied that in accordance with the provisions of Article 2 of Regulation 1484/95, representative prices were determined at regular intervals taking account of c.i.f prices on third country markets, c.i.f. prices within the Community and prices at the various stages of marketing in the Community for imported products. Member States were requested to supply information on a monthly basis. Prices recorded referred to average quality. The Commission also made use of special price recordings from the processing industry which provided rapid access to up-to-date prices. Such price recordings were carried out in those Member States which imported significant quantities of boneless chicken meat (Germany, Netherlands, Austria and Belgium). There was no predetermined formula to determine the relative weight to be afforded to the factors to be taken into account in accordance with Article 2 of Regulation 1484/95. As mentioned above, representative prices were calculated on the basis of an average of c.i.f. prices communicated by the Member States which included imports under the TRQ which tended to result in a higher representative price than that which would arise if only imports outside the TRQ were taken into account. The EC noted that importers had a free choice between the shipment by shipment approach and the representative price. The latter was a simplified version of the former and by using it, importers could avoid the need to show every time, by appropriate documentation, the exact value of the imports concerned when that value equalled or was lower than the representative price. However, the shipment by shipment approach was always available and according to the statistics available to the Community, approximately five per cent of traders used this approach. The Community did not see how importers found it impossible to supply purchasing, transport and insurance contracts, the relevant invoice, origin certificates and, where appropriate, the bill of lading especially when they had a period of up to four months to do so. These were normally available documents which were

required for the shipment of the products. There was nothing "uncertain" about the nature of the proof required.

Article X

140. **Brazil** submitted that to be able to benefit from the requirements, or constraints, of exporting either within or outside the TRQ, the traders needed to know which trade regime was applicable to any one consignment. This was a right which the traders enjoyed under the WTO transparency provisions and which was not, in Brazil's view, respected by the Community regime. Brazil claimed that Community traders used the lack of transparency in the licensing system to drive down prices for all consignments, whether within or outside the TRQ, to the disadvantage of Brazilian traders. Because of speculation in licences and the sale of those licences to traders other than those first entitled to them, all traders claimed that they were not importing under licence and within the TRQ and the Brazilian exporter had then to quote prices for over-quota trade, i.e. as if all sales were subject to duties. In practice, individual consignments were customs cleared partly within the TRQ and partly outside. This common in-TRQ and out-TRQ price was then used to determine the representative price driving this artificial price down even further. The lack of transparency in the EC trade regime for the importation of frozen chicken parts was not consistent with the underlying object and purpose of Article X of GATT. Article X addressed the publication and notification of measures affecting trade. The purpose of such publication and notification was to enable "governments and traders" to become acquainted with them. Traders, in particular, needed to become acquainted with the rules governing trade so that they could comply with, and benefit from, those measures. Brazil considered, however, that the mere publication of measures, or their notification to the WTO, was not sufficient to satisfy the requirement of ensuring that traders become familiar with them. Article X implied, and had to be interpreted so as to mean, that traders had to know, not only the rules themselves, but to which products or consignments these rules applied. If this were not so then the object of publication and notification would not be served.

141. Referring to Brazil's claims that trade in frozen poultry meat products subject to the TRQ was not transparent, the **EC** replied that the exact nature of Brazil's claim in this respect was unclear since it did not state specifically which aspects of either the administration of the TRQ or of the special safeguard provision it considered were contrary to Article X. Brazil referred to the fact that Article X of GATT "addresses the publication and notification of measures affecting trade" of which the purpose was "to enable governments and traders to become acquainted with them". However, Brazil did not indicate clearly which provision of Article X it intended to invoke. Moreover, the EC argued, the question of publication and transparency of licensing procedures was dealt with specifically in the Licensing Agreement, in particular in respect of non-automatic licensing procedures in Article 3 of that Agreement. The inter-relationship between the general transparency provisions of Article X and the specific provisions of the

Licensing Agreement was recently considered by the Appellate Body in the *Banana III* report. In that report, the Appellate Body confirmed that the Licensing Agreement took precedence over Article X of the General Agreement since it dealt "specifically, and in detail, with the administration of licensing procedures".[84] In consequence, the Community considered that the Panel should dismiss Brazil's claim as inadmissible. Should the Panel consider it necessary to address the issues raised by Brazil in respect of Article X in the light of the provisions of the Licensing Agreement, there had been no breach of the obligations under that Agreement. In summary, the administration of the poultry meat TRQ did not, in the opinion of the EC, create a discrimination, either *de jure* or *de facto*, between imported products and domestic products. The allegations by Brazil should therefore be dismissed.

142. **Brazil** submitted that the EC had misunderstood the nature of the claim under Article X. Brazil's claim under Article X was related to the administration of all the trade in frozen chickens, both within and outside the TRQ. Referring to the Appellate Body's finding concerning the Licensing Agreement in *Banana III*[85], Brazil claimed that the Appellate Body did not state that Article X was redundant when examining a Member's obligations. It stated that if a licensing system was found to be inconsistent with the Licensing Agreement there was no need to compare these practices with the terms of Article X. The finding of the Appellate Body in *Banana III* was in relation to an EC regime for the importation of bananas where there was no over quota trade. The main concern of the Appellate Body was, therefore, the examination of the TRQ licensing regime. This was, however, not the situation with respect to frozen chickens. There was over quota trade. There were, therefore, two distinct sets of rules applicable on the importation of frozen chickens from Brazil and both sets of measures were within the terms of reference of this Panel. Citing parts of Article X[86], Brazil submitted that the objective of Article X was clear: trade regulations had to be published so that traders (as well as governments) could become acquainted with them and rely on them. Once they were published, they should be administered in a reasonable manner so that traders were not subject to arbitrary behaviour. Mere publication was not, therefore, the only requirement. The underlying requirement was that publication had to be done in such a way that traders could know and be certain which trade rules applied. The applicable trade rules should not be ap-

[84] Appellate Body Report on *Banana III, op. cit.*, paragraph 204.

[85] "the Panel, in our view should have applied the Licensing Agreement first, since this agreement deals specifically, and in detail, with the administration of import licensing procedures. If the Panel had done so, then there would have been no need for it to address the alleged inconsistency with Article X:3(a) of the GATT 1994."

[86] Article X:1 provided in part that "Laws, regulations (etc.) ... shall be published promptly in such a manner as to enable governments and traders to become acquainted with them."

Article X:3(a) provided that: "Each contracting party shall administer in a uniform, impartial and reasonable manner all its laws, regulations, decisions and rulings of the kind described in paragraph 1 of this Article."

plied in an arbitrary manner. In the opinion of Brazil, the EC regime for the importation of frozen chicken did not meet the requirements of reasonableness and certainty for traders set out in some detail in Articles X:1 and X:3(a) of GATT. An exporter of frozen chickens to the EC did not know what trade rules applied to any one particular consignment of product exported. There was no certainty.

143. Brazil further argued that the obligation of uniformity, impartiality and reasonableness was not confined to ensuring, when more than one set of rules was applicable to imports of the same product, that each different set of rules was administered reasonably. There was nothing in the text of Article X to justify such a restrictive interpretation. The requirement of reasonableness applied as between the sets of applicable rules. The arbitrary nature of the administration of the frozen chicken trade rules and the lack of knowledge on the part of the trader as to which rules applied was particularly acute when price safeguards were applied. Under the of set rules applicable to imports within the TRQ, the trader did not have to be concerned with the price at which the product was exported or sold on the EC market, whereas under those applicable to the non-quota trade, the trader was obliged to ensure that a particular price was maintained both at the border and on the EC market. If the exporter did not maintain that price under one set of rules, the exporter was penalized by an additional duty while under the other set of rules the exporter was not. Brazil concluded, therefore, that the inability of the exporter to know which trade rules applied to a particular consignment of the same goods imported into the EC was a breach of the terms of Article X. A finding that the TRQ licensing rules were inconsistent with the terms of the Licensing Agreement would not address this inconsistency. Brazil's claim under Article X was separate from, and in addition to, its claims under the Licensing Agreement. There was nothing in the finding of the Appellate Body in *Banana III* which precluded the examination of the EC's frozen chicken import rules under this Article.

144. **EC** replied that imports outside the TRQ were not subject to any licensing procedure, although certain of them were subject to the special safeguard provisions. Brazil made claims for a provision which was concerned principally with transparency. The EC submitted that it had complied fully with the requirements of Article X as far as the special safeguard regime was concerned and underlined that Brazil did not allege that any specific aspects of this regime, the entirety of which had been published in the Official Journal, was contrary to the transparency requirements of Article X.

Article II of GATT

145. **Brazil** noted that schedules were provided for in Article II of GATT and were designed to reflect the commitments that Members made in respect of each other. If a schedule did not reflect the commitments made under a covered

agreement (in Brazil's case Article XXVIII of GATT), the question to be addressed by this Panel was the extent to which a Member could be required to honour its commitments. The Appellate Body in *Banana III*[87] examined the extent to which the EC's Schedule in respect of bananas was consistent with Article XIII of GATT. The Appellate Body recalled the *Sugar Headnote* case[88] and quoted that panel as saying "... Article II permits contracting parties to incorporate into their Schedules acts yielding rights under the General Agreement but not acts diminishing obligations under that Agreement". The Appellate Body then quoted paragraph 3 of the Marrakesh Protocol[89] and found that Members could not diminish rights in their schedules. Schedules had to reflect the commitments made by Members and, to the extent that they did not, the schedules were subject to multilateral review by the Members. Brazil claimed that the EC had not reflected in its Schedule the commitments made with Brazil within the terms of Article XXVIII of GATT.

146. The **EC** replied that except for preferential treatment justified under Article XXIV of GATT or Article IX of the WTO Agreement[90], the concessions that were contained in each Member's schedule, established pursuant to Article II of GATT, were the only commitments with respect to the level of duties and other charges imposed on or in connection with importation by which that Member was bound under the WTO. The text of Article II of GATT, and in particular its paragraph 1, was the expression of this basic principle which had far-reaching implications for the entire WTO system of agreements. The mere idea, suggested by Brazil's complaint, of the existence of additional obligations in relation to the duties and other charges imposed on or in connection with importation of a specific set of products, which did not flow from any preferential agreement justified under Article XXIV of GATT or Article IX of the WTO Agreement and not inserted in the schedules, ran counter to the clear provisions of Article II of GATT. More importantly, such a suggestion would introduce in the WTO system the unpredictability and instability which that provision was designed to prevent.

147. **Brazil** argued that the issuance of licences in uneconomic quantities, and the trade in these licences for value, meant that a payment had to be made to obtain licences in economic quantities prior to import. This payment or charge was in addition to that provided for in the EC's Schedule which set out that within the poultry TRQ no duty should be payable. According to Brazil, in practice, a duty of between two and three German Marks per kilo was payable prior to imports being effected. It was, therefore, in all respects, a charge payable in association

---

87 Appellate Body Report on *Banana III, op. cit.*

88 Panel Report on *Sugar, op. cit.*

89 "The implementation of the concessions and commitments contained in the schedules annexed to this Protocol shall, upon request, be subject to multilateral examination by the Members. This would be without prejudice to the rights and obligations of Members under Agreements in Annex 1A of the WTO Agreement."

90 See the Panel Report on *Newsprint*.

with import and was a clear breach of the requirement in Article II that no charges in addition to those provided for in the schedule be payable.

148. The **EC** submitted that the GATT (and other WTO agreements) were international agreements concluded between sovereign states and organizations which were binding between those parties. International responsibility for the violation of these agreements could only be engaged, except where otherwise explicitly provided, when the violation could be attributed directly to a Member as a result of a governmental measure. This was clearly the case for Article II:1(b) of GATT where a reference was made to other duties and charges "*imposed* at the date of this Agreement or those *directly and mandatorily required* to be imposed thereafter by *legislation* in force in the importing territory on that date."(emphasis added) This was confirmed by Article 19 of the DSU which indicated that "where a panel or the Appellate Body concludes that a *measure* is inconsistent with a covered agreement, it shall recommend that the Member concerned bring the *measure* into conformity with that agreement."(emphasis added) The EC stressed that there was no legislation or any legislative requirement whatsoever within the EC legal system which imposed extra charges on top of the ordinary duties and other duties and charges which were bound in its Schedule. Any payment or charge in relation to economic transactions concerning those import licences were strictly private and responsibility for such charges could not be attributed to the EC. Moreover, Article 5, paragraph 3 of Regulation 1431/94, stated expressly that import licences to be used for the Community poultry meat TRQ were not transferable. The EC urged the Panel, therefore, to reject the claims from Brazil in this respect as totally unfounded and unjustified (see also paragraphs 146 and 150.)

149. **Brazil** agreed that GATT (and other WTO agreements) were international agreements as between sovereign States. They gave rise to international obligations as between States. Brazil did not agree, however, that because the GATT was an international agreement and as the speculative charges for licences were not imposed by law, that the EC had no responsibility or obligations in respect of the extra charges that were in fact payable. Brazil was of the view that the EC's obligations in relation to Article II were not only in connection to mandatory legislation but also to "all other duties or charges of any kind imposed on or in connection with the importation in excess of those imposed on the date of the Agreement". The scope and object of the Article was not, in the view of Brazil, therefore restricted to mandatory legislation. Brazil noted that the number of licence holders was increasing as well as the incidence of speculation. The EC had accepted the need to prevent speculation. However, in Brazil's opinion, the legislative attempts to prevent speculation had not been successful.

150. Citing Article II:1(a) and (b)[91] of GATT, the **EC** submitted, Article I:1 of GATT applied equally to bound and unbound rates.[92] This wording matched the explicit reference in Article I:1 of GATT.[93] It flowed from this, the EC argued, that the *current* bound rates in the EC Schedule, including in-quota tariff rates, were the only obligations of the Community with respect to the level of duties to be applied to imported products, with the exceptions already mentioned above. The EC was obliged to apply to the results of an Article XXVIII negotiation the MFN principle which benefited *all* the other Members.

Article III

151. **Brazil** submitted that the EC regime for the administration of the TRQ had the effect of imported products being treated in a manner that was less favourable than that accorded to like domestic products. Domestic products did not require a licence for the sale on the domestic market whereas products imported within the TRQ did so require. On the assumption that licences were a valid mechanism for the administration of TRQs, Members were still obliged to ensure that the administration of licensing systems were such that they did not act as *de facto* measures giving rise to less favourable treatment. In the opinion of Brazil, the EC had failed to ensure that this obligation was respected. The issuing of licences in uneconomic amounts, the tolerance of illegal speculation in licences, the failure to ensure that exporters knew which importers were in possession of licences, and lack of knowledge of which trade regime was applicable to any one import consignment had, in combination, the effect that the imported products were competing on less favourable terms with domestic products. In addition, Brazil said, the granting of import licences to exporters which were domestic producers accorded a benefit to domestic production which imported products did not enjoy. Each of these elements by themselves, and in combination, had the effect, in the view of Brazil, of placing the imported product in a less favourable position than the domestic product in clear breach of the terms of Article III of GATT.

---

91 Article II:1(a): "Each contracting party shall accord to the commerce of *the other contracting parties* treatment no less favourable than that provided for in the appropriate Part of the appropriate Schedule annexed to this Agreement." Article II:1(b): "the products described in Part I of the Schedule relating to *any* contracting party, ... , shall, ... , be exempt from ordinary custom duties in excess of those set forth and provided therein".

92 Panel Report on *Spain - Tariff Treatment of Unroasted Coffee*, adopted 11 June 1982, BISD 28S/102, paragraph 4.3.

93 "*With respect to custom duties and charges* of any kind imposed on or in connection with importation or exportation ... *any* advantage, favour, privilege or immunity granted by any contracting party to any product originating in or destined for *any other country* shall be accorded immediately and unconditionally to the like products originating in or destined for the territories of *all other contracting parties*". (emphasis added).

152. The **EC** replied that the administration of a TRQ was effected through border measures, to which some provisions of the GATT were applicable[94], and not by internal measures to which *other* provisions applied, in particular Article III. This clear distinction corresponded, according to a long tradition in the interpretation of the General Agreement, to the acknowledged common will and understanding of the CONTRACTING PARTIES to the GATT and, by virtue of the Marrakesh protocol to the WTO Agreement, of all Members of the WTO, as confirmed in the panel report on *Italian Discrimination against Imported Agricultural Machinery*.[95] A similar approach had already been suggested by the panel report on *Belgian Family Allowances (Allocations familiales)*. The import licensing rules managing the frozen poultry meat TRQ, the EC stressed, were border measures "par excellence" and could not violate Article III of GATT, concerned only with internal measures, i.e. measures applicable after the products concerned had cleared through customs. The EC denied that any link whatsoever could be made, in substance or in the formalities, between this case and the so-called *Banana III* case in regard to Article III. The EC recalled that that panel and the Appellate Body had confirmed the value of the long-standing interpretation of the GATT which distinguished border measures and internal measures.

153. **Brazil** submitted that the payments charged by importers on the speculative sale of import licences was similar in nature to a special fee payable on imports only. Moreover, to the extent that EC legislation did provide that EC traders who exported domestic product were entitled to import licences, there was a breach of the terms of Article III. In the opinion of Brazil, it was no defence for the EC to claim that the export qualification for licence entitlement had been removed. Licence entitlement was based on past imports. Illegality in the past allocation of import rights carried forward into the present. 1997 licences were allocated on the basis of past performance in the two previous years for which statistics were available, namely 1995 and 1996. The export criteria for the allocation of import licences resulted in a current inconsistency with Article III.

154. The **EC** replied that apart from some unsubstantiated allegations concerning practices relating to the administration of the poultry meat TRQ, Brazil did not indicate any reason that could justify the claim that EC legislation applicable to the poultry products subject to this dispute *after* those products had cleared customs, treated imported poultry products in a less favourable way than domestic products. Moreover, the claim that granting import licences for the poultry meat TRQ to exporters was in breach of Article III was not only totally unsupported by motivation but showed a poor reading of the EC legislation. Whilst Article 3(a) of Regulation 1431/94 indicated that "Applicants for import

---

94 Like Article I:1, Article II, XIII and the Licensing Agreement.

95 "It was considered, moreover, that the intention of the drafters of the Agreement was clearly to treat the imported products in the same way as the like domestic products once they have cleared through customs. Otherwise, indirect protection could be given". BISD 7/S 60, adopted on 23 October 1958.

licences must be natural or legal persons who, ... can prove ... that they have imported or exported not less than ... of products within the scope of Regulation (EEC) No. 2775/75 ...", Commission Regulation 1244/95 amended that provision, eliminating any reference to exporters who were no longer entitled to apply for import licences. Thus, EC said, Brazil's claim related to a situation which as a matter of fact no longer existed and which in consequence could not entail any nullification and/or impairment of Brazil's rights under the WTO. In summary, Article III of GATT was, in the opinion of the EC, not applicable to the issue raised by Brazil. The allegations by Brazil should therefore be dismissed.

IV. ARGUMENTS PRESENTED BY THIRD PARTIES

Terms of Reference

155. Referring to the Panel's terms of reference (see paragraph 4 above), the **United States** submitted that the "covered agreements" were defined in Article 1.1 of the DSU as "the agreements listed in Appendix 1 to this Understanding". The list of such agreements in Appendix 1 was a closed list, which did not include the Brazil-EC bilateral agreement. The Brazil-EC bilateral agreement was also not one of the instruments included within GATT 1994, according to the GATT 1994 incorporation clause. The terms of that agreement, and the issue of whether EC actions had violated those terms, were therefore, in the opinion of the United States, not within the terms of reference of this Panel. The United States submitted that under Article 31(3)(c) of the Vienna Convention, the Panel should take into account "any relevant rules of international law applicable in the relations between the parties"; those "rules of international law" may include the bilateral agreement that was reached under Article XXVIII:4. The bilateral agreement could thus serve as a means of clarifying the concessions if the concessions were ambiguous.

156. **Brazil** contested the view expressed by the United States, concerning the terms of reference. This Panel had standard terms of reference under Article 7 of the DSU which made specific mention of Articles XXVIII, X, III and II of GATT, the Agreement on Agriculture and the Licensing Agreement. It was clear to both parties that this Panel had to consider the nature of the EC's commitment under Article XXVIII, as reflected in the Oilseeds Agreement. Referring to the section related to Terms of Reference in the Handbook of GATT[96], Brazil submitted that the terms of reference were defined by the complaining party which unilaterally defined the subject matter of the dispute. It was not a bilateral system. Brazil had clearly stated that it wished this Panel to consider the EC's commitments under the Article XXVIII Oilseeds Agreement and the extent to which they were not reflected in the EC's Schedule under Article II. Brazil had not only

[96] Handbook of WTO/GATT Dispute Settlement, *op.cit.*, p. 12.

cited Articles XXVIII and II in its complaint but had also made reference to the issues which this Panel should consider so as to be able to determine the EC's obligations and Brazil's rights. Panels should examine the complaint in the light of the relevant GATT provisions. This forestalled objections as to *ultra vires* in a case where a panel chose to base its findings on provisions not specifically relied on by the parties. Thus, the Panel had discretion as to what to take into consideration when examining a complaint.

157. The reference to provisions of the GATT had always, according to the author of the Handbook, been interpreted to mean not only the covered agreements but also the whole WTO legal system including secondary and supplementary GATT law.[97] Brazil maintained that the agreement agreed within the framework of Article XXVIII and submitted by the EC to the CONTRACTING PARTIES was supplementary GATT law within the terms of the standard terms of reference. In the view of Brazil, Article 7.2 of the DSU confirmed the broad scope of the standard terms of reference by providing that "Panels shall address the relevant provisions in any covered agreement or agreements cited by the parties to the dispute". Thus, panels had to look to covered agreements and "agreements cited by the parties". Brazil had cited Article XXVIII of GATT and the Oilseeds Agreement adopted within the framework of that Article. Article 3.2 of the DSU provided that the dispute settlement system of the WTO "serves to preserve the rights and obligations of Members under the covered agreements and to clarify the existing provisions of those agreements". Brazil's claim was that the EC had not complied with its obligations under Article XXVIII of a covered agreement. Those obligations were set out in the Oilseeds agreements. To know what those obligations were, the Panel had to consider the Oilseeds Agreement.

158. Brazil submitted further that there was nothing in the terms of Articles 7 and 10 of the DSU, in the Working Procedures contained in Annex 3 to the DSU, or in the standard terms of reference themselves, which gave interested third parties the right to question the terms of reference of a panel. Interested third parties may be heard by Panels within the terms of Article 10 of the DSU and Article 6 of the Working Procedures. Article 10 did not limit the issues which could be raised by interested third parties. However, more importantly, it did not give third parties the right to override the terms of reference of the Panel or to determine the proper interpretation of those terms when they had been accepted by the parties. The object of the WTO dispute settlement procedures as set out in Article 3 of the DSU, was to secure a positive solution to a dispute.

159. The **EC** submitted that the Panel was certainly entitled, in accordance with Article 10.2 of the DSU to take into consideration any relevant element that a third party submitted to its appreciation as long as this element was within the terms of reference of the Panel as adopted by the DSB. The EC considered that it was within the terms of reference of the Panel to take account of the arguments

---

97 Handbook of WTO/GATT Dispute Settlement, *op.cit.*, p. 13.

advanced in the US statement; however, the EC was not convinced that the Panel needed to address this issue prior to dealing with the questions raised by the EC concerning the application of Article 59(1) or, in the alternative, of Article 30(3) and 31 of the Vienna Convention. The EC considered that both these lines of argument would lead the Panel to the inevitable conclusion that what was applicable and applied was the current Uruguay Round EC Schedule of commitments which provided for a MFN frozen poultry meat TRQ. Consequently, the Article XXVIII Oilseeds Agreement as such was simply not relevant.

Article XXVIII of GATT

160. The **United States** submitted that Article XXVIII was a conditional provision which permitted a Member to legally renegotiate (modify or withdraw) its concessions at certain times on the condition that certain procedures were complied with in which case it was released from its obligations under Article II with respect to that concession. However, if there was no agreement, the modifying Member could go ahead and change its applied tariff, and the initial negotiating right holders, principal suppliers and substantial suppliers then were free to make counter-withdrawals on a timely basis. The only provision in Article XXVIII that spoke to the *level* of compensation was Article XXVIII:2, which was merely precatory in nature. Consequently, the United States did not see the possibility that a Member could be found to have "violated" Article XXVIII except if it had refused to negotiate with a party having rights, such as an initial negotiating right holder. The United States further submitted that nothing in the text of Article XXVIII provided any exception to Articles I or XIII. The negotiating history also confirmed that Article XXVIII concerned the unwinding or substitution on an MFN basis of concessions that were negotiated on an MFN basis.[98] Tariff compensation provided under Article XXVIII had consistently been provided on an MFN basis, as it was required to by Article I:1. Parallel conclusions had to be drawn for tariff rate quotas and the requirements of Article XIII.

161. Brazil had not even shown, the United States argued, that it had a reasonable expectation that the entire TRQ for frozen poultry was assigned exclusively to Brazil. The bilateral agreement between Brazil and the EC referred to a "global quota" for poultry meat equal to 15,500 tonnes. Nothing in the language of the bilateral agreement committed the EC to a specific quota of 15,500 tonnes exclusively to Brazil. Indeed, the contemporaneous excerpts from various EC publications that Brazil had appended to its initial Panel submission supported

---

98 "It was agreed that there was no intention to interfere in any way with the operation of the most-favoured-nation clause. This Article is headed "Modification of Schedules". It refers throughout to concessions negotiated under paragraph 1 of Article II, the Schedules, and there is no reference in the Article to Article I, which is the Most-Favoured-Nation clause. ... the intent is clear: that in no way should this Article interfere with the operation of the Most-Favoured-Nation clause." (Chairman's summing up in the Tariff Agreement Committee, 1948, EPCT/TAC/PV/18, p. 46, cited at p. 947, *Analytical Index/Guide to GATT Law and Practice* (1995 ed.))

the view that the tariff quota was intended to be available on a non-discriminatory basis. In addition, the General Agreement and the WTO provided no legal support for any expectation that concessions pursuant to Article XXVIII proceedings could be provided other than on a non-discriminatory basis. In the appellate proceedings in *Banana III*, the United States continued, the Community had argued that its market access concessions made pursuant to the Agreement on Agriculture permitted it to act inconsistently with Article XIII of the GATT 1994. The Appellate Body observed that with respect to concessions, a Member could yield rights and grant benefits, but could not diminish its obligations. The Appellate Body explained that this interpretation was confirmed by paragraph 3 of the Marrakesh Protocol.[99]

Article XIII of GATT

162. **Thailand** was of the view that any Member's agricultural tariff schedule under the Uruguay Round negotiations was part and parcel of that Member's schedule in accordance with paragraph 1 of the Marrakesh Protocol.[100] In this respect, the allocation of tariff quotas was governed by, and had to be consistent with, the provisions of Article XIII of the GATT 1994, especially Article XIII:2. Nothing in the GATT, or any other WTO Agreement, provided any special treatment to the tariff quotas derived from a negotiation under Article XXVIII of GATT. Referring to Article XIII:2(d), Thailand submitted that the interest of Thailand as a Member with a substantial interest in supplying poultry to the EC market had to be taken into account, and the allocation of the annual tariff quota of 5,100 tonnes to Thailand by the EC, if done in accordance with the provisions of Article XIII:2(d) would be consistent with the GATT. Once a quota had been established, Thailand said, the manner in which the applying country administered the quota was also very important and subject to the provision of Article XIII:2(d). The Member applying the restriction, in this case the EC, was obligated to administer those quotas in such a way that they were fully utilized. Thailand submitted that it had experienced difficulties in utilizing fully its quota due to, in Thailand's view, the excessive formalities and measures imposed by the EC, such as the fragmentation of the import quantity allotted to importers and the imposition of safeguard measures based upon its own representative price. Thailand believed that these formalities and measures were not consistent with the EC's obligations under the last sentence of Article XIII:2(d), and should be so held by this Panel. Thailand submitted further that the Agreement on Agriculture

---

[99] "The implementation of the concessions and commitments contained in the schedules annexed to this Protocol shall, upon request, be subject to multilateral examination by the Members. This would be *without prejudice to the rights and obligations of Members under the Agreements in Annex 1A of the WTO Agreement"*. (emphasis added)

[100] Paragraph 1 of the Marrakesh Protocol to the GATT 1994 stated that "... (t)he schedule annexed to this Protocol relating to a Member shall become a Schedule to GATT 1994 relating to that Member on the day on which the WTO Agreement enters into force for that Member ...".

did not change the rules regarding the allocation of tariff quotas as contained in Article XIII, especially Article XIII:2(d) of GATT as set out in the *Banana III* panel report.[101] The Appellate Body's decision in the same *Banana III* case confirmed that Article XIII, in particular Article XIII:2(d), governed the allocation of tariff quotas.

163. The **United States** submitted that no evidence had been presented to suggest that the non-discrimination provision in Article XIII was superseded by concessions negotiated pursuant to Article XXVIII. The report of the Appellate Body in *Banana III* provided, in the view of the United States, useful guidance on the nature of the non-discrimination obligation under Article XIII. There, the Appellate Body found that Article XIII required the non-discriminatory administration of quantitative restrictions and that paragraph 5 of Article XIII also applied to tariff quotas (paragraph 160). As most, if not virtually all, tariff quotas were the result of negotiated concessions, it was implicit in the legal conclusion of the Appellate Body that the origin of a particular tariff quota had no effect on the applicability of the non-discrimination obligation. A review of the bilateral agreement between the EC and Brazil incorporating their resolution of the Oilseeds dispute reflected that the parties did not agree to a method of allocating the tariff rate quota. The text of Article XIII:2(d) was clear - there was an obligation to allocate a share to Members having a substantial interest. Brazil had not identified any provision of the WTO Agreements that would permit the entire TRQ to be assigned to Brazil. In fact, the Appellate Body in *Banana III* found that Article XIII could not be construed to permit such a result.

The Licensing Agreement

164. **Thailand** submitted that a tariff quota of 5,100 tonnes of poultry meat was allocated to Thailand by the EC in 1994. This amount was also confirmed during the Uruguay Round negotiations. Therefore, Thailand's production and export plan for frozen poultry meat had been adjusted accordingly. Thailand was, however, of the view that there were uncertainty in utilizing the tariff quota and no flexibility in the quota arrangement due to (i) the lack of information concerning which importers were granted a quota and the amount of quota granted to each importer; and (ii) the allocation of import licence to each applicant in each quarter was fragmented. According to Regulations 774/94, 1431/94, 641/95 and 997/97, as last amended by Regulation 1514/97, import licences of no more than 10 per cent of the quarterly quota would be allocated to each applicant. If the quantities for which licences had been applied exceeded the quarterly quota, a reduction coefficient was applied to the quantities requested. For example, in the second quarter of 1997, the tariff quota allocated to Thailand was 1,275 tonnes. The amount of import licences was 127.5 tonnes per applicant. In the case where import applications exceeded the quarterly quota, a reduction coefficient was

[101] The Panel Report on *Banana III, op. cit.*, paragraphs 7.124, 7.125, and 7.126.

applied, at 4.9 per cent, and each importer would be granted import licences for 6.25 tonnes. This amount was, in the opinion of Thailand, not commercially meaningful. Referring to the administration of import licences, Thailand was of the view that the provisions of the Licensing Agreement should apply. Those provisions included, *inter alia*, Article 3.2, 3.3 and 3.5(h). In view of these provisions, Thailand considered that the EC import licensing procedures concerning the frozen poultry meat quota administration were inconsistent.

165. The **United States** submitted that the Appellate Body found in *Banana III*[102] that import licensing procedures for the administration of tariff quotas were subject to the Licensing Agreement. The EC did not dispute these conclusions. The EC licensing system for frozen poultry meat was thus subject to the requirement of Article 1.3 of the Licensing Agreement, which provided that Members had to ensure that the administrative procedures used to implement licensing regimes were not operated inappropriately so as to give rise to trade distortions. This general prohibition was repeated in Article 3.2 which provided that non-automatic licensing should not have trade restrictive or distortive effects on imports additional to those caused by the imposition of the restriction. If the EC's administration of the licensing regime for frozen poultry discouraged imports of poultry meat from Brazil by virtue of the alleged eligibility restrictions on licence applicants, the volume limitations imposed in individual licences, and a general lack of procedural transparency, it would seem that the Community's licensing regime then was in contravention of Articles 1.3 and 3.2 of the Licensing Agreement. If indeed the Community had conditioned access to its *import* TRQ on performance as an *exporter*, as asserted by Brazil, in the view of the United States, the Community's administration of the TRQ did introduce trade distortions which would contravene Articles 1.3 and 3.2 of the Licensing Agreement. Similarly, if licences were granted only for small, "uneconomic quantities", the licensing system was likely to have restricted trade inappropriately in contravention of paragraphs 3.2, 3.5(i) and 3.5(j) of Article 3 of the Licensing Agreement.

The Agreement on Agriculture

166. **Thailand** submitted that the Appellate Body had confirmed the decision and reasoning of the panel in *Banana III* that the Agreement on Agriculture did not change the rules regarding the allocation of tariff quotas as contained in Article XIII of the GATT[103], concluding that "For these reasons, we agree with the Panel's conclusion that the Agreement on Agriculture does not permit the European Communities to act inconsistently with the requirements of Article XIII of the GATT 1994". In light of the above, Thailand requested the Panel to find that all of the tariff quota allocations was governed by and had to be consistent with

---

[102] Paragraphs 193-194.

[103] The Appellate Body's reasons with respect to this matter appear in paragraphs 157 and 158 of its report.

Article XIII of GATT and that the EC's administration system of the tariff quota was not consistent with the provisions of Article XIII:2(d) last sentences, and the Licensing Agreement, especially its Article 3.

167. In the view of the **United States**, the language of the Agreement on Agriculture did not provide support for either of the conditions claimed by Brazil to be prerequisites to the exercise of the safeguard provisions pursuant to Article 5 of the Agreement. First, Article 5, which incorporated all of the pertinent language with respect to the safeguard measures applicable under that Agreement, contained no reference to any injury criteria. Clearly, if the negotiators had intended for such a precondition to apply, it would have been expressly specified in the Agreement. Second, Article 5.1(b) stated that the relevant import price for purposes of activation of the special safeguard should be determined on the basis of the c.i.f. import price of the imports in question. There was no suggestion in the language of Article 5 that any price other than the c.i.f. price was to be used for comparison with the applicable "trigger" or reference price. The more troublesome question posed by the EC's implementation of special safeguard provisions, in the view of the United States, was the possibility that the Community was using some amalgam of internal prices and external prices in establishing the "entry price" that was subject to comparison with the so-called "trigger" or reference price. If this was the prevailing situation, then the EC could be imposing special safeguard duties based on a methodology that was inconsistent with that expressly prescribed in Article 5 of the Agreement on Agriculture.

168. In conclusion, the United States submitted, this Panel should find that Brazil had failed to provide evidence that the bilateral agreement between Brazil and the EC justified any expectation that the EC would issue a tariff rate quota relating to frozen poultry meat that would be for the exclusive benefit of Brazil. In addition, it was clear that the EC could not have granted a tariff rate quota exclusively to Brazil with respect to frozen poultry meat without violating the obligations of Articles I, II, and XIII of GATT. The Panel should also give serious consideration to whether the licensing regime established by the EC to administer the pertinent tariff rate quota had served inappropriately to distort or restrict trade, thereby violating the Licensing Agreement. Finally, in the view of the United States, the EC might have violated the special safeguard provision of Article 5 of the Agreement on Agriculture by adopting a mechanism for establishing the applicable "c.i.f. entry" price that was inconsistent with the express language of Article 5.1(b).

Article II

169. In answer to a question by Brazil, the **United States** submitted that the protection of legitimate expectations in respect of tariff treatment of a bound item was one of the most important functions of Article II. Indeed, the importance of legitimate expectations in interpretation of tariff commitments could be confirmed by the text of Article II itself, specifically the references to "treatment contemplated" in Article II:5. This conclusion was also supported by the object

and purpose of the WTO Agreement and those of GATT 1994. The security and predictability of "the reciprocal and mutually advantageous arrangements directed to the substantial reduction of tariffs and other barriers to trade"(an expression common to the preambles of the two agreements) cannot be maintained without protection of such legitimate expectations. This was consistent with the principle of good faith interpretation under Article 31 of the Vienna Convention. It might be the case that in nearly all instances, the ordinary meaning of the terms of the actual description in a tariff schedule accurately reflected and exhausted the content of the legitimate expectations. But it should remain possible, at least in principle, that parties had legitimately formed expectations based on other particular supplementary factors. However, in this case, the concession on frozen poultry in Schedule LXXX clearly did not assign the entire TRQ exclusively to Brazil. Indeed, the contemporaneous excerpts from various EC publications that Brazil had appended to its initial Panel submission supported the view that the tariff quota was intended to be available on a non-discriminatory basis. The GATT Agreement and the WTO Agreement provided no legal support for any expectation that concessions pursuant to Article XXVIII proceedings could be provided other than on a non-discriminatory basis. Indeed, a reading of those provisions would dispel any unfounded illusions that concessions could be implemented to the exclusive benefit of a single Member.

170. The **EC** did not agree with the United States' views concerning the interpretation of Article II of GATT and the alleged existence of so-called "legitimate expectations" under that provision. This Panel was not concerned with a non-violation case under Article XXIII:1(b) of GATT. The notion of "legitimate expectations" was developed only in the framework of such cases and, therefore, it was not relevant here. The EC considered also that Article II:5 was irrelevant in the present context: that provision was, like Article XXVIII, a procedural one since it provided for the possibility to enter negotiations. It was evident, the EC believed, that none of the conditions set out in that provision were fulfilled here and Article II:5 should not be considered relevant for the resolution of the issues raised in this case.

Nullification or Impairment

171. Thailand submitted that since the EC's import licensing regime violated the provisions of the GATT and the Licensing Agreement, it constituted a *prima facie* case of nullification and impairment to the benefits of Thailand. Thailand noted that Article 3.8 of the DSU, as its predecessor the 1979 Understanding, did not refer to the adverse impact of the measures concerned. Consequently, when the *prima facie* case had been established, the actual volume of trade in the product concerned was immaterial. The past GATT/WTO jurisprudence testified to this.

V. INTERIM REVIEW

172. On 30 January 1998, Brazil requested the Panel to review, in accordance with Article 15.2 of the DSU, the interim report that had been issued to the parties on 23 January 1998. Brazil also requested the Panel to hold a further meeting with the parties to discuss the points raised in its written comments. The EC did not request a review, but indicated that it would address an issue of confidentiality in the context of the interim review. The Panel met with the parties on 3 February 1998, reviewed the entire range of arguments presented by Brazil and the EC, and finalized its report, taking into account the specific aspects of these arguments it considered to be relevant.

173. Regarding what are now paragraphs 210 and 211 of the final report, Brazil commented that the Panel had not considered the full ordinary meaning of the terms of the Oilseeds Agreement and appeared to have restricted its analysis to the meaning of the words "global tariff quota". According to Brazil, the ordinary meaning of the agreement was clear: it was an agreement which allowed the EC to withdraw concessions under certain conditions. Brazil's arguments as to the meaning of the word "global" had been only to show that this word did not alter the ordinary meaning of the terms of the agreement.

174. The Panel reviewed the relevant parts of the interim report in light of the comments by Brazil, but found no reason to change its original language. Accordingly, the Panel maintained paragraphs 210 and 211.

175. Regarding what are now paragraphs 212 to 218 of the final report, Brazil made the following comments. First, in paragraph 212, the Panel appeared to misinterpret Brazil's arguments. Brazil did not argue that Articles I and XIII of GATT never applied to compensation TRQs agreed within the terms of Article XXVIII negotiations. Brazil had argued that they did not automatically apply if the parties to the negotiations agreed that the TRQ was country-specific and the other Members did not object. Second, regarding paragraph 214, Brazil considered that it had been GATT - and was WTO - practice to create country-specific TRQs on the basis of Article XXVIII negotiations and that the Panel did not examine this practice. Third, regarding paragraph 216, Brazil recalled its argument to the effect that the oilseeds compensation package was made up of a series of elements some of which were clearly intended to be MFN and some not. Brazil claimed that this point was not addressed by the Panel. Nor did the Panel, according to Brazil, address the fact that the EC negotiated separately with the different Members having a substantial interest and that the compensatory elements of these agreements was different in each agreement. This was in Brazil's view clearly an issue which must be considered under the Vienna Convention in the interpretation of the Oilseeds Agreement. Brazil questioned why the contents of the compensation package should be different in each bilateral agreement if they had been intended to be MFN. Fourth and finally, regarding paragraph 215, Brazil recalled that it was the right and obligation of the Members themselves to monitor the results of bilateral agreements made under Article XXVIII. That was why, according to Brazil, Members which were not parties to the negotiations

were given the right to object to any agreement reached within six months. Brazil noted that no Members objected to the compensation package contained in the Oilseeds Agreement.

176. With respect to the first point raised by Brazil, the Panel considered that it had fully understood Brazil's argument. In order to avoid any impression of misinterpretation by the Panel, however, the Panel decided to insert the word "necessarily" in paragraph 212 as well as in paragraph 218, as requested by Brazil. Regarding the second point on paragraph 214, the Panel acknowledged that it was Brazil's position that such a practice existed. However, the Panel considered that its view on this point was clearly expressed in paragraph 213. Regarding the third point on paragraph 216, the Panel was of the view that Brazil was confusing the overall oilseeds package with the Oilseeds Agreement. As referred to in Chapter VI (findings) of this report, the Oilseeds Agreement is the bilateral agreement between Brazil and the EC. To clarify this point, the Panel modified paragraph 194 slightly. In the Panel's view, what had been agreed between the EC and its trading partners other than Brazil was not relevant to the present dispute. Under the Vienna Convention, such agreements could be regarded as a supplementary means of interpretation under Article 32 because they might indicate the circumstances of the conclusion of the Oilseeds Agreement between Brazil and the EC. However, in view of the conclusion reached in paragraph 216, the Panel considered that it was unnecessary to have recourse to such a supplementary source. Regarding the fourth and final point presented by Brazil, the Panel noted that in paragraph 215 it was not addressing the issue of whether the procedure for safeguarding the rights of third parties was correctly followed. Rather, it was addressing a more fundamental, systemic issue that would negatively affect all Members of the WTO, including Brazil in this case. For these reasons, the Panel did not alter its findings, except the modifications in paragraphs 194, 212 and 218 mentioned above.

177. Regarding what is now paragraph 227 of the final report, Brazil noted that on the basis of an interpretation of the text of diplomatic letters sent by the Brazilian Ambassador in Brussels to various officials in the EC Commission, the Panel found that there was no evidence of agreement between the parties on the allocation of the TRQ. Brazil commented that the Panel could not substitute interpretation of the ordinary meaning of the terms of the Oilseeds Agreement with the interpretation of diplomatic correspondence which had been cited by Brazil as evidence of the breach of the agreement.

178. The Panel noted that in the relevant section of the interim report the Panel was not interpreting the terms of the Oilseeds Agreement between Brazil and the EC. In the Panel's view, this diplomatic correspondence, contrary to Brazil's assertion, did not demonstrate the existence of an explicit agreement regarding the allocation of the TRQs. Accordingly, the Panel maintained its conclusion reached in paragraph 227.

179. Regarding what is now paragraph 239 of the final report, Brazil pointed out that it had argued in its submission that "the past performance requirement

method requires that the TRQ is allocated among supplying countries based on their past supply performance during a specific reference period due account being taken of special trade factors".

180. The Panel was aware of Brazil's reference to special factors in its submission. However, what was lacking, in the Panel's view, was identification and elaboration of those special factors which might have existed in relation to the beneficiaries of the Interim Agreements. The Panel therefore did not change its conclusion in paragraph 249.

181. Regarding what is now paragraph 249 of the final report, Brazil contested the Panel's reading of Articles 1.2 and 3.2 of the Licensing Agreement, which in Brazil's view obligated Members to ensure that the licensing arrangements did not distort trade additional to the restriction, without making distinction between trade within or outside the TRQ. Brazil recalled that it had argued that a falling market share in a growing market was in fact evidence of distortion of trade outside the TRQ since the fall in the market share began after the introduction of the TRQ licensing system. According to Brazil, it had a constant market share of around 46 per cent until 1994. It then fell off radically from 1994 onwards to reach 33 per cent in 1996.

182. The Panel noted these comments, but was not convinced that these were sufficient grounds to change the Panel's conclusion in paragraph 249 because, in the Panel's view, Brazil failed to establish the existence of trade distortion in any measurable way. As stated in paragraph 249, decline in the percentage share alone, in the Panel's view, did not constitute adequate evidence of trade distortion. Accordingly, the Panel did not alter its findings in paragraph 249.

183. Regarding what is now paragraph 257 of the final report, Brazil requested that reference be made to the fact that Brazil provided proof of speculation, which was not contested by the EC. The Panel noted that Brazil had submitted two letters (in German) in this regard. However, in the Panel's view, they did not add more information than what was already contained in paragraph 95 above.

184. Paragraph 107 of the interim report, as well as what are now paragraphs 264 and 265 of the final report, had referred to Article 3.4 of the Licensing Agreement. However, Brazil stated that its reference to Article 3.4 was due to a typographical error and requested that any reference to Article 3.4 be deleted from the final report, which the Panel accepted.

185. Regarding what are now paragraphs 267 to 270 of the final report, Brazil commented that the Panel made a restrictive reading of Brazil's arguments concerning the breach of Article X. Brazil essentially claimed that the alleged violations of the Licensing Agreement and the Agreement on Agriculture *ipso facto* constituted a violation of Article X of GATT because they were "unreasonable". The Panel considered that this was a new argument that went beyond the review of "precise aspects of the interim report" as called for in Article 15.2 of the DSU.

186. Brazil further reiterated that the very inability of traders to be able to distinguish between the two sets of measures (i.e., those relating to in-quota trade and over-quota trade) was an unreasonable administration of all measures appli-

cable to the import of frozen poultry to the EC under Article X:3(a) of GATT and a breach of Article X:1. However, as stated in paragraph 269 of the final report, in the Panel's view, Brazil's claim pertained to specific measures outside the scope of Article X. Consequently, the Panel maintained the original language in paragraphs 267 to 270.

187. In the interim report, what are now paragraphs 285 and 286 had a sub-heading entitled "reference price" and one sentence in what is now paragraph 285 referred to "reference price (trigger price)". Brazil pointed out that it did not raise any claims in relation to the reference or trigger prices regarding the specific issue of "representative price". Rather, Brazil had argued that the "representative price", which was an internal EC mechanism for the verifying or "policing" the c.i.f. price of imports of frozen poultry, was not consistent with Article 5 of the Agreement on Agriculture.

188. The Panel accordingly corrected the relevant parts of the interim report. These changes, however, did not alter the Panel's conclusions.

189. Brazil also made other drafting suggestions concerning the descriptive part of the interim report, some of which the Panel accepted and introduced in its final report. These changes are reflected in paragraphs 79 and 99 of the final report.

190. At the interim review meeting, the EC commented that it did not agree with the amendments or corrections suggested by Brazil, except those regarding paragraphs 79 and 285.

191. The interim report contained Annex III, entitled "Comparison of Additional Duties for Boneless Broilermeat (0207 14 10) Imported from Brazil in November 1997", based on information submitted by the EC. In several communications addressed to the Panel, the EC had maintained that the data included in Annex III should not be made public. At the interim review meeting, the EC stated as follows. The unfortunate breach of confidentiality which had occurred during this Panel procedure as well as other past experiences convinced the EC that there was no other way to secure an appropriate level of confidentiality after the issuance of the report than by eliminating the confidential data from the text. They should therefore be replaced by a blank page with the indication of the existence of a restricted document. In the event that a Member requested a non-confidential summary of the restricted information, the EC would provide such information in compliance with the last sentence of Article 18.2 of the DSU.

192. In light of the foregoing, the Panel deleted Annex III and references thereto in the final report.

VI. FINDINGS

A. *Claims of the Parties*

193. This dispute concerns a tariff rate quota (TRQ) for frozen poultry meat under CN headings 0207 41 10, 0207 41 41 and 0207 41 71 maintained by the

European Communities (EC). Under the EC's Uruguay Round Schedule (Schedule LXXX)[104], the quantity of the TRQ is set at 15,500 tonnes with an in-quota duty rate bound at zero per cent. Out of this total quantity, the EC has, through a regulation[105], allocated 7,100 tonnes annually to products originating in Brazil.

194. Brazil claims that the EC has failed to implement and administer the TRQ in line with a bilateral agreement between Brazil and the EC ("the Oilseeds Agreement") reached within the context of negotiations under Article XXVIII of the General Agreement on Tariffs and Trade (GATT) resulting from the EC's modification of concessions on oilseeds products because, in Brazil's view, under the bilateral agreement the tariff quota was intended to be country-specific, with Brazil being the sole beneficiary. In support of this claim, Brazil argues that Articles I and XIII of GATT do not necessarily apply to TRQs given as compensation under Article XXVIII. Brazil claims in the alternative that the EC has failed to implement the TRQ in accordance with Article XIII of GATT. Brazil further claims that in the administration of import licences, the EC has failed to comply with the provisions of Articles 1 and 3 of the Agreement on Import Licensing Procedures (Licensing Agreement), and Articles X, II and III of GATT. Moreover, according to Brazil, the EC has failed to comply with the provisions of Articles 4 and 5 of the Agreement on Agriculture in the implementation of the special safeguards that apply to imports of poultry products outside the TRQ. Finally, Brazil claims that these measures nullify or impair the benefits accruing to Brazil under the cited agreements.

195. The EC rejects these claims.

B. The Oilseeds Agreement

(i) Relevance of the Oilseeds Agreement to this Dispute

196. Brazil refers in its panel request to the Oilseeds Agreement and the alleged breach of it by the EC.[106] However, a question arises whether the agreement itself is covered by the terms of reference of this Panel because it is not a "covered agreement" within the meaning of the Understanding on Rules and Procedures Governing the Settlement of Disputes (DSU).[107] We therefore take up the

---

104 The current EC Schedule (Schedule CXL), which was negotiated as the result of the EC's enlargement to include Austria, Finland and Sweden, has not yet been certified by the Director-General. In any event, since the treatment of the poultry products in question is identical in both Schedule LXXX and Schedule CXL, we regard Schedule LXXX as the EC tariff schedule currently in force for the purposes of this dispute. See paragraph 22.

105 Commission Regulation (EC) No 1431/94 of 22 June 1994.

106 Brazil's panel request (WT/DS69/2) contains the following sentence: "The Government of Brazil considers that the EC has failed ... to implement and administer a compensation tariff rate quota in line with the bilateral agreement reached between Brazil and the EC within the context of GATT Article XXVIII:4 negotiations."

107 Article 1.1 of the DSU defines covered agreements as "the agreements listed in Appendix 1 to this Understanding".

issue of the relevance of the Oilseeds Agreement to this case as a preliminary question that has to be addressed before the examination of substantive claims.

197. First, we note that, although the United States in its third-party submission argues that the agreement is not covered by the terms of reference[108], the EC has not explicitly objected to the examination of the Oilseeds Agreement by this Panel.

198. Second, there are precedents where a bilateral agreement was examined in a GATT/WTO dispute in order to determine the scope of rights and obligations in the multilateral context.

199. We recall in this regard that in the *Banana III* case, in order to interpret a WTO waiver, the panel and the Appellate Body had to examine the Lomé Convention, which is referred to in that waiver. The following statement by the panel in that case was affirmed by the Appellate Body:

> "We note that since the GATT CONTRACTING PARTIES incorporated a reference to the Lomé Convention into the Lomé waiver, the meaning of the Lomé Convention became a GATT/WTO issue, at least to that extent. Thus, we have no alternative but to examine the provisions of the Lomé Convention ourselves in so far as it is necessary to interpret the Lomé waiver."[109]

200. Also, we recall that the arbitrator in the 1990 *Canada/EC Wheat* case, which involved a bilateral agreement establishing the time-periods for exercising Article XXVIII rights, stated as follows:

> "In principle a claim based on a bilateral agreement cannot be brought under the multilateral dispute settlement procedures of the GATT. An exception is warranted in this case given the close connection of this particular bilateral agreement with the GATT, the fact that the Agreement is consistent with the objectives of the GATT, and that both parties joined in requesting recourse to the GATT Arbitration procedures."[110]

201. Third, in the present case, the Oilseeds Agreement was negotiated within the framework of Article XXVIII of GATT.[111] Insofar as the content of the Oilseeds Agreement is incorporated into Schedule LXXX - a point not disputed by the parties - there is a close connection between the two.

---

108 Paragraph 155.

109 Panel Reports on *European Communities - Regime for the Importation, Sale and Distribution of Bananas*, adopted on 25 September 1997, WT/DS27/R, para. 7.98, cited in the Appellate Body Report (WT/DS27/AB/R) at para. 167.

110 Award by the Arbitrator on *Canada/European Communities Article XXVIII Rights*, BISD 37S/80, at 84.

111 See paragraph 8.

202. For these reasons, we proceed to the examination of the Oilseeds Agreement to the extent relevant to the determination of the EC's obligations under the WTO agreements vis-à-vis Brazil.

(ii) Relationship between the Oilseeds Agreement and Schedule LXXX

203. Since the TRQ in question is provided for in the EC's current tariff schedule (Schedule LXXX), we start with an examination of the relationship between the Oilseeds Agreement - which gave rise to the opening of the TRQ - and Schedule LXXX.

204. As noted above, the Oilseeds Agreement was concluded within the context of Article XXVIII negotiations. Under ordinary circumstances, the resulting modification of the EC tariff schedule would have been certified by the Director-General pursuant to the 1980 procedure for modification and rectification of schedules.[112] However, as the conclusion of the Oilseeds Agreement coincided with the substantive conclusion of tariff negotiations in the Uruguay Round, this procedure was not strictly followed. The EC directly incorporated the substance of the Oilseeds Agreement into its then-current tariff schedule, effective 1 January 1994, and also into Schedule LXXX at the conclusion of the Uruguay Round negotiations.[113] This procedural anomaly, in our view, does not affect the legal characterization of the Oilseeds Agreement as a bilateral agreement concluded within the context of Article XXVIII negotiations, as is evidenced by the fact that the negotiations leading to its conclusion were authorized by the CONTRACTING PARTIES. It is sufficient to note at this juncture that the EC "multilateralized" the result of the oilseeds compensation negotiations (including the Oilseeds Agreement between Brazil and the EC) through a communication to the TNC Chairman and that no GATT contracting party or other participant of the Uruguay Round raised an objection to this communication at that time.[114] In any event, the EC explains that its own tariff regulations on poultry products were first modified as a result of the conclusion of the Oilseeds Agreement and that these modifications were maintained in principle in the regulations adopted in order to implement the results of the Uruguay Round.[115]

205. The EC claims that whatever had been agreed in the Oilseeds Agreement was superseded by Schedule LXXX under the rules of Articles 59(1) or, alternatively, Article 30(3) of the Vienna Convention on the Law of Treaties (Vienna Convention). Article 59(1) of the Vienna Convention reads as follows:

---

[112] *Procedure for Modification and Rectification of Schedules of Tariff Concessions*, Decision of the CONTRACTING PARTIES on 26 March 1980, BISD 27S/25.

[113] Paragraph 43.

[114] *Ibid.*

[115] Paragraph 22.

> "A treaty shall be considered as terminated if all the parties to it conclude a later treaty relating to the same subject-matter and:
>
> (a) it appears from the later treaty or is otherwise established that the parties intended that the matter should be governed by that treaty; or
>
> (b) the provisions of the later treaty are so far incompatible with those of the earlier one that the two treaties are not capable of being applied at the same time."

Article 30(3) of the Vienna Convention further reads as follows:

> "When all the parties to the earlier treaty are parties also to the later treaty but the earlier treaty is not terminated or suspended in operation under Article 59, the earlier treaty applies only to the extent that its provisions are compatible with those of the later treaty."

206. Although we note that these provisions of the Vienna Convention (which generally pertain to the legal maxim *lex posterior derogat prior*) are codification of the customary rules of interpretation of public international law within the meaning of Article 3.2 of the DSU[116], we also note that past panels have been careful about the application of the *lex posterior* rule on tariff schedules. Indeed, in the 1990 *EEC - Oilseeds* case, which gave rise to the Oilseeds Agreement in the present case, the panel stated as follows:

> "In these circumstances, the partners of the Community in the successive renegotiations under Article XXIV:6 could legitimately assume, in the absence of any indications to the contrary, that the offer to continue a tariff commitment by the Community was an offer not to change the balance of concessions previously attained. The Panel noted that nothing in the material submitted to it indicated that the Community had made it clear to its negotiating partners that the withdrawal and reinstitution of the tariff concessions for oilseeds as part of the withdrawal of the whole of the Community Schedule meant that the Community was seeking a new balance of concessions with respect to these items. There is in particular no evidence that the Community, in the context of these negotiations, offered to compensate its negotiating partners for any impairment of the tariff concessions through production subsidies or that it accepted compensatory tariff withdrawals by its negotiating partners to

[116] See paragraph 209.

> take into account any such impairment. The balance of concessions negotiated in 1962 in respect of oilseeds was thus not altered in the successive Article XXIV:6 negotiations. The Panel therefore found that the benefits accruing to the United States under the oilseed tariff concessions resulting from the Article XXIV:6 negotiations of 1986/87 include the protection of reasonable expectations the United States had when these concessions were initially negotiated in 1962."[117]

The *Oilseeds* panel did not rule that by application of the *lex posterior* rule, the Community was bound only by the newest of tariff schedules, being released from all the previous commitments. On the contrary, the panel found that the balance of concessions negotiated in 1962 in respect of oilseeds was not altered in the successive tariff negotiations.

207. In our view, a similar situation exists in the present case. The fact that the *Oilseeds* panel dealt with a non-violation complaint does not alter the validity of this analysis. If an importing Member must respect all of its commitments in the previous rounds in respect of reasonable expectations in a non-violation case, by logical extension, such expectations would also be relevant to the interpretation of a tariff commitment in a violation case. In other words, we cannot summarily dismiss the significance of the Oilseeds Agreement in the interpretation of Schedule LXXX by recourse to the public international law principles embodied in the Vienna Convention.

(iii) The Oilseeds Agreement as Compensatory Adjustment under Article XXVIII:2

208. Now we turn to an examination of the substance of the Oilseeds Agreement. Under the terms of the Agreement, it was agreed that:

> "Duty exemption shall be applicable for cuts falling within subheadings 0207.41.10, 0207.41.41 and 0207.41.71 within the limits of a global annual tariff quota of 15,500 tonnes to be granted by the competent Community authorities".[118]

The substance of this agreement is incorporated into the relevant part of Schedule LXXX (Part I, Most-favoured-nation Tariff; Section I, Agricultural Products; Section I - B, Tariff Quotas; Minimum Access Quotas) corresponding to the

---

[117] Panel Report on *European Economic Community - Payments and Subsidies Paid to Processors and Producers of Oilseeds and Related Animal-feed Proteins*, adopted on 25 January 1990, BISD 37S/86, para. 146.

[118] Annex 1 to Brazil's first written submission. The same language can be found, e.g. in the agreed minutes between the EC and Poland, published in the Official Journal of the European Communities No L 47/22, dated 18 February 1994.

same tariff item numbers. Therefore, the analysis of the Oilseeds Agreement is equally relevant in the interpretation of Schedule LXXX.

209. Under Article 3.2 of the DSU, we are required to examine the relevant part of the Oilseeds Agreement "in accordance with customary rules of interpretation of public international law". As has been noted by many previous panels and the Appellate Body, Article 31(1) of the Vienna Convention describes such customary rules as follows:

> "A treaty shall be interpreted in good faith in accordance with the ordinary meaning to be given to the terms of the treaty in their context and in the light of its object and purpose."

Accordingly, we follow these rules in the analysis of the Oilseeds Agreement.

(a) Ordinary Meaning of the Terms

210. Brazil claims that the total TRQ under the Oilseeds Agreement should be reserved exclusively for products originating in Brazil. The ordinary meaning of the terms used in this particular provision, on its face, does not appear to support the Brazilian claim. There is nothing in this provision that suggests that this TRQ is a country-specific tariff quota with Brazil being the sole beneficiary. According to Brazil, however, the term "global" means "covering a variety of tariff lines", in this case encompassing the three listed subheadings.[119] The EC claims that the term "global" as used in this provision means "general", "universal", "comprehensive", "catch-all" or in WTO terms, most-favoured-nation (MFN) or *erga omnes*.[120]

211. Various arguments made by Brazil in paragraph 58 indicate that the term "global quota" could mean something other than MFN, but do not constitute conclusive evidence to the effect that the particular terms used in the Oilseeds Agreement must be read the way claimed by Brazil. We note, however, that the term "a global annual tariff quota" is a loosely defined, non-legal term. Pursuant to Article 31(1) of the Vienna Convention, we need to take into account the context and the object and purpose of the Oilseeds Agreement in order to determine the precise meaning of the terms used therein. Since the context of the term "global annual tariff quota" does not give us any additional guidance, we turn to the object and purpose of the Oilseeds Agreement.

(b) Object and Purpose of the Oilseeds Agreement

212. Brazil's claim that the total TRQ should be reserved exclusively for its products derives from its understanding on the object and purpose of the Oilseeds

---

[119] Paragraph 56.
[120] Paragraph 57.

Agreement as compensatory adjustment within the meaning of Article XXVIII:2 of GATT, which reads as follows:

> "In such negotiations and agreement, which may include provision for compensatory adjustment with respect to other products, Members concerned shall endeavour to maintain a general level of reciprocal and mutually advantageous concessions not less favourable to trade than that provided for in this Agreement prior to such negotiations."

Brazil argues that the MFN principle under Articles I and XIII of GATT does not necessarily apply to TRQs opened as a result of the compensation negotiations under Article XXVIII of GATT.[121] According to Brazil, since the purpose of the Oilseeds Agreement was to compensate Brazil for the modification of EC concessions on oilseeds, Brazil is entitled to an exclusive benefit in the modified tariff schedule. The EC responds that the nature of compensation cannot change the legal reality under the GATT/WTO agreements: i.e. the EC was bound, on an MFN basis, by its tariff commitments.[122]

213. First, we examine whether Brazil's argument is supported by specific provisions in the WTO agreements, decisions of the Ministerial Conference/General Council or "the decisions, procedures and customary practices followed by the CONTRACTING PARTIES".[123] We note that, despite Brazil's assertions that there are examples of country-specific TRQs in practice and that those TRQs are well recognized by academic writers,[124] there is no provision in the WTO agreements that allows departure from the MFN principle in the case of TRQs resulting from Article XXVIII negotiations.[125] Nor is there any decision of the CONTRACTING PARTIES or of the Ministerial Conference/General Council, or any adopted panel or Appellate Body report that permits such departure.

214. In our view, past GATT practice supports the applicability of the MFN principle in these situations. For instance, in response to a complaint of the Benelux countries regarding the failure by Germany to bring down to the level of the Benelux rates the German duties on cereal starch and potato flour as well as on some derivatives, a panel in 1955 made the following observation:

> "The Panel took note of the agreement reached between the delegations concerned on the basis of the offer which, in the opinion of both parties, represents a first step toward the fulfilment of the promise contained in the letter of 31 March 1951, and noted also the assurance given by the German

[121] Paragraphs 37 and 59.

[122] Paragraph 55.

[123] Article XVI:1 of the Agreement Establishing the World Trade Organization.

[124] Paragraph 54.

[125] We do not consider Brazil's reference to GATT Articles XIX:3 and XXIII:2 (paragraph 54) to be relevant to this case. Those provisions address withdrawal of concessions in specific situations involving safeguard measures or dispute settlement.

> delegation that the global custom quotas envisaged for potato starch would be administered in accordance with the provisions of Article XIII of the General Agreement."[126]

Although not technically a result of Article XXVIII negotiations, the TRQ opened by Germany in this case could be characterized as a form of compensation for not fulfilling its tariff commitments in the previous round. In the application of the TRQ, Germany followed the MFN principle contained in Article XIII and the panel (and the CONTRACTING PARTIES) accepted it as a positive move toward the solution of the dispute. Thus, we find that Brazil's argument is not supported either by the text of the WTO Agreement or past GATT practices.

215. Second, and more importantly, we note that the concessions modified as the result of the Oilseeds Agreement regarding soya beans and other oilseeds were MFN commitments to bind the tariff rates on those products as duty-free. In view of the EC's obligations under Article XXVIII:2 to "maintain a general level of reciprocal and mutually advantageous concessions not less favourable to trade than that provided for" in its previous tariff schedule, compensation for the withdrawal or modification of MFN commitments should be given in an MFN manner also. If a preferential treatment of a particular trading partner not elsewhere justified is permitted under the pretext of "compensatory adjustment" under Article XXVIII:2, it would create a serious loophole in the multilateral trading system. Such a result would fundamentally alter the overall balance of concessions Article XXVIII is designed to achieve.

216. Brazil argues that by failing to respect the balance between the withdrawal of a concession and the offering of compensation in another product, the EC has denied Brazil's rights within the multilateral system.[127] In our view, however, the balance must be sought not only bilaterally but also within the multilateral context, as required under Article XXVIII:2 of GATT. Indeed, most tariff concessions are negotiated bilaterally, but the results of the negotiations are extended on a multilateral basis. The fact that the poultry TRQ was opened as a result of bilateral negotiations between the EC and Brazil does not mean that the EC was obligated to accord the benefit exclusively to Brazil. In conclusion, we find that the object and purpose of the Oilseeds Agreement does not support Brazil's argument that the total TRQ should be reserved exclusively for its products.

(c) Preparatory Work of Article XXVIII

217. The conclusion that the EC is bound, on an MFN basis, by its tariff commitments for frozen poultry meat under the Oilseeds Agreement is confirmed by

---

126 Panel Report on *German Import Duties on Starch and Potato Flour*, noted by the CONTRACTING PARTIES on 16 February, BISD 3S/77, para. 7.

127 Paragraph 40.

the preparatory work of Article XXVIII of GATT.[128] Regarding the provision which eventually became Article XXVIII:3, the Chairman of the Tariff Agreements Committee at Geneva in 1947 concluded as follows:

> "It was agreed that there was no intention to interfere in any way with the operation of the most-favoured-nation clause. This Article is headed 'Modification of Schedules'. It refers throughout to concessions negotiated under paragraph 1 of Article II, the Schedules, and there is no reference in the Article to Article I, which is the Most-Favoured-Nation clause. Therefore, I think the intent is clear: that in no way should this Article interfere with the operation of the Most-Favoured-Nation clause."[129]

(iv) Summary

218. To sum up our findings in this section, we find no proof (either in the text or in the object and purpose of the Oilseeds Agreement) in support of the Brazilian claim that the poultry TRQ opened as the result of the Oilseeds Agreement was intended to be a country-specific tariff quota with Brazil being the sole beneficiary. In other words, we find that the EC is bound, on an MFN basis, by its tariff commitments for frozen poultry meat. We also reject Brazil's argument that Articles I and XIII of GATT do not necessarily apply to TRQs given as compensation under Article XXVIII.

C. *Legitimate Expectations*

219. Before moving on to the examination of Brazil's alternative claim on Article XIII of GATT, we address Brazil's supplementary claim regarding legitimate expectations by Brazil concerning the tariff treatment of the poultry products by the EC.[130] Brazil does not invoke particular provisions of the WTO agreements to support its claim. In this regard, we note that the Appellate Body in a recent report emphasized the importance of distinguishing between (a) the concept of protecting the expectations of Members as to the competitive relationship between their products and the products of other Members and (b) the concept of the protection of the reasonable expectations of Members relating to market access conditions. According to the Appellate Body, the former was developed in

---

[128] Article 32 of the Vienna Convention provides: "Recourse may be had to supplementary means of interpretation, including the preparatory work of the treaty and the circumstances of its conclusion, in order to confirm the meaning resulting from the application of Article 31...".

[129] EPCT/TAC/PV/18, p. 46, reproduced in the Analytical Index (1995) at p. 947.

[130] Paragraph 46.

the context of violation complaints involving Articles III and XI of GATT, while the latter was developed in the context of non-violation complaints.[131]

220. In the present case, because Brazil does not invoke specific provisions and makes no distinction between "expectations as to the competitive relationship" and "reasonable expectations relating to market access conditions", in the absence of any further elaboration, we are not able to reach a finding on this point.

D. Article XIII of GATT

221. We now turn to the examination of Brazil's alternative claim under Article XIII of GATT. The main argument presented by Brazil involves Article XIII:2, which reads in relevant part as follows:

> "In applying import restrictions to any product, Members shall aim at a distribution of trade in such product approaching as closely as possible the shares which the various Members might be expected to obtain in the absence of such restrictions and to this end shall observe the following provisions: ... ; (d) In cases in which a quota is allocated among supplying countries the Member applying the restrictions may seek agreement with respect to the allocation of shares in the quota with all other contracting parties having a substantial interest in supplying the product concerned. In cases in which this method is not reasonably practicable, the Member concerned shall allot to Members having a substantial interest in supplying the product shares based upon the proportions, supplied by such Members during a previous representative period, of the total quantity or value of imports of the product, due account being taken of any special factors which may have affected or may be affecting the trade in the product. No conditions or formalities shall be imposed which would prevent any Member from utilizing fully the share of any such total quantity or value which has been allotted to it, subject to importation being made within any prescribed period to which the quota may relate."

222. Article XIII of GATT generally requires the non-discriminatory administration of quantitative restrictions. Article XIII also applies to tariff quotas, as provided in paragraph 5, which reads:

> "The provisions of this Article shall apply to any tariff quota instituted or maintained by any Member, and, in so

[131] Appellate Body Report on *India - Patent Protection for Pharmaceutical and Agricultural Chemical Products*, adopted on 16 January 1998, WT/DS50/AB/R, para. 36.

> far as applicable, the principles of this Article shall also extend to export restrictions."

These points were affirmed by the Appellate Body in the *Banana III* case[132], and are not contested by the parties. However, the parties have divergent views on the application of Article XIII to the actual operation of the TRQ in this particular case.

(i) Agreement on the Allocation of the TRQ

223. Brazil claims that the EC reached an agreement with Brazil in 1993 on the allocation of the total TRQ to Brazil within the meaning of Article XIII:2(d).[133] The EC rejects this claim.[134]

224. Consistent with the views on the burden of proof put forward by the Appellate Body in the *Shirts and Blouses* case[135], we first examine evidence produced by Brazil to determine whether it has successfully raised a presumption that an agreement regarding the allocation of tariff quotas exists.

225. Brazil has demonstrated that it complained about the operation of the TRQ as early as 28 March 1994.[136] The first letter of complaint - from the Brazilian Ambassador in Brussels to a senior EC official - reads as follows (emphasis added):

> "I have just received information that the Council is supposedly about to decide on the allocation of the 15,500 tonnes of chicken and 2,500 tonnes of turkey resulting from the oilseeds compensation agreement. The proposal to be submitted would divide the tonnage equally into three groups (a: Brazil; b: Thailand; c: China, USA and the remaining countries), each receiving one third of the contingent. ... *[T]his distribution*, in my opinion, definitely is not compatible with the *spirit* of the oilseeds compensations agreement signed with Brazil. I would, therefore, appreciate your looking into this matter with the utmost urgency."

Another letter of 20 May 1994 from the Ambassador to another EC official reads in part as follows (emphasis added):

---

[132] Appellate Body Report on *Banana III, op. cit.*, para. 160.

[133] Paragraph 64.

[134] Paragraph 65.

[135] Appellate Body Report on *United States - Measure Affecting Imports of Woven Wool Shirts and Blouses from India*, adopted on 23 May 1997, WT/DS33/AB/R, DSR 1997:I, 323 at 337. The report also states: "... a party claiming a violation of a provision of the WTO Agreement by another Member must assert and prove its claim".

[136] Letters of complaint attached to Brazil's first written submission. We note that the EC did not respond to any of these letters in writing.

> "We have been informally advised that it would be the intention of the Commission to propose the division of that amount [15,500 tonnes for poultry meat and 2,500 tonnes for turkey meat] allocating only 45 per cent of the poultry meat quota and 71 per cent of the turkey meat quota to Brazil. It is the view of the Brazilian Government that *such quota allocation* would be a breach of the *intent and spirit* of the agreement, since it would not ensure that Brazil is duly compensated for the losses it suffered ... ."

Finally, on 15 April 1997, the Ambassador wrote to the Vice-President of the European Commission, stating (emphasis added):

> "... [W]e have *never willingly concurred with* the terms dictated by the Commission in 1994 for the distribution and management of said quotas. ... The first two letters [cited above] clearly state that, in our view, their proposed *distribution* would be in breach of the *intent and spirit* of the agreement reached in Geneva to compensate Brazil for the losses incurred as a result of the changes in the EU oilseeds regime."

226. It is also worth noting here that Brazil at this point had not explicitly claimed that the total TRQ was to be reserved exclusively for Brazil. Rather, Brazil refers to the "intent and spirit" of the Oilseeds Agreement and appears to protest against the way in which the tariff quota is distributed or allocated.

227. It appears from these letters that there was no explicit agreement regarding the allocation of tariff quotas between Brazil and the EC.

(ii) Participation of Non-Members and East European Countries in the TRQ

228. Brazil additionally claims that the EC has failed to follow the rules of Article XIII:2(d) by granting China, which is a non-Member, access to the TRQ[137] and also by allocating licences to products from Members in East Europe, which have privileged access to the EC market.[138] We address these two issues separately.

(a) Non-Members

229. We first examine the issue of non-Members. Brazil claims that the EC cannot unilaterally grant to non-Members the right to participate in a compensatory TRQ. The EC claims that there is no obligation to discriminate against non-

[137] Paragraph 66.

[138] Paragraphs 68 and 70.

Members under Article XIII:2(d). According to the EC, if the EC were to exclude non-Members from the scope of the allotment, the resulting share of Brazil would be higher than "the shares which the various Members might be expected to obtain in the absence of such restrictions" under the opening sentence ("chapeau") of Article XIII:2.[139]

230. We note that Article XIII carefully distinguishes between Members ("contracting parties" in the original text of GATT 1947) and "supplying countries" or "source". There is nothing in Article XIII that obligates Members to calculate tariff quota shares on the basis of imports from Members only.[140] If the purpose of using past trade performance is to approximate the shares in the absence of the restrictions as required under the chapeau of Article XIII:2, exclusion of a non-Member, particularly if it is an efficient supplier, would not serve that purpose.

231. This interpretation is also confirmed by the use in Article XIII:2(d) of the term "of the total quantity or value of imports of the product" without limiting the total quantity to imports from Members.

232. The conclusion above is not affected by the fact that the TRQ in question was opened as compensatory adjustment under Article XXVIII because Article XIII is a general provision regarding the non-discriminatory administration of import restrictions applicable to any TRQs regardless of their origin.

233. For these reasons, we find that the EC has not acted inconsistently with Article XIII of GATT by calculating Brazil's tariff quota share based on the total quantity of imports, including those from non-Members.

---

[139] Paragraph 71. We note that if the EC were to exclude non-Members from the basis of the calculation of tariff quota shares, such an exclusion in itself would not constitute a violation of Article XIII:2. The question we need to address here is whether the EC is *required* to exclude non-Members from the basis of the calculation of tariff quota shares.

[140] We note in this regard that in the *Banana III* case, the panel made the following observation (which was not affected by the subsequent appeal): "The consequence of the foregoing analysis is that Members may be effectively required to use a general 'others' category for all suppliers other than Members with a substantial interest in supplying the product. The fact that in this situation tariff quota shares are allocated to some Members, notably those having a substantial interest in supplying the product, but not to others that do not have a substantial interest in supplying the product, would not necessarily be in conflict with Article XIII:1. While the requirement of Article XIII:2(d) is not expressed as an exception to the requirements of Article XIII:1, it may be regarded, to the extent that its practical application is inconsistent with it, as *lex specialis* in respect of Members with a substantial interest in supplying the product concerned". See panel reports on *European Communities - Regime for the Importation, Sale and Distribution of Bananas*, *op. cit.*, para. 7.75. The quoted passage, particularly the use of the phrase "*all suppliers* other than Members with a substantial interest in supplying the product"(emphasis added), indicates that the *Banana III* panel did not take the view that allocation of quota shares to non-Members under Article XIII:2(d) was not permitted.

(b) Members in East Europe

234. Now we move on to the issue of Members in East Europe. According to the evidence submitted by the EC, licences in the "others" category are allocated to poultry products originating in East Europe, notably Hungary and Poland. We note in this regard that the EC and the then Czech and Slovak Republic, Hungary and Poland in 1992 jointly notified the CONTRACTING PARTIES that the Interim Agreements aimed at the establishment of free trade areas under Article XXIV of GATT came into force as of 1 March 1992.[141] Brazil claims that the allocation of licences to imports of poultry products from East European countries is inconsistent with Article XIII of GATT because the EC has reduced the benefit to other Members by allowing these countries to participate in the TRQ.

235. In addressing this issue, we first note that the calculation of tariff quota shares and the participation of supplying countries in the tariff quota are two distinct issues. As noted above, it is clear from the chapeau of Article XIII:2 that the share calculation must approximate the shares which the exporting Members might be expected to obtain in the absence of the restrictions. However, such calculated shares do not necessarily determine which Members are permitted to participate in the actual allocation of licences, particularly in an "others" category.

236. In the present case, the total TRQ quantity of 15,500 tonnes is a given figure for the purposes of Article XIII, not contested by the parties. Brazil has not taken a position on the EC assertion that the annual figure of 7,100 tonnes allocated for imports from Brazil corresponds to Brazil's share among the total imports into the EC during the representative period.[142] In this context, Brazil does not specifically address the calculation of tariff quota shares. Rather, it claims that the participation of East European countries in the "others" category is inconsistent with Article XIII:2.

237. We note that Brazil cites the *Newsprint* panel as a precedent.[143] The factual basis of the *Newsprint* case was as follows. The European Economic Community (EEC) opened a duty-free tariff quota of 500,000 tonnes for newsprint for the year 1984 whereas the commitment of the EEC in its tariff schedule provided for an annual duty-free tariff quota of 1.5 million tonnes. The reason for the reduction in the scope of the tariff quota was to take account of the free access to the EEC market of suppliers from the European Free Trade Association (EFTA), which was agreed upon subsequent to the tariff schedule. In response to a complaint by Canada, the EEC noted that if it were required to respect the 1.5 million-tonne level, it might count EFTA exports against that level. In respect of this course of suggested action by the EEC, the panel made the following statement:

[141] L/6992, 3 April 1992.
[142] Paragraph 53.
[143] *Panel on Newsprint*, adopted on 20 November 1984, BISD 31S/114.

> "It is in the nature of a duty-free tariff quota to allow specified quantities of imports into a country duty-free which would otherwise be dutiable, which is not the case for EFTA imports by virtue of the free-trade agreements. Imports which are already duty-free, due to a preferential agreement, cannot by their very nature participate in an m.f.n. duty-free quota. The situation in this respect could only change if the free-trade agreements with the EFTA countries were to be discontinued; in this case these countries would be entitled to fall back on their GATT rights vis-à-vis the EC, which rights continue to exist."[144]

238. There is some similarity between the *Newsprint* case and the present case regarding this specific issue. As in the *Newsprint* case, the purpose of the poultry TRQ is to allow specified quantities (15,500 tonnes) of imports into the EC duty-free which would otherwise be dutiable. However, there are three important factual differences. First, in the *Newsprint* case, EFTA suppliers were accorded duty-free access to the EEC market without restriction. In the present case, imports from Hungary and Poland under the Interim Agreements are still dutiable.[145] Second, in the *Newsprint* case, the level of the MFN duty-free quota was reduced in order to make room for preferential access while in the present case no such reduction has occurred. Third, in the *Newsprint* case, the EFTA agreement was concluded after the opening of the MFN quota whereas in this case the Interim Agreements preceded the opening of the poultry TRQ.

239. Thus, the present case lacks the basis that led to the conclusion by the *Newsprint* panel. We also note that before making the statement cited in paragraph 237 above, the *Newsprint* panel stated that "the Panel could find no GATT specific provision forbidding such action".[146] If Brazil had intended to claim a violation of Article XIII:2 on this specific issue, at a minimum, it should have elaborated on the nature of preferences accorded to poultry products imported from East Europe and should have tied it to *inter alia* "any special factors which may have or may be affecting the trade in the product" referred to in Article XIII:2(d). It has not done so.

240. Accordingly, we do not find that the EC has acted inconsistently with Article XIII with respect to the tariff quota allocation for imports from Members in East Europe.

---

[144] *Panel on Newsprint*, adopted on 20 November 1984, BISD 31S/114, para. 55.

[145] According to the annexes attached to the notification referred to in paragraph 234, one category of poultry meat (0207 41 10) originating in Hungary and Poland benefit from certain special non-MFN quotas under the Interim Agreements. However, imports under these quotas are dutiable at reduced rates. See Official Journal No L 348/1. Since Brazil has submitted no evidence regarding the nature of preferences on poultry products from East Europe, we are not in a position to know what kind of preferential treatment, if any, is given to other categories (0207 41 41 and 0207 41 71).

[146] Panel Report on *Newsprint, op. cit.*, para. 55.

E. Licensing Agreement

241. Brazil's claim regarding the Licensing Agreement can be sub-divided into issues involving (i) notification; (ii) changes to the licensing rules; (iii) distortion of trade; (iv) licence entitlement based on export performance; (v) speculation in licences; (vi) issuance of licences in economic quantities and newcomers; and (vii) transparency.[147] We examine these issues in turn.

(i) Notification

242. Brazil claims that the EC has failed to notify the necessary information regarding the poultry TRQ to the WTO Committee on Import Licensing under Article 1.4(a) of the Licensing Agreement.[148] The EC responds that it did not make a notification because it was unclear whether the Licensing Agreement applied to TRQs before the Appellate Body report on the *Banana III* case. The EC further claims that the mere fact of non-notification cannot be considered to render the whole regime illegal.[149]

243. Article 1.4(a) of the Licensing Agreement reads as follows:

> "The rules and all information concerning procedures for the submission of applications, including the eligibility of persons, firms and institutions to make such applications, the administrative body(ies) to be approached, and the lists of products subject to the licensing requirement shall be published, in the sources notified to the Committee on Import Licensing provided for in Article 4 (referred to in this Agreement as "the Committee"), in such a manner as to enable governments[150] and traders to become acquainted with them. Such publication shall take place, whenever practicable, 21 days prior to the effective date of the requirement but in all events not later than such effective date. Any exception, derogations or changes in or from the rules concerning licensing procedures or the list of products subject to import licensing shall also be published in the same manner and within the same time periods as specified above. Copies of these publications shall also be made available to the Secretariat."

---

[147] In addition to these seven issues, Brazil refers to the nature of compensation in the context of the Licensing Agreement also. See paragraph 109. However, since we have already addressed this issue in our analysis of the Oilseeds Agreement, we do not consider it necessary to repeat the discussion.

[148] Paragraph 76. We note that Brazil does not refer to Article 5 of the Licensing Agreement, which is a more general provision about notification. Article 1.4(a) only deals with the sources of publication.

[149] Paragraph 77.

[150] Footnote 3 to this subparagraph reads as follows: "For the purpose of this Agreement, the term 'governments' is deemed to include the competent authorities of the European Communities."

244. While we note the EC's explanation for non-notification, we find this omission to be inconsistent with Article 1.4(a) of the Licensing Agreement. The fact that all the relevant information is published and that the administration of all agricultural TRQs in the EC has been notified to the WTO Committee on Agriculture does not in our view excuse the EC from notifying the sources of publication pursuant to this subparagraph.

(ii) Changes to the Licensing Rules

245. Brazil claims that frequent changes to the licensing rules and procedures regarding the poultry TRQ have made it difficult for governments and traders to become familiar with the rules, contrary to the provisions of Articles 1.4, 3.3, 3.5(b), 3.5(c) and 3.5(d). Brazil further notes that not all the changes have been for the purpose of the elimination of speculation in licences and that those changes that addressed the issue of speculation have not resulted in the elimination of speculation.[151] The EC responds that there is nothing in the Agreement that prohibits changes in licensing procedures.[152]

246. We note that the transparency requirement under the cited provisions is limited to publication of rules and other relevant information. While we have sympathy for Brazil regarding the difficulties caused by frequent changes to the rules, we find that changes in rules *per se* do not constitute a violation of Article 1.4, 3.3, 3.5(b), 3.5(c) or 3.5(d).

(iii) Distortion of Trade

247. Brazil claims that its percentage share in the EC poultry market has been falling since the introduction of the TRQ in 1994, contrary to Brazil's expectations. In Brazil's view, this is attributable to the distortions of trade caused by the operation of the TRQ.[153] In particular, Brazil claims that the EC has violated the provisions of Articles 1.2 and 3.2 of the Licensing Agreement.

248. Article 1.2 of the Licensing Agreement provides as follows (emphasis added):

> "Members shall ensure that the administrative procedures used to implement import licensing regimes are in conformity with the relevant provisions of GATT 1994 including its annexes and protocols, as interpreted by this Agreement, *with a view to preventing trade distortions* that may arise from an inappropriate operation of those procedures, taking into account the economic development purposes and financial and trade needs of developing country Members."

151 Paragraph 80. See also paragraph 76.
152 Paragraph 81.
153 Paragraphs 82 and 84.

Article 3.2 of the Licensing Agreement further provides:

> "Non-automatic licensing shall not have trade-restrictive or -distortive effects on imports additional to those caused by the imposition of the restriction. Non-automatic licensing procedures shall correspond in scope and duration to the measure they are used to implement, and shall be no more administratively burdensome than absolutely necessary to administer the measure."

249. In examining these claims, we first note that Brazil's reference to the percentage share relates to its total exports of poultry products to the EC market, the majority of which consists of over-quota (duty paid) trade. The Licensing Agreement, as applied to this particular case, only relates to in-quota trade. Second, the licences issued to imports from Brazil are fully utilized, which strongly suggests that any trade-distortive effects of the operation of the licensing rules have been overcome by exporters. Third, the total volume of poultry exports from Brazil has generally been increasing (see Annex I). Therefore, we fail to understand the relevance of the decline in the percentage share in total trade to a violation of the Licensing Agreement. Thus, based on the evidence presented by Brazil regarding its percentage share of the EC poultry market, we do not find that the EC has acted inconsistently with Articles 1.2 and 3.2 of the Licensing Agreement.

(iv) Licence Entitlement Based on Export Performance

250. Brazil claims that the EC's allocation of import licences on the basis of export performance is inconsistent with Articles 1.3 and 3.5(j) of the Licensing Agreement.[154] The EC responds that nothing in the Licensing Agreement prohibits the use of a criterion relating to exports and that in any event the alleged measure is no longer in place (export performance was only taken into account for the period from 26 June 1994 to 1 June 1995).[155]

251. Article 1.3 of the Licensing Agreement provides:

> "The rules for import licensing procedures shall be neutral in application and administered in a fair and equitable manner."

Article 3.5(j) in relevant part provides:

> "in allocating licences, the Member should consider the import performance of the applicant ... ."

---

[154] Paragraph 86.

[155] Paragraphs 87 and 88.

252. Although the measure is no longer in place, Brazil claims that there are certain lingering effects.[156] Therefore, we do not reject this claim on the grounds of mootness.

253. The requirement of export performance for the issuance of import licences on its face does seem unusual. However, Brazil has not elaborated on how the export performance requirement was administered and how it has affected the in-quota exports of poultry products from Brazil.

254. We also note that the Appellate Body in the *Banana III* case made the following observation:

> "By its very terms, Article 1.3 of the Licensing Agreement clearly applies to the *application* and *administration* of import licensing procedures, and requires that this application and administration be 'neutral ... fair and equitable'. Article 1.3 of the Licensing Agreement does not require the import licensing *rules*, as such, to be neutral, fair and equitable. Furthermore, the context of Article 1.3 - including the preamble, Article 1.1 and, in particular, Article 1.2 of the Licensing Agreement - supports the conclusion that Article 1.3 does not apply to import licensing *rules*."[157]

In our view, the issue of licence entitlement based on export performance is clearly that of rules, not that of application or administration of import licensing procedures. Thus, Article 1.3 is not applicable on this specific issue.

255. Furthermore, the provision of Article 3.5(j) in this regard is hortatory and does not necessarily prohibit the consideration of other factors than import performance.

256. For these reasons, we do not find that the EC has acted inconsistently with Article 1.3 or Article 3.5(j) of the Licensing Agreement in this regard.

(v) Speculation in Licences

257. Brazil claims that speculation in licences discourages the full utilization of the poultry TRQ and that this constitutes a violation of Articles 3.5(h) and 3.5(j)[158]. The EC claims that these provisions do not impose a mandatory requirement. Furthermore, the EC points out that the relevant EC regulation stipulates that licences are not transferable with a view to avoiding speculation. Finally, the EC notes that the poultry TRQ has in fact been fully utilized.[159]

258. Article 3.5(h) provides:

---

[156] Paragraph 89.

[157] Appellate Body Report on the *Banana III*, *op. cit.*, para. 197.

[158] Paragraph 91.

[159] Paragraph 92.

> "when administering quotas, Members shall not prevent importation from being effected in accordance with the issued licences, and shall not discourage the full utilization of quotas ... ."

Article 3.5(j) in relevant part provides:

> "... consideration should be given as to whether licences issued to applicants in the past have been fully utilized during a recent representative period. In cases where licences have not been fully utilized, the Member shall examine the reasons for this and take these reasons into consideration when allocating new licences ... ."

259. While it may be true that Brazilian exporters have had additional difficulties in exporting to the EC market due to the speculation in licences, we note that the licences allocated to imports from Brazil have been fully utilized. In other words, the speculation in licences has not discouraged the full utilization of the TRQ. Thus, we do not find that the EC has acted inconsistently with Articles 3.5(h) or 3.5(j) of the Licensing Agreement in this regard.

(vi) Issuance of Licences in Economic Quantities and Newcomers

260. Brazil claims that the allocation of licences where each applicant receives a licence allowing imports of about 5 tonnes cannot be considered to be in conformity with the provisions of Article 3.5(i) regarding issuance of licences in economic quantities.[160] As a related matter, Brazil claims that the absence of a newcomer provision in the regulation regarding the operation of the poultry TRQ is inconsistent with Article 3.5(j) of the Licensing Agreement.[161] The EC claims that the licences are indeed issued to newcomers[162] and that the allocation of the licences in small quantities was made in response to an ever increasing number of importers.[163]

261. Article 3.5(i) provides as follows:

> "when issuing licences, Members shall take into account the desirability of issuing licences for products in economic quantities ... ."

Article 3.5(j) further provides in relevant part:

> "in allocating licences, the Member should consider the import performance of the applicant... Consideration shall also be given to ensuring a reasonable distribution of licences to

[160] Paragraphs 97 and 99. Brazil also refers to Article 3.5(h), which we have discussed in relation to speculation in licences. We note here again that the licences in question have fully been utilized.
[161] Paragraph 101.
[162] Paragraph 102.
[163] Paragraph 98.

> new importers, taking into account the desirability of issuing licences for products in economic quantities. In this regard, special consideration should be given to those importers importing products originating in developing country Members and, in particular, the least-developed country Members ... ."

262. We note Brazil's argument that its exporters are facing difficulties in dealing with licences for small quantities, which is echoed in Thailand's third-party submission also.[164] While the decline in the average quantity per licence may cause problems for traders, we note at the same time that the total TRQ has been fully utilized. The very fact that the licences have been fully utilized suggests to us that the quantities involved are still "economic", particularly in combination with the significant amount of the over-quota trade.

263. Thus, we do not find that the EC has acted inconsistently with Articles 3.5(i) or 3.5(j) of the Licensing Agreement in this regard.

(vii) Transparency

264. Brazil claims that there is a lack of transparency in the operation of the poultry TRQ. According to Brazil, the inability of traders to determine which consignments are being imported within or outside the TRQ means that EC is not administering the licensing system in a transparent manner.[165] Brazil specifically claims a violation by the EC of Article 3.5(a)(iii) and (iv) regarding the provision of information.[166] The EC responds that it has produced the relevant information when requested.[167]

265. Article 3.5(a) in relevant part reads as follows:

> "Members shall provide, upon request of any Member having an interest in trade in the product concerned, all relevant information concerning: ... (iii) the distribution of such licences among supplying countries; (iv) where practicable, import statistics (i.e. value and/or volume) with respect to the products subject to import licensing. Developing country Members would not be expected to take additional administrative or financial burdens on this account; ... ."

We note that Article 3.5(a) addresses specific situations in the operation of an import licensing scheme, subject to requests from Members. It is clear that Article 3.5(a) does not obligate Members to provide voluntarily complete and rele-

164 Paragraph 164.

165 Paragraph 105. Since this issue involves both in-quota and over-quota trade, we address it in Section F below when we discuss Article X of GATT.

166 Paragraph 107.

167 Paragraph 108.

vant information on the distribution of licences among supplying countries and statistics on volumes and values. Brazil has not demonstrated that there has been a case where the EC has failed to provide the required information despite a request by Brazil. Thus, we do not find that the EC has acted inconsistently with Article 3.5(a) of the Licensing Agreement in this regard.

(viii) Summary

266. To sum up our findings in this section, we find that Brazil has not demonstrated a violation of the Licensing Agreement by the EC, except for the failure to notify the necessary information regarding the poultry TRQ to the WTO Committee on Import Licensing under Article 1.4(a) of the Licensing Agreement.

F. Article X of GATT

267. Brazil claims that to be able to benefit from the requirements or constraints of exporting either within or outside the TRQ, traders need to know which trade regime (i.e. duty-free or dutiable) is applicable to any one consignment. Brazil argues that this interpretation is implied in Article X of GATT. If this were not the case, according to Brazil, the object of publication and notification would not be served.[168] Brazil argues that this is a requirement under Article X of GATT as well as under the Licensing Agreement. In response, the EC refers the Appellate Body report in the *Banana III* case[169] and argues that this claim should be rejected because the Licensing Agreement takes precedence over Article X of GATT.[170]

268. In our view, however, the factual situation is different in the present case from that in the *Banana III* case. As Brazil correctly points out, this finding of the Appellate Body was made in relation to an EC regime for the importation of bananas where there was no over-quota trade.[171] In the present case, there is significant over-quota trade, and Brazil's complaint focuses on the difficulty of differentiating between in-quota and over-quota trade. Therefore, in our view, the examination of Article X of GATT as well as the Licensing Agreement is warranted since, in the present case, the Licensing Agreement is relevant to in-quota trade and Article X of GATT is relevant to the total trade.

269. Brazil argues that the EC is obligated to establish a system that enables exporters to know in advance whether each consignment is going to be treated as in-quota imports or as over-quota imports under Article X, particularly Article X:3(a), which requires the administration of trade rules "in a uniform, impartial and reasonable manner". We note, however, that Article X is applicable only to

168 Paragraph 140.
169 Appellate Body Report on *Banana III, op. cit.*, para. 204.
170 Paragraph 141.
171 Paragraph 142.

laws, regulations, judicial decisions and administrative rulings "of general application". In this regard, we recall that the panel in the *Underwear* case stated as follows:

> "The mere fact that the restraint at issue was an administrative order does not prevent us from concluding that the restraint was a measure of general application. Nor does the fact that it was a country-specific measure exclude the possibility of it being a measure of general application. If, for instance, the restraint was addressed to a specific company or applied to a specific shipment, it would not have qualified as a measure of general application. However, to the extent that the restraint affects an unidentified number of economic operators, including domestic and foreign producers, we find it to be a measure of general application."[172]

Conversely, licences issued to a specific company or applied to a specific shipment cannot be considered to be a measure "of general application". In the present case, the information which Brazil claims the EC should have made available concerns a specific shipment, which is outside the scope of Article X of GATT.

270. In view of the fact that the EC has demonstrated that it has complied with the obligation of publication of the regulations under Article X regarding the licensing rules of general application[173], without further evidence and argument in support of Brazil's position regarding how Article X is violated, we dismiss Brazil's claim on this point.

G. *Article II of GATT*

271. Brazil claims that the issuance of licences for the poultry TRQ in uneconomic quantities and the trade in these licences is a breach of the requirement under Article II:1(b) of GATT.[174] Article II:1(b) provides:

> "The products described in Part I of the Schedule relating to any Member, which are the products of territories of other Members, shall, on their importation into the territory to which the Schedule relates, and subject to the terms, conditions or qualifications set forth in that Schedule, be exempt from ordinary customs duties in excess of those set forth and provided therein. Such products shall also be exempt from all other duties or charges of any kind imposed on or

[172] Panel Report on *United States - Restrictions on Imports of Cotton and Man-made Fibre Underwear from Costa Rica*, adopted on 25 February 1997, WT/DS24/R, para. 7.65.
[173] Paragraph 144.
[174] Paragraph 147.

> in connection with the importation in excess of those imposed on the date of this Agreement or those directly and mandatorily required to be imposed thereafter by legislation in force in the importing territory on that date."

The EC rejects this claim by asserting that there is no legislation or any legislative requirement in the EC that imposes extra charges on top of the ordinary duties and other duties and charges which are bound in its tariff schedule and that the alleged payment is not a governmental measure. On the contrary, the relevant EC regulation explicitly prohibits transfer of licences.[175]

272. We note that the WTO Agreement is an inter-governmental agreement concluded among States or separate customs territories. In order to prevail in its argument, Brazil has to demonstrate that the alleged payment is a governmental measure, and it has failed to do so. We therefore reject Brazil's claim on a violation of Article II:1(b) of GATT.

H. *Article III of GATT*

273. Brazil claims that the EC's administration of the TRQ has the effect of imported products being treated in a manner that is less favourable than that accorded to like domestic products in violation of Article III of GATT.[176] The EC responds that the TRQ is a border measure to be strictly distinguished from internal measures that are subject to the disciplines of Article III.[177]

274. We note that discrimination between imported and domestic products is prohibited under Article III of GATT, which is a rule applicable to internal measures. Conversely, certain differential treatment between imported and domestic products are permitted at the border so long as they are in conformity with the other GATT provisions that regulate measures at the border. Indeed, this has been a well-established practice followed by the CONTRACTING PARTIES. As early as 1958, the *Italian Agricultural Machinery* panel characterized the object and purpose of Article III as follows:

> "It was considered, moreover, that the intention of the drafters of the Agreement was clearly to treat the imported products in the same way as the like domestic products once they had been cleared through customs."[178]

275. Brazil has not demonstrated the existence of any discriminatory measure once the poultry products have been cleared through customs. Therefore, Brazil's claim regarding Article III of GATT is rejected.

---

175 Paragraph 148.
176 Paragraph 151.
177 Paragraph 152.
178 Panel Report on *Italian Discrimination Against Imported Agricultural Machinery*, adopted on 23 October 1958, BISD 7S/60, para.11.

I. Agreement on Agriculture

276. Brazil claims that the EC has, in its application of price-based special safeguard on the imports of frozen poultry meat, violated Articles 4.2 and 5.1 of the Agreement on Agriculture. Article 4.2 provides as follows:

> "Members shall not maintain, resort to, or revert to any measures of the kind which have been required to be converted into ordinary customs duties[179], except as otherwise provided for in Article 5 and Annex 5."

Article 5.1 in relevant part provides as follows:

> "Notwithstanding the provisions of paragraph 1(b) of Article II of GATT 1994, any Member may take recourse to the provisions of paragraphs 4 and 5 below in connection with the importation of an agricultural product, in respect of which measures referred to in paragraph 2 of Article 4 of this Agreement have been converted into an ordinary customs duty and which is designated in its Schedule with the symbol "SSG" as being the subject of a concession in respect of which the provisions of this Article may be invoked, if: ... (b) the price at which imports may enter the customs territory of the Member granting the concession, as determined on the basis of the c.i.f. import price of the shipment concerned expressed in terms of its domestic currency, falls below a trigger price equal to the average 1986 to 1988 reference price[180] for the product concerned.

(i) Article 5.1

(a) Market Entry Price and the c.i.f. Price

277. We address the issue of Article 5.1 first. Brazil claims that the market entry price under Article 5.1(b) of the Agreement on Agriculture should be the c.i.f. price plus the bound duty. Therefore, according to Brazil, the EC has vio-

---

179 Footnote 1 to this paragraph reads: "These measures include quantitative import restrictions, variable import levies, minimum import prices, discretionary import licensing, non-tariff measures maintained through state-trading enterprises, voluntary export restraints, and similar border measures other than ordinary customs duties, whether or not the measures are maintained under country-specific derogations from the provisions of GATT 1947, but not measures maintained under balance-of-payments provisions or under other general, non-agriculture-specific provisions of GATT 1994 or of the other Multilateral Trade Agreements in Annex 1A to the WTO Agreement."

180 Footnote 2 to this paragraph reads: "The reference price used to invoke the provisions of this subparagraph shall, in general, be the average c.i.f. unit value of the product concerned, or otherwise shall be an appropriate price in terms of the quality of the product and its stage of processing. It shall, following its initial use, be publicly specified and available to the extent necessary to allow other Members to assess the additional duty that may be levied."

lated this provision because it merely measures the c.i.f. price and should that price fall below the trigger price it imposes an additional duty.[181] The EC responds that the term "on the basis of the c.i.f. import price" in Article 5.1(b) means the c.i.f. price itself.[182]

278. Generally speaking, Article 5.1(b) permits the use of a special safeguard if the price of imports of the product concerned is below a defined trigger price. The relevant price of the imports concerned is referred to in Article 5.1(b) in two ways: i.e. the text of Article 5.1(b) refers to both "the price at which imports may enter the customs territory of the Member granting the concession" and "the c.i.f. import price". The ordinary meaning of the phrase "the price at which imports may enter the customs territory of the Member granting the concession" would include the payment of applicable duties since those duties must be paid prior to entry and therefore are part of "the price". The term "the c.i.f. import price" in Article 5.1(b) is qualified by the phrase "determined on the basis of", which indicates that the market entry price is something that has to be constructed using the c.i.f. price as one of the parameters. If the drafters of this provision had intended to make the invocation of special safeguards contingent solely upon the c.i.f. price, they would have simply stated "if the c.i.f. price of that product imported into the customs territory of the Member granting the concession, expressed in terms of its domestic currency, falls below a trigger price...". They could have entirely disposed of the notion of the market entry price. Thus, the ordinary meaning of the terms used in Article 5.1(b) would appear to support the interpretation advanced by Brazil, i.e. that the market entry price must include duties paid.

279. To clarify the interpretation of the terms of Article 5.1(b) further, it is also appropriate to examine the context, object and purpose of the provision.

280. The context of Article 5.1(b) is clear. It is a specific derogation from the principles contained in Article 4.2. As such, the terms of Article 5.1(b) must be construed narrowly, so as not to frustrate the attainment of the security and predictability in trade through the tariffs-only regime under Article 4.2.

281. The object and purpose of Article 5.1(b) is to provide additional protection against significant decline in import prices during the implementation period of the Agreement on Agriculture after all agricultural products have been "tariffied" under Article 4.2. By its nature, it has to address a situation that has occurred after the tariffication process. If the market entry price is equated with the c.i.f. import price, and then compared with the trigger price calculated using the c.i.f. price only, it would disregard the effect of protection granted by high duties resulting from tariffication. Thus, although the drafting of Article 5.1(b) is not a model of clarity, in light of the object and purpose of that subparagraph, it would

---

[181] Paragraphs 119, 121 and 124.
[182] Paragraph 122.

be appropriate to interpret the market entry price under Article 5.1(b) to include duties paid.

282. We therefore find that the EC has not invoked the special safeguard provision with respect to the poultry products in question in accordance with Article 5.1(b).[183]

(b) Injury Requirement

283. Brazil further claims that the EC has violated the provisions of Article 5.1(b) because it applies the special safeguards without examining injury or damage to the EC market.[184] The EC rejects this claim.[185]

284. We find that Brazil's claim on this point is not supported by the text of Article 5.1(b), which does not require a finding of injury or damage unlike in the case of ordinary safeguards under Article XIX of GATT and the Agreement on Safeguards or the transitional safeguards under the Agreement on Textiles and Clothing.

(c) Representative Price

285. Finally, Brazil argues that the mechanism for determining the representative price is not transparent and that the EC should not take an internal market price as the determinant for the external c.i.f. price. Furthermore, Brazil claims that the EC has failed to indicate how the quality element provided for in its examination of the internal market price is to be factored.[186] In response, the EC claims that the representative price is published in the Official Journal and is therefore known to traders.[187] Furthermore, the EC has submitted on a confidential basis[188] a demonstration of the way in which the additional duty is actually calculated.

286. We note that Brazil's argument on this point appears to address the issue of whether the EC has followed its own regulations concerning the operation of special safeguards. To the extent that Brazil's claim is directed to the appropriateness of the special safeguard mechanism within the EC, we are unable to find any violation of the WTO rules. Although Brazil refers to Article 5 of the Agreement on Agriculture and Article X:3 of GATT, it has not specified in what manner the EC has violated these provisions. In any event, since we have already found a violation of Article 5.1(b) by the EC, for the sake of judicial economy, we do not examine this claim any further.

---

[183] One member of the Panel does not endorse this conclusion. See paragraphs 289 to 292.

[184] Paragraphs 126, 128, 129 and 130.

[185] Paragraphs 127 and 131.

[186] Paragraph 134.

[187] Paragraph 135.

[188] See paragraphs 191 and 192.

(ii) Article 4.2

287. Brazil claims that the EC has violated Article 4.2 because the special safeguard measure on poultry products is maintained in violation of the provisions of Article 5 and therefore cannot be justified.[189] The EC claims that Article 5 is a complete, self-contained code of rules for the application of special safeguards and that it has applied those rules correctly.[190]

288. Since we have already found a violation of Article 5.1(b) by the EC, it is not necessary for us to reach a separate finding on Article 4.2.

(iii) Opinion by a Member of the Panel

289. Regrettably, I am not able to endorse the conclusion reached by the Panel in paragraph 282.

290. While one possible view of the ordinary meaning of the term "the price at which imports may enter the customs territory of the Member granting the concession, as determined on the basis of the c.i.f. import price of the shipment concerned expressed in terms of its domestic currency"(hereinafter referred to as "the relevant import price") in Article 5.1(b) could be that it means the c.i.f. price plus the duties paid, such a reading, in my opinion, is not a convincing one. The relevant import price could in principle be equal to the c.i.f. import price itself if one considers, for instance, that the expression "the price at which imports may enter the customs territory of the Member granting the concession" is a requirement so as to avoid price constructions deviating arbitrarily from the c.i.f. import price. If the drafters of this provision had intended to include customs duty, they could have referred to the "duty paid c.i.f. import price", a notion that appeared in preliminary discussion papers of the negotiators. The Panel's interpretation, in my opinion, is inappropriate in light of the context of Article 5.1(b), including its footnote 2 and Article 5.5, which unambiguously refer to "the average c.i.f. unit value" and "the c.i.f. import price" respectively. Article 5.1(b), footnote 2 and Article 5.5 must be interpreted in a consistent and coherent manner in order to have a meaningful functioning of the special safeguard provisions within the framework of tariffication process while avoiding undue restraint on the possible recourse to those provisions. I note that Article 5 does not qualify whether the safeguard should be used sparingly or not. However, when including the ordinary customs duties in the relevant import price, anomalies with the functioning of the safeguard occur.

291. The inclusion of the ordinary customs duty in the relevant import price under Article 5.1(b) creates a particular problem when the ordinary customs duty is levied as a specific duty. If the level of the specific duty is higher than the level of trigger price defined in footnote 2, the price-based special safeguard can never

189 Paragraph 116.
190 Paragraph 117.

be invoked regardless of the extent of the drop in prices because, under the Panel's interpretation, the relevant import price never falls below the trigger price. In the case of *ad valorem* duty, while with high duties the recourse to Article 5.5 is also strongly limited, this singularity does not arise. Here however, as well as in the case of specific duty, when higher duties are applied, significant price distortions can occur for different shipments due to the application of the additional duty calculated under Article 5.5. These price distortions are most prominent when c.i.f. prices are close to the c.i.f. price that triggers the special safeguard provision. In other words, a shipment having at the border a lower c.i.f. import price, compared to another shipment with a slightly higher c.i.f. price that however does not trigger the special safeguard, could have, after clearing the customs, a significantly higher price than the latter. This situation could only be corrected if one includes the duties paid in the "c.i.f. import price" under Article 5.5 in disregard of its clear wording.

292. For these reasons, I am of the view that Article 5 of the Agreement on Agriculture requires an importing Member to calculate the relevant import price within the meaning of Article 5.1(b) on the basis of the c.i.f. import price only.

J. Nullification or Impairment

293. Brazil claims that the measures discussed above nullify or impair the benefits accruing to Brazil under the cited agreements.[191] Although it may be possible to interpret the nullification or impairment claim as a non-violation complaint within the meaning of Article XXIII:1(b) of GATT, Brazil has not substantiated this claim any further. Brazil has not attempted to establish nullification or impairment of the value of concessions accruing to it in respect of poultry products, except through its claim on the violation of the various WTO rules by the EC. We thus find that Brazil has failed to establish a separate non-violation complaint.

VII. CONCLUSIONS AND RECOMMENDATIONS

294. In light of our findings in Section B and C above, we conclude that Brazil has not demonstrated that the EC has failed to implement and administer the poultry TRQ in line with its obligations under the WTO agreements.

295. In light of our findings in Section D above, we conclude that Brazil has not demonstrated that the EC has failed to implement the TRQ in accordance with Article XIII of GATT.

296. In light of our findings in Section E above, we conclude that Brazil has not demonstrated that the EC has failed to implement the TRQ in accordance with Articles 1 and 3 of the Licensing Agreement, except on the point that the EC

[191] Paragraph 15.

has failed to notify the necessary information regarding the poultry TRQ to the WTO Committee on Import Licensing under Article 1.4(a) of the Licensing Agreement.

297. In light of our findings in Section F, G and H above, we conclude that Brazil has not demonstrated that the EC has failed to comply with the provisions of Articles X, II and III of GATT in respect of the implementation and administration of the poultry TRQ.

298. In light of our findings in Section I above, we conclude that the EC has failed to comply with the provisions of Article 5.1(b) of the Agreement on Agriculture regarding the imports of the poultry products outside the TRQ.

299. We recommend that the Dispute Settlement Body request the EC to bring the measures found in this report to be inconsistent with the Licensing Agreement and the Agreement on Agriculture into conformity with its obligations under those agreements.

ANNEX I

Total EC Imports of Poultry Meat (0207 14 10, 0207 14 50 and 0207 14 70)[1]

(tonnes)

TOTAL	1988	1989	1990	1991	1992	1993	1994	1995	1996	1997p
extra-ec 12/15	15,073	21,252	34,032	32,672	44,746	47,171	60,731	53,067	86,501	37,169
Brazil	7,115	9,809	12,990	14,377	21,203	21,493	25,798	19,196	28,701	17,394
China	*	*	79	639	2,639	9,015	16,684	14,541	22,958	1,419
Thailand	1,609	4,675	13,998	12,413	16,123	12,064	13,400	9,184	15,022	10,383
Hungary	3,630	4,121	3,802	3,192	3,295	3,393	3,652	7,649	5,983	2,267
Poland	122	153	990	199			56	242	1,730	1,746
Czech Republic	*	*	*	*	*	191	2	66	144	294
Slovenia	*	*	*	*	64	46	18	*	53	60
Croatia	*	*	*	*	114	157	234	228	36	*
Romania	583	344	33	161	172	423	570	182	23	114
Bulgaria	*	*	4	5	88	1	24	6	5	*
Czecho-slovakia	1,612	1,822	1,834	961	314	*	*	*	*	*
Yugo-slavia	307	61	*	282	329	*	*	*	*	*
extra-ec not det.	*	*	*	*	*	15	*	1,070	11,112	2,978
OTHERS	95	268	303	444	405	373	294	702	733	514

[1] Submitted by Brazil.

(percentages)

TOTAL %	1988	1989	1990	1991	1992	1993	1994	1995	1996	1997p
extra-ec 12/15	100.0	100.0	100.0	100.0	100.0	100.0	100.0	100.0	100.0	100.0
Brazil	47.2	46.2	38.2	44.0	47.4	45.6	42.5	36.2	33.2	46.8
China	*	*	0.2	2.0	5.9	19.1	27.5	27.4	26.5	3.8
Thailand	10.7	22.0	41.1	38.0	36.0	25.6	22.1	17.3	17.4	27.9
Hungary	24.1	19.4	11.2	9.8	7.4	7.2	6.0	14.4	6.9	6.1
Poland	0.8	0.7	2.9	0.6	0.0	0.0	0.1	0.5	2.0	4.7
Czech Republic	*	*	*	*	*	0.4	0.0	0.1	0.2	0.8
Slovenia	*	*	*	*	0.1	0.1	0.0	*	0.1	0.2
Croatia	*	*	*	*	0.3	0.3	0.4	0.4	0.0	*
Romania	3.9	1.6	0.1	0.5	0.4	0.9	0.9	0.3	0.0	0.3
Bulgaria	*	*	0.0	0.0	0.2	0.0	0.0	0.0	0.0	*
Czecho-slovakia	10.7	8.6	5.4	2.9	0.7	*	*	*	*	*
Yugo-slavia	2.0	0.3	*	0.9	0.7	*	*	*	*	*
extra-ec not det.	*	*	*	*	*	0.0	*	2.0	12.8	8.0
OTHERS	0.6	1.3	0.9	1.4	0.9	0.8	0.5	1.3	0.8	1.4

ANNEX II

TRQ-Licences Issued under Regulation 1431/94[2]

			Quantity issued Tonnes		No of licences		Average quantity per licence
			Annual	Quarterly	Annual	Quarterly	Kg.
Group 1	BRAZIL	1994	7.100	3.550	322	161	22.050
		1995	7.100	1.775	751	188	9.454
		1996	7.100	1.775	728	182	9.753
		1997	7.100	1.775	1.260	315	5.635
Group 2	THAILAND	1994	5.100	2.550	298	149	17.114
		1995	5.100	1.275	750	188	6.800
		1996	5.100	1.275	730	183	6.986
		1997	5.100	1.275	1.256	314	4.061
Group 3	OTHER	1994	3.300	1.650	331	166	9.970
		1995	3.300	825	754	189	4.377
		1996	3.300	825	737	184	4.478
		1997	3.300	825	1.204	301	2.741

Note: In 1994, licences only issued in 2 quarters.

[2] Information submitted by the European Communities.